A COMPANION TO TANTRA

A COMPANION TO TANTRA

S.C. BANERJI

abhinav publications

Cataloging in Publication Data—DK
Courtesy: D.K. Agencies (P) Ltd. <docinfo@dkagencies.com>
Banerji, Sures Chandra, 1917-
A companion to Tantra / S.C. Banerji.
p. cm.
Includes bibliographical references (p.)
Includes index.
ISBN 8170174023
1. Tantras—Criticism, interpretation, etc. 2. Tantrism.
I. Title.

DDC 133 21

First published in India 2007

Publishers
Shakti Malik
Abhinav Publications
E-37, Hauz Khas
New Delhi-110016 (INDIA)
Phones: 6566387, 6562784, 6524658
Fax: 91-11-6857009
e-mail: shakti@nde.vsnl.net.in
website: http//www.abhinavexports.com

ISBN 81-7017-402-3

Printed at
D.K. Fine Art Press Pvt. Ltd.
Ashok Vihar, Delhi

CONTENTS

Preface		*7*
Abbreviations		*9*
Important Dates		*10*
I	**Introduction**	*11*
II	**Tāntric Elements in Post-Vedic Sanskrit Literature**	*33*
III	**Tāntric Śaivism of Kashmir**	*39*
IV	**Tāntric Lexicons**	*61*
V	**Science in Tantra**	*65*
VI	**Society Reflected in Tantra**	*81*
VII	**Tantra Abroad**	*85*
VIII	**Authors of Tantras and Commentaries**	*89*
IX	**Hindu Tantras**	*117*
X	**Buddhist Tantras**	*233*
Appendix I: Pīṭhasthānas		*247*
Appendix II: Miscellaneous Tāntric Works and Commentaries		*248*
Glossary (General)		*251*
Glossary of Scientific Terms		*298*
Select Bibliography		*307*
Index		*341*

PREFACE

The elements of Tantra are found in the *Atharvaveda* and, in a lesser degree, in the *Ṛgveda*. These relate to the mundane life of the people, and reflect their aspirations for material well-being. We see, in them, how people wanted to have long life, keep off diseases and thwart the activities of ghosts, supposed to cause harm to them. Magic, both beneficial to themselves and harmful to their enemies, figures prominently.

In course of time, side by side with the elitist works, Tantras having a populist appeal came to be composed. It seems that Tantras arose as a protest against the traditional scriptures which insisted on self-mortification and austerities, etc. as means to the attainment of emancipation of the soul from the bondage of rebirths. In doing so, they prescribed rituals which were denied to women and the Śūdras who were in the lowest rung of the social ladder.

Tantra had a different approach to life and salvation. It sought to show the way to liberation here in life not by denial of worldly pleasures. For the followers of Tantra, the body was the microcosm and was to be kept fit for Tāntric devotion. Women and Śūdras were given by Tantra many facilities for religious practices. The rigours of caste-system were considerably relaxed. The acquisition of virtues was considered more important than the accident of birth.

In the modern society of India, the traditional scriptural injunctions are yielding place to rational thinking. Those, who do not know much of Tantra, are vociferously decrying ancient Indian values categorically. For reforming the society in keeping with modern ideas, the Tantra-śāstra should be cultivated. But, in the busy life of today, with tension and turmoil, it is not possible for one to delve deep into Tantra.

The present work is designed to give, in a succinct form, the reader an idea about the highlights of Tantra. In the introduction, we have briefly dealt with the important matters relating to this literature. It is followed by short accounts of the important authors and works on Tantra. In a glossary, the difficult words and technical terms have been explained. A separate glossary of scientific terms has also been added. The bibliography is fairly exhaustive.

The labours of the author will be rewarded if the work goes some way in familiarising the readers with the contents of Tantra, both Hindu and Buddhist.

July 1999 S.C. Banerji

ABBREVIATIONS

ABORI — Annals of Bhandarkar Oriental Research Institute
AIOC — All India Oriental Conference
BEFEO — Bulletin de l'Ecole Francaise d'Extreme-Orient
BORI — (MSS in) Bhandarkar Oriental Research Institute
GOS — Gaekwad's Oriental Series, Baroda
HIL — History of Indian Literature
IHQ — Indian Historical Quarterly
IO — India Office
JAOS — Journal of American Oriental Society
JASB — Journal of Asiatic Society of Bengal
JBORS — Journal of Bihar and Orissa Research Society
JRAS — Journal of Royal Asiatic Society
JOR — Journal of Oriental Research
NCC — New Catalogus Catalogorum
NIA — New Indian Antiquary
NSP — Nirnayasagara Press
Oxf. — Catalogus Codicum Sanskriticorum Bibliothecae Bodleianae
RASB — (Des. Cat. of Skt. MSS in Govt. Collection...) Royal Asiatic Society of Bengal by H.P. Sastri
TSS — Trivandrum Sanskrit Series
ZDMG — Zeitschrift für die Kunde des Morgenlandischen Gesselschaft, Leipzig, now from Wiesbaden

IMPORTANT DATES

Abhinavagupta — 10th-11th Century A.D.

Atharvaveda — later than *Ṛgveda* (q.v.)

Atīśa — 980 (or, 982)-1053 (or, 1054) A.D.

Buddha — attainment of Buddhahood, 486 B.C. (according to Cantonese tradition)

Caitanya — 1486-1533 A.D.

Ellora sculpture — 8th Century A.D.

Haṃseśvarī Temple — 1814 A.D.

Jagannātha Temple (Puri, Orissa) — Present temple built c. 12th Century A.D. (middle)

Kālīghāṭ (Calcutta) — Image of Kālī established not later than 16th Century A.D.

Kāmākhyā (Assam) — Date of foundation of temple unknown. Renovated in 1565 A.D.

Kṛṣṇānanda — 16th Century A.D.

Liṅgarāja Temple (Bhuvaneswar, Orissa) — 11th Century A.D.

Pāla rule (in Bengal) — c. 750-1155 A.D.; (in Bihar) till Muslim conquest in 1199 A.D.

Raghunandana — 16th Century A.D.

Rāmakṛṣṇa Paramahaṃsa — 1836-86 A.D.

Rāmaprasāda — c. 1720-81 A.D.

Ṛgveda — age controversial; generally believed around 1500 B.C.

Śaṃkarācārya — c. 8th-9th Century A.D.

Vivekānanda — 1863-1902 A.D.

CHAPTER I

INTRODUCTION

WHAT IS TANTRA?

Tantra is a class of literature which does not follow the conventional or traditional Veda-based Brāhmaṇical scriptures like Dharmasūtra, Dharmaśāstra, etc. The dictionary meanings of the term 'Tantra' are *siddhānta* (conclusion), *Śruti-śākhā* (a branch of *Śruti*, i.e. the Veda believed to have been revealed and transmitted through the word of the mouth), *iti-kartavyatā* (set of duties), *prabandha* (composition) and *śāstra-viśeṣa* (a particular scripture). The last meaning suits the subject of our discussion.

The word Tantra has been derived in several ways. Derived from the root *tan* (to spread), it is taken to mean *tanyate vistāryate jñānam anena*; by it knowledge is disseminated. Some derive Tantra from the root *trai* (to save); it is so called as it protects its followers. H.P. Sastri takes 'tantra' to mean shortening. According to him, Tantra attempts to reduce long *mantras* to something like algebraic forms as in Tāntric *bījas*. Incidentally, it may be stated that, according to Mīmāṃsā philosophy, the principle of 'tantratā' means a single act performed with many acts in view (*anekamuddiśya sakṛt pravṛttis-tantratā*).

RATIONALE UNDERLYING COMPOSITION OF TANTRA

One may pose the question — when there were the Vedas and so many Veda-based scriptures like Dharmaśāstra and the six philosophical treatises, what was the necessity for a distinct class of literature, called Tantra? It is a truism that, as in all other civilised countries, in ancient India also there were the elites and the populace.

The elitist culture is reflected in the *Ṛk-*, *Yajus-* and *Sāma-vedas*. As Winternitz rightly remarks (*Hist. of Indian Lit.*, 1990, I, p. 118), the *Atharvaveda* is "an inestimable source of knowledge of the actual popular religion which is not yet influenced by the priestly religion, of the belief in numberless spirits, goblins, ghosts and demons of all kinds and of the practice of magic that is of such great importance to ethnology and the history of religion". For its populist character, this Veda had for centuries been tabooed in the upper echelons of the society, dominated by the sacerdotal class. The term 'trayī' (the triad) came to be used to indicate the three Vedas, viz. *Ṛgveda*, *Yajurveda* and *Sāmaveda*.

In the magic spells and demonology of the *Atharvaveda* lay the germs of Tantra. In fact, Tantra is sometimes described as *Upaveda* of this Veda (*Śukra-nīti-sāra*, iv.3.39). The elitist Śāstras failed to satisfy the aspirations of the common men, particularly the Śūdras and women. In the post-Vedic scriptures, Śūdras and women were marginalised. They were denied the right to perform sacrifices and to participate in other religious observances. For Śūdras, the only duty was to serve the three upper classes (*ekameva hi śūdrasya karma ... eteṣameva varṇānāṃ śuśrūṣā*, Manu, I.91). For women, the gates of heaven would be open only if they served their husband (*patim śuśrūṣate yattu tena svarge mahīyate* — Manu, V.155); they were denied the right of sacrifice, *vrata*, fast, etc. independently of their husbands (Manu, V.155). They had, however, natural cravings for religious rites.

In course of time, as life became busier and living more complicated, people felt the need for easier ways of devotion than the elaborate rituals. The orthodox Brāhmaṇical scriptures demanded self-mortification and renunciation as stepping stones to liberation. This stifled the people's natural inclination for enjoyment of sex, drinking wine and eating meat, etc. All these reasons led to the composition of Tantra, which provided easier methods of devotion without denying the satisfaction of natural human propensities. In short, Tantra taught a positive attitude to life. The idea of liberation of the disembodied soul in the other world did not appeal to the people in general. Their attitude to liberation has been eloquently voiced by Rabīndranāth Tagore. He says: *vairāgya-sādhana mukti, se āmār nay, asaṃkhya bandhan mājhe mahānandamay labhiva muktir svād*: Liberation through renunciation is not for me. Again, he asserts: *indriyer dvār ruddha kari yogāsan, se nahe āmār*, it is not for me to practise *Yoga* by shutting the senses; I shall have the taste of liberation, full of great bliss, amongst countless bonds (vide the poem Mukti in the poet's poetical work *Naivedya*).

Tantra prescribes methods for *jīvanmukti* (liberation while alive). For this purpose, the preservation of the body is indispensable. So, Tantra sets much store by the body, and ordains physical and spiritual means of maintaining it in a sound condition.

The orthodox Brāhmaṇical scriptures, by compartmentalisation of society into four castes, and by rigorous division of the people into higher and lower classes, fostered animosity among them. There was an upsurge for levelling down this invidious discrimination. Tantra came forward to reduce the rigours of the caste system, and put more premium on merit than the accident of birth. For example, a Śūdra *Avadhūta* was to be saluted even by a Brāhmaṇa. Virgin girls, with the requisite qualifications, even if they belonged to the Śūdra caste, were deemed suitable for worship even by Brāhmaṇas.

ANTIQUITY OF TANTRA

We have seen that Tāntric *ideas* are found in the Vedas, particularly in the *Atharvaveda*. But, it is not known when Tāntric literature originated. Manuscripts of some Tantras appear to have been written in the script of the Gupta Age.[1] Among them, perhaps the oldest one, the *Kubjikāmata* is available in several versions.[2] There is reference, in an inscription of Rājā-Siṃhavarman in Kailāsanātha Temple, to South Indian Śaiva Āgamas; the inscription dates back to the sixth century A.D. Four Tantras, called *Śiraścheda, Vīṇāśikha, Sammoha* and *Nayottara*, are stated, in the inscription of Sdok-Kak-Thom, to have been introduced in Kambuja (Cambodia, now Kampuchea) in about 800 A.D. The oldest *Dhāraṇīs* of Tāntric Buddhism are supposed to date from the 4th century A.D. According to G. Tucci,[3] Tantra literature originated in the time of Harivarman and Asaṅga (4th century A.D.).

Of the Buddhist and Hindu Tantras, which originated earliest cannot be ascertained with certainty.[4] Winternitz is of the opinion that Buddhist Tantra came into being in the "7th or 8th century

---

1. See H.P. Sastri, *Nepal Catalogue*, I, pp. 10, 85, 117.
2. For MSS, see *NCC*, IV, pp. 198-199.
3. *JASB*, XXVI, 1930, p. 129 ff.
4. On this question, see B. Bhattacharya, *Sādhanamālā* (Intro., p. LXXVIII) and Winternitz (*HIL*, II, 1988, p. 385).

under the influence of the Śaivite Tantras".[5] As regards Hindu Tāntric literature, perhaps the first clear reference is found in the *Bhāgavata-purāṇa* which, according to R.C. Hazra (*Studies in the Purāṇic Records*, etc., p. 55), can be assigned to the sixth century A.D.

In this connexion, it may be stated that the *Devīpurāṇa*, a Bengal work of about the seventh century A.D., shows considerable influence of Tantra. The same remark is applicable to the *Mārkaṇḍeya-purāṇa* which, according to the aforesaid Hazra, was most probably composed or compiled between the third century A.D. and the fifth (*ibid.*, p. 11 f). The *Viṣṇu-purāṇa*, which is believed to have originated not later than the fourth century A.D. (*ibid.*, p. 23), mentions the *Śakti* of Viṣṇu and several names of Durgā who is stated to fulfil all the desires of one who worships Her with wine, flesh, etc.

Winternitz comes to the conclusion that no real Tantra can be definitely said to have existed before the seventh century A.D.

PLACE OF ORIGIN OF TANTRA

The provenance of Tantra is controversial. While some suggest different places in India, others think that Tantra was of foreign origin. The following floating verse, which appears to have no foundation in history, records an interesting tradition:

Gauḍa prakāśitā vidyā maithilaiḥ prabalīkṛtā/
Kvacit kvacin-maharāṣṭre gurjare pralayaṃ gatā//

This (branch of) knowledge, which appeared in Gauḍa, was developed by the people of Mithilā, prevailed at some places in Mahārāṣṭra, and met with destruction in Gujarāt. Strictly speaking, Gauḍa was the name of a place near modern Malda in West Bengal; it, however, came to stand for Bengal. Mithilā generally indicated Bihar. Mahārāṣṭra roughly corresponds to the modern State of Mahārāṣṭra with its capital in Mumbai.

One of the arguments in support of the pro-Bengal theory is that many of the Śākta *Pīṭhasthānas* are in or near Bengal. For example, Kālīghāṭ, a prominent *Pīṭha*, is situated in Calcutta. Some other important *Pīṭhas*, e.g. Kāmarūpa, Śrīhaṭṭa, Pūrṇagiri are not very far off from Bengal. Another argument is that many of the old works on Tantra, particularly Buddhist, have been found in Bengal. The *Mahānirvāṇa-tantra*, a late but important text, is definitely known to

5. *Ibid.*

have originated here. It is also pointed out that it was a Bengali Śākta, named Kṛṣṇarāma Nyāyavāgīśa, who preached Śāktism in Kāmākhyā, a stronghold of Tantra in Assam; the then Ahom king, Rudrasiṃha, became his disciple. It is further argued that the Bengali Brahmānanda and his disciple Jñānānanda preached Tāntric philosophy and *sādhana* in the remote Hiṃlāj in Baluchistan. The Tāntric practices in Nepal appear, from some sources (e.g. K.M. Sen's *Vāṅgālīr Sādhanā*, pp. 47-48), to have been influenced by Tāntrikas from Bengal. It is widely believed that the Tāntric religion spread to China and Tibet from Bengal through Buddhism. The famous Atīśa Dīpaṃkara (c. 980-1053 A.D.) and some other scholars from Bengal settled in Tibet, and wrote several treatises on Tantra. Numerous manuscripts of works of the Tantra class, written in Bengali characters, have been found in Bengal. The pro-Bengal theory is supported by Winternitz, a stalwart in the domain of Indian literature in Sanskrit; he, however, mentions Assam also along with Bengal in this connexion.[6]

Works of the *Āgama* class, written in Śārada script, abound in Kashmir; this has led some scholars to think they originated in that region.

It is believed by some that the works of the *Saṃhitā* class originated in different parts of the country, particularly in Deccan and Bengal.

Some scholars believe that Tantra was imported by India from China. Before we examine this question, it should be stated that there is evidence of Sino-Indian contacts in remote antiquity through trade, commerce and Buddhism. Kālidāsa, the greatest poet of ancient India, who is believed to have flourished about the 4th century A.D., refers, in his drama *Abhijñāna-śakuntala* (I.31), to China silk (*cīnāṃśuka*). The names of some of the articles, growing in India, have the word 'cīna' prefixed to them. For example, *alābu* (bottlegourd) was called *Cīna-karkarika*. A kind of camphor was called *Cīna-karpūra*. The word *Cīnaja* denoted steel. A particular kind of lead was named *Cīnapiṣṭa*.

It is an erroneous impression that Fa-hien (399 A.D.) was the first Chinese pilgrim in India. I-tsing (671-695 A.D.) testifies to the fact that many Chinese visited India 500 years before him.

6. *History of Indian Literature*, II, 1988, p. 385.

There are striking similarities between Chinese Taoism and Indian Tāntrism. The Male and Female principles underlying creation were called respectively *Yang* and *Yin* in China. This idea naturally gave rise to sexual rites. The Chinese recognise the possibility of *Hsien* (immortality) through certain practices including respiratory regulation, sexual technique, etc. These ideas and practices have their parallels in Tantra. The occurrence of *Cīnācāra*, as a mode of Tāntric practice in India, lends countenance to the theory of Chinese origin of Tantra. According to the *Tārātantra*, *Cīnācāra* came from *Mahācīna*. A work is entitled *Mahācīnācāra-tantra*. In support of this theory, it is argued that the flower *Javā*, regarded as highly suitable for Śakti-worship, is called China rose in English. It is further argued that the nasal sound in the Tāntric *bījas*, like *HRĪṂ*, *KRĪṂ*, etc. is due to the influence of the nasal twang of the Chinese language (vide *Mātṛkābheda-tantra*, Paṭala 12). Another point in support of borrowing from China is that Tāntric *Yantras* and *Maṇḍalas* were designed after the pictorial scripts of the Chinese alphabet.

If the testimony of the Tibetan *Pag sam joṇ Zang* is reliable, Buddhist Tantra originated in Uḍḍiyāna.[7] Regarding the identification of Uḍḍiyāna (also spelt as Oḍḍiyāna, Oḍryāṇa) opinions differ. According to some, it was Udyāna in or near Swat Valley or Kashgarh in Central Asia. Some scholars think that Uḍḍiyāna was the region of Urain in the district of Monghyr in Bihar, near Kiul.[8] Haraprasād Śāstrī, followed by a few other scholars, locate it in Orissa. Yet others are of the opinion that it was a part of Bengal. According to Lokesh Chandra, Oḍḍiyāna was the ancient name of Kāñcī (Conjeevaram).

The aforesaid H.P. Śāstrī, relying on the following verse[9] of the *Kubjikā-mata-tantra*, thought that Tantra was of foreign origin:

gacchtvaṃ bhārate varṣe adhikārāya sarvataḥ/
pīṭhe pīṭhe kṣetre'smin kuru sṛṣṭimanekadhā//

According to Śāstrī, the idea of Śakti, the dominant figure in Tantra, was borrowed from West Asia from where it infiltrated into India along with the Magi priests of the Scythians.

---

7. See P.C. Bagchi, *Studies in the Tantras*, pp. 37-40; Grosset, *In the Footsteps of the Buddha*, pp. 109-110; *IHQ*, XI, pp. 142-144; B. Bhattacharya, *Introduction to Buddhist Esoterism*, p. 46.
8. See *Devīpurāṇa*, chap. 42.
9. See *Nepal Catalogue*, p. LXXIX.

According to Woodroffe, Tantra came to India from Chaldea around which was the Śākadvīpa of Indian tradition.[10]

The Female Energies (Yoginīs), mentioned in Hindu Tantras, include Lāmā.[11] The *Jayadratha-yāmala* mentions twenty-four types of Lāmās. The terms Ḍākinī, Hākinī, Śākinī, Lākinī, found in Tantra, are also of foreign origin.

The *Sammoha-tantra* refers to the Tāntric culture of foreign regions like Bāhlīka (Balkh), Bhoṭa (Tibet), Cīna (China), Pārasīka (Persia), Airāka (Iraq), etc.

According to a Tibetan tradition, it was through the Buddhist Asaṅga (c. 4th century A.D.) that Tāntric principles and practices were introduced into India. P.V. Kane seems to be right in not seriously taking it, because the tradition is based mainly on the *History of Buddhism* by Tāranātha (b. 1573 or 1575) who flourished more than thousand years after Asaṅga.

After the examination of the above facts, we may conclude, with P.V. Kane, that some Tāntric practices might have been exotic; but that does not necessarily mean that Tantra in general was imported into India from foreign lands. In the history of Indian Tantra, China and Tibet played prominent parts. It may be pointed out that many Sanskrit Tāntric texts were rendered into the languages of those two countries; in fact, some Indian Tantras exist only in their Chinese and Tibetan renderings, the originals being lost. Had those two countries been the original homes of Tantra, we could expect Sanskrit translations of Chinese and Tibetan Tantras.

NUMBER OF TANTRAS

There is no unanimity among the writers about the number and names of Tantras. While the number is a lac according to some, it is millions according to others. In some Tantras, the total number is 64 which is confirmed by verse 31 of the *Saundarya-laharī*, attributed to the great Advaita philosopher, Śaṃkarācārya. According to some sources, there were 64 texts in each of the three regions, called Viṣṇukrāntā, Rathakrāntā and Aśvakrāntā which will be mentioned under classification of Tantras. The testimony of the *Vīṇāśikha-tantra* (verse 9) appears to point to the number 64. There is a far larger number of Tantras according to various catalogues of manuscripts.

---

10. See A. Avalon, *Mahānirvāṇa-tantra*, 3rd ed., p. 560.
11. See G. Tucci, *JASB*, NS, LXXVI, 1930, p. 55 ff.

CLASSIFICATION OF TANTRAS

The Tantras have been classified in various ways. First of all, we should state that there are Tantras of the Hindus, Buddhists and Jainas. Hindu Tantras are broadly divided into two classes, viz. *Āgama* and *Nigama*. In the former, Śiva answers questions asked by Pārvatī; the process is reversed in *Nigama*. In accordance with the predominance of the deity, these works are classed as *Śākta, Śaiva, Saura, Gāṇapatya* and *Vaiṣṇava*. The works of the *Śāktas, Śaivas* and *Vaiṣṇavas* are called respectively *Tantra, Āgama* and *Saṃhitā*. It should be noted that the term *Tantra* is sometimes used in a general sense to indicate any of these classes. Another classification is *Rathakrāntā, Aśvakrāntā* and *Viṣṇukrāntā* according as the works belong to the regions, called Rathakrāntā, Aśvakrāntā (also called *Gajakrāntā*) and Viṣṇukrāntā respectively. [For the regions, indicated by these terms, see Glossary.]

The five mouths of Śiva are said to have originally produced ten *Āgamas*; these are:

Kāmika, Yogaja, Cintya, Mukuṭa, Aṃśumān, Dīpta, Ajita, Sūkṣma, Sahasra and Suprabheda.

These again are said to have led to the compassion of eighteen *Raudrī Āgamas*. These two classes together are the twenty-eight *Śaiva Āgamas*. According to another tradition, there are 64 Bhairava Āgamas.

The *Śākta Tantras* are divided into ten classes in accordance with the names of the ten *Mahāvidyās* (q.v.).

Tantras are divided, in another way, as

(i) *Kādi* — in which *Ka* is the symbol;

(ii) *Hādi* — in which the symbol is *Ha*;

(iii) *Kahādi* — in which the symbol is the combination of *Ka* and *Ha*;

(iv) *Sādi*.

See *Bahvṛcopaniṣad* (with commentary) *saiṣā parā saktiḥ kādividyeti vā hadividyeti vā ṣādividyeti*, and *Tāntrik Texts*, VIII (and Eng. trs.), p. 2.

According to another view, Tāntric works belong to three types, viz.

(1) *Srota* : three currents of tradition — *dakṣiṇa* (right), *vāma* (left) and *madhyama* (middle). These are supposed to represent the three *Śaktis* of Śiva as also the three qualities of *Sattva, Rajas* and *Tamas*.

(2) *Pīṭha* : collective name of goddesses, Icchā, Jñāna, etc. each representing an aspect of *Śakti*.

(3) *Āmnāya* : zone of Tāntric culture.

A mode of classification is *Kālī-kula* — a school which attaches the greatest importance to the cult of the essentially terrible Kālī; and *Śrīkula* — a school which advocates the predominance of the essentially benign Śrī or Tripurasundarī.

A class of Tantras is called *Yāmala*. One *Yāmala* belongs to each of the following: Rudra, Śakti, Viṣṇu, Gaṇeśa and others.

Again, Tantras are classified, according to mythological ages, as *Varāhakalpa, Kālakalpa*, etc.

Some divide Tāntric texts into the following groups:

(1) Āgama, (2) Ḍāmara, (3) Yāmala and (4) Tantra.

The *Vārāhītantra* mentions a class of works as *Upatantra* (minor Tantras).

According to a tradition (e.g. *Brahmayāmala*, ch. 39 — *sroto-nirṇaya* section) there is a way of dividing Tāntric works as *Dakṣiṇa* (right), *Vāma* (left) and *Madhyama* (middle) also called *Divya, Kaula* and *Vāma* respectively; each of them is subdivided as *Hārda* (internal) and *Bāhya* (external).

We have already referred to Buddhist and Jaina Tantras. Buddhist Tantras are divided in accordance with the three later divisions of Buddhism, viz. *Vajrayāna, Sahaja-yāna* and *Kālacakra-yāna*. Jaina Tantras also have been classified according to the Jaina sects.

Tantras are also classified as *Āstika* (Vedic) and *Nāstika* (non-Vedic). Those of the former class are divided according to the predominance of the deities, e.g. *Śākta, Śaiva, Vaiṣṇava*, etc. The Buddhist and Jaina Tantras belong to the *Nāstika* class.

In another way, Tantras are divided into two classes, viz. *Sadāgama* and *Asadāgama*. Opinions differ as to which are *Sat* and which *Asat*. Generally, however, those which prescribe customary worship are regarded as *Sat*, the others are *Asat*.

CONTENTS OF TANTRA — AN OVERVIEW

According to a tradition, represented by the following stanza, Tantra deals with creation, re-creation (i.e. creation after dissolution), determination of *mantras*, worship of deities and description of holy places:

> *sargaśca pratisargaśca mantra-nirṇaya eva ca/*
> *devatānāṃ saṃsthānāṃ ca tīrthānāṃ caiva varṇānām//*

A tradition, ascribed to the *Vārāhītantra*, mentions the following characteristics of Tantra: creation, dissolution, worship of deities, means of acquisition of all, the six magical acts, *puraścaraṇa* and four meditational practices.

The contents of a Tāntric work are broadly divided by Winternitz (*HIL*, I, 1990, pp. 560-561) into four parts, viz.

(1) *Jñāna* (knowledge), (2) *Yoga* (meditation, concentration), (3) *Kriyā* (action) and (4) *Caryā* (conduct).

As a matter of fact, Tāntric literature is so vast and varied that it is difficult to bring the contents of this literature under a cut and dried classification. A look over the contents of the Tāntric works, given by us, will reveal that some works deal with matters not included in the fourfold classification given above. For example, quite a few works, e.g. *Gaurī-kāñcalika*, *Kumāratantra*, etc. deal with diseases and medicines. Again, the *Sāmrājya-lakṣmī-pīṭhikā* deals, *inter alia*, with politics and statecraft. Works like the *Rasārṇava* deal with alchemy.

Thus, it is clear that none of the above descriptions of contents of Tantras is absolutely accurate. In short, however, we can broadly divide the contents into two main classes, viz. (i) philosophical and spiritual, and (ii) popular and practical.

After a general survey of the contents of Tantra literature, we shall deal with the highlights. Tantra regards liberation, rather liberation while alive (*jivanmukti*) as the goal of *sādhana*. So, it sets much store by the body of the devotee. *Mukti* is sought through *bhukti* (enjoyment). No *bhukti* is possible without the body, taste of liberation also requires it. Unlike the conventional Brāhmaṇical scriptures, Tantra does not advocate self-mortification or rigid asceticism. Generally, Tantra provides for *Pañca-makāras* or *Pañca-tattvas* as essential for the worship of Śakti, the Supreme Deity. It is not enough for the devotee to offer these to the deity. He is also to enjoy these consecrated articles. The five things are *Madya* (wine), *Māṃsa* (meat),

Matsya (fish), *Mudrā* (fried or parched cereals)[12] and *Maithuna* (sexual intercourse).

Śiva-Śakti

Śiva is the Supreme Lord. Śakti is His Female Energy. When they are united, Śakti becomes inclined (*unmukhī*) to Śiva. Then the web of *Māyā* (illusion) is rent asunder, and creation proceeds. Śakti is eternal, and pervades the universe like oil in sesame. The subtle body of the goddess is *mūla-mantrātmika* (constituted by the basic *mantra*). The relationship of Śiva and Śakti is controversial. As the *Kulārṇava* (I.110) holds, some declare it non-duality while others are inclined to characterise it as duality.

The following are stated to describe the completeness of Śiva:

Svatantratā (self-dependence), *Nityatā* (eternality), *Nitya-tṛptatā* (eternal contentment), *Sarvajñatā*.

Śakti is both *Māyā* and *Mūla-prakṛti*. Through the power of Māyā, the Supreme One conceals his own form, and appears in various manifestations. *Mūlaprakṛti* is unmanifested. In the manifest condition, She resides in the universe consisting of diverse forms and names.

The abode of Śiva-Śakti, within human body, is in the *Mūlādhāra* and *Kuṇḍalinī*. Śakti is variously called *Māyā*, *Mahāmāyā*, *Devī*, *Prakṛti*, etc. She is both *Vidyā* (True knowledge) and *Avidyā* (False knowledge or Nescience). As *Avidyā*, She causes bondage. As *Vidyā*, She causes freedom from rebirths, then leading to liberation. She is also called *Ādya Śakti* (Primeval Energy) as She is believed to have existed before creation.

As Parabrahman, Devī is beyond form and quality. Śakti exists in different forms, e.g. Lakṣmī, Sarasvatī, Durgā, Annapūrṇā, etc.

As Satī (daughter of Dakṣa Prajāpati), Umā or Pārvatī (daughter of Himālaya), She is the consort of Śiva. As Satī, She manifested. Herself as ten *Mahāvidyās* about whose names there is no consensus. According to the *Cāmuṇḍā-tantra*, they are:

Kālī, Tārā, Ṣoḍaśī, Bhuvaneśvarī, Bhairavī, Chinnamastā, Dhūmavatī, Vagalā, Mātaṅgī, Kamalā.

---

12. Cf. *Yoginī-tantra*, ch. VI. *Mudrā* is also taken to mean certain poses of hand or fingers used in worship. In *Yoga* also it denotes certain postures of the body.

As the dead body of Satī was cut to pieces by Viṣṇu[13] with his *Cakra* (disc), fifty-one pieces fell down at as many places on the earth. Each such place came to be known as *Mahāpīṭhas* which were regarded, in Tantra, as extremely holy.

Human Body — Nāḍis, Cakras, etc.

The body, considered as a microcosm, is supposed to contain, within it, three principal *Nāḍis* (arteries or veins) and six *Cakras* (mystical circles or nerve-plexuses). The above *Nāḍis* are called *Iḍā* (on the left of the spinal cord), *Piṅgalā* (on the right) and *Suṣumnā*, also called *Brahmanāḍi* or *Brahmavartman* (in between *Iḍā* and *Piṅgalā*). The *Cakras* are six, viz.

Mūlādhāra — supposed to be located at the lowest extremity of the spinal cord;

Svādhiṣṭhāna — above *Mūlādhāra;*

Maṇipura or *Nābhi-cakra* — near the navel region;

Anāhata — in the region of the heart;

Viśuddha — above *Anāhata* and in the region of the neck;

Ājñā — in between the eyebrows.

Sahasrāra is conceived as a thousand-petalled and multicoloured lotus, supposed to exist in *Brahmarandhra* which is fancied as an aperture in the apex of the cranium.

Kuṇḍalinī

Kuṇḍalinī,[14] which plays a very prominent role in Tāntric *sādhana,* is the vital energy, imagined as a serpent coiling around the aforesaid *Mūlādhāra.*

The devotee's main aim is *Cakrabheda* or *Ṣaṭ-cakrabheda* i.e. penetration of the six *Cakras*. By his *sādhana* he is to make *Kuṇḍalinī*

---

13. According to a Purāṇic legend, Dakṣa Prajāpati performed a grand sacrifice to which his son-in-law Śiva (who married Dakṣa's daughter, Satī) was not invited. Yet, Satī could not resist the desire of going to her father's house on this occasion. On her arrival there, Dakṣa began to abuse Śiva. She felt extremely insulted, and eventually died. Hearing this, the irate Śiva was determined to spoil the sacrifice. Seeing the corpse of Satī, he put it on his shoulders and began to dance violently; this spelt the destruction of the world to save which Viṣṇu, with his wheel-weapon, cut the dead-body to pieces.
14. For the scientific basis of *Kuṇḍalinī,* see Gopi Krishna, *Biological Basis of Religion and Genus* and its introduction by Weizsacker.

pierce the six *Cakras* and ultimately unite her with Śiva residing in *Sahasrāra* above — this marks the culmination of *Sādhana*.

For *Cakra* rituals, see under Society Reflected in Tantra.

Human Nature

From the point of view of *Bhāva* (mental disposition), Tantra makes a threefold division of human nature, viz. *Divya, Vīra* and *Paśu*. A person of *Divya-bhāva* has the predominance of the *Sattvaguṇa* in his nature. He is the best of men, kind, pious, pure, truthful. One with *Vīrabhāva* has the predominance of *Rajas* and is prone to indulge in such acts as lead to grief. The worst is one with *Paśubhāva*. Having in him the preponderance of the quality of *Tamas*, he is forgetful, lazy and drowsy, and has no faith in *guru* and *mantra*.

Guru,[15] Śiṣya[16]

In Tantra, *Guru* (preceptor) is regarded as indispensable for one's initiation to *mantra*, rites and practices. He is so important that he is capable of pacifying Śiva if He is angry, but when *Guru* becomes irate none can appease him. It is noteworthy that a female *Guru* is regarded as highly commendable; one's mother is the best *Guru*. One's father or husband is not regarded as fit to be *Guru*. Among the qualifications of the *Guru* are calmness, spotless character, knowledge of *Śāstras*, freedom from avarice, truthfulness, etc. Some works give warning against hypocritical *Gurus*.

Some Tantras classify *Gurus* in the following way: *Guru, Parama-guru, Parāpara-guru* and *Parameṣṭhi-guru*. For instance, according to the *Nīlatantra* (V.73), one's preceptor is his *Guru*, the *Guru's Guru* is his *Para* or *Parama-guru*, Śakti is *Parāpara-guru* and Śiva is *Parameṣṭhi-guru*. According to verses 65-66 of the same chapter, *Gurus* may be of three classes, viz. *Divyaugha* (divine beings), *Siddhaugha* (sages) and *Mānavaugha* (humans).

---

15. See *Prapañcasāra*, XXXVI; *Rudrayāmala*, Uttara II; *Kulārṇava*, XI-XIV, XVII; *Śāradātilaka*, II.143-144 (Rāghava's commentary); *Paraśurāma-kalpasūtra*, X.75 (Rāmeśvara's comm.); Kṛṣṇānanda's *Tantrasāra*, p. 3; *Prāṇatoṣiṇī*, II.2, III.1, VI.4; *Mahānirvāṇa*, X.200-201, XV.139. Several other works also deal with merits and demerits of *Guru*.
16. See, for example, *Kulārṇava*, XI, XIV; *Rudrayāmala*, Uttara II; *Prapañcasāra*, XXXVI; *Śāradātilaka*, II.745-50, 153; *Paraśurāma-kalpasūtra*, X.74; Kṛṣṇānanda's *Tantrasāra*, p. 3, etc.

The *Śiṣya* must be respectful, and regard and *Guru*, *Devatā* and *Mantra* as one. The *mantra* and *pūjā*, taught by the *Guru*, must be kept strictly secret.

Dīkṣā[17]

Nobody is allowed to take to Tāntric practices without *dīkṣā* or initiation by a *Guru*. So, *dīkṣā* has been dealt with *in extenso* in some prominent Tantras, e.g. *Prapañcasāra* (V, VI), *Kulārṇava* (14.39 ff), *Śāradā-tilaka* (Paṭala 4), *Jñānārṇava* (Paṭala 24), *Mahānirvāṇa* (X.112-119), *Prāṇatoṣiṇī* (II.4).

Several kinds of *dīkṣā* are described in some Tantras. The two broad types are

(i) *Bahirdīkṣā* — initiation to *Pūjā, Homa* and other external rites. By it, the *Sāttvika* feeling is believed to be aroused in the disciple.

(ii) *Antardīkṣā* — initiation to the internal process of awakening the *Kuṇḍalinī* energy.

According to some works, *dīkṣā* is of three types, viz.

(i) *Śāmbhavī* — by it the mind of the disciple is believed to be purified.

(ii) *Śāktī* — supposed to arouse spiritual energy in him.

(iii) *Māntrī* — it is believed to arouse the power of *mantras* and gods.

According to the *Viśvasāra-tantra*, *dīkṣā* is of four kinds, viz. *Kalāvatī, Kriyāvatī, Varṇamayī* and *Vedhamayī*. For description, see Glossary.

According to the *Kulārṇava* (XIV), the seven kinds of *dīkṣā* are: *Kriyā, Varṇa, Kalā, Sparsā, Vāk, Dṛk* and *Mānasa*. See Glossary.

The *Rudrayāmala* provides for three types, called *Āṇavī, Śāktī* and *Śāmbhavī*. See Glossary.

Besides the above modes of *dīkṣā*, three more are *Krama, Pañcāyatana* and *Ekamantra*. See Glossary.

By receiving *dīkṣā*, an aspirant is believed to advance on the way to liberation through the removal of the *malas* (impurities) in him. The *malas* are of three kinds, viz.

---

17. For details, see U.K. Das, *Śāstramūlak Bhāratīya Śakti-sādhanā* (in Bengali), 1st ed., chap. 14.

(i) *Āṇava* : it engenders the narrow jīvahood of Śiva; without its removal, it is not possible to realise the identity of Śakti.

(ii) *Buddhigata* : real knowledge can be acquired after it is removed.

(iii) *Māyīya* : it gives rise to *Ahaṃkāra* which is the root of *viṣaya* and *viṣayin*. Liberation is possible after its removal.

Puraścaraṇa

It means the rite for making the *Mūlamantra* or the basic *mantra* effective. According to the *Kulārṇava* (xvii.87), it is so called because, as a result of its performance, the desired deity moves (*carati*) before (*puraḥ*) of the worshipper for bestowing favour on him. According to another authority, it is so called as it has to be performed before the acts in which the *mantra* is to be employed. The rite consists in *dhyāna*, *pūjā*, *japa*, *homa*, *tarpaṇa*, *abhiṣeka* and *Brāhmaṇa-bhojana*.

It has been dealt with in many Tantras of which the very important are:

> *Kulārṇava* (XV.7-9, 11-12), *Śāradātilaka* (XVI.56 and Rāghavabhaṭṭa's commentary thereon, *Śaktisaṃgama*, Sundarī, III.155-56; XIV.45-46), *Puraścaryārṇava* (VI), Kṛṣṇānanda's *Tantrasāra*, *Mahānirvāṇa* (vii.76-85).

Modes of *Puraścaraṇa* vary in accordance with the nature of the devotees who may be of the types called *Divya*, *Vīra* and *Paśu*.

Abhiṣeka

It means initiation of a special type. It mainly consists in sprinkling holy waters on the neophyte while reciting *mantras* to propitiate different deities, particularly for driving away evil spirits. Different kinds of *Abhiṣeka* are meant for the disciples in the different stages of their spiritual life. Of these, *Pūrṇābhiṣeka* is regarded as the highest; for this the aspirant has to undergo severe ordeals after which he acquires divinity.

Mudrā

It generally indicates one of five *Makāras* or *Tattvas*, regarded as essential for Tāntric *Sādhana;* it denotes fried or parched cereals.

It is also used to indicate different postures of the hand or fingers used in Tāntric worship. Various *Mudrās* are mentioned and sometimes described in different Tantras. For instance, the *Śāradātilaka* describes the following *Mudrās*:

> Āvahanī, Avaguṇṭhana, Dhenu, Mahā, Sthāpanī, Sannidhāpanī, Sannirodhanī, Sammukhīkaraṇī, and Sakalīkṛti.

It should be noted that particular poses of the hand and fingers are prescribed in the works of all the sects and even in the works of the Buddhists and Jains.

Some of the Buddhist *Mudrās*[18] are *Bhūmisparśa, Dharmacakra, Abhaya, Jñāna, Vara* or *Varada, Lalita, Tarka, Śaraṇa, Uttarabodhinī*. The *Mudrās*, practised by Jains, are dealt with in two works, called *Mudrāvicāra* (71 *Mudrās*) and *Mudrāvidhi* (114).[19]

Maṇḍala[20]

Maṇḍalas or diagrams (not necessarily circles) are one of the requisites in Tāntric worship. These are of different forms. Some *Maṇḍalas* are to be drawn with coloured powders. The *Guhyasamāja* mentions a *Maṇḍala* of sixteen cubits! The names of some prominent *Maṇḍalas* are: *Sarvatobhadra, Prāsāda-vāstu-maṇḍala, Hari-hara-maṇḍala*, etc.

Yantra

It also indicates a diagram drawn on cloth, leaf, stone, metal, etc. *Yantra* is another requisite in Tāntric worship. Some *Yantras* are prescribed (e.g. in *Tantrarāja-tantra*, Paṭala 8 and verses 30-32) as amulets to be tied on the head, in the arms, neck, waist or wrist. Some well-known Tantras dealing, *inter alia*, with *Yantras* are:

> *Prapañcasāra* (Paṭalas 21, 34), *Śāradātilaka* (vii.53-56, XXIV), *Nityāṣoḍaśīkārṇava* (I.31-43), *Ahirbudhnya* (chaps. 23-26), *Mantramahodadhi* (Taraṅga 20), etc.

It should be noted that some *Yantras* are meant for malevolent purposes. For example, an *Āgneya-yantra*, drawn on a piece of garment, gathered from a funeral place, should be buried near the

---

18. For *Mudrās*, practised by Tibetan Lāmās, see Waddell, *The Buddhism of Tibet or Lāmāism*, pp. 336-37; Burgess in *IA*, 26, 1897, pp. 24-25.
19. See P. Shah, *Jour. of Oriental Institute*, VI, No. 1, pp. 1-35.
20. Vide, for example, *Jñānārṇava*, XXIV.8-10, XXVI.15-17; *Śāradātilaka*, III.113-118, 131-134, 135-139; *Mahānirvāṇa*, X.137-38; Buddhist Tantras also describe *Maṇḍalas*, e.g. *Guhyasamāja, Niṣpanna-yogāvalī, Mañjuśrī-mūlakalpa*, etc.

house of the enemy for his destruction (*Śāradātilaka*, vii.58-59). A *Yantra* is prescribed, in the *Prapañcasāra* (XXXIV.33), for rousing passion in a woman who will run to the person concerned.

Nyāsa

It means feeling the deity worshipped in the different parts of the body; without it Tāntric worship is futile. *Nyāsa* serves the dual purpose of making the worshipper feel like god, and protecting him against evil. *Nyāsas* are of various kinds, e.g. *Mātṛkā-nyāsa, Ṣoḍhā-nyāsa, Karāṅga-nyāsa, Vidyā-nyāsa, Tattva-nyāsa,* etc. Each of these is believed to produce a special result. *Mātṛkā-nyāsa* (feeling the letters of the alphabet) is twofold according as it is *Antaḥ* (internal) and *Bahis* (external); in the latter, the *Śakti* of the letters is to be felt successively on the head, face, anus, legs and the entire body. In *Ṣoḍhā-nyāsa,* six kinds of *Nyāsas* are resorted to to experience the Vidyās like Kālī, Tārā, etc. There are other types of *Nyāsa* too, e.g. *Pīṭhanyāsa* in which the different *Pīṭha-sthānas* are to be felt in different parts of the body; for example, Kāmarūpa in the heart, Jālandhara on the forehead.

Some of the important works, dealing with *Nyāsa,* are:

Gandharva, ix.2, *Tārātantra,* ii.3, *Śāradātilaka,* vii, *Tārā-bhakti-sudhārṇava,* v, p. 169; *Puraścaryārṇava,* xii, p. 1165, Kṛṣṇānanda's *Tantrasāra,* p. 93; *Saubhāgya-bhāskara* on *Lalitā-sahasra-nāma,* I.4.

Ācāra

Various modes of Tāntric *Sādhana* are recognised. These are called *Ācāras* of which the following seven kinds are generally accepted:

Vedācāra, Vaiṣṇavācāra, Śaivācāra, Dakṣiṇācāra, Vāmācāra, Siddhāntācāra, Kaulācāra.

Vedācāra, as the name indicates, consists in copious Vedic rituals. *Vaiṣṇavācāra,* the way of devotion, encourages firm faith in the saving grace of Brahman instead of blind faith. In *Śaivācāra,* the way of knowledge, there is a combination of *bhakti* and *śakti* with faith; the devotee seeks the acquisition of *Śakti*. In *Dakṣiṇācāra,* the devotee is capable of meditating on the three *Śaktis* (of *Kriyā, Icchā* and *Jñāna*) of Brahman, and acquires the ability of worshipping the triad, viz. Brahmā, Viṣṇu, Maheśvara. In *Vāmācāra,* the devotee overcomes *pravṛtti* (propensity), and proceeds to *nivṛtti* (cessation of desire). In it, he becomes free from the bonds of delusion, shame, etc.

with which a person of *paśu-bhāva* is tied. According to some (e.g. *Pārānanda-sūtra*, pp. 1-3, 13), *Vāmācāra* is twofold:

(i) *Madhyama* requiring the enjoyment of all the five *Makāras*;

(ii) *Uttama* requiring the enjoyment of only *Madya, Mudrā* and *Maithuna*.

The word *Vāma* has been taken by some to mean 'left' as distinct from 'right' (*Dakṣiṇa*). According to others, it means a woman (*vāmā*); they hold that *Vāmācāra* stresses the need of woman as an essential element for *sādhana*. This *Ācāra* prepares the aspirant for the attainment of *Śivahood* which is possible, with the help of the *Guru*, in *Kaulācāra*. In this state, he becomes liberated in life (*jīvanmukta*), and, with the knowledge of Brahman, attains the state of *Paramahaṃsa*, the highest goal of Tāntric *sādhana*.

The term *kula* has been differently interpreted by different authorities. It may mean

(i) the individual soul (*Mahānirvāṇa*, vii.97-98);

(ii) *Upāsaka* (worshipper) of Kālī (*Śakti-saṃgama*, Kālīkhaṇḍa, iii.32);

(iii) *Gotra* arising from Śiva and Śakti (*Kulārṇava*);

(iv) Śakti.

In some works, *Ācāras* are broadly divided into two classes, *Aghora* (followed by the Śaiva sect, named *Aghorin*) and *Yoga*.

Besides the above, there is mention of *Cīnācāra*, also called *Mahācīnācāra, Cīna-krama, Cīna-sādhana*. It is the name of the Chinese way of worship, chiefly relating to goddess Tārā, believed to have been brought by sage Vaśiṣṭha, and formed the basis of *Vāmācāra*. In this connection, the following texts may be consulted: *Śakti-saṃgama*, Sundarī, I.188 ff; *Puraścaryārṇava*, I.20; Kṛṣṇānanda's *Tantrasāra*, 20; *Nīlatantra*, chap. xiii.

Śava-Sādhana

Ritual with a corpse. Several Tantras deal with it. Prominent among them are:

Kaulāvalī-nirṇaya (XIV), *Śyāmārahasya* (XIV), *Tārā-bhakti-sudhārṇava* (IX), *Puraścaryārṇava* (IX), *Nīlatantra* (XVI), *Kulacūḍāmaṇi* (VI) and Kṛṣṇānanda's *Tantrasāra*.

It is described below after the *Tantrasāra*. The places, suitable for this rite, are:

> Vacant house, river bank, mountain, lonely spot, root of a *Bel* tree, cemetery and battlefield.

The appropriate time is night of the eighth and fourteenth lunar mansions in both the bright and dark fortnights. Tuesday is the most propitious for it.

The dead bodies of some men and animals are recommended for the rite. Prohibited are the body of a Brāhmaṇa, of the cow and of a woman. A human body is called *mahā-śava* (great corpse) which is stated to be the most suitable. Among the humans, the bodies of the following are prescribed:

(i) A *Caṇḍāla*[21] who died as a result of being hit with a stick, sword, spear, etc., drowning, thunder-strike, snake-bite, injury.

(ii) A bright handsome youth, killed in battle while facing the enemy, but not while running away.

The bodies of the following persons are tabooed:

(i) one who committed suicide,

(ii) hen-pecked person (*strī-vaśya*),

(iii) apostate (*patita*),[22]

(iv) untouchable (*aspṛśya*),

(v) beardless man,

(vi) one whose genital organ is not clearly visible,

(vii) leper,

(viii) old man (age not specified),

(ix) one who died of starvation in a famine.

A stale corpse is also forbidden.

Kṛṣṇānanda, following some Tāntric authorities, provides that, in the absence of the prescribed corpses, an aspirant should perform the rite on an effigy made of any of the following:

Darbha (grass), barley, rice, etc.

In the absence of suitable carcasses, the body of any animal (*jantu-mātra*) may serve the purpose.

---

21. General appellation of the lowest and most hated of the mixed castes originating from the union of a Śūdra father and a Brāhmaṇa mother; an outcaste.
22. Degraded as a result of committing a heinous act or sin.

In case the devotee gets nothing after the performance of the ritual till midnight, he should scatter sesame, walk seven steps, and perform *japa*. *Japa*, with great concentration, should be continued so long as the corpse or carcass concerned does not promise to give the desired object or to grant a boon. The devotee, having achieved his purpose, should release the hairs and feet of the dead body, which were tied before the rite commenced. Then, after washing or bathing the body, he is to throw it into water or bury it. The articles of worship are to be cast into water. Finally, he should go home.

The other rites, in connection with *Śavasādhana*, are drinking of *pañcagavya* and giving feast to twenty-five Brāhmaṇas. God is believed to reside in the body of such a devotee for a fortnight since the commencement of the rite. During this period, he is ordained to abstain from sexual enjoyment, listening to songs and witnessing dance.

Siddhi

Fulfilment or success, achieved by Tāntric *Sādhana*, may be of two kinds, viz.

(i) *Mantra-siddhi* — *mantras*, used by a *Sādhaka*, produce the desired result;

(ii) *Vāk-siddhi* — success in speech; by this the words, uttered by a *Sādhaka*, become infallible.

After reaching the peak of spiritual life by *Sādhana*, one acquires the following *Siddhis* or miraculous powers: *aṇimā* (assuming a figure of atomic size), *mahimā* (power of increasing one's size at will), *laghimā* (power of assuming excessive lightness), *garimā* (power of assuming excessive heaviness), *prāpti* (power of getting everything at will), *prākāmya* (irresistible will), *īśitva* (superiority over others), *vaśitva* (power of controlling others).

There are other minor *Siddhis* also. The greatest *Siddhi*, however, is *Mahānirvāṇa* or *Mokṣa* which is the ultimate goal of *Sādhana*.

Ṣaṭ-Karma

Six magical acts common to many Tāntric works. There are minor differences in the lists of these acts. Those commonly dealt with are: *Māraṇa* (killing), *Stambhana* (arresting the effort of the enemy or causing his physical immobility), *Uccāṭana* (expulsion), *Vidveṣaṇa* (causing dissension or creating bad blood), *Vaśīkaraṇa* (bringing others under control) and *Śānti* (propitiatory rite for averting evil).

TANTRA VIS-A-VIS VEDIC LITERATURE

It is sometimes alleged that Tantra is *Veda-vāhya* or outside the Vedic tradition. It is not wholly correct. Some hold that the omnipotent Śakti of Tantra is foreshadowed by Goddess Vāk of the *Devī-sūka* of the *Ṛgveda* (x.125); She declares: I maintain both Mitra and Varuṇa, both Indra and Agni, etc. (stanza 1). Again, She asserts: by my own greatness I have assumed the forms of these worlds (stanza 8). She combines in Herself both the efficient cause (*ārabhamāṇā bhuvanāni viśvā*) and the material cause (*etāvatī mahimā saṃ babhūvā*) of the world. The very word 'Śakti' occurs in the above Veda several times (e.g. I.31.18, III.31.14, IV.22.8). This Veda mentions magicians (VII.21.5, X.993), and refers (e.g. VII.104, X.37) to the fact that black magic was dreaded by the people. Magic, particularly black magic, is a common topic in Tantra. The concept of Mahānagnī (the Great Naked Woman), occurring in the *Ṛgveda* (e.g. *Khila* i.e. Supplement, V.22.91) and *Atharvaveda* (e.g. XIV.1.36, XX.136.6), may have suggested the Tāntric idea of Kālī.

The magical ideas and practices like *Madhuvidyā* transforming poison into nectar (I.191), bringing others under control (X.49.5, X.159.1), certain *mantras* believed to cure diseases (X.161, 163), etc. are Tāntric in character.

In an older form of the Vedic *Mahāvrata* ritual, sexual union as a fertility rite is permitted. *Maithuna* (sexual intercourse) is one of the essentials of *Sādhana*, according to some Tantras.

The *Atharvaveda* contains a part called *Ābhicārika* which deals with curses, exorcisms, etc. which are taken to be precursors of similar rites in Tantra. Hence, Tantra has been characterised (e.g. *Śukranīti-sāra*, iv.3.39) as *Upaveda* of the above Veda.

The Vedic sacrificial rites, called *Vājapeya* and *Sautrāmaṇi*, appear to foreshadow Tāntric *Cakra* (esoteric assembly of Tāntric devotees).

From some Brāhmaṇas (e.g. *Śatapatha*, V.1.2.9 and *Aitareya*, III.1.5, etc.) drinking appears to have been in vogue in sacrificial rites. This may have given rise to the practice of drinking as an essential element of Tāntric *Pañca-makāra-sādhana*.

The origin of the *Nāḍis*, so important in Tantra, can be traced to some Upaniṣads. For example, mention may be made of the *Kaṭha* (vi.16), *Chāndogya* (viii.6.6), *Praśna* (iii.6.7) and *Muṇḍaka* (ii.2.6) Upaniṣads. The *Muṇḍaka* refers (i.2.4) to Kālī though not as a goddess, but as the name of one of the seven lolling tongues of Fire-god.

An important idea in Tantra is the unity of Śakti and the Śaktimat (*Śakti-śakti-matorabhedaḥ*). This concept occurs in the Umā-Haimavatī legend in the *Kenopaniṣad*. The Supreme Power of Śakti (Female Energy) has been sought to be established in this Upaniṣad.

The *Sāṅkhāyana Gṛhyasūtra* mentions (ii.14.14) Bhadrakālī. This is a form of Kālī in Tantra.

The Tantras are not totally opposed to the Veda. For example, in the *Paraśurāma-kalpasūtra* (section X), some Vedic *mantras* are included in *Raśmi-pañcaka* (Sūtra 10). The *Kulārṇava* states (II.10.85, 104-41) that *Kulaśāstra* is based on the Veda.

From the foregoing discussion, it can be said that the remark of the great Śaṃkarācārya, made in his exposition of the *Brahmasūtras*, that Tantra is anti-Vedic, seems to be too sweeping.

As we have stated elsewhere, Hārīta, one of the twenty authoritative writers of Dharmaśāstra, characterises Tantra as one of the two kinds of *Śruti* (revealed literature), the other being the Veda (vide Kullūka's commentary on the *Manu-smṛti*, II.1). From the presence of Tāntric elements in the Vedic literature, it seems that the populist Tāntric culture ran parallel to the elitist Vedic culture.

1. Painting showing Satchakras, Rajasthan, 18th Cent. A.D.
Courtesy National Museum.

2. Painting showing yoni yantra, Rajasthan, 18th Cent. A.D.
Courtesy National Museum.

3. Painting on cloth showing Sri-Yantra, Gujarat, 17th Cent. A.D. Courtesy National Museum.

4. Painting showing Yori-Arana, Nepal, 17th Cent. A.D. Courtesy National Museum.

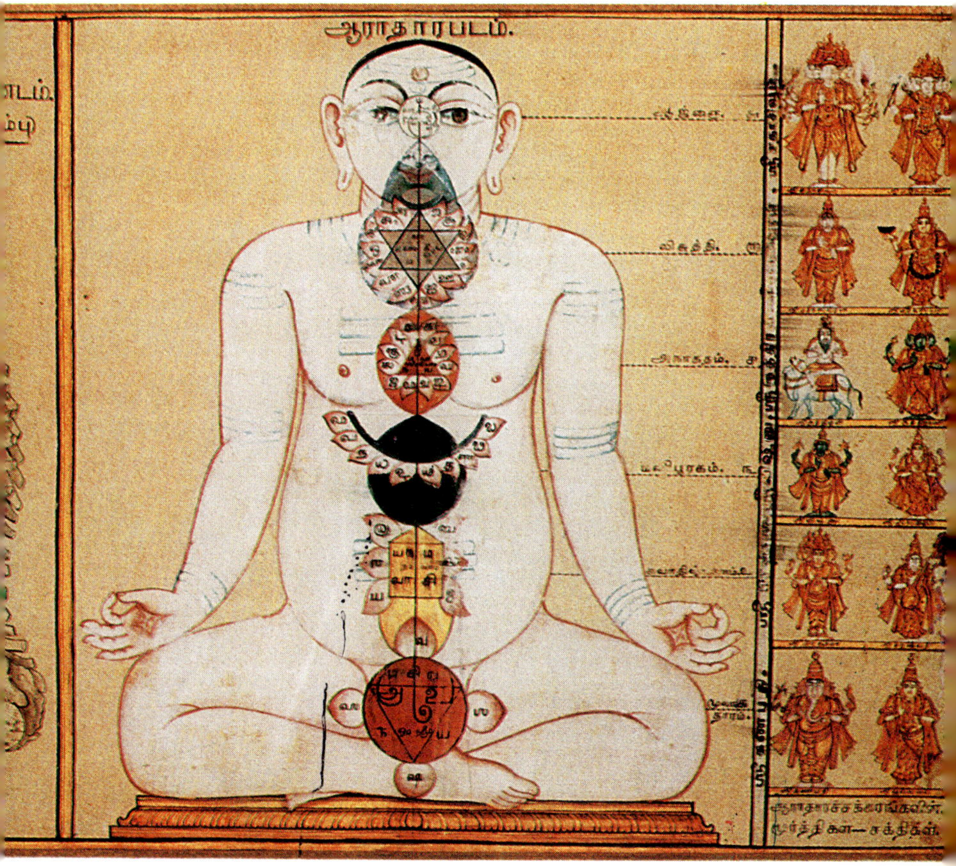

7. Painting showing Satchakra, Tanjore, 19th Cent. A.D. Courtesy National Museum.

5. Painting showing Sri-Yantra, South India, 17th & 18th Cent. A.D. Courtesy National Museum.

6. Painting on cloth showing Om Rymn, Rajasthan, 19th Cent. A.D.
Courtesy National Museum.

8. Contemporary Madhubani painting showing Kali, 20th Cent. A.D. Courtesy National Museum.

CHAPTER II

TĀNTRIC ELEMENTS IN POST-VEDIC SANSKRIT LITERATURE

THE GREAT EPICS

The *Rāmāyaṇa* (present form completed by c. 2nd or 3rd century A.D.) reflects Tāntrism at certain places. From the description of Nikumbhilā, the palladium of Laṅkā (V.24.44, VI.82.25), She appears to represent a form of the Tāntric Śakti. Her worship with wine and meat confirms this assumption. Moreover, Her worship by Indrajit with the object of causing harm to the enemy is typically like Tāntric *abhicāra*. The Uttarakāṇḍa refers, at some places, to Śiva-Śakti. Modern scholars, however, consider it to be spurious.

The *Mahābhārata* (present form completed by c. 4th century A.D.) betrays Tāntric influence. The Durgā hymns (Virāṭa, ch. vi, Bhīṣma, ch. 23) clearly contain elements of Tantra. The mention of Kālī, Mālinī, etc. as the names of *Mātṛkās* in the Vanaparvan, 190.9, reminds one of Tantra. This Parvan mentions Śakti-tīrthas like Devikā (Kāmākhyā), Kālikā-saṃgama, etc. Ādiparvan, ch. 76, testifies to the Tāntric belief that certain charms can make a dead man alive.

MISCELLANEOUS WORKS

The *Arthaśāstra*, of c. 4th century B.C., refers (v.2.59) to rites designed, for the following purposes:

annihilation of enemies, earning the love of a woman, etc.

Mantras, called *Mānava-vidyā*, were believed to produce the magical effects of a door opening automatically and making one invisible.

As early as in c. 4th century A.D., Kālidāsa appears to have been influenced by Tantra. He mentions Kālī (*Kumārasambhava*, VII.39) and Kālikā (*Raghuvaṃśa*, xi.15).

Varāhamihira (6th century A.D.), in his *Bṛhatsaṃhitā* (60.19), mentions *Mātṛkās* and *Maṇḍalas*.

Bāṇabhaṭṭa (7th century, first half) mentions Caṇḍī and Her worship with blood (*Kādambarī*, Kale's ed., 1928, p. 56). The magical practice of rendering one invisible is referred to (*ibid*., p. 339). The author's *Harṣacarita* (Kane's ed., 1918) refers to the drawing of a *maṇḍala* with different colours (ch. iii), human sacrifice (*ibid*.), measure for driving away ghosts (ii), *vaśīkaraṇa* (i), propitiation of Mātṛkās (v), etc.

Bhavabhūti (c. 7th-8th century), in his drama, *Mālatīmādhava*, refers to some Tāntric practices, e.g. offer of fresh flesh to ghosts in the cemetery, the flesh of a virgin girl for propitiating goddess Cāmuṇḍā (Acts iv, v). The worship of the hedious, dark Goddess Karālā, who appears to be the Tāntric Kālī, is mentioned in Act v. There is description also of a Kāpālika.

The Tāntric Tārā cult is referred to in the prose romance *Vāsavadattā* of Subandhu (lower limit 8th century A.D.).

The Kashmirian Kṣemendra (11th century A.D.), in his *Daśāvatāra-carita* (p. 162) sarcastically refers to the unscrupulous enjoyment of women and drinking of wine by Tāntric *Gurus* and their followers.

Kalhaṇa (12th century A.D.), in his *Rājataraṅgiṇī*, refers to the repulsive practices of Tantrokas like incest (vii.278).

Somadeva, in his *Kathāsaritsāgara* (Tawney's Eng. trs., *Ocean of Story*, ed. by Penzer), refers to several Tāntric beliefs and practices, e.g. demons flying in the air (ii, p. 299), men flying in the sky through the influence of witches (ii, p. 103), *Śavasādhana* (ii, p. 62), etc.

According to the Buddhist Sanskrit work, *Lalitavistara* (c. 1st century A.D.), the Buddha learnt from sage Viśvāmitra 46 letters of the alphabet including *aṃ, aḥ* among vowels, and *kṣa* among consonants (x). These three are mentioned as separate letters in Tantra alone.

HYMNS IN CLASSICAL SANSKRIT INFLUENCED BY TANTRA

There is a large number of hymns in Sanskrit. Hymnology forms a distinct branch of study in the history of Sanskrit literature. Hymns are addressed to different gods and goddesses. Some of them bear the deep impress of Tantra. We shall deal with just a few such hymns which will reveal that the Tāntric devotees, at least some of them, did not rest content with merely the nitty-gritty of the dry rituals; they also took to the soul-stirring music of metrical descriptions of their chosen deities to whom they surrendered themselves wholeheartedly.

Saundarya-Laharī (Wave of Beauty)

Generally attributed to Ādi Śaṃkarācārya it is in 100 (103 in one version, 104 in another) stanzas. The authorship, however, is controversial. So, the date of its composition is uncertain.

The hymn appears to be deliberately designed to present the essence of Tantra in the mnemonic form of verses. As a result, it has become a laboured composition, although there are occasional flashes of poetic art. All the verses are in the *Śikhariṇī* metre which is not very melodious.

It opens with a reference to Śiva and Śakti from whose union creation proceeds. The face of the Divine Mother (Devī) is beautiful like the full moon in autumn. She excels even the celestial nymphs, Urvaśī and Rambhā in beauty (v. 12). Verse 9 depicts the ascent of *Kuṇḍalinī* through the different *Cakras*. Different *yantras*, used in the worship of Devī, have been described. Verse 23 emphasises the oneness of Śiva and Śakti. Verse 31 refers to 64 Tantras. The next verse contains the secret sixteen-lettered *mantra* of Śrīvidyā. Verses 36 to 41 deal with worship in the six *Cakras*. Verses 42-91 give a graphic description of the Divine Mother. This description occasionally reflects poetic fancy and literary skill. For example, the parting of Devī's hairs is conceived as the outlet for the flow of the wave of Her facial beauty (44). The swans are stated to have learnt graceful gait from Devī (91).

Sublimity of thought, couched in well-chosen words, is a marked feature of the hymn. The use of the figures of words like *anuprāsa* (e.g. *dṛśa drāghīyasā dara-dalita-nīlotpala-rucā* — v. 57) and figures of sense like *śleṣa* (e.g. the words *Viśālā, Madhurā*, etc., while being place-names, at the same time, refer respectively to Devī's greatness and sweetness). Verse 63, stating that the brightness of the smile of Devi is superior to moonlight, is an excellent case of the use of the figure *Vyatireka*.

The hymn contains the main features of Tāntric *sādhana* — rousing of *Kuṇḍalinī*, its penetration of the *Cakras* and union with

Śiva, descent of *Kuṇḍalinī*, *Śrī-cakra*, the symbolic abode of Śakti (verse 11), unity of Śiva-Śakti (23), *Śrīvidyā-mantra* (32), idea of the excellence of *Antaryāga*.

The author concludes the hymn stating that the panegyric of Devī with words, learnt from Her, is similar to the worship of lights, in honour of the sun, done with its own rays, like the oblation in honour of the moon with the water emanating from the moonstone and like pleasing the ocean with its own waters.

Poet Tagore was so impressed by this hymn that he compared it with Shelley's *Intellectual Beauty*.

An index to its popularity is the existence of its several commentaries of which the most well-known are the *Sudhā-vidyotinī* and the *Lakṣmīdharā*.

Of the editions of the hymn, the following are very useful:

Ed. N. Brown, with Eng. trs., Cambridge Mass., 1958; with three comms.; Eng. trs. and notes, by P.A. Sastri and R.K. Guru, Madras, 1957; with nine expositions, Eng. trs. and notes, Hindi trs., etc. by Kuppuswami, Delhi, 1976.

Ānanda-Laharī (Wave of Joy)

Generally attributed to Śaṃkarācārya, the renowned monist. The authorship is controversial. At least two hymns of the same title exist. One of them consists of only twenty stanzas in the *Sīkhariṇī* metre. It describes the appearance and beauty of goddess Bhavānī whose compassion is zealously prayed for. There is the glorification of Śiva too.

The main topics in the longer hymn, in 103 stanzas, are: glory of Śakti, quest of Her, *Śrīcakra*, *Kulācāra*, eternality of Śiva-Śakti, origin of Tantra, worship of Devī in different *Cakras*, persons fit for Her worship, etc.

The latter version is ascribed by some to Gauḍīya Śaṃkara, the Bengal author of the *Tārārahasyavṛtti*. In this case also, the authorship is open to doubt.

It should be noted that several works of this title by different authors have been found. In some manuscripts of the *Saundarya-laharī*, the first part of 40 stanzas is called *Ānanda-laharī*.

Ed., with Eng. trs., by A. Avalon, Madras, 1961 (5th ed.).

The shorter hymn has been printed in the *Collected Works* of Śaṃkarācārya, ed. and trs. into Bengali by R. Vidyaratna, Calcutta, 1309 B.S.

For different works, entitled *Ānandalaharī*, see *NCC*, II, pp. 112-13.

Karpūrādi-Stava (or Stotra)

It is a hymn to Kālī in 22 verses of which some are composed in *Sragdharā*, while others in *Śikhariṇī* metres. The hymn contains *Dhyāna, Yantra, Sādhana* and description of Mahādevī. The chief *mantras* of Dakṣiṇa Kālikā occur in it. The greatest among them is the *Vidyārājñī* consisting of twenty-two syllables.

The text appears under different titles, e.g. *Karpūra-laharī, Karpūrādi-śyāmā, Kālīkarpūra, Kālī-svarūpa, Dakṣiṇa-kālikā, Parama-devatā-karpūrādi*, etc. Some manuscripts mention Mahākāla and Ādinātha. While some manuscripts do not mention any source, others are assigned to different sources, e.g. *Dakṣiṇakālikā-tantra, Pheṭkāriṇī-tantra, Mahākāla-saṃhitā* of Ādinātha, *Vīratantra*, etc.

There are at least 21 commentaries of which the *Dīpikā* or *Rahasyārtha-sādhikā* of Kāsīnātha, *Dīpikā* of Raṅganātha, one by Durgārāma, *Vimalānanda-dāyinī-svarūpa-vyākhyā* (1805 A.D.) of Vimalānanda appear to have been popular.

Of several editions, the most noteworthy is "Hymn to Kālīkarpūrādi-Stotra" — A. Avalon, *Tāntrik Texts*, Madras, 1953 (2nd ed.) with Eng. Intro., trs. and the commentaries, *Vimalānanda-dāyinī, Rahasyārtha-sādhikā* and *Subodhinī*.

For further details about MSS, commentaries and editions, see *NCC*, III, pp. 191-193.

CHAPTER III

TĀNTRIC ŚAIVISM OF KASHMIR

ŚAIVA WORKS AND TANTRAS

In common parlance, Kashmir is called *Bhūsvarga* (heaven on earth). It, indeed, occupies a unique position in India, not only in the panoramic scenic beauty, salubrious climate, but also in the realm of Indian culture. It produced polyhistors like Kṣemendra (11th century) and Abhinavagupta (c. the latter half of the 10th cent. to early 11th cent.). The systems of poetics, viz., *Alaṃkāra, Rīti and Dhvani,* originated in this province. The founders of these schools were respectively Bhāmaha (c. 7th-8th cent.), Vāmana (8th-9th cent.) and Ānandavardhana (9th cent.). As regards *Rasa* school, Kashmir may be said to have been the pioneer. In the *Dhvanyāloka,* Ānandavardhana, for the first time, clearly stated *rasa* as the most excellent element of poetry. In later times Viśvanātha (c. 14th cent. 1st half), in his *Sāhityadarpaṇa,* unequivocally stated *rasa* as the soul of poetry.

The *Rājataraṅgiṇī* of the Kashmirian Kalhaṇa (11th-12th cent.) is practically the only work in Sanskrit, which can claim to be historical.

The Kashmirian Dāmodaragupta (8th-9th cent.) has created a new literary genre by his *Kuṭṭanīmata,* an erotico-comic satire on courtesans.

We shall give a brief account of Tāntric Śaivism of Kashmir, which is unique in its philosophy.

The celebrated Śaiva school is called *Trika* (triad) which has been taken by different scholars to mean different things:

1. Siddha, Nāmaka, Mālinī
2. Śiva, Śakti, Aṇu
3. Pati, Paśu, Pāśa
4. Śiva, Śakti, Nara
5. Parā, Aparā, Parāparā
6. Abheda, Bheda, Bhedābheda

The literature of the *Trika* system known as Trika-śāstra, Trika-śāsana, or Rahasya-saṃpradāya can be broadly classified as

A. Āgama-śāstra

B. Spanda-śāstra

C. Pratyabhijñā-śāstra

A. ĀGAMA-ŚĀSTRA

Believed to have been revealed, it comprises eleven Tantras including *Mālinī-vijaya* and *Rudrayāmala*.

In the early stage, these works were interpreted from the dualistic, even pluralistic viewpoint.

The Trika system actually began with the *Śivasūtras*, supposed to have been revealed to Vasugupta (c. 9th cent.) to refute the dualistic view.

Śaṃkarācārya (c. 9th cent.) is said to have visited Kashmir. His visit supplied the impetus which resulted in the formulation of *Śivasūtras*.

Of the commentaries on the *Sūtras*, well-known are the *Vārtika* of Bhāskara (c. 11th cent.) and the *Vimarśinī* of Kṣemarāja, identified by some with the aforesaid Kṣemendra, by others with Kṣemendra's namesake who was a pupil of Abhinavagupta, mentioned earlier.

With the firm foothold of the *Trika* system, some of the aforesaid dualistic Tantras were interpreted from the monistic point of view.

Besides Vasugupta, several other scholar-devotees contributed to the development of Śaivism in Kashmir. Of them, famous were Kallaṭa (8th-9th cent.). Somānanda (end of 9th cent.), Utpala (9th-10th cent.), Bhāskara (c. 9th cent.), Abhinavagupta, Kṣemarāja and Jayaratha (c. beginning of 13th cent.).

B. SPANDA-ŚĀSTRA

Spanda means vibration or activity of Śiva. It is supposed to be the cause of all distinctions.

This Śāstra is based on the *Spandasūtras*, generally called *Spandakārikās* which are a sort of running commentary on the *Śivasūtras*. The *Spandasūtras*, attributed to Vasugupta by Kṣemarāja, appear to have been composed by Kallaṭa, a pupil of Vasugupta. On the Sūtras there is a *Vṛtti* or commentary by Kallaṭa.

C. PRATYABHIJÑĀ-ŚĀSTRA

For about a century following the development of the Spandaśāstra, there was a sort of interregnum in Śaiva philosophical literature.

The period that followed was marked by the onslaught of Buddhism on Śaivism. To contain the formidable foe, Kashmir developed the systematic philosophy of *Pratyabhijñā*. It is so called because it regards recognition (*Pratyabhijñā*) of reality as essential for liberation. This philosophy is based on the *Śivadṛṣṭi* of Somānanda.

Of the other works of this class, well-known are *Īśvara-pratyabhijñā* or *Pratyabhijñā-sūtra* or *Pratyabhijñā-vimarśinī* or *Laghuvṛtti* by Abhinavagupta, author also of the *Pratyabhijñā-vivṛti-vimarśinī*, a commentary on Utpala's *Vṛtti*. Kṣemarāja's *Pratyabhijñā-hṛdaya* is an important compendium. He has other works too.

In the Kashmirian school of Tantra, five *Makāras* are not taken in the literal sense, but their substitutes are prescribed.

We shall now take up the Tantras and Śaiva works of Kashmir.

ĪŚVARA-PRATYABHIJÑĀ

It is by Utpaladeva. Son of Udayakara, he had a son, Vibhramakara, and a fellow student, named Padmānanda. According to a tradition, Utpala was a native of Guptapura (Kashmiri Gotapora) not very far away from Kalāśrīpura (modern Kalaspur).

Utpala, who perhaps flourished in the first quarter of the 10th cent. A.D., must be distinguished from Utpala Vaiṣṇava, author of the *Spanda-pradīpikā*.

Besides this work, Utpala is credited with the authorship of the following works:

1. *Siddhitrayī* — the triad comprising Īśvara, Sambandha and Ajaḍapramātṛ-siddhi — these embody the main points discussed in the *Īśvara-pratyabhijñā*.
2. *Vṛtti* on *Śivadṛṣṭi* and *Īśvara-pratyabhijñā* — fragments available.
3. *Vivaraṇa* on the *Īśvara-pratyabhijñā*.
4. *Stotrāvalī*.

The *Īśvara-pratyabhijñā* is divided into four sections, viz.

1. Jñānādhikāra — dealing with cognitions. It has eight subdivisions, viz., (i) Upodghāta, (ii) Pūrvapakṣa-vivṛti, (iii) Para-darśanānupapatti, (iv) Smṛtiśakti-nirūpaṇa, (v) Jñānaśakti-nirūpaṇa, (vi) Apohanaśakti-nirūpaṇa, (vii) Ekāśraya-nirūpaṇa, (viii) Māheśvarya-nirūpaṇa.
2. Kriyādhikāra — dealing with activity. Its subsections are: (i) Kriyāśakti-nirūpaṇa, (ii) Bhedābheda-vimarśana, (iii) Māna-tatphalameya-nirūpaṇa, (iv) Kārya-kāraṇa-tattva-nirūpaṇa.
3. Āgamādhikāra — discussing the 36 *Tattvas* of Śaivism. Its subsections are: (i) Tattva-nirūpaṇa, (ii) Pramātṛ-tattva-nirūpaṇa.
4. Tattvārtha-saṃgrahādhikāra — discusses the essential nature of the Highest Being, and recapitulates the substance of the foregoing Adhikāras. Its subsections are (i) Tattvārtha-nirūpaṇa, (ii) Guruparva-krama-nirūpaṇa.

The *Īśvara-pratyabhijñā* has a commentary by Abhinavagupta, called *Vimarśinī* which exists in two forms, one shorter (*laghvī*) and the other longer (*bṛhatī*). The latter is supposed to be based on a gloss by Utpala himself, which is now lost.

The fourth Adhikāra is the epitome of the three preceding Adhikāras. Its contents are as follows: Maheśvara alone is the soul of all beings. Abhinavagupta makes it clear that He is of the nature of consciousness which has no difference in different places, times and in nature. The question may be posed — well, if Maheśvara alone is the soul, what is the bondage for releasing which this effort is made? The answer is that, through the force of ego, people think 'I am so and so'. Again, the question may be asked — whose bondage is it, who exists other than Īśvara. The reply is the real nature of oneself being unknown, one is called a *puruṣa*. *Puruṣa* creates joy and sorrow. Īśvara is *Pati* and men are *Paśus*. By practice in the prescribed manner *paśus* are freed — freed from animality and godlessness is seen. When one's identity with God is realised one becomes *jīvanmukta*. A liberated person feels that he is one with all things, whereas the fettered one feels otherwise. Paramaśiva is beyond proof, because all the *Tattvas* are merged as *Cit* (consciousness) in Him. One who realises *Ātman* as Īśvara and *jñāna* and *kriyā* as nothing beyond Him, knows what he desires and acts with this very body, he becomes *jīvanmukta*. After death he becomes Parameśvara Himself.

In conclusion, the author says that he has revealed the easy (*sughaṭa*) path declared by the *Gurus* in the *Śiva-dṛṣṭi*. Abhinava makes it clear that the path is stated to be easy because it is devoid of the path involved in external and internal rites and practices like *Prāṇāyāma*.

One, following it, realises that *Ātman* makes the world and absorbed in Śivahood attains *Siddhi*. Abhinava raises the question — if *Ātman* exists, then there is no difference between its recognition and non-recognition. When there is sprout, the seed does not remain unrecognised. The reply is — there are two things, one external like the sprouts, and the other internal like love. The former does not necessitate recognition, but the latter does. In the realisation that 'I am Maheśvara' recognition is a must. The necessity of recognition is illustrated by a very convincing analogy. The husband may be present near the wife, but so long as she does not recognise him she does not get joy. Similarly though Viśveśvara is in one's *Ātman*, His presence is unknown; as such there is no effect on the person concerned. So *pratyabhijñā* is necessary.

The author concludes the work by saying that it is written by him for the people who can attain *Siddhi* without effort. Abhinava states that it is accessible to all irrespective of caste, etc.

ŚIVA-SŪTRAS

As stated before, the *Śiva-sūtras* are traditionally believed to have been revealed to Vasugupta. It contains three sections (*prakāśas*), and a total of 79 *Sūtras*. Bhāskararāya refers to the tradition in an introductory verse (3) of his commentary on the *Śiva-sūtras*. He further records that Vasugupta handed the same to Kallaṭa, who, with the help of these, expounded the *Trika* system by his own *Spandasūtra*. Kallaṭa, in his turn, transmitted the *Sūtras* to Pradyumnabhaṭṭa, son of his maternal uncle. Pradyumna taught the same to his son, Prajñārjuna who passed them on to his pupil, Mahādevabhaṭṭa. Mahādeva gave them to his son, Śrīkaṇṭhabhaṭṭa. Bhāskara says that having obtained the same from him, he composed the *Sūtra-vārtika* at the request of his pupils. Bhāskara, in the colophon to his *Vārtika*, mentions Bhaṭṭa Divākara as his father.

The *Śiva-sūtras* were commented upon, besides Bhāskara, by Kṣemarāja who has been mentioned earlier. Bhāskara's commentary, rather explanatory *Vārtikas*,[1] names the three *Prakāśas* of the *Sūtras* as *Sāmānya-cit-prakāśa-svarūpa-nirūpaṇa, Sahaja-vidyodaya, Bibhūti-spanda* respectively.

Kṣemarāja's *Vṛtti* is a running commentary.

The contents of *Śiva-sūtras* are briefly as follows.

Caitanya or consciousness is identified with *Ātman*. The *Vārtika* states the *Caitanya* consists in *jñāna* and *kriyā*, and as it is not covered by impurities, it is Śiva.

This *Caitanya* is followed by *jñāna* or knowledge. The *Vārtika* explains the knowledge as 'I'. 'This is mine.' Kṣemarāja suggests the alternative reading *ajñāna* (ignorance). By *jñāna* or *ajñāna* he means the knowledge of the objects of senses. *Śaktis* are four, viz., Ambā, Jyeṣṭhā, Raudrī, Vāmā; these are the forms of Śiva. Their bodies are *Kalās* consisting in the letter from *A* to *Kṣa* which are the sources of word (*śabda*). This bondage of knowledge can be removed by effort (*udyama*) which is called *Bhairava*. Desire (*icchā*) of *Paramātman* is stated to be the transcendent Śakti. The entire phenomenal (*dṛśya*) world is the body of the Lord as *Cit* or consciousness is pervasive. As a means of removing the evil of ignorance the realisation of *Śiva-tattva* as the attributeless lustre is recommended. Śiva's strength and sight constitute what is called Śakti. The knowledge of *Ātman* is *Vitarka*, i.e., the feeling of one's identity with Śiva, the universal soul. *Samādhi-sukha* (the joy of concentration and meditation) is *Lokānanda*. The *Vārtika* identifies *loka* with the Eternal One, the soul of all; it is He who is joy. The attainment of the state of *Cakreśa* takes place from the rise of pure knowledge which consists in the realisation 'I am all' (*sarvāhaṃbodha*), i.e., the identification of one's ownself with everything. The state of *Cakreśa* has been explained in two ways. It may mean the eight well-known *Siddhis* called *Aṇimā, Laghimā*, etc. Or, *Cakra* is *Saṃvit* (consciousness); so the state of *Cakreśa* means the possession of excellent knowledge well-known in Yoga-śāstra. Pure consciousness is *Ātman* for the realisation of which *mantra* is necessary. Those who are very powerful spiritually can have the above realisation without *mantra*. But, those who are less powerful require *mantra*. *Mantra* is identified with *Citta* (mind) which, the *Vārtika* says, is Śiva who is devoid of attributes, is omniscient and beyond the limitations of space and time. For success in *mantra* effort

1. These are in the form of *Kārikās*, and are purported to explain what has been said, what is unsaid or said in a difficult manner.

is necessary. The *Vārtika* explains that *mantra* is the innate nature of the power of *Cit*. By incessant meditation on it Yogins attain success. *Mantra-rahasya* consists in the body in the form of *Vidyā*. When the mind, turned away from the objects of senses, is fixed in *Cit*, nescience (*avidyā*) disappears. When true knowledge of the non-dual Supreme dawns, the state of Śiva, called *Khecarī*, arises. *Khecarī* is derived thus. *Kha* is the sky in the shape of *Cit*. That which moves about there is called *Khecarī*. As it leads to the attainment of the state of the one who is meditated upon, it is called the state of Śiva (*śivāvasthā*).

Thus, *Mudrā* (*Khecarī*) and *Mantra* as means to the goal have been stated. But, how to get the power arising from these? The answer is *Guru* who represents the Śakti of Śambhu. He explains the truth, and shows the way. *Guru* leads one to the knowledge about the *Kriyāśakti* (power of doing) of the Lord. The fire of knowledge being burnt, the gross body, which is subject to the fruits of action, yields place to the divine body. The sustenance (*anna*) of this divine body is *jñāna* that is true knowledge. Here Kṣemarāja differs. He takes the body to mean the gross and subtle forms of it. Such body is offered to the fire of *Cit*. He takes *jñāna* in the sense of false knowledge that causes bondage. It is called *anna* as it is eaten up by Yogins. This *jñāna* leads to the destruction of false knowledge, and one perceives the illusory nature of things arising therefrom.

Ātmā[2] has been identified with *Citta* which is enveloped by *jñāna*, i.e., perception of passion, etc., connected with the objects of senses. *Māyā* (illusion) is want of discrimination with regard to the *Tattvas*. The idea is that attachment to the objects of senses is the obstacle on the way to the goal.

True knowledge comes from the conquest of delusion (*moha*). The *Yogin* must be ever awake spiritually; this leads to *jīvanmukti*.

Ātman is called a dancer as it throbs according to different conditions. Of this dancer the stage is the inner soul. It may be seen that *Ātman* and the *Antarātman* (inner soul) are different from each other. The *Vārtika* makes it clear that, when there is outward flash (*bahirunmeṣa*), *Ātman* is called a dancer. When there is inward wink (*antarunmeṣa*) that very *Ātman* is called *Antarātman* (inner soul). The senses are the spectators.

---

2. Kṣemarāja gives its etymological meaning as *atati sattvādivṛtty-avalambanena yonīḥ saṃcarati;* it goes from one birth to another by resorting to the qualities of *Sattva*, etc. *Ātman* is stated as *Aṇu*.

The aspirant should contemplate the *Bīja* or germ in the shape of *Cit-Ātman* which is Supreme Power, the cause of all. A Yogin, being *āsanastha*, easily sinks into the inner lake. Here *āsana* appears to mean the greatest power derived from Śakti by which he gives up all kinds of *dhyāna*, *dhāraṇā* and other activities, and, being turned inward, contemplates the Supreme Being alone. The lake is the realisation of the Highest.

The destruction of false knowledge by means of true knowledge leads to the cessation of rebirth; this is *jīvanmukti*. The text is *Vidyā-vināśe janma-vināśah. Vidyā* is taken by the *Vārtika* in the sense of *aśuddhā vidyā* (false knowledge). But, Kṣemarāja takes it to mean correct knowledge. He interprets the *sūtra* thus — *Vidyāyā avināśe*, i.e., there being no destruction of true knowledge. By *janma* he means the senses which are the cause of action accompanied by ignorance and are full of misery. One, who has acquired the correct knowledge, becomes like Śiva in life, and Śiva Himself after death.

The function of the body is the great festival (*mahāvrata*) of a powerful person; this is *Pāśupata-vrata*. The speech of one, who observes this vow, is *japa*. By this *vrata* and *japa* the knowledge of *Ātman* dawns on the *paśus* (people tied by the bonds of delusion, etc.); this dawning of knowledge is *dāna* which leads to the wearing out of the *pāśas* or bonds. Then they become fit for *Dīkṣā* which consists in *dāna* (gift of *mantra*) and *kṣapaṇa* (wearing out of *pāśas*).

A *Kevalin* is free from pleasure and pain, i.e., no thought of these enters into him.

Moha is stated to arise from *Abhilāṣā* (desire). When *Moha* disappears, a person is freed from the fruit of action. A person, who is not liberated, is enveloped by a cloak (*kañcuka*) in the form of five gross elements. By the means, stated earlier, one becomes like Śiva in this life, and one with Śiva after death.

The entire world is the manifestation of the *icchā* (desire) of the Lord. When a person, according to the instructions prescribed earlier, gets rid of the impurities, and again realises the *Ātman*, he is reunited with the Lord. When he realises his identity with the Supreme Being, he becomes Śiva, full of joy.

SPANDA-KĀRIKĀ

We have referred to it earlier. It consists of 52 *Kārikās*, divided into three *Niṣyandas* or sections called respectively *Svarūpa-spanda*,

Sahajavidyodaya and *Bibhūti-spanda*. It has a *Vṛtti* or commentary by Kallaṭa.

The contents of the *Kārikās* are briefly as follows.

Śiva, possessed of Śakti, creates the world by his *unmeṣa* (opening of eyes) and dissolves it by *nimeṣa* (closing of eyes). The question is — how is the Śivahood of a man, who is subject to rebirth, declared? The answer is this. There is no obstruction to one in whom all this phenomenal world resides and from whom all this emanates. The idea is that as he is not enveloped (by delusion, etc.), there can be Śivahood even in the state of one who is subject to rebirth. His Śivahood is not covered in any condition of *jāgrat, svapna, suṣupti*. He is beyond happiness, sorrow and delusion. He is neither *grāhya* (that which can be taken) nor *grāhaka* (one who takes).

When one's ego disappears, one attains the Supreme state. In such a condition, one becomes the knower and the doer; then one can do or know everything that is desired.

There are two *avasthās*, one *Kārya*, the other *Kartṛtva*. The former is destructible, the latter imperishable. It is only the effort for *Kārya* that is effaced. One, who is unwise, thinks himself to be effaced when that effort is effaced. In reality, one's own nature is not subject to destruction. The *bhāva*, that is turned inward and is omniscient, is never effaced. The *bhāva* as *Cit* remains. The *Cit* is felt by one who is well awake or fully possessed of knowledge *saprabuddha* in all the conditions of *Jāgrat, Svapna* and *Suṣupti*.

Possessed of Supreme Śakti in the form of *jñāna* (knowledge) and *jñeya* (object of knowledge), the Lord shines in the conditions of *jāgrat* and *svapna*. In *Suṣupti* and *Turya* conditions, He is perceived only as *Cit*.

The *Guṇas, Sattva, Rajas* and *Tamas*, do not envelop the inherent nature of the *yogin*. These *Guṇas*, obstructing the perception of the existence of *Cit*, cause the people of little enlightenment to fall into the fierce path of rebirth which is difficult to cross; because such people find *Ātman* possessed of these qualities and not as *Śuddha* (pure) and *Buddha* (enlightened). One, who always makes effort for the manifestation of the real nature of *Spanda-tattva*, even in the *jāgrat* state attains one's own nature called *turya-bhoga*. When a person becomes very angry, delighted or bewildered or when he runs, the rise of *spanda* is to be understood and should be learnt from the *Guru*. A man who, having left all other duties, is absorbed in *spanda-tattva*, realises the highest truth. In such a *yogin* the moon (*manas*) and the sun (*spana*), having left the body, a replica of the universe, set in *Suṣumnā Nāḍi*. Then, in that vast sky, devoid of the moon and the sun, a man, full of delusion by *svapna*, etc., remains confined in a state of sleep. When awakened he remains uncovered (by ignorance, etc.).

The *mantras*, which are powerful, having resorted to that power of Śakti, proceed in respective duties. With duties ceased, people, who are calm and free from the taints of *Māyā*, are merged in that sky along with the devotees' mind. So, as they are joined with Śiva, they are said to be possessed of the characteristics of Śiva. With that *Ātman*, which is all-encompassing, there is no condition in the thoughts of word and sense that does not suggest Śivahood.

So, the *bhoktā* (enjoyer) himself is present everywhere as *bhogya* (object of enjoyment). One, whose mind is of this nature that it feels that all the world is pervaded by me and looks at everything as sport, becomes *jīvanmukta*.

A devotee, by means of *mantras*, becomes one with the deity of the *mantra*. This realisation of one's own nature without the cover of false knowledge is the acquisition of ambrosia by a devotee. This, indeed, is the initiation to *Nirvāṇa* that leads to the revelation of the true nature of Paramaśiva.

A *yogin*, in the condition of *jāgrat*, finds, among various things, the very thing desired by him. In *svapna* also he sees the desired things. The fact that in *svapna* the heart is clearly manifested shows the independence of it; this is the penetration of the evil. Laying stress on effort the author gives an analogy.

Even when the mind is intent, a distant thing is hazy. Due to effort it appears clearly. So also what really exists can be soon realised by resorting to Śakti. Another analogy is this. *Ātman* pervades the body, a person can at once feel the bite even of a small louse. So, one, who realises *Ātman*, acquires omniscience everywhere.

Glāni (debility or decay) wears out the body. It arises from *ajñāna* which is avoided by the knowledge of *Ātman*.

From *Ātman* arise *Bindu, Nāda, Rūpa* (capacity for seeing in darkness), *Rasa* (taste of nectar in the mouth).

These *Siddhis*, which are obstacles, appear to men very soon. It is the *yogins* who have realised the identity of all worldly objects with the Supreme Soul that can themselves know the real truth.

One should be ever awake, comprehend by knowledge what is to be known and fix everything on one, i.e., the knowledge of the real truth. By so doing one is not tormented by *Kalās*, etc., to be described hereafter.

One who, being an object of enjoyment to forces like Brāhmī arising from the mass of words, is led astray by *kalās* in the shape of the letters beginning with *ka;* such a person is called *Paśu*.

In him the nectar of the Supreme is absent due to the rise of memory at the sight of the objects of senses. Thus, he loses independence and the capacity for going everywhere. The Śaktis Brāhmī, etc., are always ready to veil one's real nature. Without word no knowledge arises. That *kriyātmaka* (active) Śakti of Śiva, when not known, causes bondage in a *Paśu;* when known, it leads a person to *Siddhi*.

By the perception of the subtle elements of *Śabda*, etc., tied by *puryaṣṭaka* (*sūkṣmadeha*) due to the influence of *manas*, *ahaṃkāra* and *buddhi*, the feeling of joy and sorrow arises. One, who is dependent on others, feels pleasure and pain. Due to the condition of the subtle body he becomes subject to rebirth.

When a person fixes his mind on one, i.e., the gross or the subtle and effects destruction and rise of the aforesaid memory of subtle elements, etc., he becomes *bhoktā* (enjoyer); thus he becomes *Cakreśvara*, i.e., the Lord of *Mātṛs*.

The main Śaiva Tantra works are:

Ahirbudhnya-saṃhitā, Mālinī-vijayottara Tantra, Mṛgendra Tantra, Netra Tantra, Rudrayāmala Tantra, Svacchanda Tantra, Tantrāloka.

Accounts of the above works have been given under the chapter Hindu Tantras.

KRAMA TĀNTRICISM[3] OF KASHMIR

No account of Tantra in Kashmir can be complete without an examination of *Krama* Tāntricism. Advocating monistic Śaivism, it is an offshoot of the Śaiva philosophy of Kashmir. It is also called *Kramanaya*, *Mahārtha-naya* or *Mahārtha*, *Mahānaya*, *Mahāsāra*, *Atinaya*, *Devatānaya* or *Devīnaya*, *Kālīnaya*.

---

3. For details, see N. Rastogi, *The Krama Tāntricism of Kashmir*. Our account is mainly based on this work.

Originating in Kashmir, the *Krama* system spread far and wide. There is evidence of its travel as far as Coladeśa (modern Karnataka) in the south. That this system was not confined to the limits of Kashmir is proved by its association with some *Pīṭha-sthānas*, e.g. Oḍḍiyāna, Pūrṇa Pīṭha, etc.

The date and mode of origin of this system are shrouded in myth and mysticism. With Jayaratha (c. 13th cent., beginning) we stand on terra firma about the early history of *Krama* Tāntricism. In his *Viveka* commentary (III, pp. 192-93) on Abhinavagupta's *Tantrāloka*, he gives an account of the early history of the system.

The *Krama* system is believed by some to date back to the last quarter of the 7th cent. or the beginning of the 8th. This system lasted till the 18th century with varying degrees of popularity and authority. The period from the 9th century to the 12th saw the heyday of this system. After that the decline started, and the process of decadence was never arrested. Jayaratha gives ample testimony of the degeneration of the *Krama* system. The *Mahānaya-prakāśa*, attributed by some to Śivānanda I, refers (8/180, 186, 187) to the growing ignorance of the system among its followers themselves. Śitikaṇṭha (1575-1625 A.D.), author of a *Mahānaya-prakāśa*, refers to the fast fading of the system and the loss of its grip over the people.

The original *Krama* literature can be divided into two broad classes, viz. revealed and non-revealed. To the former class belong some anonymous works and the *Krama Āgamas*. The latter includes the non-Āgamic works. The *Krama Āgamas* are *Pañcaśatika* or *Devīpañcaśatika*, *Sārdhaśatika*, *Krama-rahasya*, *Krama-sadbhāva*, *Kālikā-krama*, *Krama-siddhi*. The non-Āgamic works are *Krama-sūtra*, *Siddhasūtra*, *Mahānaya-paddhati*, *Kramadaya*, *Amāvasyā-triṃśikā*, *Rājīkā*.

Prominent persons who, in some form or other, contributed to the *Krama* Tāntricism of Kashmir

(Names in English alphabetical order)

Person	*Work, if any*
Abhinavagupta	*Krama-stotra*, *Krama-Keli* comm., *Keli*

	comm. on *Kramastotra* of Siddhanātha. *Krama* philosophy has been dealt with in some other works of Abhinava, e.g. *Mālinī-vijaya-vārtika*, *Parātriṃśikā vivaraṇa*.
Bhāskara	Believed to have transmitted the doctrine of Siddha Nātha to the next generation.
Bhaṭṭa Utpala (Different from Utpala Vaiṣṇava)	No work exclusively on *Krama*. From his *Spanda-pradīpikā* commentary on the *Spanda-kārikā* he appears to have tried to interpret *Spanda* and *Yoga* concepts in the light of *Krama* philosophy.
Bhojarāja (c. 1050-1100)	Perhaps author of the *Kramakamala*.
Bhūtirāja I (Teacher of Abhinavagupta)	His contribution to *Krama* system is borne out by the following references: (i) *Tantrasāra* of Abhinava (Shastri's ed., 1918, p. 30). (ii) *Mahārtha-mañjarī* of Maheśvarā-nanda (TSS ed. No. 66, 1919).
Cakrabhānu	Highly reputed as a *Krama* teacher.
Cakrapāṇi	Supposed author of the *Bhāvopahāra* which is a *Kramastotra*.
Hrasvanātha	Head of tradition which produced important texts like *Cidgagana-candrikā* and *Mahānayaprakāśa*.
Jayaratha	*Viveka* commentary on the first, fourth, thirteenth and twenty-ninth *Āhnikas* of *Tantrāloka*. Throws light on history of *Krama* system.
Kallaṭa (No exclusive work on *Krama*. But incidental contribution to *Krama* system in the works attributed to him.)	*Spanda-kārikā*, *Spandavṛtti*, *Spanda-sarvasva*, *Tattvavicāra*, *Tattvārtha-cintāmaṇi*

Kṛṣṇadāsa	Same as Varadarāja (q.v.).
Kṣemarāja	In his *Uddyota* commentary on *Netra-tantra*, refers to *Krama* as a distinct system.
Lakṣmaṇagupta	Appears to have written on *Krama*. No work available.
Mahāprakāśa	Teacher of Maheśvarānanda. Author of several hymns mentioned in *Parimala* commentary on Maheśvarānanda's *Mahārtha-mañjarī*.
Maheśvarānanda	Appears to have written a work, called *Krama*.
Niṣkriyānandanātha	*Chummā-sampradāya*.
Pradyumna Bhaṭṭa	*Tattvagarbha-stotra*.
Ramyadeva	Author of *Vivaraṇa* commentary on the *Bhāvapahāra* (q.v.) of Cakrapāṇi. His *Akrama-kallola-kārikā* appears to have been an independent work on *Krama* system.
Siddhanātha, called Stotrakara	Supposed author of a *Krama-stuti*.
Śivānanda	Author of *Krama-vāsanā*.
Śivopādhyāya	In his *Vivṛti* on *Vijñānabhairava*, he sometimes makes remarks on the intricacies of *Krama* system.
Somānanda	*Śiva-dṛṣṭi*.
Somaputra	Śrīvatsa (q.v.), author of *Cidgagana-candrikā*, expresses indebtedness to Somaputra for revealing *Krama* secrets.
Śrīvatsa (Introduces himself as Kālidāsa)	*Cidgagana-candrikā* and comm. on *Kramastotra* of Siddhanātha.
Utpala	No work on *Krama*. From Jayaratha it is learnt that Utpala was one of the teachers from whom Abhinavagupta learnt *Krama*.
Varadarāja	His *Śiva-sūtra* indicates his *Krama* leaning.

Vasugupta	No work exclusively on *Krama*. Some of his works, particularly the *Śiva-sūtra* and *Spandakārikā*, appear to have incidentally contributed to the cause of *Krama* system.
Vātulanātha (Traditionally known, but no historical evidence)	*Vātulanātha-sūtra* (Traditionally attributed).

The main features of the *Krama* system are as follows:

A. It is Śakti-oriented

It reflects the emergence of the Śākta tendencies in the monistic Śaivism of Kashmir. This resulted in the division of the system into two schools:

(i) one emphasising the supremacy of the Śiva aspect;

(ii) the other laying stress on the Śakti aspect of the Supreme Consciousness.

B. It leans towards monistic-dualistic character of Reality

It is called *Bhedābhedopāya* as it inculcates the idea of dualism or diversity within the framework of monism or unity. It seeks to discover unity in the phenomenal duality (*bheda abheda*). While the *Pratyabhijñā* and *Kula* systems are concerned with Reality as unity or the transcendent aspect of Reality, *Krama* is concerned with the immanent Reality; according to it, immanence is an essential expression of transcendence.

C. Spiritual uplift and salvation as synthesis of *bhoga* and *mokṣa*

While the *Kula* system teaches *Sāmbhavopāya, Krama* advocates *Śāktopāya, Kula* and *Pratyabhijñā* do not countenance the idea of progression; they believe in instantaneous and immediate self-revelation. The essential feature of the *Krama* system is spiritual progression, i.e. the progressive refinement of the *Vikalpas*. So, it equally stresses each step towards self-realisation.

D. Positive epistemic bias

While the *Pratyabhijñā* and *Spanda* schools are more metaphysical, the *Krama* is more mystical. Both *Kula* and *Krama* systems have esoteric and mystical look. But, the latter emphasises the cognitive and the epistemic aspect. This, indeed, is the fundamental value of the *Krama* as a system of philosophy.

E. Linguistic peculiarity

It prefers the Prākrit languages to Sanskrit as the medium of expression. There is convincing proof that the works like the *Kramasūtra*, the *Mahānaya-prakāśa*, *Mahārtha-mañjarī*, *Prākṛta-triṃśikā-vivaraṇa*, etc., were written in some forms of Prākṛta or local vernaculars.[4]

Krama, as a Tāntric system, depends on intuition, and discourages dialectic. It does not merely argue, but experiments. It seeks fulfilment in the harmonious blending of intuition with practical realisation.

Two phases of *Krama* Tāntricism can be discerned. In the earlier phase, there was a penchant for philosophical and intuitional issues. Of the four divisions of the contents of Tantra, *Caryā* and *Kriyā* were subordinated to *Jñāna* and *Yoga*. In the later phase, however, the ritualistic aspect came to the forefront.

Experience is the pivot round which the *Krama* system revolves. The realisation of the oneness of the individual soul with the universal soul is the aim of this system of philosophy.

The *Krama* system was divided into two sub-schools, viz. (i) *Sāhasa* represented by the *Vātulanātha-sūtra* and (ii) *Chummā* represented by the work entitled *Chummā-Sampradāya*.

The main theme of the *Sāhasa* school is that a devotee's real nature is realised by firmly clinging to the pre-eminent *Sāhasa* (*mahā-sāhasa-vṛttyā svarūpalābhaḥ*, *Vātulanātha-sūtra* 1). *Sāhasa* means a sudden unexpected event. According to this school, the highest realisation or self-revelation takes place all on a sudden through divine grace; for this no previous preparation is necessary.

The exact meaning of *Chummā* is not known. It occurs in the *Tantrāloka* (4/268, 29/37). Kṣemarāja, in his commentary on the *Svacchanda-tantra* (15/1), says that *Chummakā* stands for the system to which one adheres. The chief object of the theory of *Chummā*, which appears to be a synonym of *Śarma* (vide Kṣemarāja's commentary on the *Svacchanda-tantra*, VI, p. 125), is to preserve the

4. It is interesting to note that the Buddha directed his followers to propagate his teachings in local dialects.

esoteric nature of the system adhered to. In the ultimate analysis, the *Sāhasa* and *Chummā* appear to have no basic difference.

The existence, at one time, of another sub-school of *Krama* is referred to in the *Tantrāloka* (Āhnika 29). This unnamed school is a product of the combination of two theses, one formulated in the *Devyāyāmala* and the other in the *Mādhavakula*. A feature of *sādhanā*, according to this school, is the worship of one's line of preceptors along with *Pīṭhas, Kṣetras*, etc. The *Pīṭhas* have been assigned to the different parts of the body. This system requires the aspirant to reflect upon and, therefore, visualise the *Pīṭhas* and the respective presiding deities as essentially identical with the self.

PHILOSOPHY OF KASHMIR ŚAIVISM

Here we shall give an account of the philosophy of Kashmir Śaivism in a nutshell.

Like other branches of the orthodox Indian philosophy, it recognises the changeless *Ātman* as the experiencing principle. It is called *Caitanya* or *Cit*. It is Paramaśiva underlying everything. He is both immanent and transcendental.

The universe is a manifestation of Paramaśiva. This aspect of Him is called Śakti. It has many aspects of which the following are fundamental:

- (i) Power of self-revelation — by it Śiva shines.
- (ii) Power of realising absolute bliss and joy (*Ānanda-śakti*) — satisfied in itself.
- (iii) Power of feeling oneself as Supreme and absolutely irresistible will (*Icchā-śakti*).
- (iv) Power of bringing all objects in conscious relations with oneself and with one another (*Jñāna-śakti*).
- (v) Power of assuming any form (*Kriyā-śakti*).

With these powers Paramaśiva manifests Himself or his Śakti as the universe. The manifestation of Śakti is called *Udaya, Unmeṣa, Ābhāsana, Sṛṣṭi*. This is followed by *Pralaya*. A complete cycle of *Sṛṣṭi* and *Pralaya* is called *Kalpa*.

The things and beings, constituting the universe, are called *Tattvas*. Besides the *Tattvas* recognised in Sāṃkhya, this system recognises a few others. According to Sāṃkhya, Puruṣa and Prakṛti are the final realities, but they are derivatives in Kashmir Śaivism.

The total number of *Tattvas* in this system is 36.

The process of manifestation of the universe is this. It is the experiencing out of Parama Śiva. It is similar to the psychical process in our daily lives of thinking and experiencing. The process is called *Ābhāsana*. It is *vivarta* or the illusory appearance of the Supreme — reality, according to the exponents of *Vivarta*. The teachers of the *Ābhāsa* process hold that the appearances are real in the sense that they are aspects of the ultimately Real Parama Śiva.

In the matter of universal experience, there are five principles of the universal subject-object. First, there is *Śiva-tattva*. In this aspect, the *cit* aspect of Śakti is most manifest.

Next comes *Śakti-tattva*. While *Śiva-tattva* is the very first vibration of Parama Śiva, *Śakti-tattva* checks, controls and regulates the movement of life, and acts as the principle of restraint.

From the *Śiva-Śakti* state arises the *Sadākhya-tattva,* i.e. the experience 'I am this'. It is the beginning of activity. It is the state in which, for the first time, there is the notice of being. In it, the *Icchāśakti* of the Divine is the dominant feature.

Next is the *Aiśvara-tattva* in which the experience assumes a form like 'This am I'. It is so called as in it is realised the Lordliness and the Glory of the Divine Being.

Finally, there is the *Sadvidyā* stage. In it, the experience 'I am this' is clearly felt as I identified with this. In it the true relation of things is realised.

This philosophy states the limit of individual experience, the limitation being caused by *Māyā* and her sixfold progeny, the six *Kāncukas* covering the reality.

The two principles of the limited individual subject-object are the Puruṣa and the Prakṛti. Puruṣa is put into sleep by *Māyā* by means of the limitation of *Kāla, Niyati, Rāga, Vidyā* and *Kalā*. The all-experiencer, while remaining the same, produces a number of Puruṣas who realise themselves as differentiated and separated from one another.

Each of the numerous Puruṣas becomes an *Aṇu*.

While the Puruṣa, who is sleeping as it were, experiences a vague and indefinite something, simultaneously with him Prakṛti comes into manifestation.

Puruṣa and Prakṛti are only the limited representation of the factors on the two-sided experience of the *Śuddhā Vidyā* state. For each Puruṣa, there is one Prakṛti. In his experience of Prakṛti, the Puruṣa has no specific feeling: there is no movement of thought or activity.

Prakṛti is in a state in which affective features are held in a state of equipoise; the three qualities of *Sattva, Rajas* and *Tamas* are in a state of equipoise.

The three principles of mental operation are *Buddhi, Ahaṃkāra* and *Manas*. *Manas* desires; it singles out a particular group of sensations from a whole crowd. *Ahaṃkāra* gathers, and stores up the memory of personal experiences, identifies and assimilates the experiences of the present. *Buddhi* is that which enables one to picture the mental image of objects as of a cow. It is the impersonal or superpersonal state of consciousness or experience in a limited individual.

In dealing with the means and general principles of sensible experience, this philosophy mentions five senses, five powers of action, and five general objects of sense-perception.

The five *bhūtas* are recognised as principles of materiality.

Śiva is the saviour and *guru*, assuming this form out of his love for mankind.

Paśu (literally animal) or the infinite host of souls belongs to Śiva. The soul, distinct from the body, is not created by Him; it is eternal. Individual souls are of three classes according as they are subject to three, two or one of the impurities.

The web of bonds (*pāśajāla*), that ties the soul, is divided into *avidyā, karma* and *māyā*.

Māyā is the material cause of the world, unconscious in nature, the seed of the universe.

According to the *Śaiva Siddhānta*, the universe consists of thirty-six *tattvas* including those of Sāṃkhya.

The stages of evolution are as follows:

At first, *Māyā* evolves into the subtle principles and then into the gross. The first principle evolved from *Māyā* is *Kalā*. It removes the impurities obstructing the manifestation of consciousness, and helps its manifestation according to *karma*. By *Vidyā* the soul acquires the experience of pleasure and pain.

Mūlaprakṛti of Sāṃkhya is itself a product according to the *Siddhānta*. Prakṛti is the material of which the worlds, to be experienced by Puruṣa, are made. From Prakṛti evolve *guṇas* which lead to the evolution of *buddhi*. The remaining process of evolution is like that of Sāṃkhya.

The world is not illusory. The world has a serious moral purpose. God is always engaged in preserving the souls from the bondage of matter.

The grace of God is the path to freedom.

This school recognises *jīvanmukti*. Though possessing body, the *jīvanmukta* is one with the Supreme in feeling and faculty. He continues his body until his past *karma* is exhausted, and the deeds of the intervening period are consumed by the grace of God.

The main ideas, contained in the principal works, are briefly stated below; the details may be studied in the accounts of respective works.

According to the *Kāmakalā-vilāsa, Ādyā Śakti* is the seed of all that moves and is immobile. *Parāśakti* is at once the seed and sprout as the manifested union of Śiva and Śakti. She is very subtle, and is manifested through the union of the first letter of the alphabet, i.e. *A* and the *Vimarśa* letter or *Ha*. Paraśiva is reflected in the *Vimarśa* mirror of the mass of the rays of the sun. The *Nāda-bindu* appears on the *Citta* wall illuminated by the reflected rays.

Two *Bindus*, white and red, are Śiva and Śakti — who, in their mutual enjoyment, expand and contract alternately. They are the root of the creation of the word (*Vāk*) and meaning (*artha*) which sometimes unite and sometimes separate from each other.

One, who knows the *Vidyā* of *Kāmakalā*, dealing with the *Cakras* of Devī, becomes liberated and identified with Mahātripurasundarī.

From the red *Bindu*, about to create, arose sound which is *Nāda-brahman* sprout. From sound arose the five gross elements (*bhūtas*) and letters of the alphabet. The white *Bindu* is also the source of these. The universe, from the minutest part to Brahman, consists of these five *Vikṛtis*.

The centre of *Cakra* is *Para*. At the time of evolution, it is transformed, and manifests itself as a triangle which is the source of the three *Śaktis*, *Paśyanti* and others.

The *Mṛgendra-tantra* states that Śiva is the doer of all and free from imperfections due to defilements. His functions are fivefold: evolution, sustenation, involution, potential preservation and assimilation. Śiva as Īśāna, Tatpuruṣa, Aghora, Vāmadeva and Sadyojāta, performs different functions.

The fetters (*pāśa*), which tie human beings, are fourfold. They stand in the way of true knowledge and cause defilement.

The *Rudrayāmala* lays down seven modes of *bhakti*, which are stated to cause liberation to one while alive.

It states that Śiva is both *Nirguṇa* and *Saguṇa*, the former being distinct from Prakṛti while the latter is associated with Prakṛti.

In it, the order of creation has been given. *Saguṇa* Parameśvara is stated as the first principle. Śakti is the creator of the worlds.

As stated, in connection with *Krama* Tāntricism, the main feature that distinguishes it from the *Pratyabhijñā* system is its Śakti-oriented monistic Śaivism. Another distinguishing characteristic of the *Krama* school is its belief in spiritual progression, the gradual realisation of the Supreme Reality.

CHAPTER IV

TĀNTRIC LEXICONS

There are several lexicons designed to facilitate the study of the Tāntric texts. These works generally set forth the denotation of *Om*, significance of the individual letters of the alphabet, and enumerate the *Bījas* with their meanings. The term *Mātṛkā* or *Mātṛkā-varṇa* stands for the letters of the alphabet, both vowels and consonants (from *A* to *Kṣa*). *Mātṛkā* sometimes indicate a diagram, written in a letter, supposed to have magical power. In some lexicons, *Mudrās*, appropriate for the worship of different deities, are discussed. Most of such works are of unknown authors and dates.

Some important Tāntric lexicons are:

Bījābhidhāna, Bījanighaṇṭu, Mantrābhidhāna, Mantrārthābhidhāna, Mātṛkā-nighaṇṭu of Mahīdāsa, Mudrā-nighaṇṭu, Varṇa-bīja-kośa.

Some of the above works are stated to be parts of well-known Tāntric texts. For example, the *Bīja-nighaṇṭu* is stated to follow the *Bhūtaḍāmara* (tantra). The *Mudrā-nighaṇṭu* is stated, in the colophon, to belong to the *Vāmakeśvarī-tantra*.

Some specimens of the contents of such works are given below. The *Mantrābhidhāna* lays down the significance of the following terms:

Oṃkāra — Praṇava, Dhruva, Tāra, Veda

Aiṃ — Vāgbhava

Āṃ — Pāśaka

Gam — Vighnarāja

Glau — Bhū-bīja

Hauṃ — Prasāda, Śiva

Hrīṃ — Lajjā, Girijā, Śakti, Hṛllekha, Māyā, Parā

Hum — Varmabīja

Klīṃ — Kāma

Kroṃ — Name of a *Bīja* and denotes *Śṛṇī* which means *Aṅkuśa* or goad for driving an elephant

Kṣrauṃ — Nṛsiṃha

Phaṭ — Astrākṣara

Sauḥ — Devī, Parā, Śakti

Śrauṃ — Viśva

Śrīṃ — Kamalā, Viṣṇu-vanitā

Śtrīṃ — Vadhū

Svāhā — Vahnivadhū

Svānta — Rati

Vaṃ — Toya

According to the *Mudrā-nighaṇṭu,* the following *Mudrās* please the deities, mentioned against them:

Name of Mudrā	*Name of Deity*
Śaṃkha, Cakra, Gadā, Padma, Veṇu, Śrīvatsa, Kaustubha, Vanamālā, Jñāna, Bilva, Garuḍa, Parā, Nārasiṃhī, Vārāhī, Hayagraivī, Dhenu, Vāṇa, Paraśu, Jaganmohinī, Kāmamudrās (called Liṅga, Yoni, Triśūla, Akṣamālā, Vara, Abhaya, Mṛga, Khaṭvāṅga, Kapāla)	Viṣṇu
Ḍamaru	Śiva
Padma	Sūrya
Danta, Pāśa, Aṅkuśa, Vidyā, Paraśu, Laḍḍuka, Bīja	Gaṇeśa
Pāśa, Aṅkuśa, Vara, Abhaya, Khaḍga, Carma, Dhanu, Śara, Muṣalī, Mudrikā	Durgā
Lakṣmī	Lakṣmī
Akṣamālā, Vīṇā, Vyākhyā, Pustaka	Sarasvatī
Saptajihvā	Agni
Mahāyoni	Śakti
Yoni, Bhūtinī, Bīja,	Śyāmā
Daityahūminī, Lelihā	Tārā
Veṇu	Gopāla
Nārasiṃhī	Nṛhari
Vārāhī	Varāha

Hayagraivī	Hayagrīva
Dhanuṣa-vāṇa	Rāma
Paraśu	Paraśurāma
Kāma	Jaganmohana
Kumbha	Vāsudeva

This work prescribes *Mudrās* as serving various purposes. The formations of different *Mudrās* have been described. It is stated that the *Kāmamudrā* pleases all the deities.

CHAPTER V

SCIENCE IN TANTRA

In some religious texts (e.g., *Śāktānanda-taraṅgiṇī*, 1.6 ff, ed. P. Sastri, Calcutta, 1349 B.S., p. 5 ff), there is information on embryology, anatomy and physiological development. The facts about the human body have been stated under the following categories:

Śarīrotpatti-krama (process of formation of body),

Śarīra-sthānādi-nirṇaya (location of nerves, etc., within the body),

Bhūtaguṇa (qualities of elements[1] of the body),

Śarīrastha-vāyu-nirṇaya (determination of the life-winds[2] within the body),

Śarīra-koṣa-varṇana (description of the sheaths[3] within the body).

The description of the origin and development of the foetus is basically true to life.

To chemistry and alchemy the contribution of Tantra is unique.[4] The chemical and alchemical information, contained in the Tāntric Rasa-śāstra, may be broadly stated under the following heads:

process of medicinal preparations consisting mainly of mercury, 'killing' (*māraṇa*) of mercury, transmutation of copper and iron into gold with mercury, process of 'killing' metals and minerals, methods of extracting the essence of copper pyrites and zinc from calamine, operation of metals, use of sulphuric acid, metals and alloys, recipes for cosmetics, refinement or purification of important minerals, liquefaction of mica, fixation of mercury recipe for Aethiops mineral, 'killing' of mercury, colouring of metals, purification of quicksilver, elements of composition of

---

1. The five elements are *Kṣiti* (earth), *Ap* (water), *Tejas* (fire), *Marut* (wind) and *Vyoman* (ether).
2. Named *Prāṇa, Apāna, Samāna, Udāna, Vyāna.*
3. Five, namely, *Annamaya, Manomaya, Vijñānamaya, Ānandamaya, Prāṇamaya.*
4. Vide *History of Hindu Chemistry* by P.C. Ray; *History of Chemistry in Ancient and Medieval India*, ed. P. Ray, Tāntric Period, Chapters I-XI; Iatrochemical Period, Chapters I-III.

mercury, preparation of calomel, fabrication of gold and silver, extraction of zinc from calamine, copper from blue vitriol.

TANTRA AND ĀYURVEDA

In the *Kubjikā-tantra*, there is a passage in which Śiva is represented as speaking of *pārada* (mercury) as his generative principle. The efficacy of mercury, subjected to *māraṇa* for six times, is lauded. A manuscript of this Tantra is written in Gupta script. Thus, the use of mercury in that far-off age is attested.

Some scholars believe that the original purpose of *Śavasādhana* was dissection.[5]

The *Rasa-vaidyas* propounded a philosophy of body in terms of its chemical reactions. This philosophy came to be known as *Raseśvaradarśana* or *Kāyatattva*. The chief exponents of this school are named as Mahādeva (Śiva?), Ādinātha, Nityanātha, Candrasena, Gorakṣanātha, Kapāli, etc.

Another class of physicians, who depended mainly on mercury preparations, was the *Siddha* (in Tāmil, *Sittar*) sect of South India, also called Maheśvara Siddhas of the *Śuddhamārga*. Their mode of treatment came to be known as *Siddhacikitsā*. It is learnt that one of the seven sub-sects of this school was founded by a Chinese Taoist, named Bhoga, who had miraculous knowledge of alchemy.[6]

Closely allied to the Raseśvara Siddhas were the Nātha Siddhas. Each of the nine Nātha Siddhas was usually believed to have headed a community of alchemists who were adepts in the preparation of drugs designed to retard old age, cure diseases and counteract poison.

Some Tāntric works (e.g., the *Rasa-ratna-samuccaya, Rasa-rāja-lakṣmī, Śārṅgadhara-saṃgraha*, etc.) reveal considerable knowledge of medicinal chemistry.

The minerals, having medicinal properties, are divided into four classes, viz., *Rasa, Uparasa, Ratna* and *Loha*. *Rasa* was mainly applied to the employment of mercury and metals in medicine. *Abhra* (mica), *mākṣika* (pyrite) and six other substances are the principal *rasas*. Sulphur, vitriol, alum and five other substances are the *uparasas* useful in the operations of mercury. *Ratnas* or certain gems are

---

5. N.N. Bhattacharya, *History of Tāntric Religion*, p. 17.
6. *Ibid.*, p. 18.

regarded as helpful in fixing or coagulating mercury. So also are the *lohas* (metals like gold, iron, etc.).

The *Yogasāra*[7] contains recipes for improving the physical body. The *Yogāṣṭaka*[8] gives recipes for the cure of diseases of the hair.

As in the case of alchemy, in the case of medicinal chemistry too, there is mention of laboratory, technical terms, apparatus, ingredients of crucibles, incineration of mercury, etc.

In the above works, some foreign influence is noticed. Govindācārya, in his *Rasasāra,* mentions his indebtedness to the Tibetan Buddhists for the knowledge of certain processes. For the use of opium as a drug, mentioned in some works, the authors were, perhaps, indebted to foreign countries, particularly China. The term *ahiphena*, denoting opium, is not found in the early Sanskrit lexicons. Again, Chinese drugs are mentioned in some works. Works like *Rasapradīpa*, *Rasendra-cūḍāmaṇi* mention *Phiraṅga-roga* (Syphilis) and its treatment with calomel (*rasakarpūra*) and China-root (*chobcini*, Smilax-China). This disease was imported by the Portuguese traders. The work, entitled *Dhātukriyā* or *Dhātumañjarī* (c. 16th cent.), purporting to be a part of the *Rudrayāmala*, betrays Arabic influence to a considerable degree.

TĀNTRIC THERAPEUTICS[9]

There are quite a few Tantras dealing with diseases and their remedies. The diseases can be classified as Pediatrics, Diseases of adult males, Diseases of adult females, Diseases common to men and women.

The recipes include medicines, both herbal and chemical, the former more than the latter. Aphrodisiacs and medicines for preventing or deferring physical decay as well as for rejuvenation are also prescribed. It should be noted that the greatest importance was attached to mercury as maintaining good health. Some of the terms indicating mercury, as noted below, indicate the great efficacy of this substance:

Rasa (essence or elixir), *Rasarāja* (essence par excellence, *Pārada* (that leads to the end of misery), *Mahātejas* (possessed of great

7. For MSS, see H.P. Sastri, *Nepal Catalogue*, I, 1905, p. 135; II, 1915, p. 75.
8. *Ibid.*
9. The subject has been elaborately discussed in the present author's *New Light on Tantra*, p. 168 onward.

invigorating capacity), *Śiva-bīja* (semen virile of Śiva), *Amṛta* (ambrosia), *Prabhu* (Lord), etc.

Antidotes of various kinds of poison are also prescribed.

It is noteworthy that, besides prescribing medicines for curing diseases, Tantra also advocates drugless healing. The means for such healing are Yogic; these are *Āsanas* (various postures of the body), *Mudrās* (particular positions of fingers), *Japa* (meditation), etc. and Haṭhayogic processes of *Dhauti*, *Vasti*, etc.

Some of the Tantras, dealing with Tāntric therapy, are:[10]

Arkaprakāśa, Aśvinī Tantra, Dāmara Tantra, Gāruḍi Tantra, Gaurī-kāncalikā, Kumāratantra, Kumāritantra, Matsya-sūkta, Nāgārjuna Tantra, Prayoga-cintāmaṇi, Rudrayāmala, Tārāpradīpa, etc.

TANTRA, MUSIC AND DANCE[11]

Tantra exercised influence on such a fine art as music. For example, the *Saṃgīta-ratnākara* of Śārṅgadeva mentions (chap. I.2, 120 ff) *Cakra*, *Nāḍīs*, etc., within the human body. The idea of *Nāda*, found in Sanskrit works (e.g. *Saṃgīta-ratnākara*, I.2, 1 ff, 163 ff) on music, has a close parallel to that occurring in Tantra. The idea of *Vāyu* (e.g. *Saṃgīta-ratnākara*, I.2, 59 ff) within the body, which is supposed in musicology to produce *Nāda* in conjunction with fire, is also similar to that found in Tantra.

Like Tantra, musicologists believe (e.g. *Saṃgīta-ratnākara*, I.2, 149) that *Kuṇḍalinī* or *Brahma-śakti*, coiling like a serpent, resides in *Ādhāra-cakra* or *Mūlādhāra*, and that its gradual ascent through other *Cakras* up to *Sahasrāra* in the head is the highest fulfilment of *Sādhana*.

It is believed (e.g. *Saṃgīta-ratnākara*, I.2, 140 ff) that the soul, residing in certain petals of *Anāhata Cakra*, desires success in song, etc. When resorting to certain petals of *Viśuddhi-cakra*, it gives success. Resort to some petals in *Lalanā* also ensures success. Resort to certain petals is stated to spoil music. The soul, resting in *Brahmarandhra*, becomes satisfied with nectar, and produces songs of a high order.

Like Tantra again, the science of music recognises (e.g. *Saṃgīta-*

10. For a longer list, see S.C. Banerji, *New Light on Tantra*, pp. 170 ff.
11. See Svāmi Prajñānānanda, *Bhāratīya Saṃgīter Itihās* (in Bengali), I, pp. 300 ff.

ratnākara, I.2) several sheaths (*Kośa*) within the body, e.g., *Annamaya*, *Manomaya*.

The *Mudrās* (positions of the hands and fingers) are interesting as they indicate various moods, sentiments, etc. These, perhaps, originated in the Vedic period. In Vedic rituals, different hand-poses were used by the singer of Sāmans. Tantra prescribes various *Mudrās*, e.g. *Śaṃkha* (like a conch-shell), *Matsya* (like a fish). In dance, many *Mudrās* are prescribed by theorists of whom Bharata, author of the *Nāṭyaśāstra*, is the earliest. It is difficult to say whether the *Nāṭyaśāstra* was indebted to Tantra or the latter to the former. The date of Bharata is controversial. He is generally believed to have flourished earlier than the fourth or fifth century A.D. As we shall see, though Tāntric ideas may have originated earlier, the composition of treatises on Tantra appears to have started about the fifth or sixth century A.D.

Śiva and Śakti are the pivots round which Tāntric philosophy revolves. In fact, Hindu Tantras are generally represented as dialogues between Śiva and Pārvatī. In works on music, Śiva is generally venerated. Śārṅgadeva commences the *Saṃgīta-ratnākara* with salutation to Śiva who is considered as an embodiment of *Nāda*. Śiva is supposed to please the ears of the wise through the mind following the *Vāyu* produced from *Brahmagranthi* where the Tāntric *Nāḍīs*, *Iḍā* and *Piṅgalā*, are joined with *Suṣumnā*. He is believed to reside in their heart. From Śiva emanate *Grāma*, *Varṇa*, *Alaṃkāra* and *Jöti*.

Rāgas and *Rāgiṇīs*, the very basis of vocal music, are associated with Śiva and Pārvatī. According to one tradition, one *Rāga* emanated from each of the five mouths of Śiva and one *Rāga* from the mouth of Pārvatī. *Rāgiṇīs* are supposed to be consorts of *Rāgas*.

Certain Tantras reveal close familiarity with vocal and instrumental music. For instance, in the *Uḍḍīśa-mahāmantrodaya*, sixteen musical instruments are referred to. The *Vīṇātantra* (No. 19) belonging to *Yāmalatantra* briefly traverses the entire field of music. The *Yāmalatantra* describes twelve kinds of *vīṇā;* of the thirty-two *Yāmalatantras*, several deal with *Gāndharva*, i.e., the art of music. The *Kuṇḍīśvara-tantra* (*Yāmala*, No. 18) and *Protala-tantra* (*Yāmala*, No. 28) deal with instrumental music.

TANTRA, ART AND ARCHITECTURE

The relation of Tantras to music and dance has been discussed separately. Here we shall see what impact it made on sculpture,[12] painting and architecture.

Like good poetry Tāntric art is simple, sensuous and impassioned. The sculpture and painting, inspired by Tantra, may be said to be poems in stone, paper, etc.

Tantra deeply influenced sculpture. In the sculptural delineation of Khajuraho (850-1050 A.D.), Konarak (13th cent.), Ellora (8th cent.) and at other places, Tāntric influence is marked. Nudity, various modes of coition, different ways of union of men and women are represented. Such Tāntric influence is also noticeable in the Hoysaleśvara temple (12th cent.) of Mysore the temple-walls of Middle and West India. In this connection, mention must be made of the depiction of sex-act at Sāñchi, Amarāvatī and Mathurā. In the Liṅgarāja temple (11th cent.) of Bhuvaneśvara, a couple is represented as naked and in an erotic posture. There are Tāntric images at various places.[13]

Erotic influence, perhaps derived from Tantra, is noticeable in some terracotta figures also. In some seals, this is manifest. The Rupar Seal (3rd cent. B.C.) shows the idea of copulation. A terracotta couple, found at Chandraketugarh (2nd cent. A.D.), resembles the aforesaid figure in the Liṅgarāja temple. A Tamluk terracotta shows a couple in a state of sitting coital union. An interesting figure in painted terracotta (Tibet, 18th cent.) is that of Mahākāla with a flaying knife in his headdress and a skull-cup of blood in his hand.

---

12. See M. Enlou, *Iconographic des etoffes paintes (paṭa) dans les Mañjuśrīmūlakalpa*, India, 1930.
On erotic sculptures, see D. Desai, *Erotic Sculpture of India;* K. Lal, *The Cult of Desire;* V. Prokas, *Khajuraho;* P. Thomas, *Kāmakalpa, Incredible India,* R.J. Mehta, *Konārak Sun-Temple.* Also see *Tantrayāna Art,* ed. S.K. Sarasvati, Calcutta, 1977; P. Rawlinson, *Tantra;* P. Rowson, *Erotic Art of the East;* M. Anant, Plastic situation, *Marg,* March, 1965; June, 1963; A. Roy, Sculptures of Nāgārjunakoṇḍā, *Marg,* March, 1965; S. Kramrisch, *Unknown in India* etc.; E. Zennas and J, Auboyer, *Khajuraho;* R. Lennoy, *The Eye of Love;* O.C. Ganguli, Mithuna in Indian Art, *Rūpam,* 1925, 1926.
13. See Cunningham, *Archaeological Survey Report,* IX the temple of 64 Yoginīs in Bherāghāt.

Various postures of copulation are represented in certain sculptures in caves and temples of various places, e.g., Kārlā, Koṇḍana, Badāmi (old Vātāpi), Paṭṭadakal, etc. A pillar sculpture from South India (17th cent.) represents a devotee adoring the vulva of the great Goddess.

Mithunas, regarded as an auspicious motif, are represented on some doors and at the entrance of monuments.

Even gods have not been spared in the representation of erotic motifs. For example, a celestial couple in sexual intercourse has been represented in a wooden bracket panel from a temple car (South India, 18th cent.).

In a temple of Khajuraho (c. 1000 A.D.), the erotic pleasures of heaven are depicted.

It is rather puzzling to think why such erotic motifs should be represented in temples and other holy places. Tantra provides *pañcamakāras* as indispensable for *sādhanā*. One such *makāra*, and an important one, is *maithuna*. This may have suggested the representation of such figures.

There are other suggestions too. Some think that the extreme sexuality of the rich people, who constructed the temples, was at the root of these erotic sculptures.

Others think that erotic representations were intended to attract the common people to temples.

A superstitious idea prompted the representation of such sculptures, according to some. As nobody disturbs a couple in sexual union, so Gods would not destroy or damage the temples, containing representations of copulation, with thunder, earthquake, etc.

Some think that these were designed to test the mental strength of those who were about to enter spiritual life.

Another ingenious suggestion is that the depiction of sexual union would ensure fertility of land. As such union results in child-birth, so the sculptural representation ensures the growth of crops.

A noteworthy feature in sculpture is the representation of *Mudrās*, perhaps under the influence of Tantra. *Bhūmisparśa-mudrā*, *Dharmacakra-mudrā*, *Varada-mudrā* and *Abhaya-mudrā* are associated with the Buddha.[14] It is interesting to note that the representation of *Bhūmisparśa-mudrā* is found in such remote places outside India as Ceylon. *Abhaya-mudrā* is found in the sculptures of Swat and Java.

Tāntric influence is probable in some images, e.g. Ardhanārīśvara representing Śiva and Umā who are supposed to stand for Puruṣa and Prakṛti or Liṅga and Yoni.

It should be noted that some of the sculptures, inspired by Tantra (see *Tantrayāna Art*), are absolutely free from eroticism. For example, mention may be made of the images of Tārā in various forms, e.g. Ārya Tārā of Nālandā (c. 7th cent.), Aṣṭamahābhaya Tārā of Ratnagiri (c. 9th cent.), Vajrasattva of Nālandā (c. 10th cent.), Heruka of Sārnath (c. 10th cent.), Mahāmāyūrī of Ellora (Cave No. VII, c. 7th cent.), Vajrayoginī of Bihār (c. 11th cent.), Parṇaśavarī of Vajrayoginī (Dacca, c. 10th cent.), to name only a few.

Besides stone sculptures and terracotta figures, there are some figures in bronze (e.g. a Buddhist male destroyer of death, united with his female Wisdom—Tibet, 18th century), wood (e.g. South Indian Icon of the Divine Vulva stained with the coloured powders used to worship it; South Indian wooden bracket panel from a temple showing a celestial couple in sexual intercourse), Yoginī with serpentine energy emerging from her vulva (South India, c. 1800 A.D.), worshipped as an emblem of the vulva of the Goddess (South India, 19th century).

In the domain of painting of various kinds also, Tāntric influence is obvious in certain cases.[15] Some manuscripts contain Tāntric paintings. There are also many paintings on paper, drawn in ink and various colours. Some are paintings on cloth.

The art, influenced by Tantra, seems to have got an impetus from the thoughts on aesthetics which was highly developed by the Kashmirian Abhinavagupta (c. 1000 A.D.).

---

14. See A. Coomaraswamy, *Buddha and the Gospel of Buddha*, pp. 35, 330; Grunwedel, *Buddhist Art in India* (trs. A.C. Gibson), figure 126; A. Bhattacharya, *Buddhist Iconography*, Plate XXVIII; *Memoirs of Archaeological Survey of India*, No. 66, Plate XIII (g); V. Smith, *History of Fine Art in India and Ceylon*, Plate 113; N.K. Bhattasali, *Iconography of Buddhist and Brahmanical Sculptures in Dacca Museum*, Plates VIII, XX, XXI.
15. See *Tantrayāna Art*; Rawlinson, *Tantra*; S.M. Nawāb, *Jaina Paintings*, Vol. I.

In connection with the *Ārya Mañjuśrīmūlakalpa*, we have stated that it contains a portion on *Paṭavidhāna* or picture-drawing. It may be noted that the Bengali artists, commonly called *Paṭuyās*, of whom those of Kālīghāṭ in Calcutta are very well-known, still follow the tradition of art adumbrated in the above work.

The pervasive influence of Tantra included architecture also within its ambit. In this respect, Orissa deserves special mention. This province shows remarkable originality in temple-architecture of which the two major types are *Rekha* and *Bhadra*. The former is conceived as male and the latter as female. These two, joined together, are fancied as bridegroom and the bride whose garments are tied to each other.[16]

The entire plan of a temple is Tāntric in character. The *sanctum sanctorum* is called *garbha* (womb) where the main idol is placed. A sort of corridor, through which one has to enter, connects the porch with the *garbha*.

Many temples were built in honour of Yellamma,[17] a local form of Ādi Śakti, all over North Karṇāṭaka and bordering regions of Mahārāṣṭra, the most famous being the one at Soundatti, mentioned among the Śaktisthānas in *Devī-bhāgavata*[18] (6th cent., according to some, 12th-13th cent. or earlier). From the many temples in honour of the Divine Mother, we can infer the wide prevalence and popularity of Mother-worship since the 10th century A.D.

Some West Asian shrines reveal sex-design. They are divided into three parts—the porch representing the lower end of the female organ leading up to the hymen, the hall corresponding to the organ itself and the inner sanctum symbolising the uterus.[19]

The Tāntric conception appears to have inspired at least one temple in West Bengal. That is the Haṃseśvarī temple (completed 1814 A.D.) at Bāñsberia in Hooghly district of West Bengal about fifty kilometres from Calcutta on the other side of the Ganges. The plan of this unique temple was chalked out by its builder,[20] Rājā Nṛsiṃha Devarāya, who was a Tāntric devotee.

16. N.K. Bose, *Canons of Orissan Architecture*, pp. 92, 154.
17. Also called Reṇukā. The name Yellamma is derived from the Kannada term *ellara amma* (Universal Mother).
18. See P.B. Desai, *Kallachuris of Karṇāṭaka*.
19. N.N. Bhattacharya, *History of Tāntric Religion*, p. 376.
20. Actually started by the Rājā in 1799 A.D., it was completed by his widow.

The interior of the temple is like the six *Cakras* through which *Kuṇḍalinī*, represented by goddess Haṃseśvarī, goes upward. Besides the three well-known Tāntric nerves, *Iḍā*, *Piṅgalā*, *Suṣumnā*, two more, viz. *Vajrākhya* and *Citriṇī* are indicated within the temple by ladders.

The aforesaid goddess is seated on a lotus which rests on a stem emerging from the navel of Śiva lying on a *Trikoṇa-yantra*. The goddess has a human head in her lower left-hand and *Abhayamudrā* in her upper right-hand, while, in her other hands, there are a sword and a conch.

The very name of Haṃseśvarī is Tāntric. *Haṃ* is a *Bīja*, and *Sa* stands for Śakti. The two are locked (*kīlaka*) together; the locking is believed to lead to the highest realisation.

In conclusion, it may be stated that, as D. Desai points out,[21] Tāntric representations in art and architecture appear to have been inspired by a twofold motive. One was religious, as in the case of temples. The other, a secular one, was either to give a visual expression to the passionate feelings of the artist or the sculptor or to gratify the lustful propensities of the sensual people. Examples of the latter are furnished by terracottas with sex-motif from Mathurā, Candraketugarh and those unearthed in excavated historical sites.

While Tantra may have provided the erotico-religious art and architecture, the *Kāmasūtra*, perhaps, played a significant role in inspiring the secular erotic designs to cater to the needs of the hedonistic or epicurean aristocrats or *Nāgaraka* type of men. The increasing influence of *Kāmasūtra* was, perhaps, due to the rise and firm establishment of feudalism. Before the complacent labelling of all erotic art motifs as Tāntric, we should bear in mind that esoterism is a marked characteristic of Tāntric practices so that real Tāntric devotees would not like to display ritualistic sex acts at public places. Moreover, erotic representations though they are, they are not functionally related to Tāntric *Sādhanā* or worship. In this connection, it may be noted that none of the Śākta Pīṭhas, the strongholds of Tāntric rites and practices, has any erotic depiction whatsoever.

Viewed historically, the sex-designs in art reveal different characteristics in different ages.

Of the extant specimens, the earliest ones date back to the second century B.C. During a few centuries since then, we see nude

21. *Erotic Sculpture of India*, pp. 16-17.

goddesses and females, goddesses associated with couples engaging in sexual union and making various love poses, e.g. embracing, kissing, etc. In the period between 400 and 900 A.D. secular erotic motifs appear to have been on the increase and Tāntric influence gained ground. We learn from inscriptions of the fifth century onwards about patronage extended by feudal chiefs and dignitaries to Tāntric devotees.

The period following 900 A.D. saw a spurt or explosion of erotic influence on art.

During this period coarseness and vulgarity like orgiastic depictions crept considerably into the realm of art.

Below we give a list of some noteworthy objects of art depicting erotic motifs.

Linear Representation

Daimad pot (Ahmadnagar district of Mahārāṣṭra) — Chalcolithic period, phase III, *Indian Archaeology, A Review,* 1958-59, Fig. 7.

Caves

Kupgallu cave (Mysore) D.H. Gordon, *The Prehistoric Background of Indian Culture,* p. 115.

Buddhist caves of Kondana and Pitalkhora in West Deccan — depict *mithuna* — c. 2nd-1st cent B.C. M.N. Deshpande in *Ancient India,* XV, pp. 69 ff, 81 ff.

Ellorā, Ajantā, Aurangābād — Terracottas and other objects found at Bhitā, Jhusi, Kauśāmbi in UP, Ter and Nevasa in Mahārāṣṭra, Nāgārjunikoṇḍā in Andhra Pradesh. Some terracottas of Kauśāmbi and Bhitā date from 2nd-1st cent. B.C.

Plaque from Awra-Mandasore district of Madhya Pradesh (c. 100 B.C.-300 A.D.) — Goddess Śrī with couples, on both sides, engaged in sexual intercourse, and pitchers.

Some terracottas from Candraketugarh and Tamluk dating back to a period from c. 2nd cent. B.C. probably representing wine-pots, in front.

M. Candra in *Bulletin of Prince of Wales Museum,* Bombay, No. 9, p. 25, fig. 17

Stone

Monuments of Sāñchi and Bharhut — *mithunas* associated with Śrīdevī — 2nd cent. B.C.

The art of Mathurā and Nāgārjunikoṇḍā reveals a variety of *maithuna* motifs.

Temples

Aihole, Badāmi, Mahākūṭeśvara, Pattadakal — depict poses of love-making.

Puri, Konārak, many temples of Madhya Pradesh (in Jabbalpur, Gwalior, Malwa regions), Rājasthān, Gujarāt, Mahārāṣṭra, Mysore — depict different kinds of erotic scenes.

Images[22]

Among the images, owing their conception to Tantra, the most well-known is that of Dakṣiṇā Kālī.

The form of Kālī-image, which is most popular among the Tāntric worshippers, is this. Śiva lies on His back with His male organ erect, and the goddess is seated on Him with that organ inserted into her organ in a woman-superior position.

The offer of the severed head of the worshipper before the goddess is a feature common in the Pallava (c. 4th cent. A.D. to end of 9th cent.) and Cola (c. 100 A.D. to 3rd quarter of 11th century A.D.) periods of South India.

Some other noteworthy images are those of Ekānaṃśā, the Mātṛkās, Danturā, Cāmuṇḍā, Vārāhī, Vāgīśvarī, Mahāmāyā or Tripurabhairavī, Caṇḍī, Śarvāṇī, the Yoginīs.

The Jains and Buddhists also have Tāntric icons. Among the Jains, the most popular are the images of Yakṣiṇīs, viz., Jvālamālinī, Padmāvatī and Ambikā.

Images, inspired by Tāntric Buddhism, are far larger in number. Among the images of males, well-known are those of Ratnasambhava, Amoghasiddhi, Vajradharā, Vajrasattva, Avalokiteśvara, Śaṃkhanātha, Lokeśvara, Vāgīśvara, Hevajra, Yamānta or Yamāri, crowned with a string of human heads, Jambhala, Trailokyavijaya, Mañjuśrī.

22. For descriptions of Tāntric images, see N.N. Bhattacharya, *op. cit.*, pp. 382-396. Here we refer only to those having some pronounced Tāntric features.

Among the females, the following are well-known: Kurukullā, having a garland of human skulls in one form, Parṇaśabarī, Prajñāpāramitā, Cundā. The most popular of the female deities is Tārā.

Among the Buddhist gods and goddesses, very popular is Heruka, often in a *yuganaddha* position, with his consort Nairātmā (Śakti or Prajñā).

In one image, He is represented as dancing on a corpse and having a garland of human heads.

ŚABDA AND DHVANI

Tantra has made speculations about sound. It is of two kinds, viz., *Dhvani* and *Varṇa*. *Dhvani* is sound not conveyed by letters of the alphabet, whereas *Varṇa* means such letters representing different sounds. It has been stated that difference of tone is the cause of this twofold aspect of sound. As a matter of fact, however, there is no difference in the two kinds of sound; *dhvani* is the real thing and *śabda* is its manifestation.

It is stated that the world of movable and immovable things is linked up and pervaded by the *Śakti* in the form of *dhvani*. This *Śakti* is variously called by such names as *Nāda, Prāṇa, Jīvaghoṣa,* etc.

This *Śabda-śakti* is identified with *Kulakuṇḍalinī* making indistinct sound at the *Mūlādhāra.*

It is stated that a great *Mantra* repeats itself when inspiration and expiration through the circular movement of the vital air of *Jīva* revolves round the wheel of *Dhvani*. Such a *Mantra* is called *Ajapā.* The consciousness in the *Jīva* is nothing but the eternally existing *Śakti* of *Dhvani* in the child in the womb. The vital *Śakti* of *Jīva* is only *Dhvani* in the form of *Ajapā Mantra.*

Several stages of words have been conceived. The extremely subtle state is called *parā;* it issues from the *Mūlādhāra*. The less subtle state is called *Paśyantī;* in this state it reaches the heart. The still less subtle state is known as *Madhyamā;* it exists in conjunction with *Buddhi*. The gross state is called *Vaikharī* issuing from the throat.

VALUE OF TANTRA — RISE OF SAHAJIYĀ CULT

Tantra prescribed easier rites and rituals by reducing the rigour of Brāhmaṇical practices. As stated above, it gave greater freedom of religious performances to women and Śūdras. The rigidity of the caste-system was relaxed.

TANTRA AND SUFISM

Wherever Sufism originated and flourished — in Arabia or Persia — and whatever the time of its genesis, the fact remains that it made its way into India in very early times. Like Islām, Sufism established its stronghold in Sind. It had a great appeal to the masses, the lower echelons of the society, over whom the elitist or orthodox scriptures had little hold.

By the 14th century, Sufism was closely woven into the fabric of Indian society.

The salient features of Sufism are briefly as follows: there is no God outside human mind, scriptural injunctions are not essential for realisation of the highest truth, there is the easy (*Sahaja*) way of realising it; the human body is the microcosm of the universe. The means of understanding the relation of God with the individual and with the material world consists in *tariqat* (way) and *marifat* (knowledge).

The way has seven stages, viz., service, love, sacrifice, meditation, concentration, union and equation.

Knowledge, helping God-realisation, is twofold, viz., *ilm* (gathered from experience, through perception, inference, etc.) and *marifat* (obtained through divine grace). The latter was regarded as superior to the former.

Like the Tāntrics, the Sufis believe in *Guru* (*Pīr* or *Mursid*).

Thus, even to a superficial reader, the close similarity between Tāntrism and Sufism will be obvious.

Among the leading Muslims, who followed Tāntric *rahasya-sādhana* (mystic devotion), was Gazi-Mian who, a contemporary of Sultān Māhmud (10th-11th cent.), founded a sect.

Some of the famous Sufi saints were as follows:

Shāh Karīm of Sind (17th cent). His preceptor was a Vaiṣṇava, and his followers used the symbol *Om* of the Hindus.

Sind produced another saint Shāh Ināyat.

A very popular saint was Shāh Latīf.

Sufism was so popular that, in Sind region, Hindus had Muslim preceptors and *vice-versa*.

The Jaina *Mātṛkās*, *Vidyādevīs*, *Yoginīs*, etc., recall the Mother Goddess cult of Tantra.

Some Jaina texts mention Tāntric practices prevailing in some contemporary sects. In the manner of Tantra, Jainism also refers to magical rites like *Ṣaṭkarma*, the potency of *mantras*, etc.

The same reason, which was responsible for the association of miracles with the Buddha, was also, perhaps, responsible for similar things in connection with Mahāvīra.

The extreme rigidity and rigours of Jainism made it less vulnerable than Buddhism to the infiltration of Tāntrism.

CHAPTER VI

SOCIETY REFLECTED IN TANTRA

In connexion with the rationale underlying the composition of Tantra we have got some idea about the society reflected in this Śāstra. Here we shall set forth some more information.

In breaking away from the conventional Brāhmaṇical Śāstras, Tantra did not totally reject the Veda. We have pointed out the relation between the Veda and Tantra. The *Mahānirvāṇa* prescribes Vedic *mantras* in certain rites. It is, however, curious that this work betrays a general attitude of disregard towards the above *mantras* when it declares (11.14.15, 20) that these are like poisonless serpents in *Kaliyuga*.

Post-Vedic Brāhmaṇical works were not categorically ignored in Tantra. For instance, the aforesaid Tantra prescribes the stanza iv.24 of the *Bhagavadgītā* as the *mantra* to be recited by the leader of the *Tattva-cakra* (q.v.) while pacifying and offering the five *Tattvas* or *Makāras* to the deity.

The rules of Brāhmaṇical Smṛti or Dharmaśāstra were flouted in many cases. The *Mahānirvāṇa* (viii.150) seems to recognise only *Brāhma-vivāha* instead of the eight forms of marriage mentioned in the Brāhmaṇical scriptures, e.g. Manu, iii, 27-34. This Tantra provides also for *Śaiva-vivāha* which is an innovation. This form of *vivāha,* meant for Śāktas, is as follows in the above Tantra (chap. IX). In course of a *Cakra* ritual, it is brought about, according to the mutual desire of a man and a woman, by the fellow Śāktas. The man, while repeating a *mantra,* should salute Kālī, the Supreme, for 108 times. Then the man is to ask the woman to accept him as her husband. The woman would do so with sandalpaste, flowers and rice dried in the sun. Thus she has to place her hand on that of the man. After this, the leader of the *Cakra* will pray to Kālī to protect the couple, and sprinkle over them honey or *arghya* water. At the same time, the other participants in the *Cakra* will utter *Svasti* (indicating well-being). Finally, the couple will bow down to the leader who will exhort them to act up to their promise. In such a case, both *Anuloma* and *Pratiloma* marriages are allowed. But, in Dharmaśāstra, the latter form, in which the husband is of a caste inferior to that of the wife, is prohibited.

In the Vedas and in Dharmaśāstras the *Purohita* (priest) plays the dominant role in the religious rites. In Tantra, *Guruvāda* developed to a very great extent.

While external worship, with the prescribed paraphernalia and formalities, became very important in the religious life of the people, internal worship (*Antaryāga*) was highly recommended in Tantra.

The *Manu-smṛti* vehemently condemns (XI.90) the drinking of certain kinds of *surā* (wine) for a Brāhmaṇa, Tantra prescribes wine as one of the essentials of *Sādhana*. It should, however, be noted that some Tantras forbid a Brāhmaṇa to offer wine, and provide for substitutes for it. The *Śrītattva-cintāmaṇi* (XVIII.574) is an instance in point. Substitutes, recommended for wine, are coconut water and honey.

In Dharmaśāstra, a man's sexual union with another man's wife is condemned. But, in Tāntric *sādhana*, in the absence of one's wife, another man's wife can be the Śakti, according to some works.

The Śūdras, to whom the Dharmaśāstra denied all religious observances, were eligible for Tāntric initiation.

The women, relegated to an ignominious position in Dharmaśāstra so far as religious rites were concerned, have been allowed in Tantra to have *dīkṣā* and to perform Tāntric rites. The exalted position, accorded to her, is evident from the fact that she has been designated as Śakti, the indispensable partner of one taking to Tāntric *sādhana*. As we have already stated, *maithuna* or sexual intercourse was prescribed as one of the five *Makāras* or *Tattvas* required for such *sādhana*. In the *Mahānirvāṇa Tantra* (Ullāsa viii) it is ordained that a daughter also should be brought up and educated carefully. It should be noted that Tantra allows a woman, having the requisite qualifications to give Tāntric *dīkṣā*; in fact, *dīkṣā* by a woman-*guru* is salutary. Eight times more effective is initiation by one's mother. If she gives her own *mantra* to her son, then the latter can achieve the eight well-known *Siddhis* (*Prāṇatoṣiṇī* — Kāṇḍa II, Pariccheda ii).

The orthodox Brāhmaṇical caste-rigidity was waived to a great extent in Tantra. In addition to the conventional four castes, the *Mahānirvāṇa* provides for a *Sāmānya jāti*. The son born out of the matrimonial union of a man of lower caste and a woman of a higher one has no social status according to Smṛti-śāstra. The *Mahānirvāṇa* holds that such a son will not be casteless; he will belong to the above *Sāmānya* caste. The idea of equality of all classes of people, according to Tāntric *Kulācāra*, is expressed in the following verse of the *Mahānirvāṇa* (xiv.184):

> *viprādy-antyaj-paryantā dvipadā ye'tra bhūtale/*
> *te sarveśmin kulācāre bhaveyur-adhikāriṇaḥ//*
>
> [Let all those bipeds, from Brāhmaṇa to *Antyaja* (Śūdra or Caṇḍāla), who are in this world, be entitled to this *kula* mode of worship.]

ESOTERIC RITUALS

In some Tantras, we come across the following two interesting Tāntric rituals, called *Bhairavī-cakra* and *Tattva-cakra.*

Bhairavī-cakra

According to the *Mahānirvāṇa Tantra* (VIII.54-206), it is as follows.

On a purified piece of land, a triangular figure is to be drawn with vermilion, red sandalpaste or water. A rectangular figure should be drawn outside it. The *Sādhaka* will fill a pitcher with curd, dried (not boiled) rice, fruits, leaves and scented water. After placing it in the first figure, he will meditate upon and worship the desired deity. He should keep before him the intended *tattva* (out of the *Pañcatattvas*), and sprinkle water over it with the *Bīja Mantra, Phaṭ*. The next step for the devotee is to meditate on Ānanda Bhairava and Ānanda Bhairavī. The unity of these two deities is to be reflected upon in the above pitcher. This will be followed by the purification of the other *tattvas* and contemplation that all the articles, collected there, are pervaded by Brahman. Then the devotee, with closed eyes, should offer the articles to Kālī, and eat and drink along with others assembled there. In a *Cakra*, fickleness, gossip, garrulity, spitting, etc. are prohibited. As a result of the performance of such *Cakras* for six months, one can be a king for one year, and overcome death. The daily performance of it entitles one to liberation. Also see *Kulārṇava Tantra*, VIII and *Kaulāvalī-nirṇaya*, VII.

Tattva-cakra

Also called *Divya-cakra* or *Brahmacakra*. According to the *Mahānirvāṇa* it is as follows. The leader of the *Cakra* has his mind fixed on Brahman.

Accompanied by devotees, possessed of the knowledge of Brahman, he will start the *Cakra*, and place the *tattvas* in front. Over each *tattva* he will recite the *mantra* beginning with *Oṃ* and ending with *Prāṇabīja* (i.e. *Haṃsa-mantra, so'ham*) for a hundred times. Then he will repeat, for three or seven times, the *mantra* — *brahmārpaṇaṃ brahma-havih*, etc. (*Gītā*, iv.24). The leader, along with others, will partake of the *tattvas* thus sanctified and consecrated to Brahman.

In chapter vii of the *Kaulāvalī-nirṇaya*, there is provision for worship in *Śrīcakra* (also called *Śrīyantra*). On this occasion, promiscuous sexual intercourse is allowed.

CHAPTER VII

TANTRA ABROAD

In connexion with the original homeland of Tantra, we have discussed the question of its foreign origin. Here we shall have an account of the presence of Tantra or Tāntric elements outside India.

There is a Chinese version[1] of the *Kumāratantra*. The cult of Buddhist Tārā, as Śakti of Avalokiteśvara, was present in China. Curiously enough, in pre-Buddhist Taoism and Confucianism of China, which recognised Mother Goddess, as the representative of *Yin* (the Female Principle), Avalokiteśvara[2] was transformed into a goddess. Later on, in about the seventh or eighth century A.D., Tārā was entirely merged in Avalokiteśvara who lost his male entity, and was metamorphosed as goddess Kuan-yin of China. The dual form of Tārā came to be very popular. In course of time, Taoist rituals infiltrated into the Tārā cult and Yinism or glorification of the Female Principle in Taoism. The very name *Mahācīna-tārā* suggests the existence of this goddess in China. According to the *Sammoha-tantra, Nīla-Sarasvatī* or *Ugratārā* was born in a lake, called Cola, on the west of Meru which was included in *Cīnadeśa*.

The cultural history of Tibet reveals the great impact of Tantra in that country. Some Tāntric writers, particularly of Bengal, are known to have settled in Tibet, and written Tāntric works which exist only in Tibetan, the Sanskrit originals being lost. For further information, see our accounts of the following authors in the chapter on Authors:

Abhayākaragupta, Atīśa, Bodhibhadra, Divākaracandra, Jetāri, Kumāracandra, Nāgabodhi, Śāntarakṣita, Śīlabhadra.

Goddess Tārā, as a Buddhist deity, came to be included in the Tibetan pantheon; she is called Sgral-ma or Dol-ma. Several forms of Tārā have been conceived. Siddha Nāgārjuna (c. 2nd century A.D.) is said to have revived the Ekajaṭā (= Mahācīna-tārā) cult in Tibet.

---

1. See J. Filliozat, Etude....le Kumāratantra....textes paralleles indiens, tibetains, chinois...., Paris, 1937.
2. Vide S.K. Chatterjee, *JAS*, I, 1959, p. 180.

Tāntric influence was widespread in South East Asia.[3] From an inscription of Sdak-kak-Thom it is learnt that at least four Tantras, entitled *Śiraścheda, Vīṇāśikha, Sammoha* and *Nayottara*, were introduced into Kambuja (Cambodia, later called Kampuchea) as early as 800 A.D. It is further learnt that the Royal High Priest, Simkaivalya, was initiated to Tantra by a Brāhmaṇa, named Hiraṇyadama. A few other Cambodian inscriptions mention *Śaiva Tantras* and *Śaiva Āgamas*. An inscription at Angkorvat mentions *Parameśvara-tantra*. Images of the Tāntric deity, Gaṇeśa, have been found in Cambodia.

Tāntric influence in Java is quite considerable: images of Śiva, both in his furious and benign aspects, have been found in this region. In His fierce aspect, He is called Bhairava, a name common in Tantra. Śakti also appears in both the aspects. The Batavia Museum contains images of Mahiṣamardinī (Devī as the destroyer of the buffalo-demon). Śakti of Bhairava or Mahākāla is called Bhairavī or Mahākālī. Here is a typical Tāntric image — seated on a corpse with human skulls in the neck and head and a garland of skulls on her body.[4] The Javanese Gaṇeśa is seated on human skulls; this points to his Tāntric character. The Tāntric work, *Gaṇapati-tattva* exists only in an old Javanese text.

Salutation to Maheśvara and Umā occurs in the Myson inscription (5th century A.D.) of Champa. At several places in this region, images of Devī are found; She is called Mātṛliṅgeśa-tārā, Gaurī, Mahādevī, etc.

Among other foreign countries, influenced by Tantra, mention may be made of Mongolia and Japan.

TANTRA AND JUDAISM

Like Tāntric devotees, the followers of the Jewish *Kabbah* doctrine have faith in the mystic potency of the letters of the alphabet, magic, amulets, the unity of microcosm and macrocosm, etc.

TANTRA AND CHRISTIANITY

Some scholars point out similarities between the two in certain respects. The sprinkling of water, as an essential part of the ceremony

3. See P.C. Bagchi, *Studies in Tantras*, Part I; R.C. Majumdar, *Inscriptions of Kambuja;* S.C. Banerji, *Sanskrit Beyond India.*
4. See R.C. Majumdar, *Ancient Indian Colonies in the Far East*, II, pp. 2, 102-103.

of baptism in the Anglican Church, is somewhat similar to Tāntric *Abhiṣeka*. Woodroffe finds parallelism between the sign of the Christian Cross and Tāntric *Nyāsa*. Baptism is believed by the devout to ensure the soul's residence in heaven after one's death, while the unbaptised are subjected to an ignominious existence in future life. Much in the same way, Tantra has faith in the attainment of the spiritual goal through physical means. The necessary rite in the Roman Church includes exorcism, and the use of salt, oil and lights. In Tantra, such practices are common.

CHAPTER VIII

AUTHORS OF TANTRAS AND COMMENTARIES

ABHAYĀKARAGUPTA

Perhaps born in the latter half of the eleventh century A.D. in a Kṣatriya family of Bengal. He perhaps flourished in the reign (c. 1077-1120 A.D.) of Bengal king Rāmapāla. Some think, he was a native of Orissa, while, according to others, he belonged to Bihar.

From the *Tanjur* it is learnt that he wrote 20 works on Vajrayāna, of which four are available in original Sanskrit. Besides, he wrote some commentaries, viz. on the *Buddha-kapāla-tantra* (completed at Vikramaśīla monastery in the 25th year of the aforesaid king Rāmapāla) and some other texts.

His *Ucchuṣma-jambhala-sādhana* has been edited in the *Sādhanamālā*, GOS, XLI, No. 295.

His *Niṣpanna-yogāvalī* is a well-known work.

For a list of his works, see *NCC*, I (Rev. ed.), pp. 280-281.

ABHINAVAGUPTA

A Kashmirian polymath, famous in the domains of poetics, dramaturgy, Śaiva philosophy and Tantra.

He was son of Nṛsiṃhagupta, popularly known as Cukhala, grandson of Varāhagupta, brother of Manorathagupta, disciple of Utpaladeva, Bhaṭṭa Indurāja and Bhaṭṭa Tota or Tauta, grand-disciple of Somānanda, *guru* of Kṣemarāja and Kṣemendra.

He is well-known as the author of the *Abhinava-Bhāratī* commentary on Bharata's *Nāṭyaśāstra* and *Kāvyāloka-locana* commentary on the *Dhvaniyāloka*.

Of his Tāntric philosophical works, the following have been published:

Tantrāloka, Tantrasāra, Paramārtha-sāra, Mālinī-vijaya-vārtika, Parātriṃśikā-vivṛti, Bodha-pañca-daśikā, Tantravaṭadhānikā, Īśvara-pratyabhijñā-vimarśinī.

He wrote a commentary, called *Vimarśinī,* on the *Īśvara-pratyabhijñā* of Utpaladeva.

He is assigned to a period between the last quarter of the tenth century and the first quarter of the eleventh.

See K.C. Pandey, *Abhinavagupta,* 1963.

ADVAYAVAJRA

A Buddhist, also known as Avadhūtipā or Avadhūtapāda, he was *guru* of Lalitagupta. Appears to have been a prolific writer of about 1000 A.D. Twenty-one of his works are printed in *Advayavajra-saṃgraha,* GOS, XL. Besides the above works, some other texts are also ascribed to him.

His works, available in print, are stated below:

Apratiṣṭhāna-prakāśa, ptd. in *Advayavajra-saṃgraha,* GOS, XL.

Amanasikāra
Advayavajra-saṃgraha, GOS, XL.

(Amanasikārādhāra). Also ptd. *Pro. AIOC,* XX, Vol. II Skt. and Tibetan versions by S.K. Pathak.

Kudṛṣṭi-nirghāta(na)
Advayavajra-saṃgraha, GOS, XL.

Caturmudrā
Advayavajra-saṃgraha, GOS, XL.

Tattvadaśaka
Ibid.

Tattvaprakāśa
Ibid.

Tattva-mahāyāna-viṃśati
or
Tattva-viṃśikā
Ibid.

Tattvaratnāvalī
Ibid.

Pañcakāra
Ibid.

Premapañcaka
Ibid.

Mahāyāna-viṃśikā
Ibid.

Mahāsukhaprakāśa
Ibid.

Māyā-nirukti
Ibid.

Yuganaddha-prakāśa
Ibid.

Vajravārāhī-sādhana
Sādhanamālā II, GOS, XLI.

Saṃkṣipta-seka-prakriyā
Ptd. as *Sekanirṇaya* or *Sekanirdeśa* in GOS, XL.

Saptākṣara-sādhana, Sādhanamālā II, GOS, XLI.

Siṃhanāda-sādhana
Sādhanamālā, GOS, XXVI.

Sekakārya-saṃgraha
Ptd. as Sekatānvaya-saṃgraha in GOS, XL.

Svapna-nirukti
GOS, XL.

Hevajra-viśuddhanidhi
or
Hevajra-viśuddhi-sādhana, *JBORS*, XXI.
See Viśuddhi-nidhi-nāma-hevajra-sādhana (*supra*).

Hevajrākhya-yuganaddha
JBORS, XXI.i.

Advaya's commentary on *Dohākośa* is ptd. in H.P. Sastri's ed. of *Bauddha gān o dohā*, Calcutta, 1916, the title of the commentary is *Dohākośa-hṛdayārthagīta-ṭīkā*.

AGASTYA

To him is attributed the *Śaktisūtra*.

AMARA MAITRA

A Vārendra Brāhmaṇa of Bengal, he was son of Vāsudeva and flourished in the second quarter of the 19th century. The following Tāntric works are ascribed to him:

Jñānadīpikā (Śaka 1753=1831 A.D.);
Amara-saṃgraha (Śaka 1765=1843 A.D.);
Āmarī-saṃhitā (Śaka 1768=1846 A.D.).

AMṚTĀNANDANĀTHA

Author of the *Saubhāgya-subhagodaya* and the commentary *Dīpikā* on *Yoginīhṛdaya*.

A disciple of Puṇyānanda (or Pūrṇānandanātha), he perhaps flourished in about the tenth or eleventh century A.D., according to some, 12th-13th century, according to others.

He appears to have written also the following works: *Ṣaṭ-triṃśat-tattva-sandoha, Tripurā-siddhānta-prakaraṇa, Tripura-sundarī-tantra, Tripura-sundarī-kalpa, Cidvilāsa-stuti* and *Tripurā-sāra-samuccaya-ṭippaṇa*. He is perhaps not identified with his namesake who revised Kṛṣṇānanda's *Tantrasāra*.

For MSS and further information, see *NCC*, I (Revised), pp. 355-56.

ANAṄGAVAJRA

A Buddhist pupil of Śubhākara and Padmavajra (author of *Guhyasiddhi*) and *guru* of Indrabhūti (author of *Jñāna-siddhi*, etc.). Supposed to have flourished around 705 A.D. Anaṅgavajra was one of the 84 *Siddhas*, held in high esteem in Tibet.

Of the works, ascribed to him, note worthy are the *Prajñopāya-viniścaya-siddhi* and *Hevjrasādhana*.

For his works, see *NCC*, I (Revised), p. 157.

ANUPAMAVAJRA

Author of the *Ādikarma-pradīpa* and *Suviśiṣṭa-nāma-sādhanopāyikā*, see *NCC*, I, p. 204.

ATĪŚA (or DĪPAṂKARA SRĪJÑĀNA ATĪŚA)

A native of Bengal, he was son of Kalyāṇaśrī and Śrī Prabhā. He studied under Jetāri, Ratnākaraśānti and Dharmakīrti (II). He was Principal of Vikramaśīlavihāra, and teacher of Prajñākara, author of a commentary on the *Bodhi-caryāvatāra*.

Believed to have lived from about 982-1055 A.D. At the invitation of the then king of Tibet, he went there and lived till death. He reformed Buddhism in Tibet, and founded an order, called 'Yellow

Cap Sect' or Virtue-practisers. He appears to have settled disputes between emperor Nayapāla (c. first half of 11th century) of Bengal and the Kalacuri king, Karṇa.

A contemporary of Bhūsuka and Dharmakīrti, he wrote many works in Sanskrit and Tibetan, all of which are now preserved only in Tibetan translations.

For his life and works, see A. Chattopadhyay, *Atīśa* and *Tibet*, Calcutta, 1967; P. Bose, *Indian Teachers of Buddhist Universities*, Adyar, 1923; S. Dutt, *Buddhist Monks and Monasteries of India*, London, 1962; A.K. Warder, *Indian Buddhism*.

BHAIRAVĀNANDA

Author of the *Annadī-kalpasūtra*.

BHAIRAVA TRIPĀṬHIN

Author of a commentary on the *Kramādīpikā*.

BHĀSKARARĀYA

A celebrated Tāntric author, commentator and worshipper of Śrīvidyā. He appears to have flourished sometime between 1700 and 1750 A.D. A South Indian *Ṛgveda* Brāhmaṇa of Viśvāmitra *gotra*, he was son of Gambhīrarāya, minister of a Muslim ruler of Bījāpur. Umānandanātha, author of the *Nityotasava* (q.v.), refers to his preceptor as Bhāsurānandanātha, the name of Bhāskara after his initiation. His real name was Bhāskaramakhī Bhāratī. He completed his scholarly career in Vārāṇasī, and settled in a village near Tanjore where he established contact with the court.

We are told by the aforesaid Umānanda that Bhāskara wrote a work, called *Ratnākara*. He composed the Tāntric digest entitled *Varivasyā-rahasya* and its commentary, *Varivasyā-prakāśa*. His other works are:

> *Guptāvalī*, commentary on the *Devī-māhātmya* (*Caṇḍī*); *Saubhāgya-bhāskara*, a commentary on the *Lalitā-sahasra-nāma* (a section of the *Brahmāṇḍa-purāṇa*); *Setubandha*, commentary on the *Yoginī-hṛdaya*, and a commentary of the same title on the *Vāmakeśvara-tantra* of which the *Nityāṣoḍaśīkārṇava* is a part.

In the last commentary, he mentions several Upaniṣads treating, in detail, of *Bhakti* towards Mahā-tripurasundarī, and interprets *Ṛgveda* V.47.4 as the origin of the *Śrīvidyā*. He wrote a commentary also on the *Kaulopaniṣad*.

Bhāskara's conception of *Śakti* is laid down in his *Setubandha* commentary. According to him, three forms of the Supreme Goddess, fit for worship, are generally

(i) *Sthūla* — image with anthropomorphic features;

(ii) *Sūkṣma* — in the form of *mantra*;

(iii) *Para* — form worthy of reflection.

Another form of *Mahāśakti* is beyond speech and beyond comprehension.

Bhāskara has made his comment on the list of Tantras in the *Nityāṣoḍaśīkārṇava*.

The aforesaid Umānandanātha is known for a biography of Bhāskara called *Bhāskaravilāsa*.

Bhāskara wrote a commentary also on the *Śiva-sūtra* of Kashmir.

For information about Bhāskara, see P.V. Kane, *History of Dharmaśāstra*, V, pt. 2, pp. 1044, 1071, 1145; R.K. Sastri, Intro. to ed. of the *Varivasyā-rahasya* by S.S. Sastri, pp. xvii ff; V.V. Dvivedi, Intro. to *Nityāṣoḍaśīkārṇava*, p. 15 f; Pandey, *Abhinavagupta*, pp. 583-589; C. Chakravarti, *Tantras* etc., p. 74 f; R.K. Sastri (*op. cit.*), pp. xxix-xxxiii.

See *Bhāskaravilāsa*, ptd. in the NSP ed. of *Lalitā-sahasra-nāma* with commentary of Bhāskararāya.

Also see R.K. Sastri, Intro. to ed. of *Varivasyā-rahasya* by S.S. Sastri, p. xvii f.

BHĀSURĀNANDA-NĀTHA

Another name of Bhāskararāya (q.v.).

BODHIBHADRA

Said to have lived at Somapurī Vihāra. Might be identical with Bodhibhadra of Vikramaśīla, mentioned by Tāranātha. Traditionally a Bengali.

Only Tibetan translations are available of the following works, ascribed to him:

Rahasyānanda-tilaka, Samādhi-sambhāra-parivarta, Bodhisattva-sambara-vidhi, Yoga-lakṣaṇa-satya, Bodhisattva-sambara-viṃśati-pañjikā, Kālacakra-gaṇita-mukhādeśa, etc.

BRAHMĀNANDA GIRI

Disciple of Tripurānanda and spiritual guide of Pūrṇānanda, he probably flourished in the early or middle part of the sixteenth century.

The *Śāktānanda-taraṅgiṇī* and *Tārārahasya* are attributed to him.

(Rājā) DEVĀNANDA SIṂHA

To him is attributed the *Śāktapramoda.*

DEVANĀTHA ṬHAKKURA TARKAPAÑCĀNANA

Author of *Tantrakaumudī.*

Alias Sapta-kaumudīkāra, he was son of Govinda Ṭhakkura (author of *Adhikaraṇamālā* and *Kāvyapradīpa*) and pupil of Somabhaṭṭa. Born in 1490 A.D. in Mithilā, he was patronised by Malladeva Naranārāyaṇa (1555-87 A.D.). In an introductory verse, the author says that King Govindadeva Gajapati honoured him with valuable gifts. There was another king, named Viśvasiṃha who probably succeeded the above king. The author refers to Malladeva as Lord of Kāmata which appears to have been a kingdom with its capital at Kāmatāpur, a few miles to the south of Cooch Behar in West Bengal (vide R.C. Majumdar, *Advanced History of India*, 1982, pp. 340, 382).

Besides Tantra, he wrote also on Mīmāṃsā, Smṛti, etc.

See *Hist. of Navyanyāya in Mithilā; JASB*, NS, IX (1915), 271.

DIVĀKARACANDRA

According to the Tibetan *Tanjur*, he was a Bengali, a contemporary of King Nayapāla (c. first half of 11th century A.D.) and a disciple of Maitrīpā. Divākara translated two Tāntric works into Tibetan. Divākara was author of the *Heruka-bhūta-nāma-maṇḍalopāyikā.*

See Buddhist Tāntric literature of Bengal, *NIA*, I, p. 11.

DURGĀRĀMA

Having the title Siddhāntavāgīśa, he was a Bengali scholar to whom is ascribed a *Karpūra-stotra-ṭīkā.*

GAUḌAPĀDA

A famous philosopher who was Śaṃkarācārya's teacher's teacher. According to some, he flourished in Bengal at the end of the seventh century A.D. or in the beginning of the eighth. Besides the well-known *Gauḍapāda-kārikā* and a few other philosophical works, he was the author of the Tāntric work, *Śrīvidyā-ratna-sūtra* or *Gauḍapāda-sūtra*, also called *Śakti-mīmāṃsā*.

See T.M.P. Mahadevan, *Gauḍapāda*, Madras, 1952.

GĪRVĀṆENDRA SARASVATĪ II

A pupil of Viśveśvara Sarasvatī and preceptor of Bodhendra (author of *Advaitabhūṣaṇa* and a commentary on *Ātmabodha* of Śaṃkara) as well as of Nṛsiṃhāśramin (author of *Advaitadīpikā*) and Rāmendra (author of *Vaidikācāra-nirṇaya*, he wrote the *Prapañcasāra-saṃgraha*, based on the *Prapañcasāra*, ascribed to Śaṃkarācārya.

GORAKṢANĀTHA

The most renowned teacher of the Nātha or Yogī sect of mysticism. Traditionally known as a pupil of Mīnanātha or Matsyendranātha, and teacher of Svātmārāmayogin, author of the *Haṭha(yoga) pradīpikā*.

He is traditionally assigned to different periods ranging from the eighth century to the sixteenth. Most modern scholars are inclined to assign him to the eleventh century A.D. He is generally believed to have hailed from some place in north-west India.

To him are ascribed several Tāntric works, e.g.

Gorakṣabodha, Gorakṣa-saṃhitā, Gorakṣa-siddhānta-saṃgraha.

For details about his life and works, see Briggs, G.W.: *Gorakhnāth and the Kānphaṭa Yogis*, Calcutta, 1938.

GOVINDA ŚARMAN

Author of a commentary on the *Kramadīpikā*.

GOVINDA VIDYĀVINODA

Author of a commentary on the *Kramadīpikā* of Keśava. A *Bhāgavata-sāra* is ascribed to him.

HALĀYUDHA

To him is attributed the renowned work, *Matsyasūkta*. He appears to be the same as Halāyudha, author of the well-known Smṛti digest,

Brāhmaṇasarvasva (also called *Karmopa-deśinī*), a highly authoritative work, especially in Bengal.

He was a protege of King Lakṣmaṇasena (c. 1185-1205 A.D.) of Bengal.

For further details, see P.V. Kane, *History of Dharmaśāstra*, Vol. I (2nd ed.), Ptd., 2, Section 73.

HAṂSA MIṬHU

Author of the *Haṃsavilāsa*. He refers to himself as son of Kṛpārāma and Sūrī, and born in Gujarat in Vikrama era 1794=1738 A.D.

HARAGOVINDA RĀYA

A Zamindar of Parganā Palāś in Sylhet district (now in Bangladesh) towards the close of the first quarter of the nineteenth century.

He compiled, between Śaka 1741 and 1745=1819-1823 A.D., the work, *Pañcama-veda-sāra-nirṇaya*.

For details about him, see C. Chakravarti, *Vaṅgīya Sāhitya Pariṣat Patrikā*, 59, pp. 68-72 and his book *The Tantras* etc., p. 70.

HARI

Author of a commentary on the *Kramadīpikā*.

HARIHARĀNANDANĀTHA TĪRTHASVĀMIN KULĀVADHŪTA (c. 1762-1832 A.D.)

Also called H. Bhāratī. Spiritual preceptor of Rājā Rāmmohan Roy. Some think that he wrote the *Mahānirvāṇa-tantra*.

His actual name, before resorting to asceticism, was Nandakumāra Vidyālaṃkāra.

A native of village Pālpāḍā, he is said to have written a commentary called *Kulārṇava-prakāśa* as also one on the *Mahānirvāṇa*.

HĀRĪTĀYANA

Author of *Tripurā-rahasya*.

INDRABHŪTI (-BUDDHI, -BODHI or MAHENDRABHŪTI or -OḌYĀNA-SIDDHA or OḌYĀNA-NARENDRA INDRABHŪTI or MAHĀRĀJĀDHIRĀJA INDRABHŪTI)

A Buddhist Vajrayāna Tāntric writer, believed to have flourished in the beginning of the 8th century A.D.

He was disciple of Anaṅgavajra, god-father of Padmasambhava (who went to Tibet in 747 A.D.). He was also brother of Lakṣmīṃkarā Devī.

Known to have written at least 29 works, including the *Jñānasiddhi* which appears to be the most well-known.

For a list of his works, see *NCC*, II, pp. 254-255.

ĪŚĀNA-ŚIVA-GURUDEVA-MIŚRA

A Śaiva teacher of the Mattamayūra line of *Āmarda-maṭha*, and *guru* of Vairocana (*Pratiṣṭhā-lakṣaṇa-sāra-samuccaya*). To his is ascribed the *Īśāna-śiva-gurudeva-paddhati* or *Tantrapaddhati*.

Bhoja is quoted in his *Paddhati*.

JAYARATHA (c. 12th-13th Century A.D.)

A younger contemporary of the Kashmirian king, Rājarāja who was probably the same as Jayasiṃha (c. 1200 A.D.).

Son of Śṛṅgāraratha, he was brother of Jayadratha (author of *Hara-carita-cintāmaṇi*) and pupil of Subhaṭadatta, Śiva, Śaṃkhadhara and Kalyāṇa.

He was the author of the *Viveka* commentary on the *Tantrāloka* of Abhinavagupta, and the *Vivaraṇa* on *Vāmakeśvara-tantra*.

For further details about his forefathers and family, see S.C. Banerji, *A Brief History of Tantra Literature*, p. 402.

JĀLANDHARA(I)PĀDA

A Buddhist Siddhācārya to whom the following works are ascribed:

> Cakrasaṃvara-garbha-tattva-siddhi, Mahā-kāruṇikā-bhiṣeka-prakaraṇopadeśa, Vajrayoginī-sādhana, Vimukta-mañjarī-gītā, Huṃkāra-citta-bindu-bhāvanākrama, Hevajra-sādhanasya ṭippaṇī, Śuddhi-vajra-pradīpa.

Jālandharapāda appears to have been a preceptor of Kāṇhapāda or Kṛṣṇapāda (q.v.).

A person, named Jālandharipāda, is believed to have been a preceptor of Gopīcand.

JETĀRI

A Bengali Buddhist and a scholar at Vikramaśīla Vihāra at the time of King Mahīpāla. It is not clear whether he was a contemporary of Mahīpāla I (c. 988-1038) or Mahīpāla II (reign 1070-75). Said to have been preceptor of the renowned Atīśa Dīpaṃkara (q.v.).

He appears to have written eleven works on *Vajrayāna sādhana*, which are preserved only in Tibetan translation. According to Tāranātha, he was the author of one hundred works; how many of these were on Tantra is not known.

JĪVA GOSVĀMIN

Author of a commentary on the *Brahma-saṃhitā*.

Son of Anupama, brother of Rūpa and Sanātana Gosvāmins. He settled at Vṛndāvana, and was one of the venerable six Gosvāmins of that place. His fame as a scholar-devotee was established in the 16th-17th century.

His *Ṣaṭ-sandarbha*, among other works, reveals profound learning.

For life and works, see S.K. De, *Early History of Vaiṣṇava Faith and Movement in Bengal*, Calcutta, 1961.

JÑĀNĀNANDA PARAMAHAṂSA (or GIRI)

Author of the *Kaulāvalī-nirṇaya* (or *-tantra*).

JÑĀNENDRANĀTHA or JÑANĀNANDA TĪRTHANĀTHA

Author of the *Rahasya-pūjā-paddhati* and son of Jaganmohana Tarkālaṃkāra.

KĀLIDĀSA

To him is ascribed the Tāntric work, *Cidgagana-candrikā*. It is doubtful whether the author was identical with the master-poet, Kālidāsa. At least, three persons were known by this name, as the following verse states:

eko'pi jīyate hanta kālidāsa na kenacit/
śṛṅgāre lalitodgāre kālidāsa-trayī kimu//

On the identity of Kālidāsa and the authorship of *Cidgagana-candrikā*, see S.C. Banerji, *Kālidāsa Apocrypha*, Varanasi.

KARAPĀTRISVĀMIN

Author of the *Śrī Mahātripura-sundarī-varivasyā*.

KĀŚĪNĀTHA BHAṬṬA BHAḌA

Also called Viśvanātha and Śivānandanātha. Lived in Benares. Son of Jayarāma Bhaṭṭa and Vārāṇasī, grandson of Śivarāma and pupil of maternal grandfather, Ananta. Probably flourished in the 17th or 18th century A.D.

To him are ascribed several works on Tantra, Purāṇa and Jyotiṣa. His Tāntric works are mostly of the nature of manuals; some are commentaries on well-known Tantras.

Some of his Tāntric tracts are:

Āgamotpatti-nirṇaya or *Āgamotpattyādi-vaidika-tāntrika-nirṇaya, Āmirāya-prakāśa, Kāpālika-mantra-vyavasthā, Kālībhakti-rasāyana, Kṛṣṇapūjā-taraṅgiṇī, Kaula-gaja-mardana, Tantra-siddhānta-kaumudī, Dakṣiṇācāra-dīpikā, Dakṣiṇāmūrti-kaustubha, Mantra-candrikā, Yantra-candrikā, Vāmācāra-mata-khaṇḍana, Vaidika-tāntrikā-dhikāri-nirṇaya.*

His commentaries include *Dīpikā* or *Rahasyārtha-sādhikā* on *Karpūra-stava*, commentary on *Devī-māhātmya* or *Caṇḍī*, *Gūḍhārthādarśa* on *Jñānarṇava-tantra*, *Padārthādarśa* on *Mantra-mahodadhi* of Mahīdhara, commentary on *Śāradātilaka*, *Cakra-saṅketa-candrikā* on selected verses from the *Yoginī-hṛdaya*.

For further information on the author, his works, MSS of his works, etc., see C. Chakravarti in *JASB*, Letters, 1938, pp. 455-65; *NCC*, IV, pp. 129-132.

KEŚAVA, KEŚAVA BHAṬṬA or KEŚAVA KĀŚMĪRIN

Originally belonging to the Telugu country, he was son of Śrīmaṅgala; elder brother of Ananta; disciple of Mukunda and grand-disciple of Sundara. A follower of the Nimbārka school, he is assigned to the latter part of 15th century and the beginning of the 16th. He is said to have met Caitanya.

To him are ascribed the following works:

Kramadīpikā or *Gopālamantra; Govinda-śaraṇāgati-stotra; Yamunā-stotra;* commentaries on *Kenopaniṣad, Taittiriyopaniṣad,*

Brahmopaniṣad (episode of *Bhāgavata* X.1, chaps. 11-14); *Bhagavadgītā, Vedastuti* from *Bhāgavata* X, *Muṇḍakopaniṣad, Viṣṇu-sahasranāma-stotra.*

KEŚAVA BHAṬṬA GOSVĀMIN

Author of a commentary on the *Kramadīpikā.*

KṚṢṆAMOHANA

An *Āgamacandrikā,* which is different from the work of the same title by Rāmakṛṣṇa Tarkālaṃkāra.

KṚṢṆĀNANDA ĀGAMA(or VIDYĀ)VĀGĪŚA BHAṬṬĀCĀRYA

Famous Bengal author of the *Tantrasāra* which is to be distinguished from the work of the same title by Abhinavagupta. Son of Maheśvara and disciple of Vāsudeva Sārvabhauma, he was a native of Navadvīpa, and is generally supposed to have been a contemporary of Caitanya, the renowned reformer of Bengal Vaiṣṇavism. Believed to have been born about 1500 A.D.

Besides the above work, a *Kṛtya-pallava-dīpikā* or *Kṛtyānupada-dīpikā* or *Śānti-kalpa-pradīpa* or *Ṣaṭkarma-dīpikā* is also attributed to him.

For matters relating to his life and works, see C. Chakravarti, *The Tantras* etc., pp. 66-67; B.T. Bhattacharya, *Bulletin of R.V. Res. Ins.*, Trichur, X, ii, p. 80; P.K. Gode, *Stu. in Ind. Lit. Hist.*, II, pp. 154-60; *JRASB*, XIV, pp. 74 ff; *Jour. of G. Jha Res. Inst.*, I, pp. 177 ff; *JASB*, Letters, 1948, pp. 74-80; D.C. Sircar, *The Shākta Pīṭhas*, App.

KṚṢṆAPĀDA (K. PĀDĀCĀRYA, KṚṢṆAVAJRA, KṚṢṆĀCĀRYA, KĀNHAPĀDA, or KĀLAPĀDA)

It seems there were more Buddhist writers of this name than one. Tāranātha refers to two writers of the same name, one senior and the other junior. One Kṛṣṇapāda wrote at Somapurī Vihāra. The Tāntric writer of this name was pupil of Jālandharapāda. Dates suggested range from c. 700 to c. 1200 A.D.

A *Hevajra-pañjikā* MS of Kṛṣṇa is dated c. 1200 A.D.

To Kṛṣṇapāda are attributed several Tāntric works including the *Dohākośa,* the aforesaid *Pañjikā* or *Yogaratnamālā* on *Hevajra, Hevajrasādhana,* etc.

For a list of his works, see *NCC,* IV, pp. 329-331.

For the author's life, etc., see H.P. Sastri, *Bauddha Gān O Dohā*, Calcutta; R.C. Majumdar, *History of Bengal*, I, Dacca, 1943, pp. 347-348.

KṚṢṆA VIDYĀVĀGĪŚA BHAṬṬĀCĀRYA

Identified by some with Kṛṣṇānanda Āgamavāgīśa Bhaṭṭācārya (q.v.). To him is attributed the *Ṣaṭ-karma-dīpikā*.

(RĀJĀNAKA) KṢEMARĀJA

Belonging to Kashmir, he was a pupil of Abhinavagupta and teacher of Yogarāja and Śūra. Perhaps identical with Kṣema, mentioned in Abhinava's *Tantrāloka* (ch. 37) as a son of his uncle Vāmanagupta, referred to in *Abhinava-bhāratī* (I, p. 297). He flourished in the first half of the eleventh century A.D.

Among other works and commentaries, he wrote a commentary, *Netrodaya*, on *Netratantra* and a commentary each on Abhinava's *Bhairava-stotra, Varṇodaya-tantra, Vijñāna-bhairava* (comm. called *Uddyota* jointly with Śivopādhyāya), *Śivasūtra* or *Spandasūtra* of Vasugupta (comm. called *Vimarśinī*), *Svacchanda-tantra* (comm. called *Svacchandoddyota*), etc.

See S.C. Banerji, *Cultural Heritage of Kashmir*.

KUKKURIPĀDA (KUKURĀJA, KUKKURA-RĀJA, GURURĀJA)

One of the 84 Buddhist *Siddhas*. According to a Tibetan tradition, he was a Bengali Brahmin who introduced Mahāmāyā cult in Tibet.

Believed to have lived around 693 A.D.

At least seventeen Tāntric works, including the *Mahāmāyā-sādhanopāyikā* are ascribed to him.

For songs, believed to have been composed by him, see *Bauddha Gān O Dohā;* also *Caryāgīti-kośa*, Viśvabhāratī, 1956, pp. 6, 157.

KUMĀRACANDRA

Traditionally known as a Bengali Buddhist *Avadhūta* of Vikramapurī *Vihāra*. The works, ascribed to him, are:

Ratnāvalī commentary on *Kṛṣṇayamāri-tantra*, a commentary (*Pañjikā*) on *Vajrabhairava-tantra*, and a commentary (*Pañjikā*) on *Anāvila-nāma-tantra-pañjikā*.

See *Jour. of Bihar and Orissa Res. Soc.*, XXIII, pp. 40-44.

LAKṢMAṆADEŚIKA

Author of the celebrated Tantra, *Śāradātilaka* as also of the *Tārāpradīpa*. From his own account, at the end of the work, it is learnt that he was son of Sri Kṛṣṇa, grandson of Ācārya Paṇḍita and great-grandson of Mahābala.

The commentator, Rāghavabhaṭṭa, informs us that Lakṣmaṇa was disciple of Utpalācārya, an outstanding figure in the Śaiva philosophy of Kashmir. In the line of Lakṣmaṇa's *gurus* were also Somānanda, Vasumat and Śrīkaṇṭha. The above Utpala flourished in the tenth century. So, Lakṣmaṇa perhaps lived in the 10th-11th century.

LAKṢMAṆA RĀṆĀḌE

Author of a commentary called *Sūtra-tattva-vimarśinī* (1888 A.D.) on the *Paraśurāma-kalpasūtra*.

See Intro., pp. ix-xi, to GOS ed. of *Paraśurāma-kalpasūtra*.

LAKṢMĪDHARA

A commentary called *Lakṣmīdharā* (Madras, 1957 with the original work) on the *Saundarya-laharī* is attributed to him; he appears to have been different from his namesake, author of the well-known Smṛti digest, *Kṛtya-kalpataru* (12th century A.D.).

On verse 41 of the above poetical work, the commentator clearly refers to the reprehensible practice of worshipping the female organ in its physical form. But, in the work, as in many other Tantras, *antaryāga* or mental worship is preferred to *bahiryāga* or external worship.

A Tāntric work, *Śaiva-kalpadruma*, is attributed to Lakṣmīdhara who is probably the same as the above. In the colophons to this work, the author is described as a worshipper of Śiva at Ekāmara (Bhuvaneśvara in Orissa). He was a protege of King Pratāparudra Gajapati of Orissa (1497-1539).

For references, see under *Śaiva-kalpadruma*.

LAKṢMĪṂKARĀ

Author of the *Advaya-siddhi*.

MĀDHAVĀCĀRYA

Author of a commentary on the *Kramadīpikā*.

MĀDHAVĀNANDANĀTHA

He lived at Vārāṇasī over 150 years ago, and wrote the Tāntric work, *Saubhāgya-kalpadruma* in accordance with the *Pārānanda-sūtra*. His pupil was Kṣemānandanātha.

MAHĪDHARA

Author of the *Mantramahodadhi* and its *Naukā* commentary (1588 A.D.). He is identified by some with the celebrated Vedic commentator of this name. A native of Ahicchatra (modern Rāmnagar in Bareilly district of Uttar Pradesh), he settled at Vārāṇasī.

He is well-known as a commentator of the *Śukla Yajurveda*.

MALLASENA

Compiler of the *Bhairava-Padmāvatī-kalpa*.

MATSYENDRANĀTHA

Founder of the Kaula school.

The colophons to the *Kaula-jñāna-nirṇaya* attribute the work to Matsyendranātha. Called Luipā in Tibet, and Mīnanātha in Bengal, he is traditionally known as a disciple of Ādinātha (Śiva) and *guru* of Gorakṣanātha (q.v.) and one of the 84 *Siddhas*.

He is also known as Macchendra, Machenda, Macchindra and Macchaghna. He is believed to have lived, in the earlier half of the tenth century, at Candradvīpa (modern Sandvīp in the Noākhāli district now in Bangladesh).

The *Haṭhayoga-pradīpikā* (I.5-8) names Matsyendranātha among the Mahāsiddhas.

In the Nātha cult, he is included among the nine *Gurus*.

To him and his school are ascribed the following Tāntric works:

Kaula-jñāna-nirṇaya, Akula-vīra-tantra, Akulāgama-tantra, Kulānanda-tantra, Gorakṣa-śataka, Gorakṣa-bhujaṅga, Gorakṣa-sahasra-nāma-stotra, Gorakṣa-saṃhitā, Jñānakārikā, Nityāhnika-tilaka, Śrī-kāmākhyā-guhya-siddhi, Matsyendra-saṃhitā.

MĪNANĀTHA

Same as Matsyendranātha (q.v.).

MURĀRI

Author of the *Vivaraṇa* commentary on the *Tantrapaddhati* (q.v.).

(ŚRĪ) NAḌAPĀDA

Author of the *Sekoddeśaṭīkā*.

NĀGABHAṬṬA

Author of the *Tripurāsāra-samuccaya*. He salutes Maheśvara-tejānanda-nātha. Some ascribe the *Kāmaratna* to him.

NĀGABODHI (or, -BUDDHI)

Two Buddhist Tāntric writers of this name are known —

(1) According to a tradition, he was a resident of Śiva-sera in Bengal, a disciple of Nāgārjuna (the latter?), and hailed from Uḍḍiyāna. Thirteen Tāntric works, including *Yamāri-siddha-cakra-sādhana*, *Ārya-nīlāmbara-dhara-vajrapāṇi-sādhana*, are available only in Tibetan translation in the *Tanjur*.

Some identify him with Siddhācārya Nāgabodhi, a Brahmin of western India, and a pupil of Nāgārjuna.

See *NIA*, I, p. 12 and fn.

(2) A Buddhist Tāntric writer to whom are ascribed several works including *Kṛṣṇayamāri-cakropadeśa*, *Guhya-samāja-maṇḍalopāyikā-viṃśa-vidhi*, *Yamāri-siddha-cakra-sādhana*, etc.

See *NCC*, X, p. 7.

NĀGĀRJUNA

To him is attributed the *Rasārṇava*. His identity is controversial.

NARASIṂHA ṬHAKKURA

Author of five Tāntric works, viz. *Tārā-bhakti-sudhārṇava*, *Tārāpañcāṅga*, *Tārāparicaryā*, *Tāriṇī-krama* and *Mahāvidyā-prakaraṇa*.

Son of Gadādhara, he appears to have flourished about 1668 A.D.

NĀRĀYAṆA

Of Kerala. To him is ascribed the *Tantrasāra Saṃgraha*.

NĀRĀYAṆA KAṆṬHA

Author of a commentary on *Mṛgendra Tantra*.

Son of Vidyākaṇṭha and grandson of Śaśikara Kaṇṭha, he was father of Rāmakaṇṭha. He appears to have been a Kashmirian.

He did not flourish earlier than the ninth century A.D.

NAṬANĀNANDA-NĀTHA

A pupil of Nāthānanda, he was the author of the commentary, *Cidvallī,* on the *Kāmakalāvilāsa* of Puṇyānanda.

NĪLAKAMALA LĀHIḌĪ

Author of the *Kālyarcana-candrikā.* The following autobiographical information is available in the work.

Son of Kālīmohana, the author is a lineal descendant of Nārāyaṇa who is stated to have been one of the five Brāhmaṇas brought from Kānyakubja by Ādiśūra, the then ruler of Bengal.

One of the author's ancestors, named Vallabhācārya, also known as Maṇḍana Miśra, married Līlāvatī, daughter of Udayanācārya. The original home of the author's ancestors was at village Kakaiḍ in the district of Rājshāhī (now in Bangladesh). One of his ancestors migrated to a place, called Kacuyā in aforesaid Rājshāhī, and another to Rangpur (in Bangladesh).

The author appears to have been appointed an assistant to Śivanātha, minister of the then ruler (*dharāpati*) who was probably a local chief and grandfather of the author. The author's *Guru* was named Harinātha.

NĪLAKAṆṬHA CATURDHARA (12th Century)

A native of Pratiṣṭhānpur or Paiṭhān (on the Godāvarī in Aurangābād district), he settled at Vārāṇasī. Son of Govindasūri and Phullāmtikā, he was father of Govinda Dīkṣita and disciple of Lakṣmaṇārya and Uttama-śloka-tīrtha.

He wrote a commentary (1680 A.D.), called *Aṇuparāṇu,* on *Śivatāṇḍava-tantra.*

He is renowned as the author of the popular *Bhārata-bhāva-dīpikā* on *Mahābhārata.*

See P.K. Gode, *Studies in Indian Literary History,* II, pp. 476 ff; III, p. 53.

NIRAÑJANA SIDDHA

Wrote a commentary on the *Devīkālottarāgama.*

NITYĀNANDA (NĀTHA or SIDDHA)

Author of the Tāntric work, *Ratnākara-paddhati*.

The following works also are attributed to him: *Tripura-sundarī, Mahimaḥ-stotra ṭīkā, Lalitā-stava-ratna, Śāktasūtra Agastya* and *Śrīvidyā-bhāṣya Agastya*.

NITYANĀTHA-SIDDHA or NEMANĀTHA

The *Kāmaratna-tantra, Tantrakośa* and *Śabara-cintāmaṇi* are ascribed to him.

He was son of Pārvatī. "Generally his name is found mixed up with Nāgārjuna in colophons of MSS of *Kakṣapuṭa, Rasaratnākara*, and with Ādinātha in *Śabaracintāmaṇi*", *NCC*, X, p. 119.

NITYAPRAJÑA

Author of a commentary on the *Krama-dīpikā*.

PADMAPĀDĀCĀRYA

Disciple of the great Advaita philosopher, Śaṃkarācārya. He is said to have been a native of Cidambaram.

Author of a commentary on the *Prapañcasāra*, ascribed to Śaṃkara. He is assigned to 625-705 A.D.

For his life, see Intro., pp. 36-37 of *Advaita Granthakośa;* also *Bib. of Advaita Vedānta*, pp. 228-229, Madras Uni. ed.

PADMAVAJRA

A contemporary of Indrabhūti (q.v.). Also called Saroruhavajra, he was preceptor of Anaṅgavajra and author of the *Guhya-siddhi*.

PAṆḌITA KĀṆHA

See Kṛṣṇapāda.

PĀRĀNANDA

Perhaps the same as Pārānandanātha and author of the *Pārānanda-sūtra*. Pārānanda is mentioned (pp. 72, 91 of the above work) as one of the *Gurus*. He is also mentioned in the *Mahāvidyā-tantra*, Tārākhaṇḍa, p. 164 and *Nīlatantra* (v. 67) as a *guru* of the *Mānavaugha* class. He is perhaps identical with Rāmasvāmi-paṇḍita, author of a commentary on the *Rāja-yoga-tārāvalī* of Śaṃkarācārya.

PARIVRĀJAKĀCĀRYA

Mahāmahopādhyāya P. Ācārya is the earliest known Bengal writer on Hindu Tantra, the title of his work being *Kāmya-yantroddhāra*. His real name is not known. A manuscript of the above work is dated Śaka 1297=1375 A.D. Vide H.P. Sastri, *Notices of Skt. MSS*, III.53.

PĀRVATĪPUTRA

Some ascribe the *Kāmaratna* to him.

PRAJÑĀVARMAN

He was an *Ācārya* of the Kāpaṭyavihāra of Bengal, and perhaps lived at sometime under the Pāla rulers. Two Tāntric works, *Viśeṣa-stava-ṭīkā* and *Devātiśaya-ṭīkā* are ascribed to him.

PRAKĀŚĀNANDA DEŚIKA

See Subhagānandanātha.

PRĀṆAMAÑJARĪ

Third wife of Premanidhi Pantha (q.v.).

The commentary, *Sudarśanā* on *Tantrarāja*, is ascribed to her.

PREMANIDHI PANTHA (18th Century A.D.)

Son of Umāpati and Uddyotamatī, he was a native of Kūrmācala (Kumāyun) and patronised by Malaivamnadeva, a chieftain of Nepāl. Afterwards, he lived at Vārāṇasī.

Among his various works, the Tāntric works are:

Antaryāga-ratna, Kamalā-paddhati, Dīpa-dāna-ratna, Dīpaprakāśa (1726 A.D.).

His commentaries on Tāntric texts are:

a commentary on *Śakti-samgama-tantra, Śabdārtha-cintāmaṇi* (1737 A.D.) on *Śāradātilaka, Mallādarśa* on the Śaiva Tantra, *Śivatāṇḍava*.

For a list of his works, see *NCC*, XIII, pp. 197, 198.

For a panegyric of his patron in 84 stanzas, see his commentary *Mallādarśa* on *Śivatāṇḍava; JASB*, VI, 1940, pp. 105-17; C. Chakravarti, *Tantras* etc., pp. 76-8.

PUṆYĀNANDANĀTHA

Alias Advaitānanda of Kashmir. Preceptor of Amṛtānandanātha.

Author of the *Kāmakalā-vilāsa* Tantra.

PŪRṆĀNANDA

Commonly known as P. Giri, he was actually called P. Paramahaṃsa Parivrājaka; he had also the title Yati. A native of village Kāṭihālī under Netrakonā subdivision of Mymensingh district in Bangladesh, he belonged to the *Rāḍhī* class of Brāhmins, bearing *Kāśyapa-gotra*. It is learnt that his real name was Jagadānanda and that he was son of Purandara, a Śākta, and Aparṇā. Pūrṇānanda was the name given by his preceptor, Brahmānanda Giri (q.v.).

Born in Śaka 1423 (=1501 A.D.), he was widely known as a devotee of a very high order. Kṛṣṇānanda, author of the *Tantrasāra*, was his most distinguished Bengali disciple. He was a member of the Śaṃkarite order.

Pūrṇānanda is said to have gone to Kashmir at the request of the king of that land, and succeeded in resolving disputes between the two sects, Śaiva and Śākta.

Later in life, he is said to have settled on the Himālaya.

He is said to have authored the following works:

Śyāmārahasya, Śākta-krama, Śrītattva-cintāmaṇi, Tattvānanda-taraṅgiṇī, Ṣaṭkarmollāsa, Kālikārahasya, Gadyavallarī, Subhagodaya-darpaṇa.

To him are ascribed also the following Tāntric works:

Yogacintāmaṇi, Yogavilāsa, Kālī-kakāra-kūṭa, Bhūtaśuddhi, Sarasvatītantra, Kālikādi-kālī-sahasra-nāma-stuti-ratna-ṭīkā, Kālikā-rahasya, Vāmakeśvarī-tantra, Mahā-tripura-sundarī-mantra-nāma-sahasra, Ṣaṭcakra-bheda or *Ṣaṭcakra-krama, Śāktānanda-taraṅgiṇī.*

The *Ṣaṭ-cakra-krama* has a commentary, *Dīpikā*, by Nandarāma Tarkavāgīśa.

See *NCC*, IX, p. 329.

The *Ṣaṭcakra-nirūpaṇa* (or, *-vivaraṇa*), actually a part of the *Śrītattva-cintāmaṇi*, is sometimes taken as an independent work.

He also commented on the *Ṣaṭcakradīpikā* of Brahmānanda, on the *Kakārātmaka-kālī-sahasra-nāma-stotra* and on the *Śāradātilaka*.

See D.C. Sircar, *Shākta Pīṭhas*, pp. 28, 75; C. Chakravarti, *Tantras*, p. 67 f; Bengali Encyclopaedia, *Viśvakoṣa* for Pūrṇānanda's works; *Sāhitya-varṣa-pañjī*, Calcutta, 1983, p. 45.

PUTALI or PUTTALI

Said to have been a Śūdra of Bengal, and one of the 84 *Mahā-siddhas*. His work *Bodhi-citta-vāyu-caraṇa-bhāvanopāya* exists only in Tibetan translation.

See *NIA* (Buddhist Tāntric Literature of Bengal), I, p. 11.

RĀGHAVABHAṬṬA

A renowned commentator. Son of Pṛthvīdhara-bhaṭṭa, he flourished in the fifteenth century A.D. He is well-known for his commentary, *Padārthādarśa*, on the *Śāradātilaka* Tantra, as also for his *Arthadyotanikā* commentary on the *Abhijñāna-śakuntala* of Kālidāsa.

From his autobiographical account at the end of his *Padārthādarśa* commentary (1494 A.D.), it is learnt that he was a native of village Janasthāna (Nāsik) in Mahārāṣṭra. His grandfather was Rāmeśvara. His father, Pṛthvīdhara, settled at Vārāṇasī. His great-grandfather was Mahābala.

He writes that he wrote the above commentary at Viśveśa-purī, i.e. Vārāṇasī.

A *Kālī-tattva* (*rahasya*) is attributed (for example, see *NCC*, IV, 74, *RASB* Cat., 474 f) to Rāghavabhaṭṭa who seems to be identical with the above commentator.

RAGHUNĀTHA TARKAVĀGĪŚA BHAṬṬĀCĀRYA

From his autobiographical account, contained in his work, it is learnt that son of Śivarāma, he was a lineal descendant of the famous Śākta devotee, Sarvānanda of Bengal. In the Calcutta edition of his work, his native village is mentioned as Napāḍā in Susang Parganā of Mymensingh (Bangladesh). The author refers (I.34), *inter alia*, to a *Tantrasāra* obviously of Kṛṣṇānanda. He states Śaka 1609 (=1687 A.D.) as the year of composition of his work.

The title of his work is *Āgama-tattva-vilāsa*.

RĀMAKIŚORA

Author of the *Mudrā-prakāśa*.

RĀMAKṚṢṆA TARKĀLAṂKĀRA

Son of Raghunātha Tarkavāgīśa, he abridged (1725-26 A.D.) his father's *Āgama-tattva-vilāsa;* the abridged version is entitled *Āgama-candrikā,* and contains 1,500 stanzas.

RĀMĀNANDA

Probably author of a *Bhāṣya* on the *Nityotsava-tantra.*

RĀMATOṢAṆA VIDYĀLAṂKĀRA

Author of the *Prāṇatoṣiṇī.* He was great-grandson of Kṛṣṇānanda, author of the *Tantrasāra.*

RĀMEŚVARA

To be distinguished from his namesake, mentioned by the great commentator, Rāghavabhaṭṭa as his grandfather.

He was a South Indian Brāhmaṇa of the *Kāśyapa gotra.* After initiation, he came to be known as Aparājitānandanātha. His commentary on the *Paraśurāma-kalpasūtra* is entitled *Saubhāgya-subhodaya,* or briefly *Subhagodaya.* He states Śaka 1753 (= 1831 A.D.) as the date of its completion. The commentary is marked by the author's independent views, a wide range of Tāntric knowledge, and, at places, the addition of such matters as are not mentioned in the text commented upon. Rāmeśvara is one of the stalwarts among those who represent the Śrīvidyā school. According to Rāmeśvara, one who has not restrained his senses has no right to *Kula* practices. The commentary is both lucid and informative. Rāmeśvara shows his leanings to Mīmāṃsā philosophy. This is responsible for the fact that his interpretation sometimes becomes one-sided. At some places, he assails the views of a Nibandhakāra who is Umānandanātha, author of the *Nityotsava Tantra.* The language of his criticism is sometimes vulgar and lacks restraint. For Rāmeśvara's view on *dīkṣā, Śakti* and drinking of wine, see our observations in connexion with the *Paraśurāma-kalpasūtra.*

Rāmeśvara introduces the *dhyāna* of the goddess from another Tantra in his comments on section vii of the above Tantra which does not contain any such *dhyāna.* The commentator gives an elaborate discussion on *Puraścaraṇa* in section vii.

RATNĀKARAŚĀNTI

Probably identical with Śānti to whom two Bengali songs are attributed (vide H.P. Sastri, *Bauddha Gān O Dohā*, Preface, p. 28). Born sometime in the tenth century. Said to have been a Bengali who wrote several Buddhist Tāntric works.

RĀVAṆA (of *Rāmāyaṇa* story?)

To him is ascribed the *Kumāra-tantra.*

SADĀŚIVA ŚUKLA

Author of a commentary on the *Kulacūḍāmaṇi* Tantra.

ŚAṂKARA or ŚAṂKARĀCĀRYA

Referred to as Gauḍīya. His real name was, perhaps, Śaṃkara Āgamācārya.

Son of Kamalākara and grandson of Lambodara of Bengal. From a manuscript of his *Tārā-rahasya-vṛtti,* which is dated Lakṣmaṇa Saṃvat 511 = 1630 A.D., he appears to have flourished between the latter half of the 16th century and the middle of the 17th.

The title of his work is *Tārā-rahasya-vṛtti*(*kā*).

See C. Chakrabarti, *Tantras, Studies*, etc., pp. 68-69.

Several other works on Tantra are ascribed to Śaṃkara whose identity with Gauḍīya Śaṃkara is not free from doubt. The works are *Śivārcana-mahāratna*, *Śaiva-ratna*, *Kulamūlāvatāra*, *Krama-stava*, etc.

ŚAṂKARĀCĀRYA

To him is attributed the Tāntric work, *Prapañcasāra*. He is identified by some with the great *Advaita* philosopher of this name. But, others would identify him with his namesake, author of a commentary on the *Nṛsiṃha-tāpanīyopaniṣad* which is not included among the ten principal Upaniṣads, traditionally known to have been commented upon by Ādi Śaṃkarācārya.

See *Works of Śaṃkarācārya*, Vol. X, Vāṇī Vilāsa Press.

It should be noted that no less a person than the renowned Rāghavabhaṭṭa (15th century A.D.), in his commentary on the *Śāradātilaka* (I.7, 12, etc.), attributes the *Prapañcasāra* to the Great Śaṃkarācārya. P.V. Kane, however, holds that the testimony of Rāghava, who flourished centuries later than the great philosopher

(8th-9th century A.D.), cannot be accepted as conclusive in the absence of corroborative evidence (see *Hist. of Dharmaśāstra*, V, pt. 2, p. 1105).

The *Saundaryalaharī* seems to have been composed by Ādi Śaṃkarācārya. In it, he does mention his name, and describes himself as *draviḍa-śiśu;* Draviḍa comprised the part of the Deccan from Madras to Seringapatam and Cape Comorin. He is believed to have been a native of Kerala.

The great Śaṃkara is said to have commented on several Tāntric texts including the *Śrīvidyāratna-sūtra*, attributed to Gauḍapāda.

ŚAṂKARĀNANDANĀTHA

Real name — Śambhubhaṭṭa. A pupil of the famous Mīmāṃsā scholar, Khaṇḍadeva, he was a devotee of Śrīvidyā, and wrote the well-known work *Sundarī-mahodaya*.

He flourished about 1708 A.D.

ŚĀNTARAKṢITA (705-762 A.D.)

A Buddhist Tāntric writer of Bengal. Believed to have been born in the royal family of Jahor, identified by some with Sābhār, a well-known place in East Bengal (Bangladesh). According to some, he was a native of Gauḍa-Vaṅga. He was at one time the principal *Ācārya* at Nālandā.

Appears to have written several works mainly on Buddhist Tantra. These are available only in Tibetan translation.

SARASVATĪ-TĪRTHA

Known as Paramahaṃsa Parivrājakācārya, he was a native of South India. Not to be confused with Parivrājakācārya of Bengal.

His main Tāntric work was a commentary on the *Prapañcasāra*, attributed to Śaṃkarācārya.

SARVĀNANDA (b. c. 1400 A.D.)

Son of Śambhunātha and grandson of Vāsudeva, he was father of Śivanātha and Śivānanda, and a resident of village Mehār in Tripurā district of Bengal; and the first Śākta *sādhaka* of the famous *Śaktipīṭha* of the above village. Said to have acquired *Siddhi* in 1425 A.D. He earned the sobriquet Sarvavidyā as he is said to have visualised all the forms of Goddess.

He is said to have lived for sometime at a place in the district of Jessore (now partly in Bangladesh and partly in West Bengal).

Subsequently, he migrated to Vārāṇasī, thence to Śāradā-maṭha, established by Śaṃkarācārya, and from there to Badarikāśrama (U.P.).

To him is attributed the *Sarvollāsa*.

For an account of him, see *Sarvānanda-taraṅgiṇī* by Śivanātha.

SIDDHANĀTHA

Some ascribe the *Kāmaratna* to him.

ŚĪLABHADRA (d. c. 654 A.D.)

Appears to have been a Brahmin of Samataṭa in Bengal. Initiated to Buddhism at Nālandā, he became the head of that *Mahāvihāra* when Hiuen-tsang visited it, and studied *Yogaśāstra* under him. Śīlabhadra had the sobriquet *Saddharma-nidhi*. The *Tanjur* preserves only the Tibetan translation of his Sanskrit work, *Ārya-buddha-bhūmi-vyākhyāna;* the original is lost. According to Hiuen-tsang, he wrote many works of which only Chinese translations are available.

ŚIVĀNANDA

Writer of a commentary on the *Mātṛkā-cakra-viveka*.

Is he the same as Śivānandanātha, author of the *Ṛjuvimarśinī* commentary on the *Nityāṣoḍaśīkārṇava*?

To Śivānanda, son of Sarvānanda (q.v.), is attributed the *Sarvānanda-taraṅgiṇī*. Some ascribe the *Subhagodaya* to a Śivānanda.

ŚRĪKAṆṬHA

Said to have imparted the *Brahma-yāmala* to others.

ŚRĪNAḌAPĀDA

Author of the Buddhist work, *Sekoddeśaṭīkā*.

ŚRĪNĀTHA

Some ascribe the *Kāmaratna* to him.

ŚRĪNIVĀSA

Author of the *Tātparya-dīpikā* commentary on the *Tripurā-rahasya* of Hārītāyana.

ŚRĪRĀJA DEVĀNANDA SIṂHA

Author of the *Śāktapramoda.*

SUBHAGĀNANDANĀTHA

Author of the commentary *Manoramā* on *Tantra-rāja-tantra*. The commentary appears to have been completed by his pupil, Prakāśānanda.

Originally a Brahmin from Kerala, Subhagānanda settled in Vārāṇasī. His real name was Śrīkaṇṭha. He was a contemporary of Mādhavānanda (q.v.).

According to Bhāskararāya, in his commentary on the *Nityāṣoḍaśīkārṇava*, he belonged to the Kashmir school. The *Manoramā* covers the first 22 chapters. The remaining chapters were commented upon by his disciple, Prakāśānanda Deśika.

ŚUKLA MATHURĀNĀTHA

Author of a commentary on the *Kumārī-tantra.*

SVATANTRĀNANDANĀTHA

Author of *Mātṛkā-cakra-viveka.*

TAILIKAPĀDA (also known as NĀDAPĀDA or TILOPĀ)

A Buddhist Siddhācārya to whom the following works are ascribed:

> *Acintya-mahāmudrā*, *Antar-bāhya-viṣaya-nivṛtti-bhāvanā-krama*, *Karuṇā-bhāvanā-dhiṣṭhāna*, *Gurusādhana*, *Tattva-caturopadeśa* alias *Prasannadīpa*, *Dohākośa*, *Bāhya-siddhi-pratītya-samutpāda*, *Mahāmudropadeśa*, *Ṣaḍ-dharmopadeśa.*

UMĀNANDANĀTHA

Author of the Śākta works, *Nityotsava-nibandha*, *Bhāskara-vilāsa* and *Hṛdayāmṛta*.

His real name was Jagannātha; after initiation he came to be known as Umānandanātha.

His preceptor was Bhāsurānandanātha (real name Bhāskaramakhin) who is stated to have been the author of a *Ratnākara*. Jagannātha was a pupil of Kāmākṣī-sūri alias Kāmeśvara.

From his autobiographical account, we learn that his father was Bālakṛṣṇa of Viśvāmitra gotra and mother Lakṣmiambā. It is also learnt that the author was a Mahārāṣṭra Brahmin, surnamed Śrutapetava. He was patronised by Marāṭhā kings of Tanjore, Serfoji I (1711-28), Ekoji II (1735-36), he wrote also some poetical and dramatic works.

See *NCC*, VII, pp. 136, 137; G.V. Devasthali in *C.K. Rājā Pres. Vol.*, pp. 271-284; Sāhenduvilāsa, *Tanjore Sarasvatī Mahal Ser.* No. 54, Intro., pp. 37, 59-60.

VIDYĀNANDANĀTHA

Hailing from a place south of Kāñcī, he visited the *Siddhapīṭha* of Jalandhar in north India. There he was initiated by Sundarācārya or Saccidānandanātha. Directed by the *guru*, he settled at Vārāṇasī. There he is known to have composed several works on Tantra. His commentary on the *Nityāṣoḍaśīkārṇava* is entitled *Artharatnāvalī*.

He flourished a little over 400 years ago.

VIDYĀRAṆYA

To him is ascribed the *Vidyārṇava-tantra*.

VYĀSA

Son of Janārdana. To him is ascribed a commentary on Kṛṣṇānanda's *Tantrasāra*.

YADUNĀTHA

Author of the *Āgamakalpalatā*.

UMĀPATI ŚIVĀCĀRYA

Author of the *Śataratna-saṃgraha* with its commentary, *Ullekha* (*-inī*). A commentary (*bhāṣya*) on the *Pauṣkarāgama* is also attributed to his.

A native of Chidambaram and a pupil of Maraijñāna-sambandha, he was a Śaiva teacher and writer. He belonged to the families of the Dīkṣita priests of the Naṭarāja temple of Chidambaram, and was one of the four Santānācāryas. He is known to have authored eleven works in Tamil, and two in Sanskrit on Śaivism. Three of his Tamil works are dated A.D. 1310, 1312 and 1313. The traditional biography of Umāpati occurs in two texts, entitled *Pārthavana-māhātmya* and *Rājendra-pura-māhātmya*, both of which are printed in the edition, in Grantha script, of Umāpati's *Pauṣkarabhāṣya*, published (Jñānapāda only) at Chidambaram in 1925.

CHAPTER IX

HINDU TANTRAS

ĀGAMACANDRIKĀ (1725-26)

By Rāmakṛṣṇa Tarkālaṃkāra.

To be distinguished from a work of the same title by Kṛṣṇamohana, it is an abridgement, in 1500 stanzas, of the *Āgama-tattva-vilāsa* of Raghunātha.

ĀGAMA-TATTVA-VILĀSA (1609 ŚAKA = 1687 A.D.)

By Raghunātha Tarkavāgīśa Bhaṭṭācārya.

A voluminous work, in five long chapters comprising about 14,400 stanzas (*RASB* viii, i.6214), it is professedly a digest representing the essence of a number of works, Vedic, Purāṇic, astronomical and Dharmaśāstric. It deals with the usual Tāntric topics. The highlights are *Mānasa-pūjā* (chap. ii), thirty-two kinds of offences (*ibid.*), *Śavasādhana* (*ibid.*), *Pīṭha-sthāna* (*ibid.*), Pracaṇḍacaṇḍikā, Tripura-bhairavī, Vagalāmukhī, Mātaṅgī, Dhūmāvatī (all in chap. iv), Nīlā and Śuklā Sarasvatī, sameness of Viṣṇu and Śiva (*ibid.*), genealogy and the date of composition (v).

The work mentions 160 Tāntric works. The author sometimes discusses divergent views, and gives his own conclusion.

An abridged version of the work is the *Āgama-candrikā* (q.v.), Ed. P. Sastri, Calcutta, 1985.

AGASTYA-SAṂHITĀ

It is, perhaps, the same work as that cited in such Tāntric works as the *Āgama-kalpalatā* of Yadunātha, *Nityotsava-nibandha* of Umānandanātha, *Śāktānanda-taraṅgiṇī*, etc. It appears to be a guide-book, influenced by Tantra relating to the worship of Rāma, particularly prevalent among the followers of Rāmānanda. It should be noted that the whole of chapter 26 (on the Rāmanavamī rituals) occurs in the *Caturvarga-cintāmaṇi* of Hemādri; if Hemādri (13 cent.) is the borrower, this Tantra may be assigned to an earlier period.

Ed. R.N. Das, Lucknow, 1898; K.K. Smṛtitīrtha, Calcutta, 1910. Also pub. at Mysore, 1957. On different texts of this title, see *Adyar Lib. Bulletin*, I.3, pp. 92-95.

Also see H.D. Smith in the above journal, 27, 1963, pp. 1-17 and in his *Des. Bibliography* etc., Vol. I, Baroda, 1975 (GOS Vol. 158).

AHIRBUDHNYA-SAṂHITĀ

The significance of the word *Ahirbudhnya* is obscure. *Ahi* means serpent and *budhnya* bottom. This work is represented as a dialogue between Ahirbudhnya (stated to be Śiva in His *Sāttvika* form), one of the eleven Rudras and Nārada. In some later Vedic works, Ahi Budhnya is allegorically connected with Agni Gārhapatya (Domestic Fire — vide Macdonell's *Vedic Mythology*, p. 73). It is curious that the hymn in the *Vājasaneyī Saṃhitā*, v.33, which mentions *Ahirbudhnya* (*Gārhapatya Agni* — commentary), refers to the name of Viṣṇu several times.

This work belongs to the category of *Saṃhitās* which, according to Schrader (*Intro. to Pañcarātra*, etc., p. iii), were written between 300 A.D. and the eighth century A.D. (*ibid.*, pp. 21-22, 114).

Available evidences[1] point to Kashmir as the provenance of the work.

This *Saṃhitā* contains as many as sixty chapters. The following are the highlights of the contents of the work. It is chiefly a work on the *Pañcarātra* cult, full of *mantras*, and is stated (chap. 60) to follow *Sāṃkhya-yoga*. The author informs us that it is intended for the members of the three upper castes (*ibid.*). *Śakti* is, at the same time, inseparable from God, and separate from Him. *Jīva* remains, in a potential form, in Him, and becomes separate from Him at the time of creation, and returns to Him at the time of dissolution. The liberated *Jīva* enters into Him never to be separated. It is noteworthy that, in place of ten traditional *Avatāras*, this work (v.50-57) mentions thirty-nine *Avatāras* of Vāsudeva.[2] The work sets forth the origin and development of Saṃkarṣaṇa and other *Vyūha* representatives from Vāsudeva. *Mukti* means the attainment of divinity as a result of virtuous action without selfish motive (chap. 14). The work treats of the evolution of vowels and consonants. The procedure of

1. For details, see the author's *Brief History of Tantra Literature*, pp. 378-79.
2. See Schrader, *op. cit.*, pp. 42-43.

Mahābhiṣeka is laid down in chapter 39. It is stated to be a panacea and a means of crusting enemies as well as attaining all the desired objects. This *Saṃhitā* mentions (xii.20-29) the sixty topics of Sāṃkhya, which, however, differ from those mentioned in the *Rāja-vārtika*, quoted by Vācaspati. As regards the heterodox systems (Buddhism, Jainism, etc.), these are called (xii.51) *Śāstrābhāsa* (pseudo-*śāstras*), conceived by Gods or great sages deliberately to confuse the wicked. To Sudarśana a good deal of space is devoted. Among the synonyms of Sudarśana are *Prāṇa* and *Māyā*. xii.53 mentions some names of Sudarśana, e.g. *Unmeṣa, Udyama*. The term Sudarśana has been explained (ii.7-9) as Viṣṇu's will to be (*syam iti saṃkalpaḥ*). The derivative meaning is this: *darsāna* means *prekṣaṇa* (perceptive thought); *su* (well, perfectly) conveys the idea of its being unobstructed by time and space. Sudarśana has been identified (chap. iii) with *Kriyāśakti* (force-aspect) of Lord, as distinguished from His *Bhūti-śakti* (matter aspect). Lakṣmī has been characterised as Lord's 'vibration in the form of the world', related to Him like moonlight with the moon. *Bhūti-śakti* (material cause) is the cause of creation. Among the various activities of Sudarśana are

(1) as *ādhāra*, i.e. the base or support of the world during creation and dissolution;

(2) as *pramāṇa* or regulating principle during the continuance of life (*sthiti*).

Chapter 12[3] describes the four recognised philosophical systems, viz. *Trayī*, Sāṃkhya, Yoga, Pāśupata and the Sāttvata or Pāñcarātra. Thus, it marks a departure from the tradition recognising the six systems of orthodox philosophy. It is noteworthy that the *Ahirbudhnya* refers to Sāṃkhya as *Ṣaṣti-tantra* (system of 60 topics) which is the name of the earliest extant Sāṃkhya work, usually called *Sāṃkhya-kārikā*. This chapter mentions the sixty topics[4] without explaining them. It should be added that the Pāśupata philosophy, described in this work, is not the same as the Pāśupata, usually mentioned in the philosophical works. It agrees with Āgamic Śaivism on which the later Śaivite systems of both north and south India are based. There is a vague hint (xiii.14) at the lesser philosophical sects like Kāpālika, etc. The following ten topics of the Sāttvata system are mentioned:

---

3. Analysed by F.O. Schrader in Das Ṣaṣṭi-tantra in *ZDMG*, 1914.
4. Discussed by Schrader in *ZDMG*, *op. cit*.

Bhagavat, Karman, Vidyā, Kāla, Kartavya, Vaiśeṣika-kriyā, Saṃyama, Cintā, Mārga and *Mokṣa*.

According to the work (chap. xiii), the *summum bonum* is the attainment of one's real nature which is godliness (*bhagavattā, bhagavanmayatā*, verse 11). *Jñāna* and *dharma*, the latter leading to the former, are the twofold means for reaching the highest goal.

A resume of the contents of the work is contained in parts of chapters 59 and 60.

The prominence, given to Sudarśana, is clear from a supplement enumerating 560 names of Sudarśana arranged in groups in accordance with the consonant with which the names begin.

Ed., with Eng. trs., by Nityasvarūpānanda, Calcutta, 1964; by R. Krishnamacarya, Adyar Library, Madras, 1966.

ĀKĀŚA-BHAIRAVA-KALPA

Most of the manuscripts describe it as Mahāśaiva-tantra or as a part of it. In only one manuscript, it is stated to be a part of *Mahā-lakṣmī-tantra*.

The number and order of chapters differ in different manuscripts. A Nepalese MS comprises 78 chapters. A Calcutta MS contains 50 chapters; the 50th chapter is the same as chapter 56 in the above MS.

The work contains *mantras, stavas* and ritual practices relating to various deities, e.g. Śiva as Aghora, Tryambaka, Mṛtyuñjaya, Gaṇeśa, Ṣanmukha, Durgā as Śūlinī, Bhadrakālī, Śarabha (represented in his three aspects, viz. Śārabha (or Śārabha), Sāluda or Sāluva and Pakṣirāja, etc.

A Tanjore MS of the work, containing 3,900 stanzas, divided into 136 *Paṭalas* (chapters) deals chiefly with the worship of Sāmrājya-lakṣmī (Goddess of Fortune of the empire); it is entitled *Sāmrājya-lakṣmī-pīṭhikā*.

A noteworthy feature of the treatise is that, contrary to the usual practice in Tantras, after mentioning a *mantra*, its imaginary *Ṛṣi, chandas* and *devatā* are named. It may be noted that, in the Vedic tradition, the recital of a Vedic *mantra* without knowing its sage, metre and deity was deemed sinful and infructuous. The writer of the above work resorted to this practice presumably to impart a halo of antiquity and authority to it. The very word '*Kalpa*', in the title, reminds one of the *Kalpa-sūtras* (ritualistic works) of the Vedic age.

See *NCC*, II, p. 3, for a list of contents of the work; P.K. Gode, *Literary History*, II, pp. 122-136 (paper by Gode — *A bhairava-kalpa*, an unknown source of the history of Vijayanagar.

See our account of *Sāmrājya-lakṣmī-pīṭhakas, infra*.

Also see *Karnataka Historical Review*, V, 7 (1938).

AKULAVĪRA-TANTRA

Said to have been revealed by Mīnanātha (Matsyendranātha). It is a small tract containing some statements on Tāntric *Yoga*. One MS dates back to about the 13th century A.D., and points to Kāmarūpa as the provenance of the work. According to H.P. Sastri (*Nepal Catalogue*, II, pp. xviii f, 32 f), a MS belongs to the middle of the 9th cent. A.D.

Ed. P.C. Bagchi, *Kaula-Jñāna-nirṇaya and Some Minor Texts of the School of Matsyendranātha*, Calcutta, 1934.

See *JASB* (NS), XXVI (1930), 130.

AMARA-SAṂGRAHA (1765 Śaka = 1843 A.D.)

By Amara Maitra. It, in 18 *Pādas* (sections), deals with

> *jagan-mithyātva, tattvabodha, viveka, laya-yoga, navacakra, piṇḍajñāna, Yoga-rahasya, ṣaṭ-cakra-yoga, pañcāmara-yoga, haṭhayoga, mudrā, dhāraṇā, rājayoga, jñāna-yoga, brahma-mantra-sādhana, saṃnyāsa-yoga, Kāśī-yoga, Kālajñāna, vipra-lakṣaṇa, sāṃkhya-yoga.*

See C. Chakravarti, *Vaṅgīya Sāhitya Pariṣat Patrikā*, Calcutta, 58, iii-iv.

ĀMARĪ-SAṂHITĀ (1768 Śaka = 1846 A.D.)

By Amara Maitra. In four chapters (*Upadeśas*), each of which is sub-divided into several sections, it deals with

> *Sāṃkhyayoga, mantrayoga, nāḍikā-lakṣaṇa, āsana, pratyāhāra, prāṇāyāma, dhyāna, dhāraṇā*, rules of *haṭhayoga*, procedure of *Pūjā*.

See C. Chakravarti, *Vaṅgīya Sāhitya Pariṣat Patrikā*, Calcutta, 58, iii-iv.

ANNADĀ-KALPA-TANTRA

By Bhairavānanda (13th century), it comprises 17 chapters. It mentions (XV. 2) the *Śāmbhavī Tantra*.

Goddess Bhagavatī, in Her food-giving form, is extolled as the Supreme having no god to guide her. She is *saguṇa* (possessed of attributes) to those devotees who are attached to worldly life, and *nirguṇa* (devoid of attributes) to those who are detached.

Conceived as having three forms, viz.

(i) *Sāttvika* — two-armed, beautiful and mounted on a lion;

(ii) *Rājasika* — standing with weapons on the mount;

(iii) *Tāmasika* — fierce-looking, indicating anger.

She has other three aspects, called *Parā Vidyā, Aparā Vidyā* and *Parāpara Vidyā.*

Other important matters discussed are: qualifications of *guru* and *śiṣya, *measures for infusing life into *mantras, śraddhā* (faith) as root of success, *dīkṣā*, glory of *mantra, japa*, etc., great merit accruing from the worship of a girl of seven, seventeen or eighteen, *antaryāga, cakrānuṣṭhāna,* means of acquiring scholarship, good memory, prosperity, methods of *vaśīkaraṇa*, causing harm, even destruction of enemies, acquisition of woman's love, long life, etc.

See *Jour. of Assam Res. Soc.*, III-IV, Jan., 1936, p. 121 (No. 20).

BHAIRAVA-PADMĀVATĪ-KALPA (c. 1050 A.D.)

Compiled by Mallasena of Mysore, it is concerned with Padmāvatī, a Jaina parallel to the well-known Tripurā. Written in 308 verses, it deals mainly with *mantras* and *yantras* relating to the above goddess.

Ed. K.V. Abhyankar, with comm. of Bandhuṣeṇa in Jhavery, *Mantraśāstra*, pp. 1-74.

In this work, some other minor works on the worship of the same and other Jaina goddesses are edited.

BHĀSKARA-VILĀSA

By Umānandanātha, it is a biography of his *Guru*, Bhāskararāya (q.v. under Authors).

Ptd. in the NSP ed. of the *Lalitā-sahasra-nāma.*

BHŪTA-ḌĀMARA-TANTRA

Named after Bhūtaḍāmara, name of Unmatta Bhairava. The main topics, discussed in it, are *Māraṇa-mantra, mantras* including *Mṛtasañjīvanī*, various *sādhanas* like *Sundarī-sādhana, Yoginī-sādhana*, etc., *dīkṣā, mudrā, maṇḍala* and *Sādhanādhikārī.*

See B. Bhattacharya, The Cult of Bhūtaḍāmara, *Pro. and Tr. AIOC*, 6, Patna, 1930, pub. at Patna, 1933, pp. 349-370.

BRAHMA-SAṂHITĀ

A Vaiṣṇava Tantra. It has a commentary by Jīva Gosvāmin (16th century).

Pub. in *Tāntrik Texts*, Vol. XV.

BRAHMA-YĀMALA

Existing in Nepāl Darbār library, and dated 1052 A.D. It is stated that the subject-matter was at first transmitted, in 1,25,000 stanzas, to Śrīkaṇṭha. He imparted it to others, in an enlarged form, in different countries.

It emphasises the classification of Tāntric sects according to the three currents, called *Dakṣiṇa, Vāma* and *Madhyama*. The sects are elaborately described. There are lists of gods and sages, represented as communicating the knowledge of Śiva.

According to *Jayadratha-yāmala* (ch. 41), it is the basic text of all Yāmalas. See P.C. Bagchi, *Studies* etc., p. 112.

CHINNAMASTĀ-TANTRA

Same as *Pracaṇḍa-caṇḍikā-tantra* (q.v.).

Ptd. in *Śāktapramoda*, 1890, 1893. See *10 Ptd. Books*, 1938, p. 647.

CIDGAGANA-CANDRIKĀ

Attributed, not on incontrovertible evidence, to Kālidāsa, it is in 278 verses, divided into four chapters (*Vimarśas*). It should be noted that, in the history of Sanskrit literature, at least two authors, besides the master-poet, are named Kālidāsa.

It deals with Śaiva Tantrism. The first chapter deals mainly with *Śiva-tattva, Īśvara-tattva,Brahma-svarūpa, Pratyabhijñā, Śakti-tattva, Guṇatraya, Jñāna, Dhyāna, Sṛṣṭi, Saṃhāra*, etc.

The highlights of the second chapter are: fourfold speech, *Parā*, etc., *Nāda, Bindu, Ādyaspanda, Para-tattva, Ṣoḍaśa-kalā*, etc.

The third chapter deals, *inter alia*, with *Upāsanā, Pīṭhotpatti, Kuṇḍalinī, Mantra, Mudrā, Cakra*, etc.

The main topics of the last chapter are: Caṇḍikā, *Mantra-śakti*, forms of Kālī, *Yantra, Navacakra, Guru-paramparā*, etc.

The work is like a commentary on the *Kramastuti* of Siddhanātha or Śambhunātha, a very well-known figure in the Kashmirian *Trika* school.

The work is quoted by Bhāskararāya in his commentary, *Saubhāgyabhāskara* on *Lalitā-sahasra-nāma*, pp. 53, 157, NSP ed., 1935. Also quoted by Kaivalyāśrama in commentary on *Saundarya-laharī*, Oxf. 108a.

Ed., with commentary of Dhanadānandanātha alias K.A. Sastri, Amalapuram, 1941; Svami T. Tirtha, Calcutta, 1936; in *Tāntrik Texts*, XX (A. Avalon).

For discussion on authorship, see S.C. Banerji, *Kālidāsa Apocrypha*, pp. 202-203.

In connection with the work, also see Pro. AIOC *Summaries*, XI, pp. 111-112.

DAKṢIṆĀMŪRTI-SAṂHITĀ

Of unknown authorship and date. Containing 1700 verses, divided into 65 (according to Kane, 64 according to *NCC*, viii, p. 297, 66 according to Gonda's ed. of *HIL*, II) *Paṭalas* (chapters), it deals with *Śrīvidyā-upāsanā*, the worship of different goddesses with an accent on the cult of Tripura-sundarī.

That it was regarded as an authoritative work is indicated by quotations from or references to it by, among others, Raghunandana in *Dīkṣā-tattva*, and Narasiṃha Ṭhakkura in *Tārābhakti-sudhārṇava*.

Ptd. *Princess of Wales Sarasvatī Bhavana Texts*, No. 61, 1937.

DEVĪKĀLOTTARĀGAMA

An anonymous tract in 84 verses. It states that the restlessness of mind, which is attached to the objects of sense, is the cause of one's rebirth. The meaning of liberation is *nirvikalpa-jñāna* which makes one insensate about the distinction between subject and object. One, aspiring after liberation, should fix the fickle mind; when with such mind a person realises his identity with the Supreme Brahman, he is liberated. The work decries external rites and practices. The root of salvation lies in the devotee's perception that Śiva, identified with the entire world, resides in his body.

The work has a commentary by Nirañjana-siddha.

Ed., with above commentary, by G. Kaviraj, in *Tantra-saṃgraha*, Varanasi, 1970, pp. 318-345.

GAṆAPATI-TATTVA

Found in an Old Javanese Collection. It deals with *Kāya-sādhana* resulting in the penetration of the six *Cakras* within the body, by *Kulakuṇḍalinī*, and mentions six (instead of the usual eight) accessories of *Yoga* (*Yogāṅga*). It also mentions the concepts of *Bindu*, *Nāda*, *Mantra*, *Bīja*, etc.

GANDHARVA-TANTRA

Written in 42 chapters, it appears to have been composed after collecting the essence of other Tantras. Stated to be so called as matters from all Tantras have been sung; music is called *Gandharva-vidyā*.

Highlights of the contents: Tāntric mode of *mukti* through *bhukti*, *Yoga*, *Devī-pūjā*, right of opponents of Vedic rites, of women and Śūdras to Tāntric practices, *Antaryāga*, *Bahiryāga*, *Mudrās*, *Japa*, *Kumārī-pūjā*, good and bad people (the latter including those busy with gratification of senses), *Guru* and *Śiṣya*, *Dīkṣā*, *Puraścaraṇa*, *Haṃsabīja*, *Kāmakalā*, different kinds of *mantras*, *Kulācāra*, ethical precepts, stage of *Avadhūta*, *Śakti* as partner of man in Tāntric *sādhana*, relation with another man's wife, discrimination between soul and body, *Śiva-Śakti*, *Mukti-sakalā* and *niṣkalā*, *Anuttaramantra*, 36 *tattvas*, rise and disappearance of speech.

A *Gandharva*-t appears in the collection by Rasikamohana Cattopadhyaya (1877-84 A.D.). See Bibliography (p. 98) to J.B. Chaudhuri's ed. of *Tantrarāja*-t.

Ed. Kak and Sastri, Srinagar, 1934.

GAUḌAPĀDA-SŪTRA

Same as *Śakti-mīmāṃsā* (q.v.).

GAURĪ-KĀÑCALIKĀ (-KĀÑCULIKĀ, -KĀÑJALIKĀ, -KĀÑJANIKĀ, -KAÑCUKĪ)

According to some MSS, it is a part of the *Gopāla-saṃhitā*.

An anonymous work which mainly gives recipes of herbal drugs for the cure of some diseases among which are *Bahumūtra* (a kind of diabetes), *Mūtrakṛcchra* (difficulty in urination), optical ailments like *Timira* (partial blindness), *Karṇaśūla* (ear-pain), *Śiraḥśūla* (headache), *Kuraṇḍa* (hydrocele), *Galagaṇḍa* (goitre), *Kuṣṭha* (leprosy), *Sānnipātika-jvara* (typhoid), *Romāntika* (measles), *Masūraka* (small-pox), *Kṛmi* (worm), etc.

A few recipes may be of interest and benefit to the readers:

Bahumūtra	drinking the juice of *Dhātrī* (*Barringtonia acutangula*), mixed with honey.
Eye-pain	application of a mixture of pulverised root of Badara (*Zizyphus mauritiana*), buttermilk and juice of Nimba (*Azadirachta indica*).
Śiraḥśūla	application, on the head, of the paste of the following, crushed together and boiled in mustard oil: Viḍaṅga — *Embelia ribes*, Gandhaka — sulphur, Nīlotpala — blue lotus, Cow's urine.
Kuṣṭha	application of the root of white *Aparajitā* (*Clitoria ternatea*), crushed with water.
Measles and Small-pox	drinking a decoction of the following together: *Khadira* (*Acacia catechu*), *Ariṣṭa* (*Azadirachta indica*), *Paṭola* (*Trichosanthes diocia*), *Amṛta* (*Eulophia campestris*), *Vāsaka*, (*Adhatoda vasica*) and *Triphalā* (collective name of the following: *Āmalakī* (*Emblica officinalis*), *Harītakī* (*Terminalia chebula*) and *Baheḍā* (*Terminalia belerica*).

Ptd., Calcutta, 1890; Bombay, 1907.

GAUTAMA (MI or MĪYA) (MAHĀ)TANTRA

A Vaiṣṇavite treatise, in 34 chapters, on the rituals relating to Kṛṣṇa and his worship. Prominent features of the contents:

glorification of *Kṛṣṇa-mantra*, description of Vṛndāvana, persons fit for this *mantra*, *guru*, *śiṣya*, *dīkṣā*, Kuṇḍalinī, various kinds of *āsanas* and their result, meditation on *Cakras*, importance of *prāṇāyāma*, different kinds of images of Kṛṣṇa, good and bad dreams, *Puraścaraṇa*, conduct of initiated persons, *Yoga*, etc.

The work has at least three commentaries.

Published from (i) Karnataka Press, Bombay, 1889, (ii) Vasumati Press, Calcutta, 1927-28, with Bengali trs.

GĀYATRĪ-TANTRA

In the Vārāṇasī edition (1946, 2nd ed., 1969), it comprises 815 verses, divided into five chapters. It contains a detailed account of the worship and application of the Vedic *Gāyatrī mantra* (*Ṛgveda*, III.

62.10) which, regarded as very important Tāntric *vidyā*, is highly venerated. Chapter II, however, is devoted to the significance of the Vedic *Vyāhṛtis* (*bhūr*, *bhuvaḥ*, *svaḥ*), which are mentioned before the recital of the *Gāyatrī*.

Ptd. (1) Stated above. (2) As from the *Āgama-sandarbha* (Jñāna-darpaṇa) — Ptd. (a) with *Tantrasāra* of Kṛṣṇānanda, 1877-84; (b) in *Sulabha-tantra-prakāśa*, 1886; (c) with Hindi trs., Bombay, 1916; (d) Calcutta, 1946. (3) As from *Prapañcasāra*, Madras, 1901, in Telugu script (Note: It is not found in the printed ed. of *Prapañcasāra*).

GORAKṢA-SIDDHĀNTA-SAṂGRAHA

A collection of short tracts by sages of the Nātha sect, e.g. Gorakṣanātha, Matsyendranātha, Jālandharanātha, Bhartṛhari, etc.

According to this work, Kaula Tantras were introduced on earth by nine Nātha teachers. The prominent topics of discussion are:

> non-discrimination of castes and stages of life an essential pre-requisite for liberation, nature and importance of *Yoga*, description of *Avadhūta*, salvation resulting from the attainment of the condition of Nātha (*Na* indicates one without beginning and *Tha* means that which is placed), who is the initiator of the system, description of *Kāpālika Tantra* stated to be followed by both Śaivas and Śāktas, eulogy of *Praṇava*, definition of *Paramahaṃsa*, denunciation of enjoyment of prostitutes, characteristics of good men, discussion of *Nāda*, *Bindu*, etc., *Ācāra* or Tāntric mode of conduct, way to salvation, views of dualists and non-dualists, duties of a householder, speculation about cosmogony, etc.

Ed. G. Kaviraj, Varanasi, 1925; *Princess of Wales Sarasvatī Bhavana Texts*, 18.

GUPTA-SĀDHANA TANTRA

A small tract covering 61 printed pages. It mentions *Kālī-tantra*, *Yāmala*, Viṣṇu and Nīla. It is mentioned by Kāśīnātha Tarkālaṃkāra in his *Śyāmā-saparyā-vidhi* (see MT, S 122).

The contents of its 12 chapters are briefly given below.

i. *Kulācāra*, worship of *Kulāṅganās*, viz. actress, daughter of a *Kāpālika*, courtesan, a woman of the washerman class, a woman of barber class, Brāhmaṇa woman, daughter of a

Śūdra, daughter of a cowherd, daughter of a garland-maker. They are collectively known as *Nava-kanyā*; thus, it is implied that all of them are virgins. Besides the above, any girl possessed of special qualities, who is good-looking, of good conduct, can be looked upon as *Kulāṅganā*. The devotee attains success by worshipping such a girl.

ii. *Śakti* identified with *Kula*, Śiva called *Akula*. *Kulīna* stated to be one merged in *Śakti*, *gurudhyāna*.

Dīkṣā by a female *guru* extolled as leading to the fulfilment of all desires. *Dhyāna* of such a *guru*.

iii. Daily duties of a devotee including *japa*, feeding Brāhmaṇas, worship and feeding of a virgin girl, worship of *Śakti*.

iv. Means of getting good result within a short time, good health, wealth, victory over enemies and *Aṣṭa-siddhi*. It consists in the worship of the devotee's own wife or that of another, sexual intercourse with her followed by *homa*, *japa* and *pūrṇāhuti*.

v. Modes of *japa* in each month, followed by worship of *Śakti*. Only *japa* in the company of *Śakti* stated to be beneficial. Devotee advised to avoid *Pīṭhasthānas* and to associate carefully with women. These provisions are not meant for those who follow *Paśvācāra*. Mention of following *Pīṭhasthānas*:

Badarikāśrama, Gaṇḍakī, Kāśī, Naimiṣāraṇya, Prayāga, Puṣkara, Revā, Sarasvatī, Sindhu, Utkala.

vi. Procedure of worship of Dakṣiṇa-kālikā. For worship, fit are one's *guru*, *guru's* son or *guru's* wife; in their absence, devotee himself. Appropriate *mantra* of the goddess is *Krīṃ*. Secluded place suitable for Tāntric worship. Kālī stated to live in a cemetery. Śyāmā stated to have infinite forms. Appropriate time at night for *pūjā*. After first half of night, Kālī to be worshipped with *Paśubhāva*. Different results follow from worship in different parts of night. After one *prahara* of night, it is called *Mahāniśā* for two hours, then follows *Āti Mahāniśā*. No rule about time suitable for worship with *Pañca-tattva*. *Pūjā*, after midnight according to *Kaulācāra*, called *Kula-pūjā*.

vii. Way to *nirvāṇa*. Only a devotee, worshipping goddess with *Pañca-tattva*, can reach the goal.

viii. *Siddhāricakra* described. See Glossary. Media of worshipping goddess:

Śālagrāma, any stone, jewel, diagram, image, book, any water, *puṣpayantra*, *Śivaliṅga*. Worship in an image or diagram stated to be highly effective. Worship in a *Śivaliṅga*, made of crystal, stated to be conducive to infinite result.

ix. Procedure of worship of goddess *Dhanadā* (giver of wealth), description of goddess. *Japa* of *mūlamantra* 10,000 times a day for a week stated to result in quick success. As alternative is prescribed *Śava-sādhana*. As another alternative, worship of goddess along with *Śakti* is prescribed in it, devotee should make *Śakti* drink wine, and himself drink the residue. Then, with her he should do *japa* for 1008 times.

x. *Mantra* etc. of goddess Mātaṅgī who is described.

xi. Description of rosaries for *japa* relating to different deities. Rosary of letters *A* to *Kṣa* stated to lead to supreme salvation. Human bones suitable and unsuitable for rosaries and *Śava-sādhana*.

xii. Analysis of syllables constituting *Gāyatrī-mantra*; different results obtainable by *Gāyatrī-japa* for different numbers of times.

Printed (i) with Hindi commentary by B. Mishra, Bombay, 1922-23; (ii) with Bengali trs., Calcutta, 1886.

GURU-TANTRA

In 151 verses, it discusses meditation on and the glorification and propitiation of *Guru*. The *Kulagurus* (i.e. *gurus* following *Kaulācāra*) whose names end in *nātha*:

Prahlādānandanātha, Sakalānandanātha, Sukhānandanātha, Jñānānandanātha and Bodhānandanātha.

The work is mentioned in the *Śyāmāsaparyāvidhi* of Kāśīnātha Tarkālaṃkāra (vide *RASB*, VIII, A 6303).

Ed., with Bengali trs., by J. Tarkalamkara, Calcutta, 1335 B.S.

ĪŚĀNAŚIVA-GURUDEVA-PADDHATI (or TANTRA-PADDHATI)

Attributed to Īśānaśiva; its latter part is named also *Siddhānta-sāra.*

There is a commentary, by Murāri, called *Vivaraṇa.*

The work is on Tāntric rites and rituals : It discusses the usual Tāntric topics. There are magical rites for the prevention of fever, etc. It deals also with the treatment of various diseases.

Ed. *TSS*, 69, 72, 77, 83.

Sections trs., into English, in *Jour. of the Ind. Soc. of Ori. Art*, Calcutta, IX, 1941, 151-93 and X, 1942, 210-52.

JAYADRATHA-YĀMALA

In 24000 stanzas, divided into four parts. The manuscript of the fourth part dates from the 12th century A.D., while those of the other parts appear to have originated later. The second part is incomplete. Chapters 35 and 36 have some importance in the history of Tantra. They are entitled respectively *Sambandhāvatāra* and *Sūtra-nirṇaya;* the latter names the Tantras of different traditions. Chapter 41 deals with *Yāmala, Maṅgala, Aṣṭaka* and the genealogies of the sages who taught the Tantra. The incomplete second part, containing 41 chapters, deals with duties and the rituals connected with them. Parts 3 and 4 discuss, *inter alia*, the *mantras, maṇḍalas, dhyānas,* modes of *dīkṣā*, etc.

The work is quoted by Bhāskara Miśra in *Mantra-ratnāvalī* (see 10.2580).

For a detailed notice, see P.C. Bagchi, *Studies in the Tantras*, pt. 1, pp. 109-114.

JAYĀKHYA-SAṂHITĀ

(also called *Jaya-saṃhitā* or *Jñānalakṣmī*)

A Pāñcarātra Āgama of 450 A.D., according to B. Bhattacharya. It is in 33 *Paṭalas* (chapters).

Yakṣiṇī-sādhana, Cakra-yantra-sādhana, Stambhana — these are some of the topics discussed in it.

In certain matters (e.g. *Prāṇa-pratiṣṭhā* of images), it reveals similarity with the *Śāradātilaka*. *Paṭala* xix, verses 13-33, discusses

Puraścaraṇa and its beneficial effects, indications of a devotee's attaining perfection in *mantra*. He is forbidden (xix.34-37) to disclose these things to anybody excepting the *Guru*; otherwise, he will lose *Siddhi*. It is ordained (xv.186-188) that the terms *Svāhā, Svadhā, Phaṭ, Hūṃ* and *Namas* should be used respectively in *Homa, Śrāddha*, destructive activities, creating hatred among friends and securing *Mokṣa*.

Several *Nyāsas* are described in *Paṭala* xi; *Paṭala* viii speaks about 58 *Mudrās*.

Published in GOS, 54. See *Pāñcarātra Nool Vilakkam*, p. 19.

JAYASAṂHITĀ

Same as *Jayākhya-saṃhitā* (q.v.).

JÑĀNALAKṢMĪ

Another title of *Jayākhya-saṃhitā* (q.v.).

JÑĀNA-DĪPIKĀ (1753 Śaka = 1831 A.D.)

By Amara Maitra. The title indicates the contents. It is in 23 *Prakāśas* (chapters).

See C. Chakravarti in *Vaṅgīya Sāhitya Pariṣat Patrikā*, Calcutta, 58, iii-iv.

JÑĀNARṆAVA-TANTRA

Written in 26 chapters, it contains about 2,300 verses. It mainly deals with rites and rituals relating to Tripureśvarī. Among other noteworthy topics are *dīkṣā, Śrīvidyā, Ṣoḍaśī-vidyā, Cakras*, over 30 *Mudrās* including *Khecarī-mudrā*.

It mentions the following eight prominent *Śākta Pīṭhas*:

Kāmarūpa, Malaya, Kaulagiri, Kulāntaka, Cauhāra, Jālandhara, Uḍḍiyāna, Devīkoṭṭa.

There are a few commentaries on the treatise.

The work has been extensively quoted by Kṛṣṇānanda, Brahmānanda and Pūrṇānanda, the well-known Tāntric scholar-devotees of Bengal in the 16th century.

Printed at Ānandāśrama 69, Poona.

JÑĀNASAṂKALINĪ-TANTRA

Main topics of discussion: Creation and destruction of the universe, branches of knowledge, *Brahmajñāna* as knowledge par excellence, body as microcosm, *Khecarī Mudrā*, *Śāmbhavī Vidyā*, etc., references to *Śāktas* as worshippers of *Prakṛti*, to Buddhists as nihilists, materialists as denying the existence of all things. Other main things, dealt with, are:

> *piṇḍa* (body), *brahmāṇḍa* (universe), five gross elements, 25 qualities of different things, five subtle elements; mind, tainted by sin, is freed from bondage by being engrossed in Paramātman; *Jīva*, tied to wrong ideas, when freed, becomes Sadāśiva; you are both the cause and the effect — this perception is the highest of all. Visits to holy places are futile; knowledge of *ātma-tīrtha* (one's ownself as a holy place) leads to salvation. *Brahmacarya* recognised as best penance. Real *dhyāna* is meditation on the formless, not on the form. Real *homa* is not pouring ghee into fire, but the offering of *Prāṇa* to the fire of *Brahma-yajña* which arises when mind, speech and action are destroyed, and grows without support. One, possessed of *Brahma-jñāna*, is as follows:
>
> > lonely, desireless, calm, devoid of thought and sleep.
>
> Nature of *Yoga*, steady mind means of success, threefold *Śakti* (in throat, navel and anus). Nirañjana, the untainted Brahman, beyond three *Śaktis*, resides in between eyebrows. The bodily winds named, *Nāḍis* mentioned. For salvation, the sense of unity of all, moving and non-moving, is a must; characteristics of a true devotee, all associations to be avoided; nature and significance of *Oṃkāra*, note on *Māyā*, subtle body and gross body.
>
> Ptd. with Bengali trs., Calcutta, 1891 ff.

KĀKACAṆḌĪ or KĀKACAṆḌEŚVARĪ or KĀKACAṆḌEŚVARĪ-MATA (or -TANTRA)

The work, containing about 700 stanzas, is named after Kāka-caṇḍeśvarī, an aspect of Śakti, to whom Śiva is represented as revealing the text.

In the beginning, Śiva (Bhairava) says that the Vedas are too old to bring about *Siddhi*. The goddess puts several questions to Śiva.

Some of them are about the identity of the individual soul (*jīva*), cause of its bondage to matter, the doctrine of *karman* and rebirth. In reply, Śiva says that *jīva* is *ātman*; the bondage of *jīva* is caused by *karman* leading to nescience (*ajñāna*). *Jīva* becomes subjected to *saṃsāra* due to its ignorance of immortalisation (*dravyopāya*). Thereafter, the goddess enquires about the means of acquiring *Siddhis*, i.e. such miraculous powers as flying through the sky, attracting the love of divine damsels, remaining invisible to others. She also expresses the desire to know the secrets of the elixir (*rasāyana*) which is the *sine qua non* for *Siddhi*.

Some of the matters, discussed in it, are:

the killing of mercury, transmutation of copper into gold (*Paṭala* II, 13-16, 18-20), liquefying mica (*Paṭala* III, 29-30, etc.).

Ed. R.K. Sarma, Benares, 1929, under the title *Kākacaṇḍīśvarī-kalpatantra*; V. Vaidyaraja, Etawah, 1930, with Hindi trs. under the title *Kākacaṇḍīśvarī-tantra*.

KĀLĪ-TANTRA

An anonymous work of unknown date and provenance, belonging to *Kālīkula*. It is in 21 chapters. It deals mainly with *Yoga*, *Yagāṅgas*, salvation, *Brahma-jñāna*, *Māyā*, *Dharma*, the causes and cures of some diseases, six Tāntric rites, *Mudrās*, means of purification like *dhauti*, etc., *Navagraha-mantra*, kinds of devotees, *Stavas* and *Kavacas*. As regards *Mudrās*, 25 of them are mentioned; besides 5 kinds of *Dhāraṇa mudrās* are named (ch. xiv). Great importance is attached to *Prāṇāyāma*; in this connexion, eight kinds of *Kumbhakas* are mentioned. *Āsanas* are stated to be 84 in number; of them, 32 are mentioned as the best. Of them, 4 are regarded as the most important. The remaining 28 are named.

There is another shorter work of this title in 11 chapters. It is regarded as highly authoritative in matters relating to Kālī and Her worship.

Ed. K.P. Vidyaratna, Calcutta, 1892.

Published, with Skt. gloss and Bengali trs., *Skt. Śahitya Pariṣad Ser.* 2, Calcutta, 1922. See C. Chakravarti, *IHQ*, I, p. 781.

Another text ptd. in *Śāktapramoda*, Veṅkaṭeśvara Press, 1933, pp. 1-100. A *Kālī-tantra*, with Hindi trs., pub. from Moradabad, 1902.

KĀLĪ-TATTVA (RAHASYA)

Attributed to Rāghavabhaṭṭa who seems to be identical with the famous commentator of this name (q.v.) on the *Śāradātilaka*. It contains over 2000 stanzas, divided into 21 chapters, and quotes the above commentary. The work deals, *inter alia*, with *Kaula* rituals (chs. vii, viii), *Kulācāra* (xi), virgin-worship (xvi), etc. It has a commentary by Mathurānātha.

For MSS, see *NCC*, IV.74. Also see *Indian Culture*, V, pp. 213-214. On some verses, common to this work and the *Kulārṇava-tantra* (different from the published text of this title), see C. Chakravarti, *Tantras* etc., 1963, pp. 62, 65 (fn. 27).

KĀLĪVILĀSA-TANTRA

Believed by some to have originated in eastern India (vide N.N. Bhattacharya, *History of Tāntric Religion*, p. 77). Written in 35 chapters, it deals mainly with the following matters:

> *Durgā-pūjā*, from *Bodhana* (awakening) to *Visarjana* (immersion), three types of men, viz. of *Divya* (existed only in *Satya-* and *Tretā-yugas*), *Vīra* (only in *Tretā* and *Dvāpara*) and *Paśu-bhāvas* (only in *Kali-yuga*); stress on sexual intercourse and drinking as means of Tāntric *Sādhana*. It allows (X.20-21) a *Śākta* to take to adulterous sexual union provided the woman concerned is initiated, and the man does not continue it up to the stage of the emission of semen; such a practice has been stated to result in the acquisition of supernatural power. The devotee is exhorted to practise the upward motion of semen during sexual intercourse.

Other noteworthy matters, dealt with in it, are:

> rights and restrictions relating to Śūdras, *Paśvācāra* recommended for Kali Age, *Śiva-mantras* for different castes, prohibition of *Puraścaraṇa*, *Homa*, *Athiṣeka* and *Tarpaṇa* as also of meat-eating and drinking in Kali Age, means of attaining *Siddhi*, *Pañca-tattvas* stated as suitable only in Ages preceding Kali, *Saṃvida* is allowed in this Age. Chapter XV deals with *Vaśīkaraṇa*; it is interesting that the *mantra* in this connection is in mixed Assamese and Eastern Bengali dialect as spoken in or around Chittagong (now in Bangladesh) — a fact which hints at the east Indian provenance of the work. In Chapter XXII, some *mantras* are given in the reverse forms, e.g. *Oṃ durge durge* is

read as *rgedu rgedu oṃ*. Some space is devoted to *bījas* and *dhyānas*.

A curious feature of the work is discussion on Kṛṣṇa and Rādhā. Chapters XXIII and XXIV state that Kṛṣṇa was born to Devī who was Gaurī turned dark when excited by passion. Devī tells Kṛṣṇa that, by drinking water from her breasts, He, though *Nirguṇa*, has become *Saguṇa*. Chapter XXVIII states Rādhā as beloved of Kṛṣṇa. It is further stated that Brahmā, Viṣṇu, Rudra, Īśvara and Sadāśiva are five kinds of light, and Kṛṣṇa is the Lord above them. It then speaks of Rādhā's union with Kṛṣṇa. The last chapter contains a dialogue between Kālī and Kṛṣṇa. The work appears to be an attempt at the fusion of Śāktism and Vaiṣṇavism, with an accent on the former.

It may be added that the Bengali songs of some Tāntric devotees refer to the above fusion of the two sects. For example,

Kālī hali mā rāsvihārī
naṭavar-veśe vṛndāvane/

Rāmprasād (c. 1720-81)

[Mother Kālī, thou hast become Rāsvihārī (i.e. Kṛṣṇa) in the guise of the master-dancer at Vṛṅdāvana.]

Ai ye kālī kṛṣṇa śiv-rām-sakal āmār...elokeśī/ Ibid.

[That Kālī of mine, with dishevelled hairs, is all, viz. Kṛṣṇa, Śiva, Rāma.]

Haye elokeśī-kare laye asi...
vrajapure āsi vājāiyā vānsi.../

Kamalākānta (c. 1772-1821)

[Having dishevelled hairs, and holding a sword in hand, coming to Vrajapura (i.e. Vṛṅdāvana) and playing the flute...]

Ptd. in *Tāntric Texts Series*, Calcutta, 1917.

KĀLOTTARA-TANTRA (or -ĀGAMA)

A work of unknown authorship, date and provenance. Judging by the fact that it exists in three recensions, one of which is in 1300 stanzas, and that it is quoted by such celebrities as Abhinavagupta in *Tantrāloka*, Mādhava in *Sarva-darśana-saṃgraha*, Hemādri in *Dānakhaṇḍa*, Vidyāpati in *Gaṅgāvākyāvalī*, Raghunandana in *Malamāsa-* and *Dīkṣātattvas*, etc. the work appears to have been highly authoritative.

Represented in the form of a dialogue between Śiva and Kārtikeya, it belongs to the realm of Śaiva ritual and the esoteric cult of Śiva-Śakti. Among the subjects, dealt with in it, are a number of *vratas*, Yogic elements, *guru-śiṣya* relation, significance of *praṇava*. The latter part of the work is concerned with cosmology, supernatural powers, magic and *mantras*.

See *Nepal Catalogue of MSS*, I, pp. lix, 9, 96 f. It should be noted that a recension of 350 stanzas has been edited by N.R. Bhatt, Pondicherry, No. 61.

KĀLYARCANA-CANDRIKĀ (1801 Śaka = 1879 A.D.)

By Nīlakamala Lāhiḍī. It deals with both the *Pramāṇa* and *Prayoga* relating to Kālī worship. The main topics are:

places and time suitable for worship, various kinds of *pūjā* — *nitya, naimittika, kāmya, sāttvika, rājasika, tāmasika, mānasī, antaryāgātmikā, bāhyā, siddha-pīṭhas, bhāvas, ācāras*, various images and symbols of Kālī, *puraścaraṇa, Kumārī-pūjā, Śivā-bali*, importance of *guru*, description of *Kuṇḍalinī, Ṣaṭ-cakra-bheda*, etc.

For his autobiography, see his name under Authors.

Ptd. Murshidabad, 1877-79 in Bengali script.

KĀMADHENU-TANTRA

In 24 chapters, it deals mainly with the following:

significance of letters of the alphabet, animation of *mantras, japa*, 25 *tattvas*, Brahman and *Prakṛti, dhyāna* of Brahman, effect of *Śiva-pūjā* on the occasion of *Ardhodaya-yoga* (a rare combination, in the month of Pauṣa or Māgha, of new moon on Sunday, Śravaṇā nakṣatra, etc.; regarded as a very auspicious time when devout people bathe in the Ganges).

Ptd. in *Sulabha-tantra-prakāśa* (first 21 chapters only). See *Cat. of I.O. Ptd. Books*, 1938, p. 1236.

KĀMAKALĀ-VILĀSA

By Puṇyānandanātha, also called Advaitānanda, of Kashmir and teacher of Amṛtānandanātha. It is in 55 verses. There are some commentaries of which that, called *Cidvallī*, by Naṭanānandanātha is best known.

The main topics, discussed in it, are the following:

Ādyā Śakti, seed of all that is moving and non-moving; *Parā Śakti* both seed and sprout as manifested union of Śiva and Śakti; *Paraśiva* reflected in mass of rays of the sun; *Mahābindu* appears on *Citta* wall illuminated by reflected rays; *Ahaṃkāra* is *Cit*; Śiva and Śakti respectively represented by two *Bindus*, white and red, are at the root of creation of word (*vāc*) and meaning (*artha*) which sometimes united with, sometimes separated from each other; *Bindu*, identified with *Ahaṃkāra*, is sun representing the union of above two *Bindus*.

Sun identified with *Kāma* so called as it is desirable; *Kalā* identified with two *Bindus* which are moon and fire; *Vidyā* of *Kāmakalā* deals with *Cakras* of *Devī*; one, knowing it, is liberated and identified with *Mahā-tripura-sundarī.*

From the red *Bindu*, about to create, emanated sound, the *Nāda-Brahman* sprout; sound gave rise to Ether, Air, Fire, Water, Earth and letters of alphabet; white *Bindu* also their source; universe, from minutest particle to Brahman, consists of these five *Vikṛtis*.

As above two *Bindus* are inseparable, so *Vidyā*, the indicator (*vedaka*), is identified with Devatā, the indicated (*vedya*).

Discussion on the nature and evolution of *Parā*, *Paśyantī*, *Madhyamā* and *Vaikharī* — the first three unuttered gross letters stated to have produced *Vaikharī*, i.e. the 51 letters of the alphabet.

Devī Tripurasundarī stated to reside in *Bindu-maya-cakra*, and seated in the lap of Kāmeśvara; her description — her three eyes are the sun, the moon and fire. *Śrī-cakra* of eight triangles representing the eightfold subtle body of Devī.

Description of *Yoginīs*, *Mudrās*, *Siddhi*, etc.

Paramaśiva, the Supreme One, in his *vimarśa* aspect, assumes the form of Kāmeśa. Śiva, the *guru*, imparted the *Vidyā* to his *Śakti*, *Kāmeśvarī*. She, having purified the *gurus*, revealed the *Vidyā* to them.

The work describes (verses 22, 26, 29, 30, 33) several *Yantras* (diagrams).

Ptd. (1) with commentary, *Cidvallī*, of Naṭanānanda, in Telugu script, Bellary, 1913; (2) with Eng. trs. by A. Avalon, *Tāntrik Texts*, X, 1922 (2nd ed., Madras, 1959); (3) with above commentary, *Kashmir Texts*, 12, 1918; (4) with Telugu exposition, Cocanada, 1924; (5) with

Tāmil comm. by N.S. Iyer, Madras, 1942; (6) with Telugu comm., Madras, 1934.

KĀMĀKHYĀ-TANTRA

Main contents of its 12 chapters (also available in 9 and 15 chapters):

I Description of Kāmākhyā as *Yoni*.

II Kinds of harm to enemies possible by *Kāmākhyāmantra*.

III Worship of Kāmākhyā, glorification of *Yoni*.

IV *Mantra, dhyāna, latā-sādhana* relating to Kāmākhyā.

V Merits and defects of *Guru, Śiṣya*.

VI Rites to be performed with *Pañcatattva*.

VII Application of *Kāmākhyā-mantra*, rite, involving use of urine, for the ruin of enemies.

VIII *Pūrṇābhiṣeka*.

IX Liberation of four kinds, viz. *Sālokya, Sāyujya, Sārūpya* and *Nirvāṇa* attainable only by a *Kaula* devotee; philosophy and scriptures confuse people.

X Kāmākhyā identified as Sarvavidyā, Ādyāśakti, Parāśakti; She is giver of salvation; She is Dakṣiṇa Kālī; from her universe proceeds.

XI Description of Kāmākhyā-pīṭha; mention of a number of *Pīṭhas*.

XII Description of *Kullūkās* of *mantras, Kumārī-pūjā*, worship of female Tāntric devotees, called *Latā; Durgā-pūjā* and modes of *Puraścaraṇa* connected with it; *Puraścaraṇa* prohibited for women and *Śūdras* who are eligible for *Japa* and *pūjā*; ten kinds of *mantra-saṃskāra* per month; *mantra-japa* relating to Ḍākinī, Rākiṇī, Lākinī, Kākinī, Śākinī, Hākinī — on failure of the preceding one, the succeeding one is recommended. In case of failure of even Hākinī, one is to resort to the following, one after the other that fails — *Sattva-bīja, Japa* of *varṇas* or letters, *guru-bīja*; description of the decline and degeneration of people in different *Varṣas* included in *Jambu-dvīpa*.

Ptd. in *Sulabha-tantra-prakāśa*, 1886, in *Vividha-tantra-saṃgraha*, Calcutta, 1877-81.

KĀMARATNA (variously called Kāmatantra, Kāmaratnākara or Siddha-ḍākinī)

It contains 15 or 16 *Upadeśas* (chapters); it seems to have existed in two versions, one longer, the other shorter. The number of stanzas varies from 800 to 1200, in some cases about 1900.

Ascribed, in different manuscripts, to different authors, e.g. Śrīnātha, Pārvatīputra (or, Gaurīputra), Nityanātha, Nāgabhaṭṭa and Siddhanātha. Judging from its several editions, published in different places of India, and its translations into different regional languages, it can be taken to have been widely popular.

Besides the six Tāntric acts, in which *Vaśīkaraṇa* of woman figures prominently, it contains herbal recipes for the cure of various diseases, e.g. nocturnal blindness and other optical diseases, deafness, looseness of teeth, looseness of the breasts of a woman, failing health of a pregnant woman, barrenness, venereal diseases, etc. It also prescribes antidotes for snake-bite and for counteracting the effect of the poison of plants, etc. Among the prescribed drugs, there is aphrodisiac also.

Among the supernatural powers, it lays down the means of acquiring the ability to visualise hidden treasure, make oneself invisible to others. The means of making Yakṣiṇīs favourably disposed for grant of material goods are also there.

There is a Sanskrit commentary on the work (see *NCC*, III, p. 355).

Of the several editions of the work, the following may be mentioned:

(1) with Bengali trs., Calcutta, 1884; (2) with Mārāṭhī trs., Calcutta, 1904; (3) with Hindi trs., Lucknow, 1906; (4) with Hindi commentary, Bombay, 1920; (5) with Assamese trs., Shillong, 1928.

See *IHQ*, V, p. 390.

KĀMIKĀGAMA or KĀMIKA-TANTRA

It belongs to the Siddhānta school of south Indian Śaivism. Written in verse, it is in two parts, *Pūrvabhāga* and *Uttarabhāga*, the former containing 75 chapters.

Besides matters relating to rituals, it is concerned with details about Śaiva temple-architecture, from the selection of site to the establishment of images.

It is referred to as one of the 28 Śaivāgamas in *Kāraṇāgama* and in *Siddhāntaśāstra*. The *Mṛgendratantra* is described as an epitome of the *Kāmika* or *Kāmikabheda*.

The *Kāmikāgama* is quoted, *inter alia*, by Hemādri (13th century A.D.) in his *Caturvarga-cintāmaṇi* (*Dānakāṇḍa*). It is mentioned in the *Vāmakeśvarī-mata* (*Kashmir Texts*, 66, p. 16) as one of the 64 Tantras.

Ed. (1) in two vols. with Tāmil comm. and glossary, Madras, 1898-99; (2) in Grantha script, with Tāmil explanation, Kumbhakonam, 1916; (3) Pūrvabhāga, with Tāmil meaning and Uttarabhāga Text only, by M. Alagappa Mudaliar, Madras, 1908; (4) by K.S. Mudaliar.

For MSS referring to or quoting from it, see *NCC*, III, p. 363.

KĀMYA-YANTRODDHĀRA

By Parivrājakācārya. It deals with the drawing of different *Yantras* or diagrams, used in Tāntric rites.

It is a compilation from various sources.

For MS, see Hpr. III.53-4 Śaka 1297 (= 1375 A.D.).

Also see C. Chakravarti, *The Tantras* etc.

KAṄKĀLAMĀLINĪ-TANTRA

The main topics dealt with in its five chapters are:

I Letters of alphabet called Brahman, Śiva-śakti and lords of world. Each letter given a name, e.g. *A* called *Vidyujjihvā*, *K* *Krodhīśa*. Meaning of term *Guru*, significance of *Om*.

II Description and worship of *Yonimudrā*; mention of three main *Nāḍis*; description of six *Cakras*; rise of singing Kuṇḍalinī to *Brahmarandhra* and returning to *Mūlādhāra*.

III *Guru-pūjā*.

IV *Mahākālī-pūjā*; people exhorted to be kind to women; maltreatment of women stated to harm *Sādhana*.

V *Puraścaraṇa*; wearing of rosaries of bones and *Rudrākṣa*; worship of 36 letters of alphabet stated to make *Mūlamantra* effective; great effect of *Kuṇḍalinī-dhyāna*; *Durgā-pūjā*.

Ptd. see *10 Ptd. Books*, 1938, p. 1247.

KAULA-GAJA-MARDANA

By Kāśīnātha Bhaṭṭa. Its aim is to demolish the *Kaula* school of Tantra.

See MS NW. 220.

KAULA-JÑĀNA-NIRṆAYA

Attributed to Matsyendranātha.

Divided into 24 sections, it deals mainly with meaning of *Kula*, practices prescribed for a *Kaula*, the principle *Akulavīra*, relation between *Śiva-Śakti*, *Bindu*, *Nāda*, *Kalā*, *Mokṣa*, mode of worship, meditation, *Sahaja*, means of acquisition of powers by which one can kill others and enjoy long life, denunciation of contemporary Śāstric rites and importance of *Yoga*, knowledge of *tīrthas*, characteristics of Ḍākinī and Yoginī.

Kula is that condition in which the mind and the sight of the devotee coalesce, the senses lose their independence, the devotee's own power becomes one with *jīva*, and his sight merges into the visible objects. *Kula*, meaning the same as *Akula*, is identical with Śakti. Śakti merges into Śiva, Śiva into *Kriyā* (action), *Kriyā* into *Jñāna* (knowledge) through *Icchā* (desire) which merges into supreme Śiva (12/6, 7a). *Mukti* (liberation) can be achieved with the perfect knowledge of Śiva. A liberated man can liberate others.

Ed. P.C. Bagchi, Calcutta, 1934.

KAULĀVALĪ-NIRṆAYA (or, -TANTRA)

Attributed to Jñānānanda-giri Paramahaṃsa, it appears to have come down in two recensions, the longer and the shorter. The former contains 21 or 22 chapters (*ullāsas*) and about 3,850 verses. The latter is in 9 chapters which cover the portion from ii.50 to xv of the former (as in Avalon's ed.).

According to some, the work dates back to the 16th century A.D.

Leaving aside the common Tāntric topics, the noteworthy topics, dealt with in the work of the longer version of 22 chapters, are:

Chap. I : enumeration of more than 70 Tantras of which it is stated to be the quintessence, mention of the following *Kula-gurus* (named in the same order as in the text) — Prahlādānandanātha, Sanakānandanātha, Kumārānandanātha,

Vaśiṣṭhānandanātha, Krodhānanda, Sukhānanda, Jñānānanda, Bodhānanda (verses 92-93), salutation to *Kula* trees (viz. *Aśoka, Kesara, Karṇikāra, Cūta, Tila, Nameru, Piyāla, Sindhuvāra, Kadamba, Marubaka, Campaka,* etc.; there is also an alternative list), prohibition of sleep under *Kula* trees and of causing harm to them, enumeration of numerous Tantras including Yāmalas (verses 2-14).

Chap. II : places suitable for worship of Devī:
Ekaliṅga (a place in which there is no *Śiva-liṅga* excepting one, within the radius of five *Krośas* or about ten miles), funeral ground, empty house, crossing of four roads, root of a *Bel* tree, river bank, mountain -top, solitary place, temple, *bhūgṛha* (earthen house?), near an *Aśvattha* tree, root of a *Vaṭa* tree, house in a market, one's own house, a place beyond the sight of animals, *Maṇḍapa* (a building consecrated to a deity) of a king, cave, etc.

Chap. III : emphasises the importance of *Antaryāga*, different forms of it.

Chaps. IV-V : *Pañcatattvas* and their substitutes (v. 113-123). Only the fifth *tattva,* i.e. *maithuna* or sexual union with a woman, who may even be the wife of another man excepting a *Guru* and a *Śākta* of the *Vīra* type, leads to the desired goal.

Chap. X : rules of conduct for a devotee. Among the condemned practices are theft of *Guru's* property, desire of sexual union with his wife, wasting time, slander, violence, rape, beating an offending woman even with flowers, sexual intercourse by day. Among commendable practices are service of *Guru*, respect and consideration for women, all women to be looked upon as manifestations of Great Mother (cf. *vidyāḥ samastās tava devi bhedāḥ, striyaḥ samastāḥ sakalā jagatsu*/ *Caṇḍi*, xi.6). A woman of any age, even a girl, should be bidden adieu after salutation.

Chap. XIV : direction for *Śavasādhana*.

Chap. XIX : signs of attainment of *Siddhi*.

Chap. XXII : method of making oneself invisible to others, *Śavasādhana* mentioned again; description of *Avadhūta* and of his way of life —

vāme rāmā ramaṇa-kuśalā dakṣiṇe pānapātram/
madhye nyastaṃ marīca-sahitaṃ sūkarasyāpi māṃsam//
skandhe vīṇā lalita-subhagā sad-guṇānāṃ prapañcaḥ/
Kaulo dharmaḥ, etc.

One, following *Kulācāra*, is endowed with many virtues; he has a beautiful lute on his shoulder, a woman skilled in sexual intercourse on his left, a goblet on his right, in the middle there is pork with pepper.

Some portions are similar in this work and the *Kulārṇava-tantra*, e.g. Kau I.23-31 = Ku I.7-18; Kau 9.79 f = Ku 7.42 f.

The following are some of the many Tantras quoted in this work: *Kuloḍḍīśa*, *Phetkārī*, *Yoginī*, *Tantrarāja*, *Kubjikā*, *Matsyasūkta*, etc.

About different versions of the work, see C. Chakravarti, *Indian Culture*, III, pp. 518-20.

Ed. R.M. Chattopadhyay in *Vividha-tantra-saṃgraha*, Calcutta, 1877-84; in A. Avalon, *Tāntrik Texts*, XIV, 1928.

For a comparison of the contents of the longer and shorter versions, see *RASB* Catalogue, viii, p. XIX.

KAULOPANIṢAD

Anonymous Tāntrik text in the aphoristic style. In 45 aphorisms, it deals with the following matters.

Knowledge as the only means of liberation, nature of liberation, nature of knowledge, sense-objects and their enjoyer, nature of God, Brahman, five fetters caused by false knowledge, birth, Ātman, duty, non-duty, Śakti, position of Veda in Tāntric *Sādhana*, *Guru*, sense of non-duality in a *Sādhaka*, duties up to *mantra-siddhi* including abstinence from intoxication, secrecy of worship, abjuration of talk with a person of *paśubhāva*, defiance of all opponents of *Kauladharma*.

It teaches (Sūtras 33-35) the devotee to be Śākta at heart, Śaiva in behaviour and Vaiṣṇava in society. It also inculcates (Sūtra 38) tolerance towards the followers of other faiths. Sūtra 40 forbids all *vratas* and *niyamas; niyama* is stated not to be conducive to liberation. The purport of the last two *Sūtras* is that liberation can be attained by looking upon all like one's ownself.

It has a commentary by Bhāskararāya or Bhāsurānandanātha.

Ptd., with above commentary, in *Tāntrik Texts* (A. Avalon), XI, London, 1922.

KRAMADĪPIKĀ

By Keśava Kāśmirin, it is in eight chapters (*Paṭalas*), and deals with the worship of Vaiṣṇava deities. At the outset it is stated to deal with the *Yajñavidhi* (rules of Yajña or worship) of Śārṅgapāṇi (Kṛṣṇa). The last chapter contains rules for bringing others under control.

It has several commentaries, viz. by Govinda Bhaṭṭācārya Vidyāvinoda, Keśava Bhaṭṭa Gosvāmin, Govinda Śarman (son of Jagannātha), Nityaprajña, Bhairava Tripāṭhin, Mādhavācārya, Hari, etc.

Ptd., with commentary of Govindabhaṭṭa, Benares, 1917.

KRIYOḌḌĪŚA-TANTRA

It contains 22 chapters (*paṭalas*). It deals with conventional Tāntric topics, particularly the six acts with emphasis on *Vaśīkaraṇa*. As a means of averting dangers, the worship of the Atharvavedic Kṛtyādevī is prescribed. We meet with another uncommon goddess, Hṛllekhā. Chapter XVI mentions, *inter alia*, the *Sādhanas*, called Bhūtinī, Ādyavibhūṣiṇī, Siṃhinī, Haṃsinī, Naṭī, Ceṭī, Kāmeśvarī, Kumārī, Sundarī, and Yakṣa. Chapter XX deals with *Yantras*, designed to cause different kinds of material welfare, e.g. birth of a son, release from captivity, removal of fear from Ḍākinīs, etc. The last chapter concludes with a poetical description of the deity, called Maṅgalacaṇḍī, an aspect of Durgā, well-known in Bengali *Maṅgala-kāvyas*.

Ed., in 21 chapters, by L.M. Sarma, Bombay, V.S. 1981 (=1924); 3rd rev. ed. by B.P. Misra, 1967.

KUBJIKĀ-MATA-TANTRA

It appears to have derived the title from a Śākta sect in which the worship of the Great Goddess, in her aspect as Kubjikā (the Curved One, according to some, the Hump-backed One by others), prevailed. The work exists in more versions than one. The basic version is stated to contain about 3,500 verses (2,400, according to some).

Its date is controversial; it is, however, regarded as one of the oldest Tantras. A manuscript (*Nepal*, I, p. 54) was copied about 1080 A.D. Some think that a manuscript in Gupta script exists; but others do not think so. That it was regarded as highly authoritative is indicated by the fact that Abhinavagupta (10th-11th cent.) cited it.

The above version consists of 25 chapters. The main topics are set forth below:

Chaps. I, II	: origin of Mālinī, a secret female sequence of letters of the alphabet, appearance of God as the usual male arrangement of letters; hassle between the god and goddess about their relative superiority. Devī's visit to many *Pīṭhas* to establish Her worship.
Chap. VI	: discussion on the most important *Mudrās*; nature of *Śakti*.
Chap. VII onwards	: *mantras* and manifestations of Kubjikā. The principal *mantra*, called *Samaya-mantra*, consisting of 32 syllables, stated to have six limbs, six Dūtīs presiding over them; description of Svacchanda-god of the third Aṅga, his *mantra*.
Chap. X	: connection of above six limbs with Six Ways (*Ṣaḍadhvan*); earliest *Kula* tradition about names of the six sons of Macchanda.
Chaps. XI-XIV	: six *Cakras* within the body.
Chaps. XV-XIX	: detailed treatment of four planes of meditation, viz. *Piṇḍa* (mass), *Pada* (status), *Rūpa* (form), *Rūpātīta* (One beyond form) which are identified respectively with the principal *Pīṭhas*, viz. Oḍḍiyāna, Jālandhara, Pūrṇagiri and Kāmarūpa, and imagined to be in the four centres of the body in *Yoga*.
Chap. XX onwards	: deal with 'continents' and 'holy places' within the body of the advanced *Sādhaka*.

Chaps. XXIII-XXV : insight into the nature of time, Yogic means of the passage of the soul out of the body (*utkrānti*), secret gods of the alphabet, worship of the group of deities, called *Kulāṣṭaka* (eight *Kula* goddesses, viz. Seven Mothers and Mahālakṣmī) around Kubjikā in the centre, eight *Kṣetras* or mystical abodes of the Yogin, etc.

Besides the MS, referred to earlier, there is another noteworthy MS — RASB, No. 4733. A critical edition by J.A. Schoterman is reported to be under preparation (see J. Gonda (ed.), *HIL*, Vol. II, Fasc. 2, p. 53, fn. 83).

KUBJIKĀ-TANTRA

Different from the *Kubjikā-mata-tantra*

Comprising nine chapters, it deals with the common Tāntric matters. Some topics are, however, noteworthy.

Chap. I : describes *Bṛhadyoni* (Supreme Śakti) and the *Pitṛs*. Kṛṣṇa is identified with Kṛṣṇā (Kālī). The significance of the names of *Mahāvidyās* is laid down.

Chaps. IV & V : the importance of *Kumārī-pūjā* has been stressed. Girls of the age from eight to thirteen should be worshipped as *Kulajās*. Those of the age from ten to sixteen should be looked upon as goddesses. Girls of the age from six to nine are believed to give the devotee whatever he wishes.

Chap. VI : describes *Yoni-mudrā*, i.e. the union of *Kuṇḍalinī*, rising from *Mūlādhāra* through *Cakras*, with *Sahasrāra* lotus in the head.

Chap. VII : *Kula* women are of great importance. Such a woman, of any age, even if she is a prostitute, must be saluted.

Chap. VIII : deals, *inter alia*, with *Śava-śadhana*. For this purpose, the corpse of a Brāhmaṇa or Yavana male is to be selected.

[N.B. The term Yavana may denote here the following classes of people: Greek, Ionian, any foreigner, a barbarian, etc. In modern times, it stands for a Muslim or a Christian.]

MS RASB, VII, A. 5806.

KULACŪḌĀMAṆI (TANTRA)

Literally means 'the crest-jewel of *Kula* or *Kulācåra*'. Belonging to the *Nigama* type, in which Devī answers questions by Śiva, it is included among the revealed works which are the chief among those dealing with the worship of Śakti. It is one of the 64 Tantras, mentioned by Lakṣmīdhara in his commentary on the *Saundaryalaharī* (Mysore ed., p. 81) and in *Vāmakeśvarī-mata* (*Kashmir Texts*, 66, p. 17), it appears as No. 53 in the list in the *Nityāṣoḍaśīkārṇava*. According to Sarvānanda (15th century — middle), in his *Sarvollāsa*, it belongs to *Toḍala-tantra* (*RASB*, VIII, A. 6204). That it wielded great authority is proved by reference to it in many Tantras. It refers to *Bhairavī Tantra* which is known mainly from quotations made from it.

The text, as printed, contains 430 stanzas, divided into seven chapters. Chapter one mentions 64 *Kula-sundarīs*, e.g. *Tripurā*, *Kālikā*, etc.; they are stated to be innumerable. There is a list of 64 traditional Tantras. There is, however, divergence between this list and that contained in the aforesaid *Vāmakeśvara Tantra* (see Intro. to *Kulacūḍāmaṇi*). To the inquiry of Bhairava as to why, despite His knowledge of *Kulasundarīs*, doctrines and Tantras, He does not enjoy bliss (*ānanda*), Bhairavī replies that, though the Supreme *Kula*, he cannot do so due to the influence of *Māyā*.

At this juncture, the chapter can be divided into three sections as follows:

1. Verses 16-17 — refer to the primordial state when Devī, as Prakṛti, is hidden in *Cidānanda*; in it, there is neither creation, nor preservation, nor destruction. There are no deities, not even Brahmā, Hari and Śambhu. This state is free from attachment, suffering and liberation. Piety, theism, atheism, *Japa*, *Guru* and *Śiṣya* are all non-existent.
2. Verses 17-24 — in this state, Devī, enveloped in Māyā, becomes eager (*unmukhī*) to create. In ecstasy, due to Her union with the Supreme *Akula*, She becomes *Vikāriṇī*; *Vikāras* or *Tattvas* arise in *Mūlaprakṛti*. In such a state, Brahmā, Hari and Śambhu appear; with them emerge the words and the

elements (*pāncabhūta*) constituting them. With the differentiation of Śiva and Śakti, *Guṇas* (viz. *Sattva, Rajas* and *Tamas*) start operating. Creation takes place and then dissolves.

3. Verses 24-26 — contain the lesson that all scriptures and rituals become unnecessary when Devī is recognised.

(This idea irresistibly reminds one of the following verse of the *Bhagavadgītā*:

yāvānartha udapāne sarvataḥ saṃplutodake/
tāvān sarvasya vedanga brāhmaṇasya vijānataḥ//

To a Brāhmaṇa, who has known the Reality, all the Vedas are as useless as a well when all sides are flooded.)

Devī says that She manifests Herself as a woman (*Śakti*) to know Bhairava who is united with Her. But, even when all is said, Her *Tattva* remains unknown.

The other important topics, dealt with in the work, are:

use of one's wife or any other woman by a *Sādhaka* as his Śakti, indispensability of Śakti for success in *Kulamantras*, maintenance and worship of Śaktis, who may be eight, as eight *Mātṛkās*, nocturnal performance of such rites, worship of creatures and objects sacred for a *Kaula*, *Pīṭhapūjā*, worship of Dakṣiṇakālī for controlling demons and humans, *Vetāla-siddhi* (ability to go anywhere and everywhere by means of *Śava-sādhana*, worship of Durgā, the extirpator of the buffalo-demon, declaration of Śiva-Śakti as ubiquitous and underlying the entire creation.

There is a commentary on it, by Sadāśiva Śukla.

Ptd. *Tāntrik Texts*, IV, London, Calcutta, 1915; 2nd ed., Ganesh and Co., Madras, 1956.

KULA-MŪLĀVATĀRA

Ascribed to Śaṃkara of Bengal.

It is known only from quotations or references in later works. The fact that it is referred to in such authoritative works as the *Tārā-bhakti-sudhārṇava* of Narasiṃha, *Nityotsava-nibandha* of Umānandanātha, *Prāṇatoṣiṇī*, etc. indicates the high esteem in which it was held.

An *Ajapā-japa-krama*, a part of this work, exists (RASB, VIII. B. 6520).

See *C.K. Rājā Pres. Vol.*, p. 370; *Adyar Library Bulletin*, VI, 1942, p. 205.

For details about the references to this work, see *NCC*, IV, p. 239.

KULĀNANDA-TANTRA (or -SAṂHITĀ)

Belonging to the Matsyendranātha school, it contains 60 stanzas dealing with the attainment of *Siddhis* by meditating on the power-centres within the body. The MS, on which Bagchi has based his ed., dates back to the 14th or 15th cent. A.D.

The work is mentioned in the *Āgama-tattva-vilāsa* (q.v.) of Raghunātha Tarkavāgīśa.

Ed. P.C. Bagchi, in the ed. mentioned under *Akulavīra-tantra*.

KULĀRṆAVA-TANTRA (sometimes also called KULĀRṆAVA-RAHASYA)

From the work itself we learn that it belongs to *Ūrdhvāmnāya*, and the present text represents only the fifth *Khaṇḍa* (called *mokṣapāda* or *-vāda*) of the original work, stated to have comprised 1,25,000 stanzas. It should be noted that many of the passages, cited as from the *Kulārṇava* in works like the *Kaulāvalī* of Jñānānanda, are not traceable in the present text — a fact which tends to indicate that it is not the complete form of the work. A further index to its importance and popularity is that at least two dozen portions from it have been found separately in manuscripts. A commentary on the work also exists.

The printed text contains about 2060 verses, divided into 17 chapters (*ullāsas*), and is supposed by P.V. Kane to have been composed before 1000 A.D.

Judging by quotations from it in many works, it seems to have been held in high esteem. It appears to be the foremost Tantra of the *Kaula* sect.

It is not a Tantra of the run-of-the-mill type, as we shall see from a broad resume of its contents.

Chap. I : worldly life is beset with evils resulting from the people. Liberation cannot be attained merely by austerities, external rites and study of many scriptures without realisation. One, desiring the path to liberation, should acquire true knowledge and abjure idle talk. A cause of bondage is egoism the effacement of which leads to liberation.

Chap. II : glorification of *Kuladharma* which prescribes *Yoga* without denying *bhoga*, and which is possible by *Kaula* knowledge attainable by one with a pure mind and controlled senses. The *dharma* is declared to be based on the Veda. The journey through the path of *Kula* is more perilous than walking on a sword-edge, holding on to a tiger's neck and seizing a serpent. A devotee of the *Paśu* type should shun this path. The work sounds a warning that the goal cannot be reached merely by the enjoyment of *Makāras*.

Chap. III : identifies *Parā-prasāda-mantra* with *Haṃsa*, the Cosmic Breath pervading the world. *Ūrdhvāmnāya* can be learnt not by the study of scriptures, but from the masters.

Chap. IV : shows how difficult the path is for a *Kaula* devotee.

Chap. V : usefulness of wine, Brāhmaṇas also are allowed to drink it (verse 90). Arbitrary drinking is condemned.

Verses 107-112 lay down the esoteric significance of the *Makāras* in the following way:

To drink wine means tasting the nectar oozing from the lotus within the head when *Kuṇḍalinī-śakti* is united with the moon in the form of consciousness (*cit*, Śiva) on reaching *Sahasrāra* in *brahmarandhra*.

Eating meat means merging the mind of the devotee in the Supreme Reality after he cuts the animal (i.e. ego) within himself with the sword of knowledge.

The devotee-Yogin becomes a fish-eater when, controlling the senses by his mind, concentrates them on the Self.

Maithuna means the devotee being thoroughly filled with the bliss resulting from the union of the highest *Śakti* with the Self.

The metaphysical significance of *Mudrā* is the Śakti that is roused.

The work teaches how an aspirant can rise from the realm of enjoyment to the exalted state of liberation.

Chap. VI : characteristics of the worshipper, worship, etc.

Chap. VII : eight kinds of Kula-Śakti enumerated, 36 *Śaiva Tattvas*, instead of 24 *Sāṃkhya Tattvas* referred to, v. 96 denounces excessive drinking as *paśu-pāna* (brutal drinking). It is curious that verse 128 recommends drinking till one becomes unconscious. Verse 102 recommends *divyapāna* which probably means the drinking of wine offered to a deity.

Chap. VIII : deals with *Cakras*.

Chap. IX : devoted to *Yoga*, recognises Vedāntic monism. Verse 88 defines a *Kaulika*.

Chap. X : worship on special days.

Chap. XI : rules of *Kulācāra*. Qualifications of *Guru* and *Śiṣya*. The eight bonds, tying a *Paśu* type of man, are: *ghṛṇā* (hatred), *śaṃkā* (apprehension), *bhaya* (fear), *lajjā* (shame), *jugupsā* (aversion), *kula* (family), *śīla* (conduct), *jāti* (caste).

Chap. XVII : gives the meanings of some words like *dīkṣā*, *mudrā*, *yantra*, *madya*, *surā*, *māṃsa*, *guru*, *ācārya*, *deśika*, etc.

Some of the noteworthy features of the work are the following.

Women have been accorded a very honourable position. A woman, though committing faults, should not be beaten even with a flower. One should speak only of her virtues (xi.64-65). Warning against hypocritical *gurus* (imparting *dīkṣā* out of avarice (xiii.128). Of all kinds of devotees, *Kaula* has been declared as the best; he knows the secret of both *Kula* (Supreme Śakti) and *Akula* (Parama Śiva).

According to P.V. Kane, this Tantra was composed before 1000 A.D.

Of several editions, the most well-known is the one in *Tāntrik Texts*, V, Calcutta and London, 1917. For various details about the work, see G. Carlstedt, *Studies in Kulārṇava-tantra*, Upsala, 1974.

For a different text of the same title, in 12 chapters, see C. Chakravarti in *Saṃskṛta Sāhitya Pariṣat Patrikā*, XIV, pp. 269-274, Calcutta and in *ABORI*, XIII, pp. 208-11.

KUMĀRA (KAUMĀRA or BĀLA) -TANTRA

Attributed to Rāvaṇa (obviously the formidable foe of Rāma in the *Rāmāyaṇa*) or to his son (in some works), it contains twelve chapters. It may be characterised as a medico-tāntric work. The work deals with paediatrics. Children's diseases are supposed to be caused by certain evil female spirits for the appeasement of which some rites are prescribed.

The text occurs in Cakrapāṇi's (11th century A.D.) *Cikitsā-sāra-saṃgraha*. A resume of this Tantra is found in Trimalla's *Yogataraṅgiṇī* (ch. LXVII, Bombay ed., 1888).

The *Kumāra-tantra* prescribes herbal remedies of various child-diseases, besides recipes for the general health and growth of children. Among the ailments of children, mentioned in it, are: swelling of the navel, *jvarātisāra* (diarrhoea with fever), ulceration in the mouth, post-teething troubles, excessive thirst, *atisāra* (dysentery), *chardi* (vomiting), hiccup, etc.

This work deals, in extenso, with the symptoms of *Bālagraha* (any demon or unfavourable planet teasing or injuring children). It also prescribes remedies including the recital of incantations and magic formulae. An interesting remedy for fever is fumigation over the body of the child with the smoke of the following burnt things: snake-slough, garlic, ghee, faeces of a cat, goat-hairs, honey and certain herbs including Vaca (*Acarus calamus*).

Ed. (1) Calcutta, 1872; (2) in Grantha script, Madras, 1904; (3) with Hindi comm., Bombay, 1911; (4) with Telugu notes, Madras, 1917; (5) J. Filliozat, *JA*, 1935, CCXXVI, pp. 1-66, with French trs.; (6) J. Filliozat, La Kumāratantra de Rāvaṇa, text with other parallel Indian texts including Tāmil and parallel texts in Tibetan, Chinese, Cambodian and Arabic, and a detailed study, *Cahiers de la Soc. Asiatique*, IV, Paris, 1937. For further information, see *NCC*, IV, p. 203.

KUMĀRĪ-TANTRA

An anonymous Tantra comprising about 300 stanzas divided into nine chapters (*Paṭalas*) the main contents of which are given below:

(i) Glorification of *mantras*;

(ii) Mental worship;

(iii) Diagram, called *Kālikā-yantra*, and external worship;

(iv) Materials for worship of Kālī. Among animals, to be sacrificed, are sheep, buffalo, hare, porcupine, boar, deer; human sacrifice declared best;

(v) *Puraścaraṇa*. Prescribed for *Devīpūjā* is blood of a human being, sheep, buffalo, mouse and cat. *Mantras* are to be recited while looking at a naked *Kaula* wife of another person. Sexual union with a woman indispensable. *Kula-sādhana* is stated to be the best of all *sādhanas*;

(vi) *Kulācāra* is described. Sexual intercourse with any of the following women is recommended: actress, Kāpālika woman, prostitute, washerwoman, barber woman, Brahmin woman, Śūdra woman, cowherdess, a woman of the garland-maker class;

(vii) Places suitable for worship: Kāmarūpa, Pūrṇaśaila, Vindhya, Uḍḍiyāna, Vārāṇasī, Lauhitya (Brahmaputra), Karatoyā (river), Prayāga, Brahmāvarta.

If it is not possible to go to these places, worship can be performed in *latā-gṛha* which may mean creeper-bower or the house of a woman designated as *Latā* (see Glossary) in Tantra, on a sword, trident, bow, knife, chowrie, fan, canopy (i.e. a place under a canopy), flag, a place lighted with lamps and surrounded by beautiful women including prostitutes. Both in this a *Paṭala* vi, worship of goddess is recommended in a cemetery; in this chapter, worship of Kālī in a cemetery is declared to be more effective than worship even in a *Pīṭha* (see Glossary).

(viii) Description of *Kaula Ācāra*.

(ix) Discussion on Kālī. Of all forms of Kālī, *Śmaśāna-Kālī* stated to be the best.

The work appears to have a commentary by Śukla Mathurānātha, and to be quoted, *inter alia*, by Kṛṣṇānanda in

Tantrasāra, by Rāmatoṣaṇa in his *Prāṇatoṣiṇī*, by Raghunātha Tarkavāgīśa in his *Āgama-tattva-vilāsa*.

The text is called Pūrvabhāga in some MSS.

The KT is mentioned as No. 6 in the list of Tantras in the *Āgama-tattva-vilāsa*.

There are at least three other Tantras of this title (see *NCC*, IV, p. 225). One text ptd. in *Śāktapramoda*. Compiled by Devānandasiṃha, 1890, 1893; Veṅkaṭeśvara Press, Bombay, 1932.

LAKṢMĪ-TANTRA

It is an anonymous metrical work in 57 chapters; the 56th one is, however, lost. In the chapter-colophons, it is described as *Pāñcarātra-sāra*. This Tantra, though betraying a *Śākta* overtone, is a must for the study of Tāntric Vaiṣṇavism. Lakṣmī has been represented as Viṣṇu's *Śakti*.

It is supposed by some to date back to sometime between the 9th century and the 11th or 12th.

It deserves notice that the work mentions *Vāmācāra sādhana* in which a woman is required as the partner of a devotee.

Leaving aside the mythical and traditional Tāntric matters, discussed in it, we shall highlight the main contents:

> description of the nature of the six guṇas, viz. *Jñāna, Icchā, Śakti, Bala, Bharaṇa* and *Vīrya* (chap. 2); description of Vāsudeva and other *Vyūhas*, emergence of Mahāmāyā and Mahāvidyā from Mahālakṣmī (4), creation of *Pradhāna, Kala, Hiraṇyagarbha, Mahat, Ahaṃkāra, Pañca-tanmātras, Pañcabhūtas*, senses; also creation of Manu, Mānava, etc. (5); great *Vyūhas* of Nārāyaṇa associated with *Sākti*, Lakṣmī incarnated according to various *quṇas* (8); incarnations of Mahālakṣmī as Mahiṣamardinī, Durgā, etc. (9); nature of the Supreme, determination of stages of *Suṣupti, Svapna, Jāgrat* (10); *Vyūhas* and necessity of their *Avatāras* (11); discussion on goddess's Śaktis like *Tirobhāva* (12); *Lakṣmī-svarūpa-prakāśa* (14); *Karma-sāṃkhya-yoga, Sarva-saṃnyāsa* as means of salvation, *Prakṛti-tattva* (15); assumption, by Śabda Brahman, of the forms of *Nāda, Bindu, Madhyamā* and *Vaikharī* (18); *Varṇotpatti* or description of the letters of the alphabet (19); classification of *mantras* as *Uttama, Madhyama* and *Adhama* (22); discussion on Tārā and *Tārā-mantra* (24); *Antaryāga* (36); summary of *Lakṣmī-tantra* (51); nature of *Parā, Paśyantī*, etc. (57).

Another recension of the work appears to comprise 49 chapters (vide N.N. Bhattacharya, *History of the Tāntric Religion*, p. 48).

Ed., with Hindi commentary of C.L. Gautam, Varanasi, Eng. trs., with notes, by S. Gupta, Leiden, 1972.

MAHĀ-CĪNĀ-CĀRA-TANTRA or KRAMA (also called CĪNĀCĀRA-TANTRA, MAHĀCĪNA-KRAMĀCĀRA, ĀCĀRASĀRA-TANTRA)

It contains five or six (according to some, seven) chapters, and is named *Mahā-cīnā-cāra-sāra-tantra* in the colophon.

It should be noted that chapter 9 of a version of the *Nīla-tantra* is named *Mahā-cīna-krama* which is also the subject-matter of chapter 6 of the *Tārārahasya (vṛttikā)* of Śaṃkara Āgamācārya of Bengal.

The important topics discussed are as follows.

It is stated in chapter ii that Vaśiṣṭha, having gone to Mahācīna, saw young Buddha drunk and surrounded by a thousand girls. Then the sage thought, "What is this done by Viṣṇu incarnated as Buddha? It is unbecoming of Him?" An aerial voice declared that it was *Cīnācāra* befitting a worshipper of Goddess. Thereupon, the Buddha narrated this *Ācāra* the main features of which are: mental worship, worship of women who should not be maligned or beaten, merit accruing from *Śava-sādhana*, worship by a devotee who is naked.

Chap. iii : of wine and woman, as means of devotion, the latter is superior, because she is the abode of all gods. Worship of Devī in *Yoni-pīṭha* (i.e. Kāmākhyā in Assam) best means of pleasing Her. Mode (including some vulgarities) of worship of a woman. Women suitable for worship: *Kāpālika* woman, prostitute, washerwoman, woman of the barber class, woman of cowherd class. Brāhmaṇa woman, Śūdra woman, accomplished woman of any caste. Sexual union with a woman prohibited except at the time of worship. Also condemned is drinking wine except on such an occasion.

Chap. iv : characteristics of good meat, rules about preparation of *Kula*-substance (i.e. *Pañcatattva*).

Chap. v : ethical rules to be followed: avoidance of sight on an ill-dressed woman, non-enjoyment of a woman who is not to be enjoyed, etc. Though generally drinking wine and enjoyment of others' wives are regarded as unethical, yet these practices are allowed for Tāntric worship according to *Cīnācāra*. [Note: China was called Mahācīna in medieval times.]

Ptd. in *Vividha-tantra-saṃgraha* in 5 chaps.

MAHĀNIRVĀṆA-TANTRA

An anonymous Śākta Tantra. Believed by some to have been written by Hariharānandanātha, preceptor of Rājā Rāmmohan Rāy (1772?-1833 A.D.). It is in fourteen chapters (*Ullāsas*) the main contents of which are given below:

I. Liberation, II. Meditation on Brahman, III. Supreme Brahman, IV. Meditation on Supreme Prakṛti, V. *Mantroddhāra*, purification of *Tattvas*, VI. *Śrīcakra*, *Homacakra*, VII. Description of hymns, protective spells and *Kula* principles, VIII. Duties of castes and stages of life, IX. Rules regarding *Kuśaṇḍikā* and ten sacraments, X. *Vṛddhiśrāddha* and other obsequial rites, *Pūrṇābhiṣeka*, XI. Expiation of sin causing harm to one's ownself and others, XII. Secular law, XIII. Matters relating to *Vāstu*, *Grahayāga*, consecration of tanks, etc., temples, gifts and consecration of all gods, XIV. Establishment of *Śiva-liṅgas*, four kinds of *Avadhūtas* (see Glossary).

Some important matters, contained in the work, are as follows:

1) Śakti is the Supreme Prakṛti of Brahman, and, at the same time, is everything from the *Mahattattva* to the atom.

2) *Tattvas* of Sāṃkhya, e.g. Prakṛti, Mahat, etc. and Vedic *mantras* have been incorporated.

3) *Pañcatattvas*, i.e. *Madya*, *Māṃsa*, etc. are allowed only to the circle (*Cakra*) of the initiated (for details, see text vi.1 ff.

4) Warning against abuse of the *Pañcatattvas*. Women should only smell wine. A devotee should enjoy only his own wife, and never that of another. Alternatives to *Pañcatattvas* are prescribed for those who are unable to control their senses, e.g. sweet substances like milk, honey as substitutes for wine.

5) *Kaula* mode of devotion declared best.

6) Ethical principles very much the same as those prescribed in Smṛtis. Besides four castes, a *Sāmānya* caste is recognised; it was supposed to originate from the intermixture of castes. Of four stages of life, only *gārhasthya* (householdership) and *bhaikṣuka* (asceticism) are stated to be suitable in Kali Age.

7) Of the eight forms of marriage, prescribed in *Smṛti*, only *Brāhma* appears to be recognised. Besides, a particular kind of marriage, called *Śaiva Vivāha* (see Glossary), is prescribed for *Śāktas*.

8) It ordains (*Ullāsa* viii) that one's daughter also should be brought up and *educated* carefully.

9) Esoteric assemblies of Tāntric devotees, called *Bhairava-cakra* and *Tattva-cakra*, described in vii.154-176 and vii.203 ff respectively. These have been described in the introduction to this work.

Published by Ādi Brāhma Samāj, Calcutta, 1876; with commentary of H. Bharati and ed. Woodroffe, Madras, 1953 (3rd ed.), with comm. and Bengali trs., M. Bhattacharya, Prose Eng. trs. by M.N. Datta, Calcutta, 1900.

MĀLINĪVIJAYOTTARA TANTRA[1]

From the introductory portion, it appears to be an abridged version of a voluminous work. According to Jayaratha, in his commentary on the *Tantrāloka* (Vol. I, p. 35 of No. xxix of Kashmir Series of Texts, verse 17), the *Mālinīvijayottara* is so called as, owing to the glory of Mālinī (i.e. the series of letters of the alphabet), it occupies a pre-eminent place among the schools of Śaiva Tantra to all of which it is superior. The work, belonging to the Āgama class, is of unknown authorship and date. Abhinavagupta, in his *Tantrāloka*, holds that the *Mālinīvijaya* is the essence of the Trika system (of Kashmir) which itself is the quintessence of the different teachings of the Lord, laid down in different schools of Tantra.

The *Mālinīviyayottara* is in 23 chapters (*Adhikāras*) with a total number of 1,267 verses. The main contents of the work, particularly its distinguishing features, are briefly set forth here.

1. For a detailed account, see S.C. Banerji, *A Brief History of Tantra Literature*, p. 386 ff.

The objects of knowledge are twofold: 1. Acceptable — Śiva, Śakti, Vidyeśa, Mantra, Mantreśvara and *Jīvas*; 2. Avoidable — impurity, actions, *Māyā*, the entire world as the creation of *Māyā*.

In the spheres of both matter and soul, success depends on the correct discrimination between the acceptable and the avoidable.

Śākta is the stage that can be attained by contemplating on the object of meditation along with speech. *Śāmbhava* is the stage that can be attained by deep and penetrating spiritual insight; in it there is absolute absence of concentration on any particular object.

The kinds of inspiration, dealt with in the work, can be explained in the light of the five states, called *jāgrat* (waking), *svapna* (dream), *suṣupti* (deep dreamless slumber), *turya* (*mantramaheśa*) and *turyātīta* (beyond the fourth state: *Śivaśakti*).[2] These five states are synonymous respectively with *Piṇḍastha* = *Sarvatobhadra*, *Padastha* = *Vyāpti*, *Rūpastha* = *Mahāvyāpti*, *Pracaya* = *Rūpātīta* and *Mahāpracaya*.

The transcendental Self has three manifestations, viz. average self, energy and Śiva. These three make the triad of fundamentals forming the principal theme of the *Trika* philosophy of Kashmir.

The usual order of the alphabet, from *A* to *Kṣa*, is called *Pūrvamālinī*, popularly called *Mātṛkā* or *Siddhā*. *Śakti* appears as *Pūrvamālinī* representing the entire gamut of the alphabet. Aghora is urged by Parameśvara to act. In deference to His desire, Aghora vitiates *Māyā* from which proceed the letters of the alphabet; these are the source of knowledge in general.

Śakti has endless forms. Of them, the chief are *Aparā* or *Ghoratarī*, *Parāparā* or *Ghorā* and *Parā* or *Aghorā*. *Aparā* prods *jīvas* in their downward march by causing them to be attached to the objects of sense. *Parāparā* hinders the progress of *jīvas* towards the goal of their life, and attaches them to the mixed fruit of pain and pleasure. *Parā* guides *jīvas* to the attainment of the *summum bonum*, i.e. Śivahood.

Yoga, according to the work, means union of the individual soul and the universal soul. Like *Jñāna* (true knowledge) *Yoga* leads to the attainment of the goal of life. The *Yogin* has to pass through four stages. He is (i) *Saṃprāpta* when he has received initiation through successive teachers, and lives upto it; (ii) *Ghaṭamāna* when he repeatedly restrains his mind, withdraws it from external objects,

2. For details, see M. Kaul's introduction to *Mālinīvijayottara Tantra*, p. xxi.

and concentrates on the truth; (iii) *Siddha* when, by ceaseless effort, he succeeds in disciplining the mind which is concentrated exclusively on the truth; (iv) *Siddhatama* when he is entirely identified with the highest principle, loses his own individuality in utter disregard of the condition in which he is placed. It is in this stage that the *yogin* becomes capable of rescuing humanity, sunk in the morass of depression.

This work, while emphasising the value of the practice of *mudrās*, names the following *mudrās*: (i) Amṛta, (ii) Aṅkuśa, (iii) Avāha, (iv) Cakra, (v) Daṃṣṭrā, (vi) Daṇḍa, (vii) Dravyatā, (viii) Ghaṇṭā, (ix) Hala, (x) Kapāla, (xi) Karālā, (xii) Khageśvarī, (xiii) Khaṭvāṅga, (xiv) Mahāmudrā, (xv) Mahāpreta, (xvi) Mahodayā, (xvii) Nati, (xviii) Padma, (xix) Pāśa, (xx) Rodhā, (xxi) Śakti, (xxii) Sthāpanī, (xxiii) Triśikha-mudgara, (xxiv) Triśūla, (xxv) Vajra, (xxvi) Yogamudrā.

Besides providing for external worship, this work gives details of *antaryāga* (mental worship).

Nirvāṇa means the unity of the *Guru*, *Śiṣya* and the world. The *Guru* will bring the *jīva* of his disciple into his own self. Then, the preceptor will awaken the *Kuṇḍalinī* in him, and cause its ascent penetrating the *Cakras* and resting in *Brahmarandhra*. The disciple, thus united with the Supreme Reality, finds himself free from his bondage to *Māyā*. As a result, he is never reborn, and never becomes a *Paśu*.

There is a *Mālinīvijayottara-vārtika* by Abhinavagupta.

Mālinīvijayottara-tantra, ed. M.S. Kaul, Delhi, 1984.

Mālinīvijayottara-vārtika, ed. M.S. Kaul, 1911.

MANTRAMAHODADHI

A Tāntric work, attributed to Mahīdhara, in twenty-five sections (*Taraṅgas*). It consists of *mantras* of different deities.

Ptd., with elaborate introduction, author's commentary, *Naukā*, Delhi, 1981. Text with Eng. trs., by R.K. Rai, two vols., Trs., with Hindi comm., by S. Chaturvedi, Varanasi, 1981.

MĀTAṄGA-PĀRAMEŚVARĀGAMA

An *Upāgama* of the Pārameśvara, the 26th of the 28 Āgamas of Śaiva Siddhānta school. It is in four sections (*pādas*), viz. *Vidyā*, *Kriyā*, *Yoga* and *Caryā*. Of these, the *Vidyā* section is the longest, containing 1,537 stanzas, divided into 26 chapters (*Paṭalas*) in the printed edition. It has a commentary by Rāmakaṇṭha, son of Nārāyaṇakaṇṭha. The contents of this section are briefly indicated below.

I	Mythical origin of the Śāstra.
II	Uddeśa-prakaraṇa. Matters discussed are: *Karman* as bond, nature of *bhoga*, special feature of *mukti*, propounded in it.
III	Examination of *Tattva, Laya* and *Bhoga*, discussion on *Pati, Śānti, Vidyā, Pratiṣṭhā, Nivṛtti*, etc.
IV, V	*Adhikāra-tattva-prakaraṇa, Śakti-vicāra*. Description of five *Śaktis* of Bhagavat, nature of *Śaktipāta*.
VI	Puṃ-pāśeśvara-prakaraṇa. Refutation of *Śūnyavāda, Nirālambana-vādi-mata*, confirmation of *Satkāryavāda*, determination of *Pāśas*.
VII	Vidyā-tattva-prakaraṇa. *Parā* and *Aparā vidyās*.
VIII	Māyā-tattva-prakaraṇa.
IX	Kalā-tattva-prakaraṇa. Solution of problems about *Māyā*, discussion on *Kalā*.
X	Vidyā-tattva-prakaraṇa. Much the same as VI above, origin of *Vidyā* from *Kalā-tattva*.
XI	Rāga-tattva-prakaraṇa. *Rāga* here means attachment which is the cause of happiness or sorrow, happiness resulting from attainment of *Parameśvara-pada, Karman* as means to cessation of *rāga*.
XII	Kāla-tattva-prakaraṇa. Three kinds of *Kāla*, refutation of Nyāya doctrine, *Kāla* as the driving force, *Kāla anitya* and *asarvagata*, refutation of Maṇḍana Miśra's view.
XIII	Niyati-tattva-prakaraṇa. Refutation of view that *mokṣa* arises from *Śaktipāta* alone, *dīkṣā* etc. are indicators of that; *Niyati-tattva* inferior to *Kāla-tattva*.
XIV	Puṃstattva-prakaraṇa. *Utkaṇṭhā-yoga, Pañca-tattva-yoga*, union of *Prakṛti-Puruṣa* cause of creation.
XV	Avyakta-tattva-prakaraṇa. Nature of *Avyakta* — refutation of Sāṃkhya view that *Vṛttis, Sattva* etc. are *Avyakta*; refutation of *Pāñcarātra* view about eternality of *Avyakta*. *Avyakta* denoted by *Pradhāna*.

XVI	Guṇa-tattva-prakaraṇa.
XVII	Buddhi-tattva-prakaraṇa. Kinds of *dharma, yama, niyama,* nature of *jñāna, vairāgya, ajñāna,* etc.
XVIII	Ahaṃkārādi-saptadaśa-tattva-prakaraṇa, nature of mind.
XIX-XXIII	Discussion on the *Pañca-mahābhūtas* (five gross elements).
XXIV	Adhva-saṃkhyā-prakaraṇa.
XXV	Sakalādhva-saṃharaṇa-prakaraṇa, discussion on *Pralaya.*
XXVI	Bhoga-padārtha-nirūpaṇa. Effect of different kinds of *Karman.*

Ed. Vidyāpāda, with commentary of Rāmakaṇṭha, by N.R. Bhatt, Pondicherry, 1977.

MĀTṚKĀBHEDA-TANTRA

It is available in two forms, one containing 14 chapters and the other 15. The work has some characteristics which distinguish it from Tantras in general. For instance, chapter i lays down alchemical processes of making gold, silver, gems, etc. It also states the process of transforming wine into milk and of rendering wine odourless. Chapter v contains the method of making mercury-ash. Chapter ii deals with genetics; it is stated that a daughter is born if a woman's reproductive element exceeds the quantity of the husband's. If the reproductive fluids of both are of equal quantity, then an eunuch is born. Chapter viii glorifies mercury. In the word *pārada* (mercury), *p* is stated to indicate Viṣṇu, *a* Kālikā, *ra* Śiva and *da* Brahmā. So *pārada* alone is the soul of Brahmā, Viṣṇu and Śiva. Chapter xii describes Tārā, Tripurā, and gives the cause of the insanity or disease of people even after initiation, and prescribes suitable remedies.

According to P.C. Ray, this work originated earlier than the 4th cent. A.D.

It is mentioned in the list of Tantras, contained in *Nityāṣoḍaśīkārṇava* (No. 38) and *Kula-cūḍāmaṇi-tantra* (No. 35 — named as *Mātṛbheda*).

It mentions *Cīna-tantra* (i.7), *Kālī-tantra* (i.7), *Toḍala-tantra* (vii. 60), *Nityā, Vāmakeśvara* and *Gupta-sādhana* Tantras.

Ed., in 15 chapters, by R.M. Chattopadhyay in *Vividha-tantra-saṃgraha*, Calcutta, 1881-86; in 14 chapters and 600 stanzas by C.M. Bhattacharya, Calcutta, 1933; in 15 chaps. by B. Sarma, Prayāg, V.S. 2017 (= A.D. 1960/61). There are other editions, particularly from Bengal. A MS in Jammu is in 19 chaps. (*Paṭalas*) — see *HIL*, ed. J. Gonda, Vol. II, fasc. 2, p. 96, fn. 16.

Eng. trs. by M. Magee.

MĀTṚKĀ-CAKRA-VIVEKA

By Svatantrānandanātha. It has a commentary by Śivānanda.

Pub. in *Sarasvatī-bhavana Series*, Benares, 1934.

MATSYA-SŪKTA

It is in 64 chapters, and attributed in some manuscripts to Halāyudha who was, perhaps, the same person as *Dharmādhyakṣa* (Chief Judge) of King Lakṣmaṇasena (c. 1185-1205 A.D.) of Bengal. In some later works, it is referred to as *Mahātantra*. The word 'matsya' in the title may indicate Matsyendranātha, founder of the *Kaula* school.

The *Ugratārā-kalpa* or *Tārākalpa*, a part of the above work, contains about 650 verses, divided into ten chapters. The final colophon attributes the work to Virūpākṣa (Śiva); it is a guide to the Tārā-worship in its various aspects. The work, however, has a Vaiṣṇava background. It contains an invocation of Kṛṣṇa; Nandavaṭuka enquires of Parāśara about the secret ritual of Tārā.

The *Matsya-sūkta* has been quoted in many works.

The work has not yet been printed. For some MSS, see RASB 5997; Mitra, *Notices*, II.608, describes a MS of about 4000 verses in 26 chaps. This MS is stated to contain chaps. XXXV-LX of the second part; this portion deals mainly with *Aśauca*, *Prāyaścitta* and *Vrata*.

MEGHAMĀLĀ

Declared to be a part of the *Rudra-yāmala-tantra*, it contains, according to MS no. 5875 of Asiatic Soc., Calcutta, 1075 stanzas divided into eleven chapters. Its contents are rather unusual. It deals with prognostications by observing meteorological phenomena like nature of clouds, the influence exercised by them on plants, planetary effects and the cries of crows, etc.

Ptd., Varanasi, 1878; ed. R.V. Sarma, Bombay, 1911.

MERUTANTRA

Of unknown authorship and date.

It exists in a large number of manuscripts, and is stated, in the introduction, to have been narrated by Śiva to gods who found a refuge on Mt. Meru against the onslaught by a demon. The number of *Prakāśas* (chapters) varies as 25, 35 or 50. The number of stanzas is 15,000 according to some, 16,000 according to others. The text is accompanied by a commentary (*Pañjikā*).

It is considered, by some, to be a late work because of the mention of London in it. From the number of its manuscripts and the fact that it is mentioned in the *Siddha-nāgārjuna-kakṣapuṭa* as one of the sources, drawn upon, it seems that the nucleus of the work was not very late.

The work may be characterised as an overview of *Kaula* rituals in respect of *dīkṣā*, *puraścaraṇa*, etc. and an eclectic conglomerate of the traditions of different schools.

Ptd., Venkatesvara Press, Bombay, 1908 (Rep. 1940). List of contents in I.O. Cat., IV, p. 380 f (No. 2570).

MṚGENDRA-TANTRA

This Tantra, as available to the present author, consists of two sections — *Vidyāpāda* and *Yogapāda*. It was compiled at the instance of Hari Singh, King of Kashmir, and published in 1930. References to the frequent use of surgical instruments in operations, as in *Paśu-lakṣaṇa-prakaraṇa* (verse 18) seem to hint at the origin of the Tantra in the age of the *Suśruta-saṃhitā* (early centuries A.D.) or sometime later.

It is a shorter form of the *Kāmika Tantra*. Indra is said to have come across the doctrine of *Kāmikāgama* at a time when he put on the lion (*mṛgendra*)-shaped armour; this explains the significance of the title.

The system of philosophy, contained in it, agrees to the *Pāśupata* system. The *Vidyāpāda* section, in 13 *Paṭalas* (chapters), describes the three main fundamental categories, viz. *Paśu*, *Pāśa* and *Paśupati*. *Paśu* (fettered being) has the limitations which lead him to the lowest position in life. When, as a result of evolution, the individual soul comes to perceive the radical opposition of matter, then it becomes free from its domination never to return to its fold. *Pāśas* (fetters) are of four kinds, viz. *Prāvṛti*, *Īśabala*, *Karma* and *Māyākārya*; the last one is the influence exercised by *Māyā* over the fettered soul. *Paśupati* or

Pati is Śiva who, omniscient and the doer of all, is unaffected by defilements and is known by the five names of Īśāna, Tatpuruṣa, Aghora (or Ghora), Vāmadeva and Sadyojāta. He is ever busy with the five functions, viz. evolution, sustenance, involution, potential preservation and assimilation.

The other section, called *Yogapāda*, discusses the eightfold path (the eight *Yogāṅgas*) of concentrative practice which enables one to acquire various powers.

It is learnt from the text that the Śaivites of yore had to overcome tough opposition in rationalising the worship of Śiva personified.

The work has a commentary by Bhaṭṭa Nārāyaṇa Kaṇṭha.

(*Vidyāpāda-Yogapāda*), with commentary of Bhaṭṭa Nārāyaṇakaṇṭha, ed. M.S. Kaul, 1930; *Mṛgendrāgama* (on *Yoga*), with above commentary and *Dīpikā* of Aghora Śivācārya, ed., with trs. and notes, by H. Hutin, Pondicherry, 1980; *ibid.* (*Kriyāpāda* and *Caryāpāda*), with the above commentary, ed. N.R. Bhatt, Pondicherry, 1962.

MUDRĀ-PRAKĀŚA

By Rāmakiśora, in six chapters and nearly 500 stanzas. Besides some general Tāntric matters, it deals with the *mudrās* of the five well-known principal deities.

Ptd., Varanasi, 1941 V.S. = 1884-85 A.D.

NIḤŚVĀSA-TATTVA-SAṂHITĀ

A Tantra of the *Śaiva Āgama* class. The work consists of five *Sūtras*. Here, *sūtra* is not used in the general sense of aphorism, but to indicate a current of thought. It is stated to have been transmitted by the word of mouth (through which wind or breath passes); this is the significance of the word *niḥśvāsa*. The word *saṃhitā* means collection, the following five *Sūtras* are collected in this work:

1. *Laukika-dharma*, 2. *Mūla-sūtra*, 3. *Uttara-sūtra*, 4. *Naya-sūtra* and 5. *Guhya-sūtra*. Their contents respectively are:

(i) Initiation and the initiated,

(ii) Sacrifice and worship of Śiva,

(iii) *Mukti-maṇḍala*,

(iv) *Mukti-dīkṣā,*

(v) Nature of *Mantras.*

Laukika-dharma comprises four chapters. The main topics discussed are:

Chaps. 1-2	:	merit accruing from the performance of various ceremonies fixed for certain days of the year, bathing of *Śiva-liṅga* ensures the result of many Vedic sacrifices; Brahmā and Viṣṇu got Śiva's favour by worshipping his *Liṅga;* kinds of gifts to Śiva.
Chap. 3	:	holy places and worship on specified dates.
Chap. 4	:	exposition and good result of Vedic *dharma;* brief account of Sāṃkhya and Yoga philosophies, a passage on *Pāśupata-vrata;* description of the pure way.

Mūla-sūtra contains eight chapters dealing, *inter alia,* with initiation to Śaiva esoterism; Śiva's manifestations as Tatpuruṣa, Aghora, Sadyojāta, Vāmadeva and Īśāna.

Uttara-sūtra — in five chapters deal mainly with the following ten *Śaktis* (*Tattvas*) underlying Śiva's manifestations:

Prakṛti, Puruṣa, Niyati, Kāla, Māyā, Vidyā, Īśvara, Sadāśiva, Dehavyāpin and Śakti.

Origin of the letters of the alphabet and Śaiva tradition.

Naya-sūtra (4 chapters): More details of the above *Tattvas* excepting *Śakti* with the corresponding symbols in the forms of letters of which *A* has been regarded as the most important.

Chap. I	:	different fetters (*pāśa*) figure prominently.
Chap. II	:	discussion on the four qualities of *dharma, jñāna, vairāgya* and *aiśvarya.*
Chap. III	:	discussion on five gross elements.
Chap. IV	:	discussion on *Praṇava.*

Guhya-sūtra — 17 chapters. The noteworthy matters discussed are: kinds of *Sādhanas, Siddhi-kṣetras* (holy places conducive to success in devotional pursuit), types of *dīkṣā,* cosmography, discussion on *mantras* — their esoteric elements, mastery of them, particularly the *mantras* relating to the Five Brahmās, the Śaiva form of the Sāvitrī, etc.

The work has some importance for two reasons: one, it mentions (fol. 9b, 42) several holy places and rivers; two, it names a number of Tantras, and describes (fol. 24a, b) the Śaiva Tantras.

The Nepal MS of the work is written in the Gupta script of the 8th century A.D. which, therefore, is the lower terminus of the date of the original text. Some scholars, however, think that the MS was written around 900 A.D.

For further details, see P.C. Bagchi, *Studies in the Tantras*, pp. 3 ff, 92-96; J. Gonda (ed.), *HIL*, vol. II, fasc. 2, pp. 33-36.

NETRATANTRA

An anonymous Tantra of unknown date.

According to M.S. Kaul, it was, perhaps, modelled on the *Svacchanda-tantra*. It deals with the worship of Śiva as Amṛteśvara and Mṛtyujinnātha. The significance of the title is that the *mantra*, peculiar to the deity glorified in the work, is as important among *mantras* as the eyes in the human body. The philosophy relating to the eyes of Śiva is discussed in it. Bhairavī asks Bhairava how His eyes simultaneously perform the contradictory functions of protection and destruction, and how the third eye, usually regarded as watery, could emit fire which reduced Cupid to ashes. In reply, Bhairava says that his real nature is of the triune form of will, wisdom and work. It is also stated that His eyes are the sun, moon and fire.

It is interesting to note that this work mentions Tāntric traditions of three currents — *Dakṣiṇa* (right), *Vāma* (left), and *Siddhānta* (established), associated respectively with Bhairava, Tumburu and Sadāśiva, the three manifestations of Śiva (ix.11 with Kṣemarāja's commentary, ch. xi, xvi.2 etc.).

It contains 22 chapters (*Adhikāras*) which deal with the following topics:

- I Unity of real nature,
- II Mystic statement of *Amṛteśvara-mantra*,
- III Mode of offering sacrifices,
- IV Initiation to the worship of the deity,
- V Anointing ceremony,

VI	Gross form of divine meditation,
VII	Its subtle form,
VIII	Its supreme form,
IX	Some forms of the deity,
X	Attendants of the deity,
XI-XII	Worship according to *Uttarāmnāya* and *Kulāmnāya*.
XIII	Worship open to all humans,
XIV	Superiority of the *mantra* over other Tantras,
XV	Its efficacy in protection,
XVI	Objects which can be attained by the worship of Amṛteśvara,
XVII	Use of *Amṛteśvara-mantra* in amulets for different purposes,
XVIII	Amṛteśvarī and Her worship,
XIX	Purificatory rites for the obsessed,
XX	Yoginīs, their functions,
XXI	*Mantras* — their nature and significance,
XXII	Glorification of *Amṛteśvara-mantra*.

This Tantra has a commentary by Kṣemarāja (11th century A.D.).

The *Amṛteśa-tantra* (MS. of 1200 A.D. in *Nepal Catalogue*, I, p. LVII, 11, 125 f) is the same as the *Netra-tantra*.

Ed. V. Dvivedi, with commentary, Delhi, 1985; J. Das, with Bengali trs., Calcutta, 1388 B.S.; M.S. Kaul, Bombay, I, 1926; II, 1939.

NĪLATANTRA

It appears to exist in a shorter and a longer version, the latter having the title prefixed by *Mahā* (as in MS L 235) or *Bṛhat* (as in the printed ed. of this work). The shorter version seems to have undergone more redactions than one. For example, the MS RASB VIII.A. 5959 is in 17 chapters, MS no. 5950 contains 15 chapters whereas the Calcutta ed. of the *Nīlatantra* contains 22 chapters. One, however, feels inclined to think that the last one represents the longer text although the title does not give any such indication. The problem can be solved only by comparing the Śrīnagar ed. with the Calcutta ed.

The significance of the name of goddess Nīlasarasvatī is puzzling in view of the fact that the general idea about Sarasvatī is that She is all-white (*sarva-śuklā*). The *Tārā-bhakti-sudhārṇava* (Taraṅga I) states: *līlayā vākpradā ceyaṃ tena nīla-sarasvatī* — Nīlasarasvatī is so called as She delivers speech effortlessly. The same line occurs in the *Kubjikā-tantra*. The *Tārā-rahasya* equates this deity with Kālī and Tārā.

For the present, we give an account based on the Calcutta edition. Leaving aside the trite Tāntric topics, dealt with in it, the following features may be noted.

Supreme Ādyāśakti has been conceived as *Nīla* (ch. i). *Gurukrama* is a noteworthy feature (v). Difference in the rules regarding drinking stated to depend on the mental attitude (*Divya, Vīra* or *Paśu*) of the devotee (ix). Eight *kulavṛkṣas* (trees auspicious for the followers of *Kulācāra*?) have been mentioned; these are *Śleṣmāntaka* (Dillenia indica), *Karañja*, (Pangamia glabra), *Nimba* (Azadirachta indica), *Aśvattha* (Ficus religiosa), *Kadamba* (Anthocephalus chinensis), *Bilva* (Aegle marmelos), *Vaṭa* (Ficus bengalensis), *Aśoka* (Saraca asoca) (xi.119). *Mahā-cīna-cāra* has been explained (xiii). Chapter xiv lays down the means of achieving success of *mantras* without *japa* and *puraścaraṇa*. *Amṛtas* are declared to be three, viz. *Praṇava*, *Mātṛkā* and *Devī Hṛllekhā*, in association with which even a fallen *mantra* becomes effective. Chapter xv attaches great importance to *Kumārī-pūjā* in Tāntric rites. *Kumārīs* of different ages are designated in the following way:

One year — *Sandhyā*,
Two years — *Sarasvatī*,
Three years — *Tridhā-mūrti*,
Four years — *Kālikā*,
Five years — *Subhagā*,
Six years — *Umā*,
Seven years — *Mālinī*,
Eight years — *Kubjikā*,
Nine years — *Saṃvarṣā*,
Ten years — *Aparājitā*,
Eleven years — *Rudrāṇī*,
Twelve years — *Bhairavī*,
Thirteen years — *Mahālakṣmī*,
Fourteen years — *Pīṭhanāyikā*,
Fifteen years — *Kṣetrajā*,
Sixteen years — *Tāriṇī*.

It is ordained that a *Kumārī* of any age, before the start of menstruation, may be worshipped. Great result is stated to follow *Kumārī-pūjā*, performed on a dead body. In emphasising the importance of *Kumārī-pūjā*, the author states that she should be given, as *dakṣiṇā*, in gold, silver and/or pearls. Moreover, the devotee concerned should bear the expenses of her marriage. Chapter xvi lays down details about *Śava-sādhana*.

Another noteworthy matter in this chapter is some ethical precepts to be followed by a man in respect of women.

Chapter xix is devoted to *Sādhana* and conduct of the *Vīra* devotees, *Avadhūtas*, suitable flowers for Tāntric worship, drinking, etc. Chapter xx deals with mental worship, kinds of *Āsanas*, kinds of rosaries for *japa*. Among other things, chapter xxi discusses the erotic sentiment and practices, denounces a man with *paśu-bhāva*, practices of *śāktas*, both *Antaryāga* and external worship, eulogy of *japa*. Chapter xxii describes the worship of Ugratārā, extols Nīla Sarasvatī. *Jñāna* (true knowledge) is accorded the highest place; formal rites are to be performed so long as *Jñāna* does not dawn. *Bhakti* is stressed.

This Tantra is important in more respects than one. First, it mentions (xix.2-5; xxi.20-22, 45) several Tantras, thus helping the determination, however tentatively, of the chronological relation of it with the Tantras mentioned. Chapter v divides *gurus* into three broad classes, viz. *Divya*, *Siddha* and *Mānava*. Those of the last class appear to have been human beings (v.67-68). What is striking is that, under this category, some female *gurus* also have been named. Among the animals, whose flesh or meat can be offered to the goddess, are mentioned hare, *godhikā* (a kind of lizard) and porcupine. What is rather unusual is the provision also for *Mahāmāṃsa* or human flesh.

Among the *Pīṭhasthānas*, mentioned in the work, are Devīkoṭṭa (xi.96), Kāmabhūmi (xi.97), Kāmākhyā (xi.86, 97), Kāmarūpa (same as Kāmākhyā? — xi.85, 97), Uḍḍiyāna (xi.96).

The *Śrīvidyārṇava Tantra*, which is believed to have been written after the first half of the eleventh century A.D., refers to the *Nīlatantra*. Of the works, mentioned in the *Nīlatantra*, the *Kulārṇava* is believed to have been composed before 1000 A.D. So, the *Nīlatantra* can, perhaps, be assigned to about the first half of the eleventh century.

Ed. J.L. Das, Calcutta, 1388 B.S. (in Bengali script) with Bengali trs. *Bṛhannīlatantra*, ptd., Srinagar, 1938.

NIRUTTARA-TANTRA

An anonymous text in about 800 stanzas, divided into 15 chapters (*paṭalas*). It is in the form of a catechism, Devī asking questions and Śiva replying. According to some, the title suggests that Śiva's replies are *niścita* (definite) so that no further reply or *uttara* is necessary. According to others, the work is so called as Devī, after Her first inquiry about the basic form (*Prakṛti*) of all Tantras and Mantras, requests Śiva to tell Her of the right way so that she may attain the Supreme (*Niruttara*, than which nothing is greater).

The bare contents of the chapters are as follows.

Chap. I	: Nature of *Siddhavidyās* and meditation on them in the manner of *Divya* and *Vīra Sādhakas*.
Chap. II	: *Mantra* and *Pūja* of Dakṣiṇa Kālī, result of *Pūjā*, *Guru*, *Puraścaraṇa*.
Chap. III	: *Kavaca* and *Stotra* of Dakṣiṇa Kālī.
Chap. IV	: Modes of worship, *Puraścaraṇa*, *Prāṇāyāma*, *Dhāraṇī*, *Dhyāna*, *Samādhi*.
Chap. V	: *Tattva* and *Pūjā* of Rajanīdevī.
Chap. VI	: Means of quick *Siddhi* by *Rajanī-pūjā*.
Chaps. VII-VIII	: *Abhiṣeka*.
Chap. IX	: Description of *Cakras* and *Pūjā* in them.
Chap. X	: Different *Cakras* and rules regarding worship of various Śaktis.
Chap. XI	: *Sādhana* of Yogins, description of female devotees, rules of worship, etc.
Chap. XII	: Procedure of best form of *Puraścaraṇa*.
Chap. XIII	: *Rahasya-pūjā*.
Chap. XIV	: Different kinds of *Veśyās*.
Chap. XV	: Consecration of wine, mention of *Siddhavidyās* and *Mahāvidyās*, their worship.

Some important matters, discussed in the work, may be dealt with now.

The basic form (*Prakṛti*) of all *Siddhavidyās* is Dakṣiṇakālī who should be meditated upon according to *Divya*- or *Vīra-bhāva*. Verse i.9 provides for Kālī-worship in a creeper (*latā*) and for the worship of Nīlasarasvatī in a blue object. A burning ground is suitable for

Dakṣiṇakālī (i.26). It is of two types, *Yoni* (Śakti) and *Liṅga* (Śiva). Dakṣiṇakālī does not give anything without the connexion of these two (i.27-28). The *guru*, who gives instructions about the worship of deities, belonging to *Kālīkula* and *Śrīkula*, is designated as Kulanātha (i.11).

The following are the characteristics of Rajanī Devī:

> devoid of greed, desire, shame; stoical attitude to pleasure and pain, auspicious nature possessed of *Sattva-guṇa*, indifference to worldly life (v.3-4).

Only those Brāhmaṇas, who have undergone *Abhiṣeka*, are allowed to drink wine as a part of *Sādhana*. No *dvija* should drink wine without having *Abhiṣeka* (v.33). One, who becomes intoxicated, is forbidden to drink (v.34). In the absence of wine, a *dvija* is asked to offer cow's milk (v.37). One should drink the residue of wine drunk by a female, called *Śakti*, and eat the remnant of fish, etc. eaten by a *Vīra* devotee who is senior (in Tāntric initiation, not in age) (v.42). The following verse provides that one should drink the residue of wine drunk by one's wife, and condemns that drunk by another person's wife. In *Cakra-pūjā*, one is debarred from sitting in the same seat with even one's own *Śakti*.

A devotee becomes fit for instant success by the acquisition of the knowledge that all men are Śivas and all women Śaktis (vi.4).

A *Vīra-sādhaka* is forbidden to enjoy women (ix.24).

The following five kinds of *Cakras* (ritual sessions) are mentioned (x.7): *Rāja, Mahā, Deva, Vīra* and *Paśu*. Worship in these *Cakras* is ordained for *Sādhakas* of the *Vīra* class as also for *Brahmacārins* and *Gṛhasthas*. Yogins are allowed to worship women in all *Cakras*. The following women are to be worshipped in a *Rājacakra* (x.10): mother, sister, daughter, daughter-in-law, preceptor's wife.

Wines of the *Gauḍī* and *Mādhvī* types are recommended (x.11). X.25 states *gauḍikaṃ phalajam* (produced from fruits). But, Kullūka, under *Manu-smṛti* (xi.94), explains *gauḍī* as *guḍena kṛtā* (prepared with molasses). In the same context, Kullūka explains *Mādhvī* as *madhūka-vṛkṣo madhus-tat-puṣpaiḥ kṛtā*, i.e. produced from the flowers of *Madhūka* (*Madhuka longifolia*).

In a *Mahācakra*, the following women are recommended to be worshipped: mother, sister, daughter-in-law, daughter and wife of a *Vīra Sādhaka*. X.15 and 28 forbid an aspirant to touch such a woman on pain of infernal suffering.

Among the articles, necessary for worship, is mentioned *Kukkuṭodbhava* (literally meaning 'produced from a cock'). Its meaning is not clear. Does it mean cock-meat? It may be noted that, though domestic cock is a taboo, wild cock's meat has been allowed as food in the scriptures. X.25 refers to it as *pakṣi-sambhava* (derived from birds); this seems to support our conjecture. It is interesting to note that even now in Nepal, cock-meat and hen-eggs are offered to Goddess Kālī. The translator of the Calcutta edition of the work (1385 B.S.) explains *Kukkuṭodbhava* as a kind of wine produced from a cock. Among *matsyas* (fish), as one of the *Makāras*, mention is made (x.25) of *Rohita* (*Labea fimbariatus*) and *Sāla* (*Channa striatus*).

For *saṃnyāsins* (those who have renounced the world), instead of the abovementioned five women, *veśyās* (see our observations on chapters XIII and XIV below) of the four castes are recommended. It seems, as an alternative, the following kinds of women are stated (x.32) as corresponding to the aforesaid five kinds of women:

> princess, Caṇḍāla woman, *Kāpālika* woman, daughter of a washerwoman, one's own wife.

According to x.40, in a *Vīracakra*, the best *Sādhaka* may offer any kind of wine, fish, *mudrā* and any kind of *Puṣpa*. In such a *Cakra*, the devotee has to worship one's own wife, and drink the residue of the wine drunk by her; sharing a common seat even with her is prohibited. In a *Paśu-cakra* (x.51), a devotee should worship his step-mother, daughter, sister, daughter-in-law or his own wife, and satisfy them like a *paśu* (animal).

In chapter XI, it is stated that a devotee of the *Vīra* or *Divya* type can be an *Avadhūta* by means of *Abhiṣeka*. It should be noted that Tāntric initiation, to which usually all, irrespective of caste and sex, are entitled, is denied to such women (xi.44).

The worship of Goddess Kāmākhyā has been highly extolled, so much so that no *Śakti-mantra* is stated to be effective without it (xi.48).

It is curious that no *Kālī-mantra* is stated to be effective without a barber woman, no *Tārā-mantra* can be effective without enjoying a Caṇḍāla woman. *Śrīvidyā* cannot be fruitful without sexual union with a Brāhmaṇa woman (xiii.3).

The unique feature of this Tantra is the elaborate classification of *Veśyās*. It is rather peculiar that while, elsewhere, low-born women have been recommended as partners in Tāntric *Sādhana*, xiv.60-61 explicitly prohibit sexual union with such women; even thought about such a woman is forbidden.

The main contents of chapter XIV are briefly as follows. *Viparīta-rati* (apparently meaning sexual intercourse in the reverse order or woman-superior position) is praised for a woman. The real meaning of the above expression, according to some, is *nivṛtti* or restraint on the part of a woman. Cohabitation of a man with a woman other than his own, and of a woman with a man other than her husband are condemned. In *Kulārcana* (a particular Tāntric rite), a woman is allowed to have sex with a person other than her husband. A *Kula* woman should choose her *Guru* as her husband. If, however, such a woman does not do so, then Śiva will be her husband. As the consort of Śiva, she will be

(i) Powerful Kālī — if she is 16 years old,
(ii) Tārā — if 15 years old,
(iii) Ṣoḍaśī — if aged 14,
(iv) Unmukhī — if aged 13,
(v) Bhairavī — if 12 years old.

If she is aged 11, she will be designated as *Brahma-veśyā*, reputed as extremely chaste, and rare in the three worlds.

The following kinds of *Veśyās* are declared to be holy like the places mentioned against them:

Brahma-veśyā — Dvāravatī,
Deva-veśyā — Dvārakā,
Gupta-veśyā — Ayodhyā,
Kula-veśyā — Māyā,
Mahā-veśyā — Mathurā,
Mahodayā — Kālikā,
Rājaveśyā — Kāñcī.

The above *Veśyās* are described as follows:

Brahma-veśyā	A *Deva-veśyā* who is *Kulīna*, i.e. observing the practices prescribed for the *Kaulamārga*.
Deva	A woman who is at first united with the deity in a *Cakra*, and then semen is emitted into her by a person who has done *japa*, kisses again and again her female organ and forehead.

Gupta	Born in the family of a Tāntrik devotee and is devoid of shame, passionate, resorting to a man of *Paśubhāva* as her husband.
Kulā	Born in the family of a householder.
Mahā	*A Kula-veśyā* who becomes naked of her own accord.
Mahodayā	A *Kula-veśyā*, devoted to Tāntrik *sādhana*, becoming the wife of a man of *Vīrabhāva*, and willingly taking to the path of detachment or cessation of desire.
Rāja	Free and independent like a king.

The above are designations of *Veśyās* belonging to the four castes. XIV.8 makes it clear that they are not *Veśyās* in the ordinary sense of prostitutes. They are so called as they wander about like *Veśyās* (*veśyāvat*). A woman, who is chaste and pious and devoted to the worship of Śiva-phallus, is a *Veśyā*. The *Veśyā*, taking to the *Kula* path of devotion, is the giver of liberation. One is ordained to shun, in a *Kula* rite, a *Veśyā* who resorts to many *Vīra-sādhakas*; he should avoid also a *Veśyā* who resorts to a *Sādhaka* of the *Paśu* type. This work categorically condemns a man who has sexual union with an unchaste woman.

Depending on the diversity of their functions, women are differently designated; the designations are not to be taken in their ordinary sense. They are:

Naṭī	A beautiful woman of any of the four castes, who begins to dance at the sight of the articles of worship.
Kāpālikā	A beautiful woman of any of the four castes.
Veśyā	A beautiful woman of any of the four castes, who desires sexual union at the sight of the articles of worship.
Rajakī	A handsome woman of any caste, who, at the sight of the articles for worship, declares that she is in her monthly impurity.
Nāpitaṅganā	Not defined.
Yoginī	A woman in whom Śiva and Śakti are united. According to the translator of the

	Calcutta edition, 1385 B.S., a woman who meditates upon the union of Śiva-Śakti.
Svapacī (*Caṇḍālī*)	A *Kulajā* woman who, at the sight of articles of worship, shuns a *Sādhaka* of *Paśubhāva*, and resorts to one of *Vīrabhāva*.
Śauṇḍī	A beautiful woman of any caste, who questions a worthy *Sādhaka*, indulges in *Viparīta-rati* (see *supra*) with her husband.
Bhūmīndra -tanaya (daughter of a king)	A beautiful woman of any caste, whose *Yantras* for *Pūjā*, etc. are always refined.
Gopinī	A beautiful woman of any caste, who, when a problem arises about a *Sādhaka* of *Paśubhāva*, conceals (a *Vīra-sādhaka*).
Mālikā	A beautiful woman of any caste, about whom a *mantra* is recited at the sight of the articles of worship.

In the absence of Śakti (devotee's own wife), one may choose any one of the above.

This work is No. 59 in the list of Tantras in the *Kulacūḍāmaṇi-tantra*.

Ed. D. Tripathi, with Bengali trs., Calcutta, 1385 B.S.; B. Sarma, Prayag, V.S. 2017 (=A.D. 1960-61).

NIRVĀṆA-TANTRA

Containing a little more than 500 verses in 14 chapters, according to some manuscripts and 18 according to others. It should be noted that it is conspicuous by its absence in the ancient list of Tantras; it is quoted in comparatively later Tāntric works.

The important topics, discussed in it, are:

Parama-guru supposed to reside in the Great Lotus within the head (iii), cosmogony and cosmology (i, iv-vii), liberation of *Sāyujya* type attainable in the regions of *Tapas*, *Mahas*, *Jana*, etc. (ix), disappearance of fear of death on hearing the name of Ādyā Śakti Mahākālī (x), description of the five *Tattvas* of Vaiṣṇavas, viz. *Guru*, *Mantra*, *Varṇa*, *Deva* and *Dhyāna* (xii), Tāntric *Pañcatattva* to be resorted to after controlling the six internal enemies (viz. *Kāma*, *Krodha*, etc.) — xiii, nature and duties of *Avadhūtas*, *Paramahaṃsa*, attainment of liberation by Brāhmaṇas and others by means of *Vīrabhāva* (xiv).

It should be mentioned that, in the beginning, the Supreme Being is stated to be a formless female, and is called Vaikharī who is the same as Kālī. The text refers (chap. iv) to seven *Kula-parvatas* (mountains holy for the *Kaulas*?) which are: Nīlācala, Mandara, Candraśekhara, Himālaya, Suvela, Malaya and Bhasma.

The work is so called perhaps because it mentions (x.49) Kālī as *Nirvāṇadā*.

Ed. N. Smṛtitīrtha, with Bengali trs., Calcutta, 1385 B.S.; G. Kaviraj (Tantra-saṃgraha, II) in 15 chaps.; B. Sarma, Prayag, V.S. 2021 (=1964-65 A.D.), 14 chaps.; Mitra, *Notices*, 3181 (describes a manuscript of 524 stanzas in 18 chaps.).

NITYĀṢOḌAŚĪKĀRṆAVA TANTRA

See *Vāmakeśvara-tantra*.

NITYOTSAVA-TANTRA (or -NIBANDHA)

By Umānandanātha.

In seven chapters (*Ullāsas*) which are named after the seven states of ecstasy, described in the *Kulārṇava-tantra*. It appears to be a supplement to the *Paraśurāma-kalpasūtra* (q.v.) and written in 1745 (according to Gonda, *HIL*, II, p. 151). Though it is like a work on ritualistic procedure, it enjoyed great popularity. It was criticised by Rāmeśvara. It has a *Bhāṣya* probably by Rāmānanda.

Ed. *GOS*, Vol. 23, 1923; 3rd ed., 1948.

PĀNCAMA-VEDA-SĀRA-NIRṆAYA

A huge digest by Haragovinda Rāya, it contains six *Kandas* (Sections) each of which is divided into several sub-sections. The six sections are called respectively *Sṛṣṭi*, *Dīkṣā*, *Karma*, *Jñāna*, *Sādhana* and *Yoga*. It deals mainly with the worship of Dakṣiṇa Kālikā and *Kula* rites. The object of the compiler, as stated by himself in the beginning of the work, is as follows:

tantrāṇyoekāni vicārya....sāraṃ samuddhṛtya,
karotyayaṃ pañcamaveda-sāra nirṇayam//

For details about the work, see C. Chakravarti, *Vaṅgīya Sāhitya Pariṣat Patrikā*, Calcutta, 59, pp. 68-72, and his book *Tantras* etc., p. 70.

PARAMĀNANDA-TANTRA

It appears to be the title of two distinct works, one on Śrīvidyā and the other on Śāktism. The former (MS RASB VIII. A. 5998) is divided into 25 chapters (*ullāsas*) comprising a total of about 3600 verses.

In the first chapter, the special feature of this work has been stated among the different Sundarītantras of the sects, Vaiṣṇava, Śaiva, Saura, Gāṇapatya, Śākta, etc. Chapter II mentions the number of sectarian Tantras as follows:

> Vaiṣṇava — 6000, Śaiva — 10,000, Śākta — 100,000, Gāṇapatya — 1,000, Saura — 2,000, Bhairava Tantras — 7,000, Yakṣa-bhūtādi-sādhana — 2,000.

In addition, there are Tantras classed as *Yāmala, Siddhānta, Arṇava, Rahasya, Tantra, Sūtra, Āgama, Sāra, Upadeśa*, etc.

Tantras are stated to be innumerable.

The Tantras of the following classes are divided into three classes, viz. *Sāttvika, Rājasika* and *Tāmasika*:

> Digambara, Vāmana, Kapāla, Kṣapaṇaka, Aghora, Vāmakeśa, Nagnikā-mata, Kālaka, Vārdhuṣa, Pūrvakaula, Miśraka, Cāmuṇḍa, Śuddhaśākta, Dakṣiṇa, Samaya, Paramata, Avadhūta, Kaulika.

The other noteworthy topics, discussed in the different chapters, are as follows:

> Śrīvidyā-svarūpa, Tripurā-mantropadeśa, Bala-mantra-sādhana, Pūjā-mandira, wine in worship, Sādhaka-dharma, Antarhoma, Kaulamārga, Ajapā-japa, Nyāsas, Anukalpa (substitutes) of Pañca-makāras, good and bad dreams, Yantras.

The 18th century may be tentatively fixed as the lower limit of the date of the work.

The work is professedly an epitome of all Tantras: *sarva-tantra-sārabhūtam* (25/17).

See *NCC*, XI, pp. 180 f.

The second work of the same title is divided into chapters, called *Udrekas*. Its colophon mentions the title of the work as *Pārānanda-tantra*, and states the extent as one and a quarter lakh stanzas.

PARĀTANTRA, PARĀTANTRĀGAMA or (MAHĀ)KARAVĪRA-MAHĀYĀGA

It is represented as a dialogue between Śiva and Devī (Kulasundarī) at the Karavīra funeral place; the latter asking questions to which the former replies. The contents are briefly as follows. It declares that Goddess, cause of the cosmic order, reveals Herself as the five gross elements; Her highest form, however, is Brahman. There is the mention of the six *Āmnāyas*, viz. Eastern, Southern, Western, Northern, Upper and Lower. Their deities respectively are Pūrṇeśvarī, Kubjikā, Kālī, Śrīvidyā and Vajrayoginī. Their *mantras* are also stated. The last three chapters are devoted to Kālī, Guhyakālī being regarded as transcendent. The fourth chapter deals chiefly with the ritual, performed by a a Vīra devotee, along with his Śakti, at night.

Ed. (9 chaps. containing 526 verses) by D.S. Jang Bahādur Rāṇā, Prayag (Allahabad), 2016 V.S. (1959-60 A.D.). The editor takes the six sections of chap. I as separate chapters.

PĀRĀNANDA-SŪTRA

It seems to have been authored by Pārānanda who is mentioned (pp. 72, 91) as one of the *Gurus*. Pārānanda or Pārānandanātha is mentioned also in the *Mahāvidyā-tantra* (Tārākhaṇḍa, 164) and *Nīla-tantra* (v. 67) as a *Guru* of the *Mānavaugha* class.

The highlights of its contents are as follows:

> three ways of devotion, viz. *Dakṣiṇa, Vāma* and *Uttara*, each succeeding being superior to the preceding one — *Dakṣiṇa* declared to be based on the Veda, Smṛti and Purāṇa, *Vāma* on the Veda and *Āgama, Uttara* on the Veda and teachings of the *Guru* who is *jīvanmukta; Vāmācāra* may be *Madhyama* (in which all the *Makāras* are used) or *Uttama* (concerned with one, sexual union and poses of hand or finger); *jīvanmukti* means visualising the deity worshipped; a young woman or courtesan is *Śakti* incarnate; high eulogy of women; drinking beyond the prescribed limit is animality; the *mantra* — *īśvarātman, tava dāso'ham* may be given to or taken from even a Caṇḍāla.

In emphasising the importance of drinking, the author urged a *jīvanmukta* person to drink again and again till he falls on the ground, rises and drinks again; freedom from rebirth is thus ensured; otherwise, a devotee has a fall.

Woodroffe gives the following esoteric interpretation of the above provision:

Being thus awakened, *Kuṇḍalinī* enters *Suṣumnā*, penetrates the *Cakras*, climbs up to *Sahasrāra* where it enjoys communion with the Supreme Lord. Again, it comes down, through the same passage, to *Mūlādhāra*. Nectar flows from such union. The devotee thinks of it, and becomes happy. This is the wine, called *Kulāmṛta* which a spiritually advanced devotee drinks. It is with reference to such a devotee that the work states 'drinking again and again' and 'rebirth does not occur'.

It is noteworthy that the work mentions the following Tāntric teachers:

Amṛtānanda (pp. 54, 73), Unmādānanda (pp. 54, 72, 76), Jñānānanda (pp. 54, 73, 91), Devānanda (p. 44), Pārānanda (pp. 72, 91, the author of the present work), Surānanda (pp. 54, 70, 72).

The following teachers, whose names end in 'bhairava', have been frequently quoted:

Ākāśa-bhairava, Unmatta-, Kāla-. A Bhairava, as an author, is also mentioned (p. 66).

Nyāsa and animal-sacrifice, though generally regarded as indispensable for *Śakti*-worship, are forbidden in an incomplete MS of *Pārānanda-mata* or *Pārānanda-mata-saṃgraha*, published in *JRASB*, 1939, with a brief summary of the contents in English. It is a metrical work, with occasional prose passages, giving clearly the views of the Pārānanda school. Some of its verses occur also in the *Pārānanda-sūtra*. At some places, the language is the same in both the works.

Pub. in *GOS*, vol. 56, 1931.

PARAŚURĀMA-KALPASŪTRA (or KALPASŪTRA or VIDYĀ-KALPASŪTRA or PARAŚURĀMA-SŪTRA)

The title may lead one to think that it belongs to the class of Vedāṅgas (Vedic accessories), called *Kalpasūtra* which originated in pre-Christian times. It is, in fact, a Tantra which, contrary to the usual practice, is composed mainly in the aphoristic style.

The oldest available manuscript (in RASB) is dated 1675 A.D. The work is assigned by some to about 1300 A.D. It has two commentaries, one undated and anonymous and the other, called *Saubhāgyodaya* (Śaka 1753 = 1831 A.D.), by Rāmeśvara.

The work appears to be a compilation of various Tāntric matters, presented in its own special style.

The contents of the work, in the order of its ten sections, are: *Dīkṣā*, *Gaṇanāyaka*, *Śrīkrama*, *Lalitā-krama*, *Śyāmākrama*, *Vārāhī-krama*, *Parā-krama*, *homa* and *Sarva-sādhana-krama*. The total number of *Sūtras* is 336.

Sections xi and xii appear to be later additions containing a number of additional *mantras*.

Though not included in the old lists of Tantras, yet it must be said to its credit that it contains systematic descriptions of the worship of Tripurā.

In x.84, there is mention of another division of the contents into five parts beginning, respectively, with the words *Atha*, *Evam*, *Atha*, *Ittham*, *Atha sveṣṭa*. Thus, each of the divisions is divided into two sections. In x.83, the work is described as *Mahopaniṣad* and *Mahātraipura-siddhānta*. According to Satish Siddhāntabhūṣaṇa, the work is based on the *Tripurā-mahopaniṣad* (vide *Kaula-mārga-rahasya*, p. 242, fn. The work is considered to be important for the philosophy of Tantra (see G. Kaviraja, Pref. to the first ed. of *Tripurā-rahasya*).

Some noteworthy features of the work are stated below.

In the worship of *Śrīvidyā*, according to *Kaulas*, the five *Makāras* are a must (i.12). i.26 declares that proper performance of *homa* leads to the realisation of *Ātman* or knowledge of the attributeless *Cit* (consciousness, i.27); this is liberation.

Rāmeśvara, the commentator, rejects the view that *dīkṣā* makes one fit for worship. He argues, on the authority of the *Tantrāloka* of Abhinavagupta, that *dīkṣā* dispels merely *pauruṣa ajñāna* (human ignorance) but not intellectual ignorance (*bauddha ajñāna*). The latter causes the perception of differences between individual Soul and Supreme Soul; this error can be eradicated by scriptural knowledge. So, *jīvanmukti* is attainable by means of knowledge of scriptures following *dīkṣā* which may be of three kinds, viz. *Śāktī*, *Śāmbhavī* and *Māntrī*.

The worship of Gaṇeśa (section ii), which is a part of the worship of Lalitā or Śrīvidyā, differs from the worship according to Smṛti in that, in the former, animal-sacrifice and use of *Pañcamakāras* are prescribed.

Section v describes *Śrīyantra* or *Śrīcakra*, and provides for the worship of *Navavaraṇas* constituting the above *Yantra*.

In connexion with *Śakti* worship, as a part of Lalitā-worship (v. 21), Rāmeśvara lays down a discussion on *Śakti*. It is noteworthy that the *visarjana* or farewell to the goddess after worship is to be given so that She can reside in the heart of the worshipper.

In section vi, Śyāmā appears to be identical with Mātaṅgī or Mātaṅgeśvarī. She is called *Saṃgīta-mātṛkā* (source of music). Among practices, forbidden for the worshipper of Śyāmā, are: slander of singers, apathy or aversion to the playing of musical instruments like the lute, flute as also vocal music and dance. It is curious that the devotee of Śyāmā is debarred from uttering the word Kālī. *Sūtra* 39 requires a devotee of Lalitā not to think of Vārāhī, not to speak ill of the five *Makāras*, not to chew sugarcanes, not to be rude to women, not to ignore a woman who wants to speak, not to drink for the gratification of the senses.

Section viii provides that the devotee should reflect on the merger of all *Tattvas* into the fire of *Cit*. Another requisite is the meditation on the 36 *Tattvas* in the navel.

An interesting fact is that, in section x, some Vedic *mantras* are included (Sūtra 10); thus, it is not correct to say categorically that Tantras are opposed to the Veda.

Some of the practices, prescribed for a devotee, are: not to cut *kula* trees, friendliness to all creatures, gradual abjuration of hatred, apprehension, fear, shame, disgust, truthfulness, non-attachment to others' wealth and wives, not to entice an indifferent woman by money and the like, salutation of the following: an assemblage of women, one who has attained success in *Sādhana*, a host of virgin girls engaged in sports, mango-tree, *Aśoka* tree, cremation ground, a courtesan intoxicated or in blooming youth, any woman in the prime of youth, etc. Among the prohibited practices are: forcibly enjoying an unwilling woman, deserting a woman who is attached, self-applause, blaming others, exposing others' faults, use of harsh words, ridicule, reproach, abuse, coercion.

Among the kinds of wine recommended are that distilled from rice, produced from molasses, produced from flowers like *Madhūka*. It may be noted that these three kinds of wine are unequivocably prohibited for Brāhmaṇas by Manu (xi.94). On section iii, Rāmeśvara justifies drinking in a Tāntric rite. He, however, adds that it is applicable only for those who are self-controlled.

Ed., with Rāmeśvara's commentary, in GOS, Vol. 22, 1923; 2nd rev. and enlarged ed. by S.Y. Dave, 1950.

PHEṬKĀRIṆĪ-TANTRA

A typical Tantra in 20 chapters, according to some, in 21 according to others. In the edition of G. Kaviraj, the number of stanzas is about 1400. It professes (colophon to chapter VI) affiliation to the *Paścimāmnāya*.

Predominantly a work on magic, it deals mainly with the following topics: invocation to Ugrakālī in Her manifestation as Kṛtyā and mention of the sources, particulars of *mantraśāstra*, six conventional magical acts, *mantras* of *Ucchiṣṭa-caṇḍālinī*, *Dhūmāvatī*, *Ugratārā*, *Ceṭikā*, tenfold *saṃskāras* of *mantras*; chapter XVI (*Lavaṇamantra*) bearing close similarity with chapter XXXIV of the *Prapañcasāra-tantra*.

The Tantra describes some weird rites, e.g. worship in a funeral place with human or animal flesh, cat's fur, menstrual blood, etc.

It prescribes superstitious practices like wearing amulets, casting dry leaves to the wind to be carried by it for driving away the enemy, etc., sacrificing symbols representing an enemy. An interesting practice is to meditate on oneself as representing a fierce deity.

This work appears to have enjoyed great popularity in view of the fact that it is quoted, *inter alia*, by such stalwarts as Kṛṣṇānanda in his *Tantrasāra*, Narasiṃha Ṭhakkura in *Tārā-bhakti-sudhārṇava*, Pūrṇānanda in *Śyāmā-rahasya*, Sarvānanda in *Sarvollāsa*.

Ptd. in *Vividha-tantra-saṃgraha*, Calcutta, 1877-84; *Sulabha-tantra-prakāśa*, Calcutta, 1886.

The latest ed. is by G.N. Kaviraj, in *Tantra-saṃgraha*, Varanasi, 1892 Śaka = 1970 A.D.; Vol. II, pp. 161-306.

PIṄGALĀMATA

It is in 19 sections (*Prakaraṇas*). The main contents of the work, as found in the MS (dated 1174 A.D.), preserved in Nepal Darbār Library (Catalogue, II, pp. 69-70), are:

> explanation of the terms *Āgama*, *Śāstra*, *Jñāna*, *Tantra* etc., reason for communicating Tāntric knowledge to others, definition of *Liṅga*, list of *Ācāryas* fit for worshipping it, general and particular types of worship, materials of *Liṅga*, places suitable for the establishment of a *Liṅga*.

It is included in the *Kalpārtha* subdivision of the *Kriyāsūtra*, mentioned in it as one of the seven classes of Tantra. Describing itself as a Tantra of an extraordinary (*asādhāraṇa*) type, it aims at explaining *abhidhāna* (denomination), *nimitta* (cause), *kartā* (maker), and *parimāṇa* (extent) by which things are conditioned.

It appears to belong to Jayadrathādhikara of *Brahmayāmala-tantra*.

It is quoted, among others, by Kṛṣṇānanda in his *Tantrasāra*.

PĪṬHA-NIRṆAYA or MAHĀPĪṬHA-NIRṆAYA

It claims to be a part of the *Kula-cūḍāmaṇi-tantra* in one MS, or of the *Tantracūḍāmaṇi* in several MSS. In 80 stanzas, it deals with *Piṭhas*. Of the 51 *Pīṭhas*, mentioned in it, those located in Bengal figure very prominently. D.C. Sircar assigns it to a period earlier than 1752 A.D.

For a study, see D.C. Sircar, *Śākta Pīṭhas*, particularly pp. 3 and 23.

For MS, see RASB, VIII. A. 6141.

PRĀṆATOṢIṆĪ (or -TOṢAṆĪ)

It is so called as it was written by Rāmatoṣaṇa Vidyālaṃkāra under the patronage of Prāṇakṛṣṇa Viśvāsa. It is a huge compilation made (1743 Śaka=1821 A.D.) from the following Tantras:

> Muṇḍamālā, Matsyasūkta, Mahiṣamardinī, Māyā, Mātṛkābheda, Mātṛkodaya, Mahānirvāṇa, Mālinīvijaya, Mahānīla, Mahākāla-saṃhitā, Merutantra, Bhairavī, Bhairava, Bhūtaḍāmara, Advaya, Vīrabhadra, Bījacintāmaṇi, Ekajaṭī, Nirvāṇa, Tripurāsāra, Kālīvilāsa, Viśvasāra, Varadā, Vāsudeva-rahasya, Vārāhī, Bṛhad-gautamīya, Varṇoddhṛti, Viśvasāra (appears to be a repetition, see above), Viṣṇuyāmala, Bṛhannīla, Bṛhadyoni, Viṣṇu-rahasya (?), Vāmakeśvara, Brahmajñāna, Brahmayāmala, Adavita, Varṇa, Varṇavilāsa, Pheṭkāriṇī, Puraścaraṇa-candrikā, Puraścaraṇollāsa, Pañcadaśī, Picchilā, Prapañcasāra, Haṃsa-parameśvara, Nava-ratneśvara, Nityā, Nīla, Nārāyaṇīya, Niruttara, Nāradīya, Nāgārjuna, Dakṣiṇāmūrtitantra, Dakṣiṇā-mūrti-saṃhitā, Dattātreya-saṃhitā, Aṣṭāvakra-saṃhitā, Yakṣiṇī, Yoginī, Yoni, Yogasāra, Yogārṇava, Yoginī-hṛdaya, Yogi-yājñavalkya, Yoga-svarodaya, Ākāśabhairava, Rājarājeśvarī, Rādhā, Revatī, Rudrajāmala, Rā (Vā?)mārcana-candrikā, Śavara, Indrajālaka, Kālī, Kāmākhyā,

Kāmadhenu, Śrīkālī-kula-sarvasva, Kumārī, Kṛkalāsa-dīpikā, Kaṅkāla-mālinī, Kālottara, Kubjikā, Kuloḍḍīśa, Kulārṇava, Kulamūlāvatāra, Kalpasūtra, Gaurī, Gandharva, Śrī-gaṇeśa-vimarśinī, Guru, Gautamīya, Gāyatrī, Gavākṣa, Gorakṣa-saṃhitā, Śrīkrama, Jñānārṇava, Jñāna-bhāṣya, Annadākalpa, Utpatti, Uttara, Uḍḍīśa, Yakṣaḍāmara, Sarasvatī, Śāradā, Śaktisaṃgama, Śaktikāgama-sarvasva, Ūrdhvāmnāya, Svarodaya, Svatantra, Sammoha, Cīnācāra, Toḍala, Ṣaḍadv(?)aya-mahāratna, Siddhyaika-vīra-tantra, Nigama-kalpadruma, Latā, Tārārahasya, Śyāmā-rahasya, Skanda-jāmala.

Besides the above, among the sources are also mentioned Purāṇa, Śruti, Smṛti, etc.

The work comprises seven books (*Kāṇḍas*) each of which contains several chapters. The contents are briefly indicated below:

Kāṇḍa	*Name*	*Chapter*	*Subject*
I	Sarga	1	Bīja-svarūpa-śabda-prādurbhāva-rūpākara-kathana
		2	Śabdārtha-svarūpa-brahma-kathana-garbhākṣara-jāta-jagat-kathana
		3	Caturvidha-deha-sṛṣṭi-kathana
		4	Annamaya-koṣātmaka-manuṣya-deha-kathana
		5	Manuṣya-janma-kathana
		6	Varṇotpatti-krama-kathana
		7	Akṣara-lekhanādi-prakāra-kathana; Korako nāma
		8	Varṇābhidhāna-kathana
		9	Āmnāyabheda-rūpa-kesara-kathana
		10	Phala-kathana-rūpa
II	Dharma	1	Saṃskāra-rūpa-granthi-kathana
		2	Guru-śiṣya-prakaraṇa-rūpa-sakha-dvaya-kathana
		3	Guru-śiṣya-vicārā-dya-ṅkurā-ropaṇādi-kathana
		4	Adhivāsa-rūpa-puṣpa-kathana

		5	The heading of the chapter shows it is the fifth, but chapter-colophon shows that it is the sixth. It reads — dīkṣā-rūpa-phala-kathanā-tmaka-ṣaṣṭha-pariccheda
III	Artha	1	Ācāra-saptakādi-guru-paṃkti nirūpaṇānta-rūpa-granthi-kathana
		2	Prātaḥkṛtya-vidhi-rūpa-śākhā-kathana
		3	Snānādi-tilakānta-praśākhā-kathana
		4	Gandhādipātra-sthāpanānta-rūpa-pallava-kathana
		5	Not mentioned. It discusses *Bhūtaśuddhi*, the materials, flowers, *Bel* leaves, for worship, *Liṅga-pūjā*, etc.
IV	Kāmya	1	Granthi-kathana
		2	Śākhā-kathana
		3	Praśākhā-kathana
		4	Kukkoṭocchiṣṭa-caṇḍālinī-dhūmāvatī-kṛtyā-parimala-jayadurgā-gṛdhragaṇa-parivṛta-jvālāmukhī-prayoga-rūpa-pallava-kathana
		5	Durgotsava-prakaraṇa pratipadādi-kṛtya-rūpa-stava-kathana
		6	Durgā-mantra-stuti-nāma-māhātmya-śatanāma-bali-homī-yānukalpa-parimāṇā-tmaka-durgotsava-prakaraṇa-rūpa-puṣpa-kathana
		7	No description. It, however, deals with the rites and observances during the twelve months from Āśvina.
V	Bhakti	1 and 2	mixed up into one. The colophon shows the conclusion of the second chapter which is named *Śākhā-kathana*.
		3	Śiva-prakaraṇa-kathana
		4	Śālagrāma-prakaraṇa-kathana
		5	Viṣṇu-pūjādi-kathana
		6	Mahāvidyādi-kathana

		7	No description. It deals with Kūmārī-pūjā, and eulogises Brāhmaṇas, glorification of Agastya-gayā, pilgrimage, glorification of Kāśī (Vārāṇasī)
VI	Jñāna	1	Pañcāmarādi-mudrā-daśaka-rūpa-granthi-kathana
		2	Svara-jñāna-rūpa-śākhā-kathana
		3	Rājayoga-rūpa-pallava-kathana
		4-6	Appear to be mixed up into one The main topics are: Six *Cakras* within the body, praise of *jñāna*, *ātmatattva*, liberation, *brahmatattva*, various matters relating to *mantra*, rules about daily prayer (*sandhyā*), *puraścaraṇa*, *varṇa-svara-cakra*, discussion on *tithi*, *vāra*, *nakṣatra*, *svara*, etc., *śikṣā-gurūpadeśa*, etc.
		7	Diagrams like *Sarvatobhadra*, etc.
VII	Nirguṇa	1	Paśubhāvādi-nirṇayādi-rūpa-granthi-kathana
		2	Pūrṇābhiṣekādi-kathana
		3	Vīrācāra-pūjādi-ṣaṭkarmānta-karma-kathana
		4-5	Appear to be mixed up into one and no description of contents. Main topics discussed are: Kulācāra, Antaryāga, Madya-prabhedādika-phala, Kula-pūjāṃ vinā pānādau doṣah, Pūjaka-lakṣaṇa, Ānanda-svarūpa, Pañca-tattva, Cakrā-nuṣṭhāna, Kula-śakti, Śakti-praśaṃsā, Ṣodaṣa-prakāra-bandha-lakṣaṇa (16 ways of sexual union), etc.

There appears to be a supplement on drugs as cures of various diseases. In this portion, some magical processes are laid down for achieving certain purposes, e.g. victory in dispute, protection against theft, etc.

Ptd. (latest) by Navabhārata Publishers, Calcutta, 1991 (in Bengali characters).

PRAPAÑCA-SĀRA(-TANTRA)

The title means "the essence of the phenomena or of the diversity of objects".

Attributed to Śaṃkarācārya who is identified, without definite evidence, with the celebrated Advaita philosopher of this name (c. 8th-9th century A.D.). Rāghavabhaṭṭa, the famous commentator (15th century), in his commentary on the *Śāradātilaka* (I.7,12 etc.), refers to the author of this Tantra by using the honorific epithet *Ācārya*. P.V. Kane, in his *History of Dharmaśāstra*, V, pt. 2, p. 1105), holds that the testimony of Rāghava, who flourished centuries after the great Śaṃkarācārya, cannot be accepted without corroborative evidence. The omission of the Buddha in the list of *Avatāras* (*Prapañcasāra*, XX: 59) and the existence of a commentary on the Tantra, by Śaṃkarācārya's disciple, Padmapāda, are pointed out by the pro-Śaṃkarācārya scholars in support of their contention. But, the mention of *mantras* for black magic (XXIII .5), the mention of means (XXXIV.33) of rousing passion in a woman and to draw her near and the use of ungrammatical forms tend to go against the authorship of the renowned philosopher.

The *Prapañca-sāra* contains 36 chapters (*paṭalas*). The highlights of the contents of the important chapters are briefly given below:

Chap. I : Discourse on the creation of the world; *Śabda-brahman* (verses 41 ff); description of the successive stages through which a foetus grows; creatures divided into three classes, viz. *Audbhida* (growing by piercing the ground), *Aṇḍottha* (issuing from eggs) and *Jarāyuja* (born out of uterus).

Chap. II : Functions of the three elements in the body, called *Vāyu* (wind), *Pitta* (bile) and *Kapha* (phlegm), causes of some diseases and their cures, formation of stool and urine; discussion on sound — *Parā*, *Paśyantī*, *Madhyamā* and *Vaikharī* — origin of letters of the alphabet; observations on *Kuṇḍalinī*, *Yantra*, *Oṃkāra*, *Bīja*, etc.

Chap. III : Discussion on *Kalās*, *bhūtas*, etc., images of Viṣṇu, Rudra.

Chap. IV	:	*Bīja Hrīṃ* and its different names.
Chap. V, VI	:	Discussion on initiation, significance of the term *mantra*, *Maṇḍalas*, *Guru*, *Nyāsas*.
Chap. VII	:	Rules relating to the *sādhana* of Goddess of Speech and *Japa* of Her *mantra*.
Chap. VIII	:	Hymn to Sarasvatī (verses 47-60).
Chap. IX	:	Discussion on Tripurā (stated to be so called as She creates the three *Mūrtis*, viz. Brahmā, Viṣṇu and Rudra) and Her worship; role of erotic element in Tāntric *sādhana*.
Chap. X	:	Description and worship of *Mūlaprakṛti*.
Chap. XI	:	Worship of Śrī or Lakṣmī.
Chap. XIV	:	*Durgā-pūjā*.
Chap. XV	:	Worship of sun.
Chap. XVIII	:	*Kṛṣṇa-mantra*; *dhyāna* of Kṛṣṇa as a child in the morning, Mukunda in midday and the invincible one in the evening.
Chap. XIX	:	*Yoga*; eight *Siddhis* the possession of which is declared to make a devotee *jīvanmukta*.
Chap. XX	:	Verse 60 names ten incarnations among which Kṛṣṇa is substituted for the Buddha.
Chap. XXI	:	*Yantras* of the twelve zodiacs; a fire hymn to Viṣṇu.
Chap. XXX	:	Deals in detail with *Gāyatrī-mantra*.
Chap. XXXVI	:	Childlessness — its causes and cure.

An index to its popularity is the existence of over a dozen commentaries of which *Prapañcasāra-vivaraṇa* by Padmapāda has been referred to earlier. This commentary has a gloss, called *Prayoga-krama-dīpikā*.

There is a compendium, called *Prapañca-sāra-saṃgraha* by Gīrvāṇendra Sarasvatī.

Besides being a rich source of information on *mantras* (of *Agni*, *Gaṇeśa*, *Kāma*, *Kṛṣṇa*, *Viṣṇu*, *Rudra*, *Sarasvatī*), it contains occasional flashes of the poetic art. We find in it verses composed in some metres other than the common *Anuṣṭubh*. For example, verses 48-67 of chapter XI are in *Bhujaṅgaprayāta*. There are also stanzas in *Āryā*, *Śārdūlavikrīḍita* and *Vasantatilaka*, etc.

This work has been quoted, *inter alia*, by Kṛṣṇānanda in *Tantrasāra*, Raghunandana in *Āhnika-tattva*.

For application of *mantras* contained in this Tantra, see *Anuṣṭhāna-dīpikā* or *Prapañcasārokta-mantra-anuṣṭhāna-paddhati*, NCC, I, Rev. ed., p. 214b.

Ed. (1) T.N. Vidyaratna, Calcutta, London, 1914 (*Tāntrik Texts*, 3) with introduction by A. Avalon. (2) A. Sarasvati, with commentary of Padmapāda and intro. by Avalon, Delhi, 1981.

There are other eds. also.

Regarding the authorship of the philosopher, Śaṃkara, see A.B. Ghosh, *Cultural Heritage of India*, IV, 1956.

On commentaries, see C. Chakravarti, *Tantras*, etc., p. 65 and NCC, XIII, pp. 3-5.

RĀDHĀ-TANTRA

An anonymous work of unknown date and provenance. The fact that most of its MSS are written in Bengali characters, and available in Bengal seems to point to Bengal as its place of origin. The number of chapters varies from 32 to 37. According to the chapter-colophons, it is called *Vāsudeva-rahasya*.

The work narrates the story of Kṛṣṇa and Rādhā. It lays down the *mantras* and the rites in a Śākta mould. Vāsudeva Kṛṣṇa worships Tripurā who addresses him as son, and confers Her grace on Him. In chapter XVIII, Kṛṣṇa has been represented as an incarnation of the Supreme Prakṛti. She initiates Him to *Kulācāra* which is to be followed by Kṛṣṇa, accompanied by Padminī, i.e. Rādhā who has been represented as one of Her own manifestations.

The work appears to be an attempt at a fusion of Vaiṣṇavism and Śāktism.

Among several editions, the latest is that by Puri Dasa, Calcutta, 1954, as informed by S.C. Mukherji in his *A Study of Vaiṣṇavism*, etc., p. 195. Of the earlier editions, the latest one appears to be by K.P. Vidyaratna, Calcutta, 1313 B.S. = 1906 A.D.

RAHASYA-PŪJĀ-PADDHATI

By Jñānendranātha or Jñānānanda Tīrthanātha.

As the title indicates, it deals with *Rahasya-pūjā* which means worship with *Pañcamakāras*. A noteworthy topic of discussion is *Cakrānuṣṭhāna* (see *Bhairavī-cakra* and *Tattva-cakra* in Glossary).

RASĀRṆAVA

A standard work and the most well known among the Tantras dealing with alchemy. Containing over 2,300 stanzas, divided into 18 chapters (*Paṭalas*), it deals partly with conventional Tāntric topics, but mostly with matters relating to chemistry and alchemy. It is attributed to Nāgārjuna who is much later than the famous Buddhist philosopher (c. 2nd century A.D.); this Nāgārjuna is believed by some to have flourished about the 12th century A.D.

The highlights of its contents are:

methods of processing mercury for different uses, preservation of metals, their killing, colouring, test of purity, etc., distillation of alum, eight *Mahārasas* or great chemical substances, etc. The following six metals are mentioned in it: gold, silver, copper, iron, tin and lead.

Ed. P.C. Roy and H. Kaviratna, Calcutta, 1910 (Bib. Ind.).

RUDRAYĀMALA (UTTARATANTRA)

It is an anonymous metrical work in 66 *Paṭalas* (chapters); additional 27 chapters are found in some manuscripts. The sub-title *Uttara-tantra* obviously implies that a *Pūrva-tantra* also existed; it is not available now. It should be noted that the additional portion is found in some of the Bengali manuscripts, as observed in the Preface to the Vārāṇasī edition of 1986.

This huge work, besides dealing with the usual Tāntric topics, some of which have been discussed in a more detailed manner, treats of some matters not generally occurring in Tantras. Some of the important common Tāntric topics are *Kaulācāra* (chapter 2), *Kumārī-pūjā* (6-10), *Ṣaṭ-cakra-bheda* (19), science of the movement of *Kuṇḍalinī* (60), *Manasā-pūjā* (26), method of controlling sense-organs, etc. Among the uncommon topics are details about *Yoga* and *Yogāṅgas* (17, 22, 23, 24, 25, 26, 27, 32, 43, 46 etc.), elements of *Haṭhayoga*, e.g. *Dhauti*, *Neti*, etc. (34, 35, 54), *Pañca-śava-vidhāna* (51, 55), matters relating to Rākiṇī (41, 42), Lākinī (45, 50, 52), Śākinī (61, 62), Kākinī (58, 59, 64, 65), *Mahācīnācāra* (17), matters relating to the worship, etc. of Kṛṣṇa (37, 38, 39, 42), Vedas and the sacrificer (15), glory of *Atharvaveda* (17), worship of the Lord of *Vārāṇasī-pīṭha*, *Vārāṇasī-pañcapīṭha*, etc.

Ptd. with Hindi comm., Bombay, 1983. *Uttara-tantra*, ed. R.K. Rai, Varanasi, 1986.

ŚAIVA-KALPADRUMA

Attributed to Lakṣmīdhara, it contains about 3,300 stanzas, divided into eight chapters (*Kāṇḍas*).

The title is self-explanatory.

See RASB Cat., p. 623 f; G. Kaviraj, T. Sāh., p. 643; C. Chakravarti, *Tantras* etc., p. 72 f; P.K. Gode, *Lit. History*, I, p. 475.

ŚĀKTAKRAMA or TANTRACŪḌĀMAṆI (c. 1571 A.D.)

By Pūrṇānanda Giri. In seven chapters (*aṃśas*) it deals, in the metrical form, with Śākta practices. It contains 1500-1700 stanzas. The main topics, chapterwise, are:

I. Daily worship, II. The three *bhāvas* or mental dispositions, III. *Kumārī-pūjā*, IV. Equanimity, V. *Kāmakalā*, VI. Ideal condition of Nirvikalpa, VII. Six acts.

RASB, VIII. A. 6197-99; Baroda II. 10624.

ŚĀKTĀNANDA-TARAṄGIṆĪ

By Brahmānanda Giri, it consists of eighteen chapters (*Ullāsas*).

The main topics of the chapters are given below:

I : Condition of foetus in the womb; *avidyā* (nescience); cause of liberation is meditation on Mahāmāyā in the form of *Vidyā* or True knowledge; body a microcosm; condition after death.

II : Dīkṣā, Guru, Śiṣya.

III : Saguṇa and Nirguṇa Brahman, merit of *dhyāna* which leads to *bhukti* (enjoyment) and *mukti*.

IV : Daily duties of a Tāntric devotee, role of *guru*, description of *Cakras* within the body.

V : Sitting postures and their effects.

VI : Antaryāga.

VII : Worship of Śakti — procedure of.

VIII : Rosaries for *japa*.

IX : Japa, mantras, beads for rosaries.

X : Different kinds of mantras in respect of different deities.

XI : Mukha-śodhana mantras for different deities.

XII-XIII : Puraścaraṇa.

XIV : Substances prescribed for different kinds of offerings to gods; flowers permitted and prohibited for worship of different deities.

XV : Kulācāra and offerings to jackals, Japa as a means of expiating sins.

XVI : Persons association with whom is prohibited.

XVII : Rules for construction of maṇḍapa and kuṇḍa.

XVIII : Rules regarding Kuśaṇḍikā and *Homa*.

Ed. P. Sastri, with Bengali trs., 1349 B.S.; R. Chattopadhyay in *Vividha-tantra-saṃgraha*, Calcutta, 1881-86.

ŚĀKTA-PRAMODA

Attributed to Rājā Devānanda Siṃha of Muzaffarpur, it deals, in 17 chapters (*Tantras*), with the worship of the ten Mahāvidyās, Śiva, Viṣṇu and some other deities. At least two reprints (1893, 1973) of the *editio princeps* indicate its popularity.

First ptd., Bombay, V.S. 1947 = 1890 A.D.

ŚAKTI-MĪMĀṂSĀ

Also called *Gauḍapāda-sūtra* or *Śrīvidyāratna-sūtra*, attributed to Gauḍapāda. In 101 *sūtras*, this Śāktāgama lays down the mystic significance of the letters of *Śrīvidyā-mantra*, the deities represented by them, and the cardinal principles of Śāktism.

Ptd. Sarasvatī-bhavana Texts, No. 11, Benares, 1924.

ŚAKTI-SAṂGAMA-TANTRA

One of the most popular and comprehensive Śākta Tantras. From the text (1, 1.9 f) we learn that the entire work was formerly known as *Tantrarāja*.

The extant work is in four *Khaṇḍas* (Sections), viz. Kālī-khaṇḍa (20 chaps. with a total of 1860 stanzas), Tārākhaṇḍa (71 chaps. comprising 3,409 stanzas), Sundarīkhaṇḍa (21 chaps.) and Chinnamastā-khaṇḍa (10 chaps. and nearly 1582 verses). The number of chapters varies in different MSS. It is assigned by some between 1555 and 1607 A.D., by others between 1530 and 1700 A.D.

Leaving aside the topics, commonly dealt with in Tantra, the following are the noteworthy matters, discussed in it.

Kālī-khaṇḍa: The object of the work is stated as the eradication of heretical faiths, particularly Buddhism, preservation of the sect concerned and of Brāhmaṇism as well as the inculcation of *Mantra-siddhi*. Theory of evolution. *Trailokyākarṣaṇī mantra* (incantation capable of attracting the three worlds). iii.32 explains the term *Kula* as denoting the multitude of the worshippers of Kālī.

Tārā-khaṇḍa: In 36.18-20, *Kulācāra* is taken to mean worship with *Pañca-tattvas*. Verses 24-26 of the same chapter declare that the Veda, Śāstras and Purāṇas are exposed like courtesans. It is ordained that Tāntric *mantra* should be carefully kept secret as the wife of a family is kept in seclusion. The gods bestow favour; otherwise one is destroyed. Different kinds of *yoga* are stated.

Symbolic interpretations of some *Makāras*; *Mudrā* has several meanings — mixture of jaggery and ginger, or of salt and oil-cake or of garlic and tamarind fruit or of wheat and *Māṣa* beans. *Śaktyālāpa* (*Kuṇḍalinī-kūjana*?) is the fifth kind of *Mudrā*.

Madya means the experience (*rasa*) of Śakti when effort is made to rouse *Kuṇḍalinī*.

Maithuna is the union of *Kuṇḍalinī* with the deity in the thousand-petalled lotus within the head.

Both the *Kālī* (iii.142-144) and *Tārā* (xiii.43.50) *Khaṇḍas* eulogise women in eloquent terms. The latter declares *striyo devāḥ striyaḥ prāṇāḥ striya eva hi bhūṣaṇam*.

Sundarī-khaṇḍa: The oldest section, according to some. Chiefly deals with the rituals relating to *Śrīcakra*. It also lays down the effects of the worship of different deities. There is discussion on *Nityās*.

Chinnamastā-khaṇḍa: Also called *Sammoha* or *Sammohana Tantra*. It is mentioned, under *Sammoha Tantra* in a Sanskrit inscription of Cambodia, dating back to 802 A.D. The important topics, discussed in it, are as follows.

Chapter I: The following traditions of *mantras* are mentioned: Kubjikā, Mahākhila-deveśī, Pratyaṅgiras, Saṃkarṣaṇī, Siddhakālī, Śeṣamantra, Śeṣikā, Śrīmat-siddha-karālikā, Sundarī.

In accordance with the above nine, Guhyakālī is stated to have nine faces.

Chapter III: Mentions the following nine *Pīṭhas*; the word *Pīṭha* is used not in its ordinary sense, but to mean modes of Tāntric practices: Bauddha, Cāndra, Cīna, Gaṇeśa, Śaiva, Śākta, Svāyambhuva, Vaidika, Vidyā.

Chapter V: *Kādi-mata* stated to be in vogue in specified regions, e.g. Ābhīra, Aṅga, etc. (56).

Hādi-mata is stated to prevail in 56 regions; e.g. Andhraka, Cola, Gandhāra, etc.

Each of the above two schools is stated to have nine divisions which are not named.

Again Tāntric tradition is stated to be four according to the geographical divisions of East, West, South and North. The four principal sects, according to this division, are *Gauḍa, Kāśmīra, Kerala* and *Vilāsa*. The *Gauḍa* sect appears to have been from Śilahaṭṭa to Saindhava, *Kāśmīra* from Madra to Nepāla, *Kerala* from Aṅga to Mālava and *Vilāsa* in all countries.

In another way, Tāntric sects are divided into three classes, viz. *Divya, Kaula* and *Vāma*. Each of these is subdivided as *Hārda* (inner) and *Bāhya* (outer).

The number of Tantras, prevailing in different regions, is mentioned below:

Cīna	: 100 principal and 7 subsidiary Tantras;
Drāviḍa	: 20 principal and 25 subsidiary Tantras; the Jainas have 18 principal and 20 subsidiary ones;
Kerala	: 60 principal, 500 subsidiary;
Kāśmīra	: 100 principal, 10 subsidiary;
Gauḍa	: 27 principal, 16 subsidiary.

There is a sixfold division of *Āmnāyas*, as stated earlier.

Chapter VI: Contains names of the kinds of literature belonging to the sects, called *Śaiva, Vaiṣṇava, Saura* and *Gāṇapatya*.

Chapter VII: Mentions Tāntric *Sādhana*, divided into six kinds from various points of view; under each, mention is made of the *Vidyās* in the above six *Āmnāyas*.

Some other interesting topics, discussed in this work, are: the origin of ten *Mahāvidyās*, *Śaṃkarite Daśanāmī* tradition, identification of Kṛṣṇa and Rāma with Lalitā and Śiva respectively.

Ed. B. Bhattacharya — *Kālīkhaṇḍa*, GOS, 61, Baroda, 1932; *Tārākhaṇḍa*, GOS, 91, 1941; *Sundarī-khaṇḍa*, GOS, 104, 1947; Ed. V.V. Dvivedi — *Chinnamastā-khaṇḍa*, GOS, 166, 1979.

See *Poona Orientalist*, XXI, pp. 47-49; P.C. Bagchi, *Studies in the Tantras*, I, Calcutta, 1939.

ŚAKTISŪTRA

Also called *Śāktasūtra* or *Agastya-sūtra*.

It contains 113 sūtras and commentary on nineteen of them.

"It contains a series of 113 pronouncements on Śākta doctrine, modelled after the *Śivasūtras*" — *A Hist. of Indian Literature*, ed. J. Gonda, II, p. 166. For the different titles, see *NCC*, I (Rev.), p. 27.

See *Adyar Library Bulletin*, I.iii, p. 95; *Sarasvatī Bhavana Studies*, X, pp. 182-187.

SAMMOHA TANTRA

See under *Śakti-saṃgama Tantra*.

SĀMRĀJYA-LAKṢMĪ-PĪṬHIKĀ

In connexion with the *Ākāśa-bhairava-kalpa*, we have seen that the *S-la-pīṭhikā* forms a part of that work. This is confirmed by the chapter-colophons of the MSS of the above title. This work, of unknown authorship and date, contains 139 chapters.

Its special feature is that, besides dealing with the conventional Tāntric topics, it contains considerable material about *Rājadharma*, as hinted at by the word *Sāmrājya* in the title. It deals with following topics:

> forts and the capital city (31-45), coronation (46-61), elements of the state (63), royal duties (65, 70-81, 100-105), battle (137-138), etc.

There is much information about chariot-making, elephant-lore, horse-lore, infantry, archery, various kinds of arrows, etc.

It is noteworthy that the work reveals some departures from the information about forts, contained in the *Manu-smṛti* (vii.70) and the *Arthaśāstra* (ii.3). In it, *giridurga* has been divided into eight classes.

There are some personal copies of it, inscribed with the names of a few Marāṭhā kings of Tanjore, in the Sarasvatī Mahal Library of that place; it seems that it served as a useful manual for the rulers.

SARVĀNANDA-TARAṄGIṆĪ

Attributed to Śivānanda, it, in about 325 stanzas, gives a biographical account of the life of the author's father, Sarvānanda (q.v.).

Ed., with Bengali trs., by A.B. Tarkatirtha, Calcutta, 1932.

SARVOLLĀSA

By Sarvānanda.

It deals mainly with Tāntric *Sādhana*, particularly *Vīrasādhana*. In it, verses are compiled from different Tantras. From the portion on *Ullāsa-nirṇaya* (determination of topics in different chapters), it appears to contain 64 chapters. But, in the extant MSS, 63 chapters are available. According to a tradition, chapter 64 contained the *mantra* by which the compiler attained *Siddhi*; that was why he kept it a close secret, and took it away while renouncing the world.

The main topics, discussed in it, are Creation, *Bhāva* (mental attitudes of devotees), *Kumārī-pūjā*, *Vaiṣṇava Ācāra*, characteristics of *Sādhanas*, *Śaiva Ācāra*, substitutes of *Pañca-makāra*, *Yantra*, *Śākta Ācāra*, *Sādhakacakra*, *Śrīcakra*, *Bāhya Pūjā*, *Abhiṣeka*, *Dakṣiṇācāra*, *Vāmācāra*, *Kula-lakṣaṇa*, *Siddhāntācāra*, *Divyācāra*, *Kulācāra*, *Brahma-jñāna*.

Ed. G. Kaviraj; R.M. Chakravarti and D.C. Bhattacharya, Comilla (now in Bangladesh), 1941.

ŚATA-RATNA-SAṂGRAHA

By Umāpati Śivācārya who probably flourished towards the end of the 13th century and the earlier half of the 14th. A Śaivite writer, he belonged to the families of Dīkṣita priests of the Naṭarāja temple at Chidambaram, and was one of the four Śaiva Santānācāryas. He lived in Kottaṅguḍi on the outskirts of Chidambaram. His traditional biography occurs in two texts, called *Pārthavana-māhātmya* and *Rājendrapura-māhātmya*, both about the above place and printed in the beginning of Grantha script edition of Umāpati's *Pauṣkara-bhāṣya*. Umāpati is known to have authored 13 works on Śaivism, 11 in Tāmil and 2 in Sanskrit.

The *Śata-ratna-saṃgraha*, an epitome of the Śaiva Āgamas, with the commentary, *Ullekh(inī)*, was written by Umāpati. Its main contents are concerned with Śaiva philosophy, ethics and religion. The following lines from the Introduction (p. 1) of the text clearly bring out the nature of the work:

It "attempts to harmonise the different ideals of self-realisation and to restrain their extravagance. Intellectual apprehension of the *Tattvas*, strenuous self-sacrifice, unflinching devotion to Śāstras and their teachings, ceremonial observances, rituals and Yaugic practices all regarded as effective methods of approach to Śiva (Supreme Self)."

According to the author, liberation cannot be attained merely by philosophising. The truth of the following *Mahāvākyas* has also to be realised:

Prajñānamānandaṃ brahma (Brahman is perfect knowledge and bliss).

Ahaṃ brahmāsmi (I am Brahman),

Tat tvamasi (That thou art),

Ayamātmā brahma (This self is Brahman).

Ed. A. Avalon, *Tāntrik Texts*, XXII, Calcutta, 1944.

ṢAṬ-KARMA-DĪPIKĀ

Variously called *Kṛtyā-pallava-dīpikā*, *Kṛtyānupada-dīpikā*, *Śāntikalpa-pradīpikā*, etc., it is ascribed to Kṛṣṇa Vidyāvāgīśa Bhaṭṭācārya (*NCC*, IV, p. 358). The author or compiler is identified, not on definite evidence, with Kṛṣṇānanda Āgamavāgīśa Bhaṭṭacārya, the most well-known Tantra-writer of Bengal.

As the title suggests, it deals with the conventional six Tāntric acts. It appears to be a compilation of passages from some sources. For instance, the first chapter has many verses in common with the 23rd chapter of the *Śāradātilaka*.

Ptd., with Bengali trs., along with *Dattātreya-tantra*, Calcutta, 1885.

Ed. J. Vidyasagara's sons, in *Indrajāla-vidyā-saṃgraha*, Calcutta, 1915.

ṢAṬKARMOLLĀSA

By Pūrṇānanda Giri. Besides the six well-known magic rites of Tantra, it deals with *āsana* and *kuṇḍa* (receptacle of sacrificial fire).

Hpr. IV. 308.

SĀTVATA-TANTRA

Not to be confused with the *Sātvata-saṃhitā*.

It is a Vaiṣṇava work in the form of a dialogue between Śiva and Nārada, the former's reply to the latter's enquiry about the incarnations of Kṛṣṇa. Also called *Tantra-bhāgavata*, it comprises nine chapters (*paṭalas*) the contents of which are briefly stated in the work itself.

I : Creation of the universe.

II : Incarnations of Viṣṇu.

III : Division of incarnations as *Sampūrṇa*, *Aṃśa* and *Kalā*.

IV : Kinds of devotion; characteristics of different kinds of devotees.

V : Release from rebirth by service of Viṣṇu in ways suitable in different Ages.

VI : Thousand names of Kṛṣṇa.

VII : Glory of Viṣṇu-nāma; offences relating to the service of Viṣṇu and the recitation of His name; offences committed by Vaiṣṇavas and means of redemption.

VIII : Secret of devotion, the essence of all.

IX : Cause of the origin of Tantra.

Some important matters, discussed in the work, are the following.

Viṣṇu has three forms, called *Puruṣas*; the first creates *Mahat*, the second remains in the water in the midst of *Brahmāṇḍa* and the third exists as the inmost thing among all creatures. The knowledge of the third one leads to liberation.

The *aṃśāvatāras* of Brahmā, Viṣṇu and Rudra have been enumerated. Hari's *Līlāvatāras* are loved by people.

How can Kṛṣṇa, who is Brahman devoid of attributes, be divided as *Aṃśa* and *Kalā*? The reply is that owing to their difference in knowledge and capacity, people describe such divisions as *Pūrṇa*, *Aṃśa*, *Aṃśāṃśa* and *Kalā*.

Bhakti is of three kinds, viz. *Jñānamayī* (when the mind is incessantly attached to Hari; it is superior to *mokṣa*), *Bhāgavatī* (when all the senses are firmly attached to Viṣṇu) and *Premamayī* (resulting from listening to *Hari-līlā* from good people).

Bhakti is rooted in the refuge in Kṛṣṇa. Sincere quest of such a refuge, in body, mind and speech, is called *Śaraṇāgati*. It is of three types: the first protecting *dharma*, *tīrtha* and gods from sin, etc.; the second consists in diverting one's attachment from wife, son, friend, money, house, cattle, etc. to Kṛṣṇa. The third and highest form of *Śaraṇāgati* is that in which the mind, identifying the body with the self, becomes attached to Kṛṣṇa. *Śaraṇāgati* is further divided into six types, viz. resolve to have things favourable to *Bhakti*, avoidance of what is unfavourable to *Bhakti*, unshaken faith in Kṛṣṇa as the protector, acceptance of Him as Lord, self-surrender and telling Him of distress.

Hindrance to *Bhakti*: possession of material things in excess of what is necessary for leading one's life. Causes of destruction of *Bhakti*: violence to creatures, pride, hatred towards the pious, especially the *guru*.

Bhaktas are divided into three categories, viz.

(1) *Nirguṇa* : having pure mind, devoid of pride and attachment, abiding by the Śāstra, friendliness to all creatures, non-violence to one who is violent to all creatures.

(2) *Bhakta-bhāgavata* : free from attachment, hatred, pride, sense of insult; not loving anything except service of Hari; resorting to Vāsudeva in body, house and sense-functions.

(3) *Premika-bhakta* : possessed of love for the pious, pure conduct, free from attachment to those who are addicted to wealth, passion, etc., eager to listen to the glory of Kṛṣṇa, saluting all, careful in singing the glory of the Lord.

The love of devotees is the means to the release from rebirth.

The thousand names of Kṛṣṇa are given. If it be not possible to recite all the names, only Kṛṣṇa may be recited.

Śiva's advice is that one should resort to the Lord's feet alone after giving up faith in gods, holy places and religion. Condemned is the worship of all other gods and goddesses with animal-sacrifice for fulfilling desires. Abstinence from animal-sacrifice is better than this practice which has, however, not been categorically banned.

Ed. A.S. Phadke, Varanasi, 1934.

SAUBHĀGYA-SUBHAGODAYA (or -SUDHODAYA)

By Amṛtānandanātha. The title indicates its subject-matter. In six chapters, of which chapters III-V are devoted to *Śrīcakra*, it is a manual of rites for acquiring material prosperity.

In some MSS, the author's name is Vidyānandanātha. But, Amṛtānandanātha's own statement (*mayā saubhāgya-subhagodaye*) on *Yoginī-hṛdaya*, ii.17 confirms his authorship.

Ed. V.V. Dvivedi in his ed. of *Nityāṣoḍaśīkārṇava*, pp. 306-321.

SAUBHĀGYA-KALPADRUMA

Written by Mādhavānandanātha in accordance with the *Paramānanda-tantra*.

ŚRĪ-TATTVA-CINTĀMAṆI (1499 Śaka = 1577 A.D.)

By Pūrṇānanda Giri, it is a metrical work in 26 chapters (*Prakāśas*). The sixth chapter, called *Ṣaṭcakra-nirūpaṇa*, was so popular that it came to be regarded as a separate work. Many manuscripts of it are found at different places.

The *Śrī-tattva-cintāmaṇi* deals with the following topics:

Brahma-svarūpa, Tattva-jñāna-pratibandha-kāraṇa, Śabda-brahma-svarūpa, Tattva-jñāna-svarūpa, Dīkṣā, Mantra, Mantriṇāṃ daśa-saṃskārāh, Vāstuyāga, Maṇḍapa, Ṣaṭ-cakra, Kuṇḍa, Homa, Mantrabheda, Śakti, Ṣoḍaśīvidyā, Prātaḥkṛtya, Snāna, Antaryāga, creation, Śrī-cakra, Mudrā, Yantra, Sparyākrama, Tripura-sundarī-stotra, Puraścaraṇa, Prāyaścitta, Jñāna-dūtī-yāga, Tripura-sundarī-vidyā-jīvana-prāptyupāya, Devatā-stava-pāṭha, Śrī-mahātripurasundarī-stotra, Mahāyantra-saṃskāra.

Some interesting observations of the author are the following. The causes of loss of longevity are acceptance of gifts from those who fail to do the duties prescribed for their castes and stages of life, lust for others' wives, greed for others' money, non-study of Vedas and other scriptures, deceiving the *guru*, unrestrained sense-indulgence (i.26-27); threefold *Dīkṣā*, viz. *Śāmbhavī* (ii.16-17), *Śākteyī* (ii.14-15) and *Māntrī* (ii.10-13); highest goal can be attained only by *Sākṣāt-tattva-jñāna* (i.47-51) or direct knowledge of reality and not by austerities; *mokṣa* means merger of the individual soul into the Supreme Soul (i.64); *Jñāna* alone leading to salvation is twofold — arising out of *viveka* (discrimination) and arising out of *āgama* (i.67) or scriptures; *Antaryāga* (mental worship) highly extolled, and stated to be performed through absence of illusion, pride, passion, conceit, delusion, arrogance, jealousy, agitation, malice, greed, restraint of senses, kindness, forgiveness, knowledge, non-violence (stated to be the best). These are called *Bhāva-puṣpas* (chapter xvi).

Construction and worship of *Śrīcakra*, called *Cakrarāja* which is conducive to all material happiness, have been dealt with.

The author clearly forbids a Brāhmaṇa to offer wine to goddess (xviii.574). A Brāhmaṇa, adopting *Vāmācāra*, must not even eat meat and drink wine (*ibid.*). Wherever wine is prescribed, a Brāhmaṇa should offer, as substitutes, coconut water and honey.

The following flowers are called *Śākta* (suitable for worship of Śakti):

Ambhoja	— Same as Utpala (q.v.)
Aparājitā	— *Clitoria ternatea*
Aśoka	— *Saraca asoca*
Bandhujīva	— *Pentapetes phoenicea*
Campaka	— *Michellia chamaka*
Droṇa	— *Leucas cephaloles*
Hayāri	— ?
Jāti	— *Jasminum officinale*
Javā	— *Hibiscus rosasinensis*
Kubja	— ?
Kunda	— *Jasminum pubescens*
Kuraṇṭha	— *Barleria prionitis*
Madana	— ?
Mandāra	— *Erythrina variegata*
Nāga	— ?
Pāṭala	— *Stereospermum suaveolens*
Punnāga	— *Calophyllum inophyllum*
Ramā	— ?
Utpala	— *Nymphaea lotus*
Vijaya	— ?
Yūthi	— *Jasminum auriculatum*

The offer of certain flowers in certain seasons is condemned, e.g. *Śephālikā* and *Kahlāra* excepting in autumn.

The work mentions some gems, jewels and pearls, e.g. *Prabāla*, *Marakata*, etc. the use of which is stated to produce good result.

In chapter xxii, it is laid down that, to ensure the acquisition of learning by a man in future, within three days of his birth, a particular *mantra* should be written on his tongue with honey and white *dūrvā* grass or a golden pencil.

Chapter xxiii contains procedure of practice of magic, both white and black. In white magic are included power of being murder-proof, dear to the king, being like Cupid, counteracting the effect of poison at sight, attracting goddess of prosperity, etc. Tāntric black magic is too well known to be repeated.

Among the creatures to be sacrificed in worship are also human beings whose meat is stated to give the greatest satisfaction to goddess (ch. xxiv).

Critically ed. by B.M. Sāṃkhyatīrtha and C. Bhattacharya, with introduction by P.C. Bagchi, Calcutta, 1936; Tāntrik Texts Series, No. 2.

ŚRĪVIDYĀ-RATNA-SŪTRA

Same as *Gauḍapāda-sūtra* (q.v.).

SUBHAGODAYA

Attributed to Śivānanda (son of Sarvānanda of Bengal?) by some, to Gauḍapāda by others, it is a short tract of 52 stanzas dealing with the subject-matter of the *Nityā-ṣoḍaśīkārṇava* (q.v.). In view of the fact that it is quoted, *inter alia*, by Amṛtānanda in his *Dīpikā* and by Maheśvara in his own commentary, *Parimala*, on his *Mahārtha-mañjarī*, it seems to have been authoritative.

Ed. V.V. Dvivedi as an Appendix to his ed. of *Nityā-ṣoḍaśīkārṇava*. For a list of quotations from the *Subhagodaya*, see G.N. Kaviraj, *Luptāgama saṃgraha*, pp. 157 f.

SUDHĀ-VIDYOTINĪ

Title of a commentary on the *Saundarya-laharī*.

SVACCHANDA-TANTRA

Of unknown authorship and date. From the introduction, it is learnt that it is an abridged form of the original work containing one hundred crore verses. *Svacchanda* means free will which is the keynote of Kashmir Śaivism. Belonging to the *Trika* system of Kashmir Śaiva philosophy, it is a leading Tantra of *Dakṣiṇācāra*, and one of the best *mantra-śāstras*.

This work mentions free and pure *Cit*, and is monistic. Its approach is totally different from that of the *Mṛgendra* and *Mataṅga* Tantras of *Dakṣiṇācāra*; they advocate dualistic philosophy. Kṣemarāja, the well-known commentator, gives a monistic interpretation.

This Tantra is singularly devoid of the treatment of the six malefic acts of *Māraṇa* etc., so common in Tantra. It stresses *upāsanā* (worship, meditation) and *Kriyā* (ritual).

It comprises fifteen chapters.

Ed., with Kṣemarāja's comm., by K.V. Dvivedi, Pt. I, II.

ŚYĀMĀ-RAHASYA

By Pūrṇānanda Giri, in 15 or 16 chapters, according to some, 22 chapters according to others. It lays down the practices of the worshipper of Kālī. It is the most well-known and popular among his works. The important topics discussed are:

> mantroddhāra, morning duties, bath, daily prayer, tarpaṇa, nyāsa, etc.; pūjā-vidhi, stava and kavaca, puraścaraṇa, various dhyānas and mantras relating to Kālī, Śmaśāna-kālī, etc.; Kulācāra, Kuṇḍa-golodbhava, svayambhu-kusuma-grahaṇādi-vidhi, dūtīyāga, Śivābali, mantra-siddhi, kāmyaprayoga, Mahiṣa-mardinī-pūjā, vīra-sādhana, Kālī-stava, kavaca.

The work prescribes expiation for incest including sexual intercourse with one's mother. In ii. 22, worship with the following *viṣaya-puṣpas* (ii.24-26):

> *Amoha, Amāyā, Anahaṃkāra, Aśabda, Apada, Adambha*, the qualities of *Sattva, Rajas* and *Tamas, Amātsarya, Alobha, Ahiṃsā, Indriya-nigraha, Dayā, Kṣamā, Jñāna*.

Under *Guru-krama*, the *gurus* (all males) of the *Mānavaugha* category were perhaps historical personages; they are called *Kali-kāla-gurus*.

The work refers to more than sixty Tantras, besides referring to others as tantrāntare, *anyatra*.

It mentions Padmapādācārya (under iii.78) and Rāghavabhaṭṭa (under iii.165).

The work appears to be partly modelled on the *Tārārahasya* of the author's preceptor, Brahmānanda.

Ed. P.C. Pal and ors., Calcutta, 1948 Vikrama Saṃvat 1891-92; J. Vidyasagar, Calcutta, 1896; P.K. Sastri, Calcutta, 1313 B.S.; R.M. Chatterji, *Vividha-tantra-saṃgraha*, Calcutta, 1874-84; S. Tirthanatha, with Bengali trs., Calcutta, 1389 B.S.

TANTRA-CŪḌĀMAṆI

Alternative title of the *Śākta-krama* (q.v.).

TANTRĀLOKA

By Abhinavagupta. Written in 37 chapters, and primarily based on *Mālinī-vijaya-tantra*, it deals elaborately with the principles and practices relating to Kashmir Śaivism.

In this huge treatise, the speculative element is predominant in the earlier part and the ritualistic in the latter. In the speculative part, the author deals with the *upāyas* or means of attaining the divine self. This is followed by a discussion on the *adhvams* or systems of cosmic powers used as the paths of access to the state of liberation. The charming activity of Śakti is described in chapter XIII. Chapter XXIX deals with the esoteric rituals of the followers of *Kula* tradition. The work has some historical importance in the fact that a lengthy portion at the end (37, 33-85) contains an autobiographical account of the author and his family as well as his *Guru-paramparā*.

It has two commentaries, one being the *Tantrāloka-viveka* by Jayaratha.

For details, see K.C. Pandey, *Abhinavagupta* (2nd ed., 1963), pp. 52 ff; N. Rastogi, *Intro. to the Tantrāloka*, Delhi, 1987.

Ed., with commentary of Jayaratha, by M.K. Shastri, Srinagar-Bombay, 1918-38 (12 vols.). An ed., by Dwivedi and Rastogi, in 8 vols., pub. by Motilal Banarsidass, Delhi, 1986. Trs. into Italian by R. Gnoli "Luce delle sacre scritture", Torino, 1972.

TANTRA-PADDHATI

Alternative title of *Īśāna-śiva-gurudeva-paddhati* (q.v.).

TANTRARĀJA-TANTRA

Of unknown authorship and date. It comprises three sections, viz. *Kādi, Hādi* and *Kahādi* (also called *Śakti-saṃgama*); each section represents a distinct *Mata* or school of opinion about the way of regarding and worshipping the *Devatā*. The *Kādi* section, also called *Kādi-mata-tantra* and *Ṣoḍaśa-nityā-tantra*, has been published. It consists of 36 chapters, each containing one hundred stanzas.

It has at least three commentaries. One of these is the *Manoramā* (1660 VS = 1603-4 A.D.) by Subhagānandanātha (chaps. I-XXII), and completed by his pupil, Prakāśānandanātha (XXIII-XXXVI). Another commentary, called *Sudarśanā* is by Premanidhi Pantha (ascribed to his wife Prāṇamañjarī). The third commentary is by one Śivarāma.

Another indication of its popularity is the existence of about 30 MSS in different parts of the country (see *NCC*, VIII, p. 92).

The following important matters have been dealt with in this work.

Chap. 1 : Meaning of *Kādi*, summary of the work, 25 defects of *mantras* to be removed by *Guru*. The union of the first letter A with the last one *H* makes *Aham* which represents all the letters and, therefore, in terms of *mantra*, the full expression of the Self. The Tantras of the *Kādi* class are stated to be nine which, according to the commentary, are: *Sundarī-hṛdaya, Nityā-ṣoḍaśīkārṇava, Candrajñāna, Mātṛkā, Sammohana, Vāmakeśvara, Bahurūpāṣṭaka, Prastāra-cintāmaṇi* and *Meruprastāra*.

Chap. 2 : *Gurus* of *Divya, Siddha* and *Mānava* classes named in verses 2-5. *Maṇḍalas* and *Yantras* described.

Chaps. 4-5 : Rites relating to Lalitā. Nine *Cakras* under three heads, viz. *Sṛṣṭi, Sthiti* and *Saṃhāra*. The Yoginīs in the *Cakras* mentioned. Nine names of Devī, e.g. Tripurā, Mahā-tripura-sundarī, etc. Nine

	principal *Mudrās*. *Mātṛkās* divided into nine groups. Verses 79-80 give ethical principles, e.g. avoidance of desire for or denunciation of wife, not to be angry with women, not to beat them even when they are wicked.
Chap. 6	: Final aim of worship — realisation of the unity of Devī, the self, *Cakra*, *Devatās* therein and the surrounding *Śaktis*.
Chap. 7	: Devoted to the worship of the first to the ninth *Nityās*; Chaps. 15-21 deal respectively with the tenth to the sixteenth *Nityās*.
Chap. 8	: A devotee should drink wine only so long as the mind is not entirely absorbed in Devī; to drink more is sinful. Verses 30-32 provide that different *Yantras* should be engraved, painted or drawn on pieces of gold, silver, copper, cloth, birch-leaf with sandal-paste, camphor, musk, saffron, etc.; these should be worn on the head or arms or neck, waist or wrist.
Chap. 10	: Verses 81-85 state *Trailokya-mohana-vidyā*.
Chap. 26	: Unity of the 16 *Nityās* and the *Mātṛkās*.
Chap. 28	: States the identity of the universe with 16 *Nityās*.
Chap. 31	: Incidentally, many trees are mentioned.
Chap. 33	: It is stated that there are 960 *Yantras* of Ādyā Nityā, Lalitā.
Chap. 34	: Verse 84 states that Lalitā assumed the form of Kṛṣṇa who was surrounded by His *Śaktis*. He assumed six forms, called Siddhagopāla, Kāmarāja-gopāla, Manmatha-gopāla, Kandarpa-gopāla, Makaraketana-gopāla and Manobhava-gopāla. The last five are stated (28-33) to have been created by Lalitā. Verses 96-99 mention some herbs the use of which, in the prescribed manner, enables one to visualise *Devatās*.
Chap. 35	: Deals with the *vāsanā* of words. It does not convey the etymological meaning of a

particular word, but what the devotee understands or ought to understand by it. Verse 1 speaks of the *vāsanā* which indicates the oneness of the 16 *Nityās* with the self of the devotee. Verse 6 states that the worship of *Śrīcakra* is unification of the Knower, Knowledge and the Object of knowledge. The identity of the different parts of the devotee's self with the different parts of *Śrīcakra* has been stated. Verses 27-30 state that a *mantra* of one letter is called *Piṇḍa*, of two letters *Kartari*, of three to nine letters *Bījapa*, of ten to twenty letters *Mantraka*; that which exceeds that number is called *Mālā*.

Verses 91-100 name fifty herbs (*oṣadhi*), one for each of the fifty letters of the alphabet. These are classified into five groups of ten each. Each group belongs to one of the five gross elements (*bhūta*).

Chap. 36 begins with twenty questions put by Devī to Śiva about the following:

(i) True nature of the *Nityās*, (ii) means of knowing them, (iii) form of the universe, (iv) *puṇya* and *pāpa* of creatures, (v) causes of *puṇya* and *pāpa*, (vi) causes of rebirth, (vii) liberation, (viii) world of birth and death, (ix) one who attains liberation, (x) cause of bondage, (xi) means of liberation, (xii) root of *saṃsāra*, (xiii) *Tattvas*, (xiv) intelligence, (xv) senses, (xvi) *prāṇas*, (xvii) *jīva*, (xviii) *para* (beyond *jīva*), (xix) *Kāla*, (xx) *Graha*.

It is stated that one cannot get anything without a *Sadguru* (good preceptor) and personal effort.

Each chapter of the work is named after a *Tattva*. The *Tattvas* of the successive chapters are:

Bhūmi (earth), *Toya* (water), *Vahni* (fire), *Vāyu* (air), *Vyoman* (ether), *Gandha* (smell), *Rasa* (fluidity), *Rūpa* (form), *Sparśa* (touch), *Śabda* (sound), *Yoni* (genital organ), *Pāyu* (anus), *Pāda* (foot), *Pāṇi* (hand), *Vāk* (speech), *Prāṇa* (vital breath), *Jihvā* (tongue), *Netra* (eye), *Ghrāṇa* (sense of smell), *Śrotra* (ear), *Ahaṃkāra* (ego), *Buddhi* (intellect), *Manas* (mind), *Prakṛtyātmā*, *Puruṣātmā*, *Niyatātmā*, *Kālatattva*, *Rāgatattva*, *Vidyātattva*, *Kalātattva*, *Māyātattva*, *Śuddhavidyā*, *Īśvarātmā*, *Sadāśiva*, *Śaktitattva*, *Śivatattva*.

Ed. L. Sastri, Pt. I (chaps. 1-18) with *Manoramā* commentary, London, 1918 (*Tāntrik Texts*, viii); Pt. II (chaps. 19-36) with same commentary, ed. S. Misra, Calcutta/London, 1926 (*Tāntrik Texts*, xii). An Introduction, covering both parts, by A. Avalon, reprinted in 1952 under the title *Tantrarāja-tantra, a short analysis*.

See C. Chakravarti, *Tantras*, etc., p. 77; K.V. Sarma, *Gode Comm. Vol.*, pp. 185-188.

The *Tantrarāja* is referred to, *inter alia*, in Kṛṣṇānanda's *Tantrasāra*. Also quoted by some other writers, e.g. Narasiṃha Ṭhakkura in *Tārā-bhakti-sudhārṇava*, by Navamīsiṃha in *Tantracintāmaṇi*, by Gīrvāṇendra Sarasvatī in his *Prapañca-sāra-saṃgraha*, etc.

TANTRASĀRA (c. 1580 A.D.)

(1) By Kṛṣṇānanda Āgamavāgīśa Bhaṭṭācārya

It contains the essence of the Tantras of all sects, viz. Śaiva, Śākta, Vaiṣṇava, Saura, Gāṇapatya, etc. It appears that the original text has undergone many changes.

Besides the main topics, usually discussed in Tantras, it contains also hymns addressed to several deities. The author quotes from various Tāntric works, both original and digest; of these works, some are known only by name.

To him belongs the credit of conceiving the image of goddess Kālī, which has been widely popular in Bengal. He is believed to have introduced the worship of Kālī in Bengal.

An index to its popularity even beyond the confines of Bengal is that its manuscripts exist in several scripts besides Bengali.

Although contrary to the conventional Brāhmaṇical Śāstras, Tantra allows considerable latitude to women and Śūdras, yet Kṛṣṇānanda debars them from certain *mantras*, e.g. *Gāyatrī, Oṃkāra* and *Lakṣmī-mantra* (Śrī).

The author insists on *Kumārī-pūjā* (worship of virgin girls) as indispensable in certain rites, particularly in *Durgāpūjā* (on the *Mahānavamī tithi*).

The different forms of Kālī, described by the author, are called *Dakṣiṇa-kālī, Bhadra-, Guhya-, Śmaśāna-, Mahā-*.

Amṛtānanda Bhairava and Rāmānanda Tīrtha (18th century) prepared separate revised versions of the *Tantrasāra*. Rāmānanda's version is preserved in a complete manuscript in Asiatic Society, Calcutta.

The Vaṅgavāsī ed. of the work and Rāmānanda's version contain references to Pūrṇānanda and his *Śrī-tattva-cintāmaṇi*. It is doubtful whether these references occurred in the original work of Kṛṣṇānanda.

The work has a commentary by Vyāsa, son of Janārdana.

For further details about the work, see S.C. Banerji, *Tantra in Bengal*, Delhi, 1992.

Ed. (i) P. Tarkaratna, with commentary and Bengali trs., Calcutta, 1927. (ii) R. Chattopadhyay, with Beng. trs. (iii) S.C. Mukhopadhyay, Vasumatī, Calcutta, 1334 B.S. It is entitled *Bṛhat-tantrasāra*.

See D.C. Bhattacharya, in *P.K. Gode Comm. Vol.*

(2) By Abhinavagupta

It is an epitome of the author's *Tantrāloka* (q.v.).

Ed., with notes, by M.R. Sastri, Srinagar, 1918. Reprint, Delhi, 1983.

TANTRASĀRA-SAṂGRAHA

By Nārāyaṇa, son of Umā and Nārāyaṇa of Sivapurana and a native of Kerala, belonging to the 15th or 16th century. This work is to be distinguished from its namesake by Ānandatīrtha. In 32 chapters, it is a manual of popular medicine and worship of certain deities, mixed with magic. Antidotes for counteracting the effects of various kinds of poisoning have been dealt with in the first ten chapters which, together, are sometimes called *Viṣa-nārāyaṇīya*. The remaining chapters deal chiefly with the subjects stated below:

XI-XIV : Remedies for ailments, caused by planets;

XV-XVI : Cures of other maladies;

XVII-XVIII : Destroying the effects of hostile magic;

XIX : Causing illusion; worship of deities for achieving various results.

Remarkable similarity is noticed between the portions of this work from chapter XI onward and the second book of the *Īśāna-śiva-gurudeva-paddhati* (q.v.). The portions concerned of both these works are called *Mantrapāda*. Similarity is found also between chapters I-X of the *Tantrasāra-saṃgraha* and chapters XXXIX and XL of the other work. It is difficult to ascertain who exercised influence on the other writer.

The first part of *Tantrasāra-saṃgraha* has resemblance with the 13 chapters of the *Kāśyapa-saṃhitā* (Triplicane, 1933).

Ed. M.D. Aiyangar, Madras, 1950, with a commentary.

TĀRĀ-BHAKTI-SUDHĀRṆAVA (c. 1680 A.D.)

By Narasiṃha Ṭhakkura (c. 1668 A.D.), son of Gadādhara. The author is the fifth lineal descendant of Govinda Ṭhakkura, author of the *Pradīpa* commentary on the *Kāvyaprakāśa* of Mammaṭa.

Written in 20 chapters (*Taraṅgas*), it deals elaborately with the worship of Tārā who is not to be identified with the Buddhist goddess of this name. This Tārā is one of the ten Vidyās, connected with Śakti.

In Taraṅga 6, passages, quoted from the *Kūrmapurāṇa* (I.12.261-263), state that various Śāstras like *Bhairava, Yāmala, Vāma*, etc. opposed to Veda and Smṛti, were written for deluding (*mohāya*) people. The author of the *Tārā-bhakti-sudhārṇava* observes that the Purāṇas aim at glorifying the Veda, and not disparaging the Tāntric *Āgamas*.

In glorifying the *Guru*, it betrays the barbarous provision (Taraṅga iv, p. 116) for offering one's sister, daughter or wife to be enjoyed by a *Kulayogin* who is drunk.

It appears to have been compiled from various Tantras, e.g. *Rudrayāmala, Tattvabodha, Tantracūḍāmaṇi, Matsyasūkta, Tārārṇava*, etc.

Ptd. in *Tāntrik Texts*, xxi, Calcutta, 1940.

TĀRĀRAHASYA

By Brahmānanda Paramahaṃsa.

In four sections (*Paṭalas*), it deals mainly with rites and practices in connexion with the worship of Tārā, various images of this deity, daily duties, *mantra* and *gāyatrī* relating to Ekajaṭā, Ugratārā and Nīlasarasvatī, worship of Śiva phallus, *antaryāga*, *yantras* relating to the above deities, rosaries, expiatory rite in case of forgetting *mantras*, purification of *Pañcatattvas*, *Yoga*.

Ed. J. Vidyasagar, Calcutta, 1896.

Several other works have the same title. Of these, one is a part of the *Rudrayāmala-tantra*.

TĀRĀ-RAHASYA-VṚTTI(KĀ) or VĀSANĀ-TATTVA-BODHIKĀ

Attributed to Gauḍīya Śaṃkara. In the colophon, he is referred to as son of Kamalākara and grandson of Lambodara. From the date of a MS, belonging to Darbār Library of Nepal, given as Lakṣmaṇa Saṃvat 511 (= 1630 A.D.), the author may be supposed to have flourished in 16th-17th century.

In 15 chapters, comprising an estimated (by Stein) number of 2,500 stanzas, it describes daily worship, *dīkṣā* and *puraścaraṇa* in a general way. The author pays special attention to matters relating to the worship of Tārā. The sixth chapter deals with *Mahācīna-krama*, the Tibetan mode, the ritualistic practices concerning the worship of Tārā.

The work is probably the same as the *Tārā-rahasya-vṛttikā*, mentioned by Narasiṃha Ṭhakkura in his *Tārā-bhakti-sudhārṇava*, p. 141.

It has a commentary, called *Vṛtti*.

Pub. from Varendra Research Museum, Rajshahi (now in Bangladesh, 1961). For information about the author, see C. Chakravarti, *Tantras*, p. 68 f.

TĀRĀTANTRA

A short tract of six chapters and 150 stanzas, it lays down the *mantra* for the worship of *Ugratārā*. The Buddha and Vaśiṣṭha are stated to have done *sādhana* with this *mantra*.

It has some historical importance as it names nine *Kaula Gurus* whose names end in *-nātha*. It mentions *Mahācīnākhya Tantra*, and states that *Cīnācāra* came from Mahācīna.

This work deals in detail with the worship of Tārā (without giving Her *dhyāna*) according to *Vāmācāra* in which *Pañcamakāras* are indispensable. The connexion of *Cīnatantra* with the worship is recognised. The devotee is required to offer his blood to Goddess. In chapter V, even a drop of the worshipper's blood is declared to be better than a pitcherful of the blood of animals.

Ptd. Varendra Res. Soc., Rajshahi (now in Bangladesh), 1913; ed. A.K. Maitra, Delhi, 1983.

TATTVĀNANDA-TARAṄGIṆĪ

By Pūrṇānanda Giri. In 6 *Ullāsas* (chapters), it deals with the common Tāntric topics of *bījoddhāra, mantroddhāra*, etc.

RASB, VIII. A. 6200; BORI, 387 of 1882-83.

TOḌALA-TANTRA

It is in ten chapters (*Ullāsas*) containing a total of about 500 stanzas. The meaning of the title is not known.

It begins with the determination of Bhairava. The main topics of discussion are:

> corpse as the mount of the goddess, Jñāna-yoga, seven svargas, seven pātālas, nāḍi, mudrā, mantras of Kālī and Tārā, Kālī-pūjā, puraścaraṇa, deha-yoga, description of body as a microcosm, navārṇa-mantra, means of getting long life, Ṣaṭcakra, mantra and dhyāna of Bhūta-kātyāyanī, daśāvatāra. Great stress is laid on japa according to prescribed methods.

Mentioned in *Mātṛkābheda*, *Sarvollāsa* of Sarvānandanātha, *Śāktānanda-taraṅgiṇī* and *Āgama-tattva-vilāsa* of Raghunātha Tarkavāgīśa.

Ed. B. Sarma, Prayag, V.S. 2018 (=A.D. 1961/62); G. Kaviraj in *Tantra-saṃgraha*, II, pp. 53-94.

TRIPURĀ-RAHASYA

An anonymous work existing in three parts (*khaṇḍa*), called *Māhātmya*, *Jñāna*, and *Caryā*; the last one has not yet been published. Traditionally, it contains about 12,000 stanzas; the total number of verses in the two extant parts is 6687 + 2163 = 8,850. The work is in the form of a discourse, delivered by Hāritāyana to Nārada, the discourse is represented as a reproduction of the teachings of Dattātreya to Paraśurāma.

Tripurā, the Supreme Goddess, is variously called Sundarī, Lalitā, Ṣoḍaśī, Śrī Vidyā, Kāmeśvarī, etc. The significance of the name Tripurā is that Her body is supposed to consist of three Śaktis, Brāhmī, Vaiṣṇavī and Raudrī.

It has a commentary, called *Tātparya-dīpikā* by Drāviḍa Śrīnivāsa, son of Vidyānātha Dīkṣita of village Mahāpuṣkara in Drāviḍa country; it is dated Kali era 4932 = 1831 A.D.

The *Jñānakhaṇḍa*, comprising 22 chapters, is briefly described below.

The Supreme Reality, of the nature of Pure Intelligence, is self-luminous and free from the limitations of time, space and causality. Possessed of unrestricted Power of Will, it is fully free. This freedom means that the essence of consciousness is basically distinct from matter.

As regards the aforesaid Power, Creation follows its manifestation; Dissolution follows in the wake of the abeyance of the Power.

Caitanya (consciousness), the self-luminous light, may shine on itself when it is known as *Ahaṃtā* (I-ness). Or, resting on non-ego, it may express itself as *Idaṃtā*.

The work is highly philosophical. Its philosophy will be understood by showing the main points of its difference from the Vedāntic standpoint. In the Tantra, Śiva and Śakti are two aspects of the same Reality, i.e. Pure Consciousness. In Advaita Vedānta, Brahman is corresponding to the Tāntric Pure Consciousness; Vedāntic Śakti, known as *Māyā*, is material but not of the nature of Brahman. On the other hand, Tāntric Śakti or Pure Freedom is non-material. Its spiritual essence is indicated by its designation, *Cit Śakti*. In Tantra, *bāhyābhāsa* (external manifestation) is of non-Ego (*anahaṃbhāva*) within Pure Ego, appears external to it. In Vedānta, we have Radical Nescience (*mūlāvidyā*); the so-called *Avyakta* (unmanifest) or Jaḍā Śakti (matter) is the aforesaid non-Ego. In Tantra, however, the Lord's freedom or the Spiritual Power (*Cit Śakti*) is above the aforesaid Nescience.

In Vedānta, we have the doctrine of illusory appearance of the world (*vivarta-vāda*). According to the Tantra, the world is real. It is the expression of the Free Will (*Cit Śakti*) of the Lord.

According to Vedānta, the world resolves itself into Māyā which, being different from Brahman, is material. In Tantra, the world is resolved into the above *Cit Śakti* which remains even after the dissolution of the world.

Ed. Jñānakhaṇḍa by G. Kaviraj and N.S. Khiste, Varanasi, 1925-28; 2nd ed. by G. Kaviraj, 1965, with comm., *Tātparya-dīpikā*.

Eng. trs. by A.U. Vasavada, Varanasi, 1966.

TRIPURĀSĀRA-SAMUCCAYA

Ascribed, in the colophon, to Nāgabhaṭṭa. In it, there is salutation to Maheśvara-tejānandanātha. Divided into ten chapters (*Paṭalas*), it deals mainly with Bhūta-śuddhi, Mantra-svarūpa, Prāṇāyāma, and its effect on health, Yonimudrā resulting in the removal of defects like *chinna* of *mantras*, special kinds of Yoga in the six Cakras, Svayambhuliṅga, Bāṇalinga, etc. in Mūlādhāra, Ājñā, etc., Yantras, Bāhya-pūjā, Maṇḍapa, Kuṇḍa for homa, Sthaṇḍila for homa.

It has commentaries by Nāgabhaṭṭa, Harisinghji, Satyāvāsa, Gaṅgārāma and Govindācārya.

Quoted, *inter alia*, in the *Tantrasāra* of Kṛṣṇānanda, the *Durgotsava-tattva* of Raghunandana.

Ptd., with Govindācārya's comm., Calcutta, 1897 (2nd ed.).

UḌḌĪŚA-TANTRA

(Also called U-mahātantra, U-śāstra, Rāvaṇoḍḍīśa, Rāvaṇoḍḍīśa-ḍāmara-tantra-sāra, Uḍḍāmara-tantra, Vīrabhadra-tantra, U-vīratantra.)

It seems to have been designed as a handbook for those who perform tāntric rites for causing harm to the enemy, preventing abortion and barrenness of semen, attaining *Siddhi*, etc. The following are some of the interesting topics dealt with in the work.

Chapter IX contains, *inter alia*, the procedure of *Śava-sādhana* and the application of *Mṛta-sañjīvanī-mantra* (for reviving a dead person). Chapter X contains some other rites for prevention of troubles caused by mice, serpents, etc. For example, having made a paste of goat's dung and urine as well as *haritāla* (yellow orpiment) along with onions, one should besmear a mouse with it. Seeing or smelling it, other mice will run away. By burning a mixture of white molasses, sandal, Viḍanga (a kind of vegetable and medicinal substance, largely used as a vermifuge), Triphalā (the three myrobalans taken together, viz. Āmalakī — *Emblica officinalis*, Harītakī — *Terminalia chebula*, Baheḍā — *Terminalia belarica*), lac and flowers of Arka (*Calotropis gigantea*) one can prevent serpents and scorpions. By scattering a mixture of sand and white mustard in the field, one can drive away the birds and beasts damaging crops.

One should collect a *Sarpākṣī* (?) plant with roots and leaves on Sunday, and make a paste of it with the milk of a cow of one colour. This should be taken by a woman in her monthly illness. She should eat light food consisting of *Śāli* rice and *Mudga* (*Phaseolus aureus*). Thus, a woman can conceive within seven days. She should avoid tension, shocks, fear, day-sleep, work, cold and heat. An alternative is to take a mixture of equal quantity of pasted *Mustā* (*Cyperus rotundus*) grass, *Priyaṅgu* (*Aglaia odoratissima*), *Sauvīra*, lac, honey and water with which old rice has been washed.

After feeling sudden pain in the first month of pregnancy, crush *Padmaka* (*Prunus puddum*), *Uśīra* (*Andropogon squarrosus*) and sandal, and mixing the powder with cow's milk, take one *pala* of it — this prevents abortion.

Easy delivery is ensured by inserting, into the female organ, the pulverised root of white *Punarṇavā* (*Boerhaavia repens*) plant. An alternative recipe is to drink water boiled with *Dasamūla* (?), mixed with ghee and rock-salt.

We have noted only some of the recipes, given in the work.

That this work was regarded as authoritative is proved by its mention in such works as Nāgārjuna's *Kakṣapuṭa*, Narasiṃha's *Tārā-bhakti-sudhārṇava*, *Sarvollāsa* of Sarvānanda, etc.

The existence of about 80 MSS, representing different versions, found in different parts of the country (vide *NCC*, II, p. 291 f) and several editions indicate the popularity of the work.

It may be noted that the first 11 stanzas of chapter II of the Tantra are identical with I.1-11 of the *Mahānirvāṇa Tantra*. There is an *Uḍḍīśa-tantra* ascribed to Śrīnātha (*NCC*, II, p. 291).

Some editions are (1) by R.M. Chattopadhyay, in *Indrajālādi-saṃgraha*, Calcutta, 1879; (2) in *Sulabha-tantra-prakāśa*, Calcutta, 1887; (3) with Hindi trs., Moradabad, 1898.

ŪRDHVĀMNĀYA

It is curious that it seems to have been the title of two works, one Vaiṣṇava and the other Śākta; the latter has the alternative title Kālyūrdhvāmnāya-tantra, and is ascribed to Mahādeva.

The one, available in print, is called *Ūrdhvāmnāya-saṃhitā*, Ed. A.C. Tarkanidhi, Calcutta, 1285 B.S. = 1878 A.D., with Bengali trs.

See *NCC*, III, p. 3.

VĀMĀCĀRA-MATA-KHAṆḌANA

Ascribed to Kāśīnātha Bhaṭṭa. The title indicates its contents.

See MS RASB, VIII. A 6446.

VĀMAKEŚVARA-TANTRA

Of unknown authorship, date and provenance, it is a misnomer. Consisting of eight chapters (*Paṭalas*). The first five chapters together are called *Nityāṣoḍaśīkārṇava* or *Catuḥśatī* (because of the total of 400 stanzas) and also *Vāmakeśvarīmata*. The last three chapters are collectively called *Yoginī-hṛdaya*. In later times, the *Nityā* and the *Yoginī* have been treated as two separate works.

The main contents of the first five chapters are briefly stated below.

I The Goddess who questions Śiva, sums up the 64 Tantras containing secret *mantras*; appearance and disappearance of *Saṃsāra*, Parameśvarī, the receptable of the world, 16 *Nityās*, *Cakrapūjā*, various *vidyās*, *japa*, etc.

II *Yantras* — their nature and the good effects of wearing them, supernatural powers attainable by a devotee, etc.

III *Mudrās*.

IV *Akṣarādi — sādhana*, nature of *jñāna*, Supreme Power of Śakti, cosmogony, glorification of *vidyās*, etc.

V *Japa-homa-vidhi*, *mālā-nirūpaṇa*, etc.

The work has one commentary each by Bhāskararāya (*Setubandha*), Vidyānandanātha (*Artharatnāvalī*), Śivānanda or Śivānandanātha (*Ṛjuvimarśinī*). To Jayaratha is ascribed a commentary, called *Vivaraṇa*, on the *Vāmakeśvara Tantra* (NCC, VII, p. 187). Jayaratha appears to have flourished in the 12th-13th century. Jayaratha states that the first commentary on the *Nityā* was by Īśvaraśiva, a Kashmirian author of the 9th century (vide M.K. Sastri's edition of the *Nityā*, p. 47). Thus, the 9th century is, perhaps, the lower terminus of the date of the *Nityā*.

Ed. (1) V.V. Dvivedi, with a learned introduction and commentaries of Śivānanda and Vidyānanda, Varanasi, 1968; (2) K.S. Agase, Poona, 1908, with Bhāskara's commentary (rev. ed., 1970); (3) M.K. Sastri, Srinagar (under the title Vāmakeśvarī-mata) with Jayaratha's comm.

VARIVASYĀ-RAHASYA

It is attributed to Bhāskararāya who is renowned in the realm of Tantra. The title means 'secret of *Varivasyā*' which means *sevā, pūjā, upāsanā*, etc. Consisting of 167 verses, it deals with *Śrīvidyā* as in *Kādimata* — its interpretation and the worship of the deity adored by the author. The Vedic nature of *Śrīvidyā* is mentioned (6-8), the four *bījas* constituting it are referred to (32), the presiding deities are found (32-36). It dwells on the existence, within it, of the five stages of consciousness (viz. *Jāgrat* — waking, *Svapna* — sleep, *Suṣupti* — deep slumber, *turīya* — being one with Brahman and the stage beyond), etc. It is important that the work identifies the *Vidyā* with Vedic *Gāyatrī* (60 f). The symbolic exposition of the 15 syllables, constituting the *Śrīvidyā*, have been discussed.

There is a commentary, called *Prakāśa*, by the author himself.

Ed. (1) with author's comm., Eng. trs. and notes, by S.S. Sastri, Adyar (Madras), 1948; (2) I.C. Sastri (with *Bhāvanopaniṣad*), Calcutta, 1917.

There are other eds. of which mention may be made of the one pub. at Amalapuram, 1908 (in Telugu script).

(ŚRĪ) VIDYĀRṆAVA-TANTRA

Attributed to Vidyāraṇya (to Śivānanda Gosvāmin, by some) who may or may not be identical with the renowned Advaita philosopher (14th century) of that name, it is a compilation of quotations from different texts with brief connecting prose lines. Among the Tantras, drawn upon by him, important are the *Kulārṇava, Jñānārṇava, Tantrarāja, Rudrayāmala* and *Tripurārṇava*. From certain evidences, he seems to have flourished after the middle of the 11th century.

The work is in two parts — Pūrvārdha and Uttarārdha. The earlier part deals with the details about the threefold worship of Mahā-tripurasundarī as *Sthūlā* (gross), *Sūkṣmā* (subtle) and *Parā* (transcendental). The latter part describes the worship of other gods and goddesses. It is interesting to note that Buddhist deities, Ekajaṭā, Tārā, Nīlasarasvatī and Mañjughoṣa are also mentioned.

The compiler mentions the line of *Gurus* through which he was initiated to the lore of Mahātripurasundarī. The line of teachers is divided into two parts, the first part mentions 71 persons, headed by Kapila, ending with Śaṃkarācārya. The second part names the Gurus from Śaṃkara downwards. There is mention of 14 disciples. The compiler is declared to be a great grand-disciple of Śaṃkara (I.71 f).

The work, in its printed form, contains at least 11 chapters (*śvāsas*); it ends abruptly after stanza 78 of ch. 11. The work appears to have been compiled at the request of Ambadeva, son of Prauḍhadeva and king of Vidyānagara (=Vijayanagar).

Some of the noteworthy features of this Tantra are as follows. In chapter 19, there is vehement condemnation of the *dvijas* who bow before the image of Viṣṇu or the Śiva phallus established, worshipped or even touched, by Śūdras. The prohibited persons include *Pāṣaṇḍas* (heretics), *Ābhīras,* women and uninitiated *dvijas*. Śūdras and women are debarred from touching a *Śiva-liṅga,* duly consecrated by Brahmins, versed in *Mantras*. Not to speak of reciting Vedic and Purāṇic *mantras,* women and Śūdras have no right to hear their recital. A *dvija* is forbidden to enter the house of a Buddhist on pain of eternal suffering.

This chapter gives a detailed description of good and bad *Śālagrāma* stones which are worshipped as symbols of Viṣṇu or Nārāyaṇa.

On the authority of the *Haya-śīrṣa-pañcarātra,* the Vaiṣṇava images of Vāsudeva, Saṃkarṣaṇa, Pradyumna and Aniruddha are mentioned. On the authority of the *Siddhārtha-saṃhitā,* 24 Viṣṇu images are described; thus, it has importance in the history of Indian sculpture.

The Veda is highly extolled. It is ordained that the Tāntric worship of the five deities, beginning with Gaṇeśa, should be preceded by their worship with Vedic *mantras*. Brahmins, taking to the Tāntric way out of passion or greed, leaving aside the Veda, become *Mlecchas* and doomed to perdition.

In this chapter, *antaryajna* (mental worship) has been regarded as extremely important.

In chapter 24, Kālī, variously named as Śyāmā, Dakṣiṇa, Bhadra, Guhya, Śmaśāna and Mahākālī, has been highly eulogised, and great importance attached to devotion to Her.

Among the magical practices, contained in chap. 25, there is a process for ensuring the easy delivery of an issue. Of other magic rites, one is concerned with making oneself invisible to others.

It is, indeed, interesting that, though *Guru* has been accorded an exalted position in Tantra, this work does away with the indispensability of the preceptor for Tāntric initiation. It has been declared (ch. 34) on the authority of the *Rudrayāmala* that, in the absence of *Guru*, one should, in the thirteenth lunar mansion of the dark fortnight, write the *mantra* on a palm-leaf, and place it before Dakṣiṇāmūrti. Then, after worshipping Her, he should recite the *mantra* for 108 times; such a *mantra* is stated to be better than one obtained from *Guru*. In the Kali Age, often faults are likely in *mantras*, learnt from the *Guru*.

It describes (ch. 35) *jīvanmukti* (liberation while alive), and states how it can be acquired.

The work lays down that a person, though devoid of knowledge, can attain *Siddhi* by *bhakti* alone. It sets forth the characteristics of a *bhakta*, who is entirely free from sin. Thus, it has considerable importance in the history of the *Bhakti* cult.

VIJÑĀNABHAIRAVA (TANTRA)

Consisting of 162 *Kārikās* (memorial verses), it is in the form of catechism, Goddess Bhairavī questioning and Lord Bhairava replying. The work characterises itself as *rudrayāmalīya* (belonging to the *Rudrayāmala*).

The important topics, dealt with in it, are:

Bhakti in non-dualistic philosophy, characteristics of *sādhana*, means of liberation — the awakening of *Kuṇḍalinī*, the stages of *Kuṇḍalinī's* ascent along the Supreme Path, *Prāṇa* in *Āgama*, *Oṃkāra-sādhana*, *Japa*, penetration of the six *Cakras*, *Nāda*, *Ajapā*, *Śūnya*.

In reply to Bhairavī's enquiry about His identity, Bhairava says that He is indescribable, beyond space and time (*dik-kāla-kalanātīta*), and cannot be named (*vyapadeṣṭum aśakya*). Bhairava is a combination of *Parāpara* and *Parā Devī*. As *Śakti* and *Śaktimat* are identical, so also the Supreme Śakti is identical with Śiva.

The means of reaching the goal is threefold, viz.

(1) *Śāmbhava*: for a devotee of a superior type. By this means, God is realised by (a) concentration in which all thoughts, destabilising the mind, are abjured, (b) the perception that the soul is not tarnished by the taints of the body, etc.

(2) *Śākta*: for a devotee of the medium type. In it, there is rectification of wrong ideas and development of right perspective by means of truth-finding argument, salutary scriptures and instruction of competent preceptors.

(3) *Āṇava*: for a devotee of an inferior type. For the purification of thought, he has to depend on *Buddhi, Prāṇa, Deha* or some external object.

Verse 132 lays down that the immutable soul is devoid of knowledge. The external conditions are dependent on knowledge. So, this world is *Śūnya*.

The aspirant should shun all thoughts like 'I', 'Mine', 'By me', etc., and discard all objects of sense; it is through the senses that the feelings of pleasure and pain arise. Bhairava emerges when the mind, perceptions etc. wear out due to the dawning of consciousness and destruction of delusion (verse 136).

The awakening of *Kuṇḍalinī* is emphasised as the means of perfect bliss. *Kuṇḍalinī* being awake and conscious the entire world assumes the form of consciousness and the person concerned realises non-duality (see particularly verses 17, 78, 80, 82, 91, 92, 98, 99, 107, 117, 120, 126, 129, 130). The ascent of *Kuṇḍalinī* results in the effacement of all thoughts and propensities obstructing the unfolding of one's humanism; this paves the way to the realisation of the attributeless One (verses 15, 43, 45, 98, 107, 123).

Great importance is attached (verses 152-155) to spontaneous *japa* (i.e. *Ajapā*, a term not mentioned in it) which is stated to go on in all the three states of *jāgrat, svapna* and *suṣupti*. Verse 154 mentions the unconscious and ceaseless repetition of the *mantra haṃsa* in an individual for 21,600 times throughout day and night. Exhalation proceeds with the sound *haṃ* and inhalation with *sa*.

According to this Tantra (verse 151), no formal worship is necessary, because the Supreme Being, the article for worship and the worshipper are all one and the same.

The aspirant should reflect upon the soul like the limitless sky. Then *Śakti*, as supportless consciousness (*nirāśrayā citiśakti*), will reveal Herself (verse 91). The devotee should look upon the world as unreal and Śiva as real.

Some methods of spiritual discipline are mentioned. Among them are the concentration of mind, with closed eyes, on the forehead (i.e. the point of the junction of the eyebrows); suppression of all the motor organs (speech, hands, feet, anus and genital organ) as a result of which the vital energy, ascending from *mūlādhāra* to *brahmarandhra*, produces the experience of bliss (verse 66). A process of obtaining tranquillity is to place oneself on a seat, partly contracting the anus and to get the mind absorbed there (verse 78). Calmness may be experienced by mentally pronouncing *Ha* with the tongue placed in the open mouth (verse 80). By reflecting on the body as supportless (*nirādhāra*), the mind is purged of the objects of knowledge; thus, the *Yogin* becomes devoid of desires (verse 81).

Joy results from looking upon the world as magic or a painting and everything as transient (verse 101).

A devotee of Śiva can become Śiva by the confirmed notion that he is identical with the Supreme Lord, the maker of all and omniscient and immanent (verse 108).

The work insists on mental purity and not external purification. It is stated that outward purification of a jar, filled with excretion, is useless. *Japa* and rituals are external gross things. Essential is the reflection on the Supreme. What is needed is contemplation on the abstract, not on the body and limbs of the deity. Mental offering of the elements (*bhūta*), sense-organs, and the world of diversities into the fire of *Mahāśūnya* (the Great Void) is real *homa*. The true *Kṣetra* (holy place) is the union of Rudra and Śakti, because it destroys all fetters (*kṣapaṇāt sarva-pāśānām*) and saves all (*trāṇāt sarvasya*). Real bath is the perception of independent blissful consciousness as the essential element of the soul and the reflection of merger into it:

svatantrānanda-cinmātra-sāraḥ svātmā hi sarvataḥ/
āveśanaṃ tatsvarūpe svātmanaḥ snānamī-ritam//

Verse 150

Some ideas in this work have parallels in the *Bhagavadgītā*. For example, this work speaks (verse 31) of fixing the mind between the eyebrows. This idea occurs in the *Gītā* (viii.10). Verse 88 speaks of the suppression of the senses, an idea found in the *Gītā*, ii.59. Verse 134 holds that, by suppressing the functions of the senses, contact with which generates the feelings of pleasure and pain, one can rest in the soul in its pristine form. A similar sentiment is expressed in the *Gītā*, ii.14.

Ed. (1) with sub-title *Samagra Bhāratīya Yogaśāstra*, Skt. and Hindi comm., by V.V. Dvivedi, Delhi, 1978; (2) with comm., French trs. and notes, by L. Silburn, Paris, 1961; (3) with Bengali trs. and exposition, by R.C. Adhikari, Burdwan (W. Bengal), 1980; (4) with Eng. trs., by J. Singh; (5) with Kṣemarāja's comm. (up to verse 23), Śivopādhyāya's comm. (on the rest) and notes, by M.R. Shastri, 1918.

On the work, see J. Gonda, Medieval Religious Literature (*A History of Ind. Lit.*, Vol. II.1), Wiesbaden, 1977, p. 208 f.

VĪṆĀŚIKHA TANTRA

It is the only surviving work out of the four Tantras (the other three being the *Śīraścheda, Nayottara* and *Sammohana*) mentioned in an inscription of Sdok Kak Thom, dating back to about 1052 A.D., in Cambodia. From the epigraph, it is learnt that one Śivakaivalya in the court of King Jayavarman II, in the ninth century, introduced for the King a cult derived from the doctrine contained in the above four Tāntric texts, brought from outside. The above four works represent the four faces of Tumburu, a manifestation of Śiva. These works are the sources of the *Vāmasrotas* (left current) of Tantra.

This work calls itself a *Yāmala* Tantra, but the Śiva-Śakti symbolism which characterises the *Yāmalas* is not conspicuous. It concerns itself with the description of details about the worship of Tumburu and his four *Śaktis*, Jayā, Vijayā, Ajitā and Aparājitā.

The title suggests the nexus of the work with the *Śikhās*, a small group of early Tantras which are mostly lost. Mention is made by Jayaratha, in commentary on the *Tantrāloka* (I.18), of eight of these works, including *Vīṇā*.

The highlights of the *Vīṇāśikha* are briefly given below. The contents may be divided into two parts:

(1) Stanzas 1-118. It represents Tumburu as a manifestation of Śiva with four faces, eight arms and the four *Śaktis*, mentioned earlier, and prescribes the ordinary procedure of His worship.

(2) Stanzas 119-396 (the total number of the stanzas of the work is 396). It lays down the special procedure of the worship including Yogic mysticism and magic rites. In stanzas 51-67 are discussed *Prastāra* (arrangement and the five main *bījas*).

In stanzas 240-250b, we have explanation of *Haṃsa*, Śiva residing in the respiratory system.

Stanzas 250c-259b describe Śakti within the body. The course of God is characterised by a fiery *Śikhā* (tuft of hair on the head) which is of the nature of *jyoti* (flash); He resides at its upper end, and is the source and ultimate goal of the material and phonic creation.

He has two aspects:

(1) Fiery during the period of progression (*ayana*); then He resides in the *Piṅgalā Nāḍī*.

(2) Like nectar during the period of regression (*viṣuva*) when He resides in *Iḍā*.

The way through *Suṣumnā* leads to final release.

St. 323-363b — Doctrine of *Ekākṣara* (monosyllabic) *mantras*.

It is the only work dealing exclusively with the worship of Tumburu. Its influence transcended the bounds of India, as is attested by the aforesaid Cambodian inscription. Moreover, stanzas 349c-351b of the Tantra are identical with stanzas 18 and 19 of the *Māyā-tattva* fragment from Bali (see ed. in *Stuti* and *Stava*, by Goudriaan and Hooykas, Amsterdam, London, 1971).

As regards the language of this work, it may be pointed out that it contains quite a few grammatical and metrical irregularities. Some of these have been mentioned in the present author's *New Light on Tantra*, p. 80 f.

The *Vīṇāśikha* is included in the list of 64 *Āgamas* in the *Nityāṣoḍaśīkārṇava*.

Ed. T. Goudriaan, Delhi, 1985 with intro., Romanised text. Eng. trs., notes, index of verses and of Sanskrit words.

VIṢṆU-SAṂHITĀ

A Vaiṣṇava Tantra in 30 chapters (*Paṭalas*).

Pub. in *Trivandrum Skt. Ser.*, 1925.

YOGINĪ-HṚDAYA-DĪPIKĀ

By Amṛtānandanātha. The title indicates the contents.

Ptd. in *Sarasvatī Bhavana Series*, 1923.

YOGINĪ-TANTRA

Of unknown authorship and date, it appears to have been regarded as highly authoritative. Besides a good number of its MSS, there are at least five editions, and we find quotations from or references to it in various works. The work refers to Viṣṇusiṃha, ruler of Coochbehar early in the sixteenth century which, therefore, is the *terminus a quo* of its date. From the detailed treatment of Kāmarūpa in it, it has been suggested by some that this Tantra might date back to a period after 1560 when the temples of Kāmākhyā and other deities were renovated. An examination of its contents shows that it is a rich source of traditions and legends and perhaps some historical facts also about Kāmākhyā and the people who lived there. It has some geographical importance as it mentions several holy places, especially *Pīṭhas* along with topography in certain cases.

This Tantra consists of two parts (*khaṇḍas*), the first comprising 1290 stanzas divided into nineteen chapters, the second containing 1514 stanzas arranged in nine chapters.

The following Tantras are mentioned in it:

Sarasvatī, Pheṭkāriṇī, Nīla, Uttara, Kulārṇava and *Śiva*.

We shall briefly indicate the noteworthy matters dealt with in the different chapters of the work.

PART I

Chap. i: Detailed description of the form of Kālī.

Chap. ii: Matters relating to Kālī. *Brahma-vidyā* called *Kālikā-vidyā*. Great importance attached to *japa* with a rosary of human bone. Best time for *Pūjā* stated to be *Mahārātri*, i.e. the last two hours of the middle watch of the night.

Chap. iii: Discussion on *Kavacas* and rites for various purposes.

Chap. iv: Six conventional Tāntric rites.

Chap. v: Different kinds of *Sādhana* for fulfilment of different desires, including *muṇḍa-sādhana* on *Pañcamuṇḍa āsana* (consisting of the skulls of a jackal, a serpent, a dog, a bull and a man; as an alternative are prescribed five human skulls). This *sādhana* is stated to bring about all kinds of success.

Chap. vi: *Yoga*, both *divya* and *vīra*, the performance of the former being called *divya-kaula* and the latter *vīra-kaula*. *Pañcamakāras* are meant for the devotees of *paśubhāva* (animality). *Kaula* rites extolled.

For devotees of the three upper castes, the substitutes for wine are respectively mixture of molasses and ginger-juice, coconut water and bee-honey. Fried rice is called *Mudrā* (one of the five *Makāras*, referred to above). For *Maithuna*, a woman of the same caste, in her absence, one of a lower caste is recommended. For an ascetic, *Maithuna* means the union of *Kuṇḍalinī* with the apex on the thousand-petalled lotus with the head. For an *Avadhūta*, there is no restriction as to the kinds of wine, fish, meat. He is allowed to have *Maithuna* with any woman excepting his mother, a maiden and a spinster. A Yogin is advised to drink the juice exuded from the place of contact of *Kuṇḍalinī* with the highest point within the head.

Chap. vii: Deals with various *Vidyās*, called *Svapnavatī* (by which one can see every thing in dream), *Mṛta-saṃjīvanī*, *Madhumatī* and *Padmāvatī*.

Chap. viii: On the origin and description of Yoginīs.

Chap. ix: Legend of how Mahādeva came to fall near the feet of Kālī.

Chap. x: Kālī stated to have given will force to Viṣṇu, power of action to Brahmā and power of knowledge to Śiva. Discussion on *Brahmāṇḍa*.

Chap. xi: Deals with holy spots and places conducive to success and salvation. *Mahāpūjā* at the following nine *Pīṭhas*, called Yonis, is stated to produce great result:

Upavīthi, Vīthi, Upapīṭha, Pīṭha, Siddhapīṭha, Mahāpīṭha, Brahmapīṭha, Viṣṇu-pīṭha, and Rudrapīṭha.

Glorification of Kāmākhyā.

Varying degrees of merit stated to result from *japa* at the following places:

Jālandhara, Uḍḍiyāna, near Nīlakaṇṭha in Nepal, Ekāmrakānana, Rāḍha, Vikaṭākṣā, Puṣkara, Prayāga, Drauṇa mountain, Jvālāmukhī, Virajā, Himālaya, Kedāra, Kailāsa, Jayantī, Ujjayinī, Mandara hill.

Chap. xii: Reasons why, in Kali Age, there is neither *Śiva-jñāna* nor *Mantra-siddhi*.

Chap. xiii: Among other places, stated to have been visited by Śiva, mention is made of Koca, near Yonigarta.

Chap. xiv: Describes how and where the *Mlecchas*, born to *Plavas*, *Yavanas* and *Saumaras*, came to be the protectors of Kāmarūpa. *Bāhlīkas* are also mentioned. The *Mlecchas* are stated to have become rulers of Kāmarūpa after Śaka 981 (= 1059 A.D.). There is a prophecy that they will bring more lands under their control. We are further informed that the *Saumaras* ruled in the east, *Kuvācas* in the west, *Yavanas* in the south and *Plavas* in the north.

Chap. xv: Glorification of Kāmākhyā, identified with Kālī.

Chap. xvi: Legend narrating how Goddess assumed the form of Kālī, glorification of Vārāṇasī and description of good result accruing from residence and death there.

Chap. xvii: Glorification of Brāhmaṇas and praise of *Kumārī-pūjā* irrespective of the caste of the *Kumārī* worshipped.

Chap. xviii: Glorification of the river Ganges, salvation stated to be the result of dying in it.

Chap. xix: Eulogy of *Kulācāra*.

PART II

Chap. i: Effect of worship in the different *Pīthas* which are:

In the southern part of Madhyadeśa Bhadrapīṭha, in the west Jālandhara, in the east Pūrṇapīṭha, in the north-east Kāmarūpa, in the north-west

Jālandhara (repeated), in the north Kulapura, in the north-east Vihāra, a little to the north Mahendra and in the east Śrīhaṭṭa.

[It should be noted that, according to Manu, ii.21, Madhyadeśa was the name of the region between the Himālaya and Vindhya-mountains, to the east of the place where the river Sarasvatī disappeared, and to the west of Prayāga. About the place of disappearance of the Sarasvatī, N.L. Dey, in his *Geographical Dictionary*, 1971, p. 37, writes "the spot in the great sandy desert in the district of Sirhind (Paṭiālā) where the river Sarasvatī loses itself after taking a westerly course from Thaneswar."]

Upapīṭhas (minor Pīṭhas) — Oḍra, Śakṭākāra-pīṭha comprising Sindhu-bhadraka-pīṭha, Ādipīṭha, Madhyapīṭha, Trikoṇa, Pravarapīṭha, Aśoka-pīṭha, Navapīṭha, Kola-pīṭha, Saumara, Śiva-talpa-pīṭha, seven *Pīṭhas* called Brahmakṣetra, Kalākṣetra, Raghukṣetra, Nandana, Pārijāta, Śivāraṇya, Deśāraṇya. Other Pīṭhas — Nāthapīṭha, Vārāhī, Dharmapīṭha, Mahāpīṭha, Puṇyākhaya, Nīlapīṭha, Hayatāmrākhya, Śrīpīṭha. Several other places, rivers, forests, mountains and lakes are also mentioned.

Chap. ii: Deals with the time propitious for journey to holy places. The sight of the following persons and things, among others, is stated to the auspicious for one undertaking a journey:

On the right: flower, food prepared from barley, conch-shell, drum, deity, king, cows, chariot, any vehicle, parboiled rice, meat, rice, brittle vessel, best food.

On the left: girl, married couple, courtesan, full pitcher, woman, moving beast and bird.

In front: curd, fruit.

The work mentions auspicious time for various kinds of work, e.g. visiting a deity, marriage, etc.

Chap. iii: Various matters relating to Kāmarūpa Mahāpīṭha. It is stated that a sin, committed elsewhere, is destroyed at a holy place, but a sin, committed at a holy place, is never destroyed. Several holy places are mentioned. Importance of Gayā as a *tīrtha* is mentioned.

Chap. iv: Various names of Śiva.

Chap. v: Importance of Vārāṇasī.

Chap. vi: Various practices appropriate at various places.

Chap. vii: Procedure and materials for drawing diagrams. Three kinds of *mantras* — masculine (for male deities), feminine (for female deities) and neuter. A feminine *mantra* is called *Vidyā*. Rules about bathing Goddess and offerings to Her. Among creatures, to be offered by a Śūdra, is a human being. A brief description of Goddess in autumn presumably referring to *Durgā-pūjā* which term, however, is not used.

Chap. viii: Effects of bath, worship, etc. at various places and near various deities.

Chap. ix: Description of Viṣṇupuṣkara as a holy place. Importance attached to mental purification without which a holy place can do nothing. Speciality of Puruṣottama-tīrtha (Puri), non-observance of conventional rules about *Upanayana*, intercaste marriage, etc. allowed. Women are allowed to talk or lie with people other than their husbands.

Practices prevailing at the following places: Jālandhara, Sarveśu-yoginī-pīṭha, Kāmarūpa, Saumara, Kolva-pīṭha, Mahendra, Śrīhaṭṭa.

Description of Apunarbhava Tīrtha and praise of it as a holy place.

Of several eds., the following may be noted:

Ed., with Hindi trs., by K. Misra, Bombay, 1983; with intro. in Eng., by B. Sastri.

For date, etc., see J.N. Farquhar, *An Outline of Rel. Lit. in India*, London, 1920, p. 354; C. Chakravarti, *Tantras*, etc., p. 23; M. Neogi, *Śaṃkaradeva and his Times*, Gauhati, 1965, p. 82, n. 97.

YONI-TANTRA

An anonymous work in eight chapters (*Paṭalas*). The *Bṛhad-yoni-tantra,* still in MS, is a different work.

It should be noted that many of the verses of the *Yoni-tantra* are found in other Tantras, viz. *Bṛhad-yoni-tantra, Rudrayāmala, Yoginī-tantra, Kulārṇava, Śyāmā-rahasya*. It is not yet certain whether the *Yoni* borrowed them from the other Tantras or the latter from the former. The possibility of all these texts borrowing from a common source cannot be ruled out.

We briefly note below the main contents chapter by chapter.

Chap. i: It states that the Tantras number 64, but does not mention their names. *Yoni-pīṭha* declared as the best of all *Pīṭhas*. Worship, according to *Kaula* rites, of one's own wife or that of another is recommended.

Chap. ii: Women, fit for being worshipped, are: actress, *Kāpālika* woman, prostitute, washerwoman, barber woman, cowherd woman, woman of the garland-maker class, Brāhmaṇa woman, Śūdra woman. They are called *Nava-kanyā*. An accomplished (*vidagdha*) woman of any caste is suitable. Sexual union is forbidden with *mātṛ-yoni* which means mother, according to others, a woman who has given birth to a child. Daily worship of a woman aged above twelve years up to sixty years, with *Pañca-tattvas,* is recommended. Among the things, to be offered in worship, are mentioned burnt fish and hen's egg. The devotee should be naked, and have dishevelled hairs.

Chap. iii: Among animals, to be sacrificed in worship, are deer, camel, elephant, cow, jackal, lion, horse, etc. For ritual enjoyment, a virgin is prohibited.

The *Yoni* is divided into the following ten parts (14 ff) each of which is related with a manifestation of Devī:

Yonimūla — Devī,
Yoni — Naganandinī,
Yoni-cakra — Kālī,
Yoni-cakra — Tārā,

Yoni-Kuntala — Chinnamastakā,
Yonisamīpato — Vagalā,
Yonisamīpato — Mātaṅgī,
Yoni-garta — Ṣoḍaśī,
Yoni-garta — Bhuvaneśvarī.

Caṇḍālī mentioned as the most important among the *Yonis* and as a *Gaṇanāyikā* (verse 20). It may be noted that, in the *Kulārṇava* (vii.42), *Caṇḍālī* is one of the *Kula-śaktis*. She figures prominently in the Buddhist and *Sahajiyā* cults.

Chap. iv: Japa etc. should be done in accordance with the rules laid down in *Mahācīna-tantra* or with *Mahācīna-cakra*. The Tantra mentions a *Yoni-pīṭha*, called Mādhavī, in *Koca-deśa* to the west of the Ganges. *Kumārī-pūjā* and *Kaula-bhojana* are recommended.

Avadhūtāśrama stated to be the best for *Saṃnyāsa*.

It recommends the reprehensible practice of sexual intercourse with one's daughter, *vadhu* (daughter-in-law?), sister, female disciple in the absence of other women (?).

Chap. v: Sexual union with preceptor's wife and one's mother is prohibited. Among the disabilities of a Śūdra are: intercourse with a Brāhmaṇa woman, worship of *Śālagrāma*, performance of *homa* and the recital of *Oṃkāra*.

Chap. vi: Women of the three upper classes are forbidden for ritual enjoyment. (Is the prohibition for Śūdras alone?)

Chap. vii: Practices for devotees of the *Vīra* type. Mental worship is emphasised. According to verse 17, for ritual sexual union, another man's wife is preferable to one's own.

Chap. viii: *Maithuna* stressed as indispensable in a Tāntric rite. *Cīnācāra* regarded as important. *Yoni-pūjā* is the best of all *pūjās*.

The work appears, on some grounds, to have originated in Bengal.

Yoni-garta, mentioned several times (e.g. i.15, iv.2, v.11), is taken by some to denote a particular part of the vulva. Others would take it to refer to the shrine of goddess Kāmākhyā, in Kāmarūpa, which is a cave mentioned as *manobhava-guhā* in *Yoginī-tantra* (xi.35) and *Kālikā-purāṇa* (LXII.88).

The *Yoni-tantra* may be regarded as a Vaiṣṇava Tantra with Śaivite leaning. It is, as pointed out earlier, based on the worship of Mādhavī who seems to be a counterpart of the Śaiva Kāmākhyā. The Tantra advocated *Kulācāra* presumably to popularize it beyond the Vaiṣṇava community. Another means perhaps adopted for the same purpose was the provision of *Yoni-pūjā* on a *Liṅga* which usually denotes a *Śiva-liṅga*.

Some similarities between this work and the Vaiṣṇava *Sahajiyā* cult may be pointed out. In both, *Caṇḍālī* plays a prominent part. As regards the term *gaṇa-nāyikā*, used in the Tantra, it may be observed that *Nāyikā*, in the Vaiṣṇava *Sahajiyā* cult, denotes a woman highly suitable for ritual purpose. As we have seen, the Tantra betrays a predilection for another man's wife as *Śakti*. *Parakīyā* figures in the above *Sahajiyā* cult.

According to some, *Caṇḍālī* is the designation of a woman on the first day of her menstruation.

For further details, see Schoterman's introduction to his edition of the work.

Ed. J.A. Schoterman, New Delhi, 1980.

CHAPTER X

BUDDHIST TANTRAS

ĀDIKARMA-PRADĪPA

By Anupamavajra, it is a Buddhist Tantra of *Kriyā-tantra* class. Written in the form of *Sūtras* with a running commentary. Deals with ceremonies and pious acts to be performed by the Ādikarmika-Bodhisattva, i.e. the follower of Mahāyāna and aspiring for enlightenment. The topics discussed are:

> initiation ceremonies for the disciple (who may be a layman or a monk), daily duties including *Pitṛ-tarpaṇa*, giving alms, meals, worship of the Buddhas and other sacred beings, study of the *Prajñāpāramitā*, meditation, etc. Meant for the beginner, and not for the accomplished Yogin. Corresponding to the Brāhmaṇical manual on *Nityakarma*.

Ed. La Valleė Poussin, Bouddhisme Etudes et Materiaun, Mem. Ac. Belgique, 1897. See same scholar in *JRAS*, 1895.

ADVAYA-SIDDHI

A Buddhist *Sahajayāna* Tantra (c. 729 A.D.) by Lakṣmīṃkarā. It teaches a novel monistic doctrine, called *Sahajayāna;* it is still in vogue among the Bāūls of Bengal (West Bengal and Bangladesh taken together). The work rejects asceticism, rites and worship of images. It recommends only meditation on the body, the abode of all gods.

Ed. in *Jour. of Oriental Institute,* MS Uni., Baroda, XIII, i, Appendix. Text in Devanāgarī, with Tibetan trs., Eng. trs. and Intro.

See B. Bhattacharya, *Sādhanamālā*, II, pp. liv-lvi.

ĀRYA-MAÑJUŚRĪ-MŪLAKALPA

A Buddhist Tantra containing parts of different dates ranging from the 4th century A.D. to the 9th. B. Bhattacharya assigns it to the 2nd century A.D. The early origin of the work is indicated by the absolute absence of the term *Vajrayāna*, and the occurrence of *Mantrayāna*, *Vajrayāna* represents a later phase of Buddhism.

In the extant form, it contains 55 chapters; the Trivandrum edition, however, contains two parts with a total of 49 chapters of which the first three are called *Parivartas* and the rest *Paṭala-visaras*. Jayaswal gives the text of *Paṭalavisara* (53). It contains 1003 verses of which verses 6-344 narrate the biography of the Buddha up to his attainment of *Nirvāṇa*. Verses 345-980 deal with real history from about 78 A.D. to the 8th century.

The instructions, contained in the work, are represented as dialogues between Śākya Muni and Kumāra Mañjuśrī, between Śākyamuni and the *Parṣanmaṇḍala* (councillors), between Mañjuśrī and *Parṣanmaṇḍala*.

The topics discussed are broadly as follows: *Mantra* texts relating to Kumāra Mañjuśrī Bodhisattva Mahāsattva; these are believed to cause long life, health, wealth and other kinds of material happiness, acquisition of desired objects, means for the acquisition of Māntric power, astrological matters, omens and portents.

It is not only an important work of Tāntrik Buddhism, but has also value in the realm of arts. The *Paṭavidhāna* portion contains guidelines for drawing pictures of the Buddhas, Bodhisattvas, Tārā and other goddesses as also of Yakṣas, etc. There are drawings of *Maṇḍalas* and methods of painting abstract ideas.

The enumeration of holy places has some importance for the topography of ancient India.

Ptd. in *TSS*, Trivandrum, 1920-25.

AṢṬAMĪ-VRATA-VIDHĀNA

A Buddhist Tantra of the Kriyā-tantra type. Deals with rites to be performed on every eighth day of every fortnight. It prescribes the use of mystical *Yantras*, *Mudrās*, sacrificial gifts and prayers with *Bījas* like *hruṃ*, *phaṭ*, etc. In it are addressed not only the Buddhas and Bodhisattvas, but also some Śaivite deities.

MS Oxf. II. 1446 (1) has a commentary in Newāri dialect.

Vide Wilson, *Works*, II, p. 31 ff.

(ŚRĪ) CAKRA-SAṂVĀRA (or -SAṂBHĀRA)-TANTRA

It describes the ritual of *Mahāsukha* (Great Bliss). It seeks to teach the *Mantras*, the *Japas*, the figures of the divine couples one has to imagine, the sacrificial ritual and the symbolical significance of the *Mantras* relating to *Mahāsukha*. It is available only in Tibetan.

See Kazi Dawa-Sandup (Introduction and Eng. trs.) in *Tāntrik Texts*, VII, Calcutta, 1919. Tibetan Text in *Tāntrik Texts*, XI.

See H. Zimmer, Kunstform und Yoga im indischen Kultbild, Berlin, 1926, 67 f, 74 ff.

EKALLAVĪRA-CAṆḌA-MAHĀROṢAṆA-TANTRA (also called EKALLAVĪRA-TANTRA, EKAVĪRA-TANTRA or CAṆḌA-MAHĀROṢAṆA TANTRA)

A Buddhist Tantra in 25 chapters (*Paṭalas*). Main contents: The Mahāyāna philosophical doctrine, called *Pratītya-samutpāda* (dependent origination), explained in chapter XVI. Recommendation of the cult of Yoginīs, e.g. Mohavajrī, Piśunavajrī, Rājavajrī, etc. Also recommended is the cult of female deities with sexual actions. The work lays down how the six perfections (*pāramitās*) are attainable by sexual intercourse. The attitude of the author is that enlightenment is achieved through bliss, and no bliss is possible without a woman. All women in the world are looked upon as incarnations of Bhagavatī (cf. *vidyāḥ samastās-tava devi-bhedāḥ striyaḥ samastāḥ sakalā jagatsu* — all women , O Goddess, are different manifestations of yours; *Devī-māhātmya* or *Caṇḍī* included in *Mārkaṇḍeya Purāṇa*).

Caṇḍaroṣaṇa is regarded as an emanation of Akṣobhya. See B. Bhattacharya, *Indian Buddhist Iconography*, p. 60 ff.

For excerpts from MSS of this work, see H.P. Sastri, *Des. Cat. of Skt. MSS in Asiatic Soc. of Bengal*, I, pp. 131-141.

GUHYA-SAMĀJA

Also called *Tathāgata-guhyaka* (c. 300 A.D.); one of the earliest (according to some, the earliest) Buddhist Tantras of the *Vajrayāna* school. According to Tibetan traditions, it came into being in South India. The title means a secret society which is believed to have introduced, for the first time, the *Vajrayāna* doctrines into Buddhism.

In two parts — Pūrvārdha (18 chapters, called *Paṭalas*), also called Aṣṭādaśa-paṭala; Uttarārdha or Aparārdha (in 15 *Paṭalas*), said to be spurious.

Sometimes confused with *Mahāyāna* text, *Tathāgata-guhya-sūtra* from which it is actually different.

The authorship of the work is controversial. Some ascribe it to Asaṅga, the renowned Buddhist scholar. A comparison of the refined language of Asaṅga, in his undisputed work, *Mahāyāna-sūtrālaṃkāra*, with the barbarous language of this work leads P.V. Kane to reject the theory of Asaṅga's authorship. P.C. Bagchi is opposed to the identification of the author of the *Sādhanamālā*, No. 159, with the celebrated *Yogācāra* philosopher.

The work prescribes an easy way of attaining liberation and even Buddhahood in a short time and in one's lifetime. Bodhisattvas and Buddhas are stated to have obtained the seat of *Dharma* by enjoying objects of pleasure as they pleased.

Contrary to the Buddhist principle of *Ahiṃsā*, etc. it allows several kinds of flesh, e.g. that of elephant, horse, dog, even human beings (Paṭala 6). Among the revolutionary practices, repugnant to civilised taste, it allows unrestrained sexual intercourse with even one's own mother, sister and daughter (Paṭala 5). It allows one to speak the untruth and even to steal another person's wealth. It provides for the quick means to the acquisition of *Siddhis* (miraculous powers). For the acquisition of powers, association with females is a must.

It is curious that the work advocates the enjoyment of women as the panacea for sick men. Jīvaka, the master physician, is stated to have formed a girl out of all medicaments. The ailing people, who came to him for treatment, were made to cohabit with the girl; they were eventually cured. It may be noted that the MS, described by R.L. Mitra (*Nep. Buddh. Lit.*, p. 226 ff), prescribes, as a means to the attainment of the highest perfection, the eating of meat as also daily sexual union with young and beautiful Caṇḍāla girls.

Of the eight accessories of *Yoga* (*Yogāṅgas* — see Glossary), it omits *Yama* (self-restraint), *Niyama* (which includes Vedic study and contemplation on God) and *Āsana*.

A novel feature is the theory of the five *Dhyānibuddhas* emanating from the Bhagavat (vide B. Bhattacharya's Intro. to *Guhyasamāja-tantra*, p. xix and his Intro. to *Buddhist Esoterism*, pp. 32, 33, 70, etc.). They represent the five *Skandhas* or fundamental principles underlying creation; each of them is associated with a *Śakti*.

The work deals with the conventional Tāntric *Ṣaṭkarmans*.

An index to its authoritative character is the fact that it is quoted by Indrabhūti in his *Jñānasiddhi* and by Advayavajra in his *Advaya-vajra-saṃgraha*. The *Guhyasiddhi* of Padmavajra also recognises its authority. Moreover, there are as many as twelve commentaries on it.

Ptd. *GOS*, LIII, 1931. Its portion, called *Pañcakrama*, which prescribes means for attaining the five stages of Tāntric Yoga, has been ed., with intro., by La Vallée Poussin, Etudes et Textes Tantriques, 1896.

For text-problem, see *IHQ*, IX.1, pp. 1-2; L.M. Joshi, *Jour. of Ori. Inst.*, MS Univ., Baroda, XVI, pp. 138 ff.

GUHYASIDDHI

A Buddhist Tāntric work by Padmavajra, a contemporary of Indrabhūti. The work describes and recommends the secret rites of *Vajrayāna*. It is written in *Sandhyā-bhāṣā* (literally, the twilight language, i.e. a mystic language). According to some, it was the language of the borderland between the ancient Āryāvarta (vide *Manusmṛti*, ii.22) and the actual Bengal. According to others, it was *Sandhā-bhāṣā* i.e. language with a secret motive (see *Viśvabhāratī Quarterly*, 1924, p. 265 and *IHQ*, IV, 1928, p. 287 ff).

Vide B. Bhattacharya, *Sādhanamālā*, II, pp. xlvi, cvi ff, *NCC*, VI, p. 93; XI, p. 149.

HEVAJRA-TANTRA

A Buddhist work the Sanskrit MSS of which are divided into two parts (*Kalpas*), each containing ten chapters. In the Chinese translation, however, the number of chapters is continuous.

According to Snellgrove, the editor of the printed work, it existed towards the end of the eighth century A.D. He thinks that the *Advaya-vajra-saṃgraha* and *Sekoddeśaṭīkā* are indebted to the *Hevajra*.

Hevajra is the Supreme Being in the state of non-duality. It particularly stands for Heruka, united with Śakti in the *Yuganaddha* form. *Hevajra* is invocation to Vajra; 'He' indicates (Pt. II, p. 2) *Mahākaruṇā-vajraṃprajñā*. So, this work teaches both *Upāya* (means) and *Prajñā* (wisdom).

Some important features of the work are the following. It mentions (Pt. 1, p. 70) the *Pīṭhas*, named Jālandhara, Oḍḍiyāna, Pūrṇagiri and Kāmarūpa, several *Upapīṭhas* and *Upakṣetras* are also mentioned. Instead of *Śakti*, *Prajñā* is mentioned. The work states (Pt. II, p. 70) how the followers of this Tantra enjoyed sexual union with women, called *Mudrās*, and thereby attained *Siddhi*. A ritual for winning over a young woman is laid down in Pt. I, p. 54. Among the topics, dealt with in it, is *Kāyasādhana*. The body is stated to contain 32 *Nāḍis* which take the *Bodhicitta* (mind turned towards perfect enlightenment) upward till it reaches the region of great bliss (*Maha-sukha-sthāna*). Instead of *Iḍā*, *Piṅgalā* and *Suṣumnā*, the commonly known *Nāḍis* in Tantra, principal *Nāḍis* in this work are: *Lalanā*, *Rasanā* and *Avadhūtī*. With these are associated respectively *Prajñā*, *Upāya* and the absolute non-duality which is beyond *grāhya-grāhaka* (what is to be taken and one who takes).

A noteworthy topic in this Tantra is the *Sandhyā-bhāṣā* which is described as *Mahāsamaya* of the Yogins and as a *Mahābhāṣā*, full of significance. *Mahāsamaya* is the doctrine of the *Hevajra* school. (On *Sandhyā-bhāṣā*, see Glossary.)

The work has a commentary, called *Yogaratna-mālā* by Paṇḍita Kāṇha.

Ed. D.L. Snellgrove, with Eng. trs., 2 vols., London, 1959.

JÑĀNASIDDHI (variously called O BUDDHI O BODHI, MAHENDRABHŪTI, OḌYĀNASIDDHA, OḌYĀNA-NARENDRA of MAHĀRĀJĀDHIRĀJA INDRABHŪTI)

A Buddhist Vajrayāna tantra, by Indrabhūti who appears to have been author of *Kurukullā-sādhana* (*Sādhanamālā* No. 174). Many other Tāntric works are attributed to him; of these 23 are translated in the *Tanjur*. Indrabhūti, a king of Uḍḍiyāna, was teacher or disciple of Anaṅgavajra and (god?) father of Padmasambhava, the founder of Lāmāism. Indrabhūti (c. 687-717 A.D.) is stated to have been brother of Lakṣmīṁkarā Devī.

The work briefly sets forth the principal doctrines of Vajrayāna, which are the following.

The very practices, leading an ordinary person to hell, may help a Yogin attain liberation. One, without any desire, can acquire the highest enlightenment in this very life. The killing of animals, speaking the untruth and theft are condemned. As regards women, it holds that one attains *Siddhi* by enjoying a woman of a despicable family. One should not look down upon even a woman who is uncouth in every part of her body. A woman of any family should be worshipped, provided she is a holder of *Vajra*. This is especially applicable to a Dombikā, born in a Caṇḍāla family.

A person, to be *Guru*, must be highly qualified; one is warned against a hypocritical *Guru* who initiated disciples out of greed.

A procedure of *Abhiṣeka* is laid down.

Ptd. in *GOS*, 44, 1929. For various Tāntric works, attributed to Indrabhūti, see B. Bhattacharya in *Sādhanamālā*, II, pp. xi ff, xii ff, xcviii f; *NCC*, II, p. 254; VII, p. 342.

KĀLACAKRA-TANTRA

This metrical Buddhist work belonging to *Kālacakrayāna*, an offshoot of *Vajrayāna*, and variously called *Śrī-kālacakra-tantra-rāja*, *Śrī Mahākāla-cakra* and *Laghu-kālacakra-tantra*, contains, according to Banerjee's critical ed. (1985), 1047 verses, divided into five chapters (*Paṭalas*) which are named *Lokadhātu-paṭala*, *Adhyātma-paṭala*, *Abhiṣeka-paṭala*, *Sādhana-paṭala* and *Jñāna-paṭala*.

In the colophon to chapter V, in the above edition, the total number of verses is stated as 12,000. The words *tantraṃ śrīkālacakraṃ laghutaramakhilaṃ*, in verse V.261, clearly indicate that it is an abridged version.

According to a traditional account, we gather that Sucandra, king of Śambhala, was present when the Buddha revealed the *Mūla-tantra* of the *Kālacakra*. Sucandra explained the text in its abridged form to one Sūryaratha. King Yaśas (Yaśorāja) is credited with introducing the shorter version, and converting the Brāhmaṇical sages of Śambhala to the principles of *Kālacakra*.

There is a commentary, called *Vimalaprabhā*, by Puṇḍarīka who is said to have written it at the instance of his father, Yaśorāja.

The contents, chapterwise, are briefly as follows:

I Sucandra approaches the Buddha for a discourse on *Kālacakra*; the Lord's preachings, description of the universe (*Lokadhātu*); various activities of the Lord including the eradication of the religion of *Mlecchas* and establishment of Buddhism.

II Existence of Lord *Kālacakra* in rites of impregnation (*garbhādhāna*), semen, menstrual flow, in the growing womb, as ten incarnations beginning with that of Fish, nature and purification of four *kāyas* and four *vajras*, breast, *Nāḍis*, vital winds, five *skandhas*, *dhātus*; in short, in religions, agreeable to different beings.

III *Guru*, *śiṣya*, village, direction, land etc., sacrifice, rosary, meditation, 36 *Kuladevīs* — all pervaded by the Lord.

IV Existence of Lord in *Śūnyatā*, three refuges, self-mortification, acquisition of *Bodhicitta*, resort to Noble Path (*Mārga*), *maṇḍala*, *Yoga* of *bindu*, etc.

V Lord's existence in purification of *dhātus* like bones of the body, *mantra* groups like *Ādi*, *Kādi*, *Prajñopāyas*, *Kriyā-yoga*, fourth *Abhiṣeka*, acquisition of knowledge of *Mahāmudrā*, *Bodhicitta*, actions of body, mind and speech, description of Buddhakṣetra (place in which the Buddha appears) and *vajra*, Bodhisattvas, benefit of all beings, *Śūnyatā*, etc.

The system developed with Time (*Kāla*) as the central theme to be realised for the eradication of ignorance and attainment of liberation. So, the work deals elaborately with astronomical matters like the movement of planets, etc. Astrology also has a part to play.

Yantras have been dealt with in considerable details (I.127-147).

The language of the work bristles with solecisms. It seems that such texts were not written by elites, but by men who were more anxious to propagate the ideas among the *hoi polloi* than to produce learned treatises. It should be noted that the mathematical and astronomical portions of the work betray jargon, not easily intelligible to readers. Might be, these were current coins of Tantric preachers in those days.

Though traditionally a work of very high antiquity, it actually is a late work. It mentions Mecca and Islam (vide Winternitz, *History of Indian Literature*, 1983, II, p. 387); the *terminus ad quem* is fixed by the mention of the work by Abhayākaragupta (1084-1130 A.D.) in his *Vajrāvalī-nāma-maṇḍalaupāyika* (see *NCC*, IV, p. 15).

The provenance of the text is Orissa, according to some.

Ed. (1) Tibetan text, with Mongolian trs., by J. Schubert, in *Mitteilungen des Instituts für Orient forschungen*, I, 1953, pp. 424-73; (2) Raghuvira, New Delhi; (3) B.N. Banerjee, Asiatic Soc., Calcutta, 1985. The editor of the Asiatic Soc. ed., in the editorial note, informs us that he will publish two more vols.; the second vol. will contain the *Vimalaprabhā* commentary and the third vol. will contain a study based on the text and the commentary.

For various matters, relating to the work, see Intro., *A la histoire du Buddhisme Indien*, 2nd ed., Paris, 1876, p. 480 fn., Winternitz, *Hist. of Ind. Lit.*, 1983, II, p. 387; S.B. Dasgupta, *An Intro. to Tantric Buddhism*, Calcutta, pp. 64-69; *JASB*, 1907, pp. 225-27; *Nepal*, II, Preface, pp. ii-iv; *JASB*, Letters, 1952, pp. 71-76; AIOC, 1955, *Summaries*, p. 104. For mention of a Chinese trs., see *AR*, XX, 488, *JA*, 1849, p. 356, *JRAS*, 1880, p. 167. The *Sekoddeśa-ṭīkā* (GOS, XC) is an exposition of its *Seka* section.

MAHĀKĀLA-TANTRA

Appears to be influenced by Śaivism. Written in the form of conversation between Śākyamuni and a goddess. Stated to be proclaimed by the Buddha. Among contents are explanations of the mystical significance of the letters forming the name Mahākāla (Śiva). Among other things are mentioned the means of discovering hidden treasure, acquiring a kingdom, getting a desirable wife, learning *Mantras* and magic rites by which a man can be made insane, enslave and kill him.

See R.L. Mitra, *Nep. Buddh. Lit.*, p. 172 ff; E.B. Cowell and J. Eggeling, *Cat. of Buddh. Skt. MSS*, p. 37 f.

MAÑJUŚRĪ-MŪLAKALPA

Describes itself as a *Mahāyānasūtra* and as a part of the *Avataṃsaka* (*Buddhāvataṃsaka-mahā-vaipulya-sūtra*).

Śākyamuni represented as giving instructions to Mañjuśrī about magic rites with *Mantras*, *Mudrās*, *Maṇḍalas*, etc.

Chap. IX teaches the *Mantra* of Mañjuśrī, which includes all science in itself and is the means to the attainment of all things; it renders ineffectual all *Mantras* of enemies, washes off all sins, etc. This Great *Mantra* is called *Killhuṃ*.

Chap. XIV attributes the same powers to the *Bhruṃ Mantra*.

The work reveals little of Buddhism excepting the fact that the worship of the "Three Jewels" is mentioned in chap. 47.

Ed. T.G. Sastri in *TSS*, Nos. LXX and LXXVI, 1920, 1922.

See J. Przyluski in *BEFEO*, t. XXIII, 1923, p. 301 ff, and B. Bhattacharya, *Sādhanamālā*, II, p. xxxiv f.

Trs. into Chinese as a *Mahāvaipulyasūtra*, between 900 and 1000 A.D. Trs. into Tibetan as a Tantra in 11th cent. A.D.

NIṢPANNA-YOGĀVALĪ-NĀMA

Attributed to Abhayākaragupta, it contains 26 chapters, each dealing with a *Maṇḍala*. Many of the deities of Tāntric Buddhism, mentioned in it, do not appear anywhere else. The descriptions of the deities have importance from the point of view of iconography. Also valuable are religious and philosophical matters discussed in it.

According to a MS (Cordier, III, p. 230), its full title is *Mañju-vajrādhikramābhisamaya-samuccaya-niṣpanna-yogāvalī*.

Ed. B. Bhattacharya, Baroda, 1949.

PAÑCAKRAMA

Said to be a part of the *Guhyasamāja* (q.v.). It deals more with *Yoga* than with Tāntric observances. In it, the means of attaining the five stages of Tāntric *yoga* are laid down. The means consist in *Cakras*, magic formulae, mystic syllables and worship of Mahāyānist deities and Tāntric deities. To the Yogin, who reaches the highest stage, all differences disappear, and no duality of any sort exists.

The work comprises five sections of which section III is ascribed to Śākyamitra who is mentioned by Tāranātha as a contemporary of King Devapāla of Bengal of the earlier half of the 9th century A.D.

The other four sections of the work are attributed to Nāgārjuna who seems to be a Tāntric scholar rather than the Nāgārjuna, author of the Buddhist work, *Mādhyamika-kārikā*, who probably flourished in the latter part of the 2nd century A.D.

Ed., with intro., by La Vallée Poussin, *Etudes et Textes Tantriques*, 1896.

PRAJÑOPĀYA-VINIŚCAYA-SIDDHI

Attributed to Anaṅgavajra, it is a Buddhist *Vajrayāna* text, believed, by B. Bhattacharya, to have been composed about 705 A.D. The highlights of its contents are as follows.

It is declared (v.16) that a devotee, by adhering to the instructions, can acquire the highest enlightenment in this very life. The condition, attainable by following the *Vajrayāna* method, is stated (i.20) to be neither duality nor non-duality. It is full of peace, capable of being experienced by one who is steady, undisturbed and full of *prajñā* (wisdom) and *upāya* (activity with compassion). It is provided (v.22-23) that an aspirant for liberation must, by all means, achieve perfection of wisdom. This perfection exists everywhere in the form of woman. *Prajñā* has connexion with the state of rapturous emotion, called *Sukha* and *Mahāsukha*. Of the nature of unlimited bliss, *Mahāsukha* is salutary in all respects, pre-eminent, and gives rise to full enlightenment (i.27), *Prajñā* and *Upāya* are conceived as female principle and male principle respectively. In keeping with the usual Tāntric practice, *Prajñā* is identified with a woman of flesh and blood. *Mahāsukha* is declared as sexual symbolism. In iii.9-16, there is an eloquent eulogy of the *Guru* who is identified with the Buddha, described as omniscient.

An outrageous statement (v.25) is that a Yogin, desirous of sexual union with his mother, sister or daughter, would attain *Siddhi*.

Ptd. in Two Vajrayāna Works, *GOS*, XL, iv, 1929. For exposition of the relevant passage (v.25 referred to above), see Guenther, *Yuganaddha*, pp. 106-209.

For a study of *Prajñā* and *Upāya*, with reference to this work, see *Jour. of Indian and Buddhist Studies*, II (1952-53), 512-13.

SĀDHANA-MĀLĀ

A composite *Vajrayāna* work containing 312 Tāntric tracts believed to have been composed between the third and the twelfth centuries A.D. Many of the works are anonymous, and known to the Tibetan *Tanjur*. Some of the authors, mentioned in it, are credited with the authorship of other works on Tantra.

The main contents of the works are magical. The principal topics are: worship of *Prajñā-pāramitā*, attainment of *Siddhi* or perfection — the nature of the *Siddhis* and methods of acquiring them, use of *Mudrās*, meditation, detailed description of the deity to be meditated upon. Among deities, to be worshipped, are Dhyāni-Buddhas and their families, innumerable forms of Tārā and other female deities, a Buddhist god of love, Vajranāga, an incarnation of Mañjuśrī.

Language of the *Sādhanas* generally defective Sanskrit and metres of the verses very irregular. Some *Sādhanas* are in prose and short, others are longer with metrical *mantras;* some are wholly metrical.

The dates of the authors, to whom different *Sādhanas* are attributed, appear to range between the 7th century A.D. and the 11th. One manuscript of the *Sādhanamālā* dates back to 1165 A.D.

The prominent authors mentioned are: Asaṅga, Nāgārjuna (perhaps different from his namesake, the renowned founder of the Mādhyamika school of Buddhist philosophy), Indrabhūti (687-717 A.D.), Padmavajra, Lakṣmīṃkarā, Sahaja-yoginī Cintā (c. 761 A.D.).

The detailed descriptions of the deities, contained in the *Sādhanamālā*, inspired many sculptors and painters in conceiving the images of them. Thus, the works were of great importance to Buddhist iconography.

Ed. (under the title *Sādhana-mālā* or *Sādhana-samuccaya*) by B. Bhattacharya in *GOS*, Nos. XXVI, XLI, Baroda, 1925, 1928. See B. Bhattacharya, The Indian Buddhist Iconography mainly based on *Sādhanamālā* and other cognate Tāntric Texts and Rituals, Oxford, 1924; P.C. Bagchi in *IHQ*, 6, 1930; N.K. Bhattasali, *Iconography of Buddhist and Brāhmaṇical Sculptures in Dacca Museum*, 1972.

SAṂVARODAYA-TANTRA

In the form of conversation between the Buddha and Bodhisattva Vajrapāṇi. It, however, appears to be predominantly Śaivite; it recommends the cult of Liṅga and the worship of Śaivite deities.

See Burnouf, *Introduction*, p. 479 ff.

SEKODDEŚAṬĪKĀ

A Buddhist Tantra, attributed to Śrīnaḍapāda.

Ed. M.E. Carelli, with introduction in English, *GOS*.

ŚRĪCAKRA-SAṂBHĀRA-TANTRA

A Buddhist Tantra available only in Tibetan and English translations. Its importance lies in the description of *Mahāsukha* (Great Bliss). In relation to *Mahāsukha*, it provides *mantras*, *japa*, imaginary figures of the divine couples the devotee has to keep before his mind's eye, sacrifice, the symbolical significance of the *mantras*.

See K. Dawa-Sandup (Introduction and Eng. trs.) in Avalon's *Tāntrik Texts*, VII; *ibid.*, XI (Tibetan texts).

Also see H. Zimmer, Kunstform und Yoga im Indischen Kultbild, Berlin, 1926, 67 f, 74 ff.

TĀRĀ-TANTRA

A Buddhist Tāntric digest in 6 chapters (*Paṭalas*). In it, the Buddha and sage Vaśiṣṭha are referred to as great Bhairavas. The Buddha, an incarnation of Viṣṇu, is stated to have got the position of Creator, after being initiated to the *Mantras* of Ugra Tārā. The Buddha's Śakti, Tārā, is of the form of wisdom (*Prajñā*). Vaśiṣṭha is said to have obtained the knowledge of Tārā, in China, from the Buddha. In this connexion, the following verse from the *Rudrayāmala* is worth quoting:

Vaśiṣṭho brahmaputro'pi cirakālaṃ susādhanam/
jagāma cīna-bhūmau ca yatra buddhaḥ pratiṣṭhitaḥ//

See Woodroffe, *Shakti and Shākta*, p. 104 ff.

Ptd. Varendra Research Soc., Rajshahi (now in Bangladesh), 1913.

APPENDIX I

PĪṬHA-STHĀNAS

Holy place of Śakti. Such places are generally held to be fifty-one in number. Each of these places is believed to contain a limb of Śakti.[1]

Pīṭhas are usually divided into two classes, viz. *Mahā* (major) and *Upa* (minor). A great Tāntric devotee is said to have attained the goal of *Sādhana* at each of the *Pīṭhasthānas* (*Pīṭha* means seat); so, these came to be very holy to their respective followers.

There is no consensus among the different Tantras about the names and number of these places.

In some Purāṇas and Tantras of the early medieval age, only four *Pīṭhasthānas* are mentioned. These are Jālandhara, Uḍḍiyāna, Pūrṇagiri and Kāmarūpa; some works read Śrīhaṭṭa for Jālandhara.

The *Rudrayāmala Tantra* mentions two lists of *Pīṭhasthānas*, one containing 10 main *Pīṭhas* and the other 18 *Pīṭhas*. 42 and 50 *Pīṭhas* are mentioned in the *Kubjikā Tantra* and *Jñānārṇava Tantra* respectively. Kṛṣṇānanda's *Tantrasāra* follows the list in the latter. But, instead of Merugiri Pīṭha, Kṛṣṇānanda reads Merupīṭha and Giripīṭha; thus, the number of *Pīṭhas* in this work is 51. Some works mention 108 *Pīṭhasthānas*. A late work, called *Pīṭha-nirṇaya* or *Mahāpīṭha-nirṇaya*, however, mentions 51.

Of the 51 places, now recognised as *Devī-pīṭhas*, many are minor holy places in Bengal (West Bengal and Bangladesh taken together); for instance, Caṭṭala, Tripurā, Kālīghāṭ, Yaśohar, etc. Curiously enough, these places are conspicuous by absence in the works of the early medieval age.

---

1. In this connexion, see the legend, relating to *Dakṣa-yajña* set forth under the caption Śiva-Śakti.

APPENDIX II

MISCELLANEOUS TĀNTRIC WORKS AND COMMENTARIES

Religion and spirituality were essential parts of the lives of ancient Indians. In fact, their daily life was a round of rituals and prayers. Ever since Vedic times, the Indians chose poetry as a medium of eulogising gods and praying to them. The entire *Ṛgveda* is a collection of hymns to various gods and goddesses.

The *Mahābhārata,* as we have seen in the chapter on Tāntric Elements in Sanskrit Literature, contains hymns to Durgā, which unmistakably reveal Tāntric bias.

The Purāṇas contain many hymns. Of such hymns, quite a number are tinged with Tāntric hue. In this connection, the *Devīmāhātmya* or *Caṇḍī,* contained in the *Mārkaṇḍeya-purāṇa,* deserve special mention. There are several hymns in it, which bear the clear imprimatur of Tantra. For instance, the *Argalāstotra* opens with a verse containing the words Cāmuṇḍā and Kālarātri. The word 'Kālī' has been used in a verse. Verse 21 describes Cāmuṇḍā as *Śavavāhanā* (mounted on a corpse). The typical words Ḍākinī and Śākinī occur in verse 54. In the eulogy of the Goddess by the demons, she is designated as Ādyā Prakṛti, a Tāntric conception (verse 7). She has been called *Vidyā* (verse 9) and Śabdātmikā (verse 10, of the nature of sound). The *Kuñjikastotra* provides, in the manner of Tantra, that the hymn, which is very secret, should be concealed like one's own genital organ. Verse 4 of this hymn contains the names of the important Tāntric rites of *Māraṇa, Mohana, Vaśīkaraṇa, Stambhana* and *Uccāṭana.*

Some Tantras contain hymns. For example, Abhinavagupta, in his *Tantrāloka,* has given us eulogistic and prayerful hymns.

As regards the number of *Pāñcarātra* texts, we find lists in the following works:

Kapiñjala-, *Pādma-*, *Viṣṇu-* and *Hayaśīrṣa-saṃhitās* and *Agnipurāṇa*.

The total number of texts, mentioned in the above works, is 210. Besides the above, the following Saṃhitās are extant:

Upendra-saṃhitā (different from the *Upendra*, mentioned in the above list), *Kāśyapottara-saṃhitā*, *Paramatattva-nirṇaya-prakāśa-saṃhitā*, *Pādma-saṃhitā-tantra*, *Bṛhad-brahma-saṃhitā*.

In addition to the above, many Saṃhitās have been quoted or mentioned by name, which seem to be different from those mentioned in the above list. The following may be mentioned, but there may be many more:

Citraśikhaṇḍī, *Maṅkaṇa*, *Vaiśampāyana*, *Śukapraśna*, *Sudarśana*, *Saumantava*, *Haṃsa*, *Haṃsaparameśvara*.

The earliest source of information about the *Pāñcarātra* is believed to be the Nāradīya (more familiar, Nārāyaṇīya) section of the Śānti Parvan of the *Mahābhārata* though the possibility of its earlier existence cannot be ruled out.[1]

It is generally believed that this system originated in northern India, and gradually spread to the south.[2] The earliest extant South Indian *Pāñcarātra* text appears to be the *Īśvara-saṃhitā* which probably dates back to about the time of the great Śaṃkarācārya (c. 9th cent. A.D.). The oldest work of North India, quoting the *Pāñcarātra*, seems to be the *Spanda-pradīpikā* of the Kashmirian Utpalavaiṣṇava (10th cent. A.D.).

The ideal and complete *Pāñcarātra Saṃhitā* consists of the usual Tāntric topics, viz., *Jñāna*, *Yoga*, *Kriyā* and *Caryā*. To be more explicit, the subjects, treated in this system, are as follows:

1. Philosophy, 2. Linguistic occultism (*mantra-śāstra*), 3. Theory of magical figures (*yantra-śāstra*), 4. Practical magic.

This Tantra, in both its versions, is divided into three parts. The subject-matter is presented in the form of discourses either by Śākyamuni or Vajrapāṇi. The instructions given relate to the evocations and arrangements of various *maṇḍalas* and the rites of initiations and consecrations which are given in them, as well as the descriptions of the ritual known as *homa* in Sanskrit and *Sbyin-Sreg* in Tibetan and funerary rituals of different kinds.

---

1. See F.O. Schrader, *op. cit.*
2. *Ibid.*

GLOSSARY (General)

[For scientific terms, used in Tantra, there is a separate glossary.]

The vast Tantra literature contains a large number of technical terms and words which are not commonly used. Here we have noted only such words as are often necessary for the study of Tantras.

For the convenience of those who are interested only in the scientific elements in Tantra, we have given a separate list containing exclusively the scientific terms, based mainly on the *Rasārṇava*.

In English Alphabetical Order

Abhicāra
: A rite designed to harm others. *Śāradātilaka*, XX. 111, 123-25. *Śaktisaṃgama*, Kālī, VIII. 102-105.

Abhiṣeka
: Consecration of the Tāntric devotee who has holy water sprinkled over him. It is of two broad kinds:
Śāktābhiṣeka and *Pūrṇābhiṣeka*.
Śāradātilaka (Rāghavabhaṭṭa's comm. iv. 1).
Prāṇatoṣiṇī, II. 5.
Śaktisaṃgama, Kālī, XI. 29-37.

Ācāra
: Rules of conduct as means of spiritual attainment. There are generally seven kinds of such rules; e.g., *Veda*, *Vaiṣṇava*, *Śaiva*, *Dakṣiṇa*, *Vāma*, *Siddhānta*, *Kaula*.
These are comprised in two main categories, viz., *Vāma* and *Dakṣiṇa*.*Kaulamārga-rahasya*, p. 11.
Prāṇatoṣiṇī, vii. 4, p. 582.
Mātṛkābheda, p. 6.

Ādhāra
: Literally, receptacle.
The *Cakra* (q.v.), supposed to exist in the lowest extremity of the spinal cord, is called *Mūlādhāra*.
Nīlatantra, IV. 9.

Adhaḥ-āmnāya
One of the six geographical divisions believed to be presided over by Buddhist and Jain deities, Vāgīśvarī, Vajrayoginī, Nairṛteśvarī, etc.
Prāṇatoṣiṇī, I. 9, p. 64.
Śaktisaṃgama, Sundarī, III. 182-84.

Adhvaśodhana
Procedure of purifying the body consisting of six *adhvas*, viz., *varṇa*, *pada*, *mantra*, *kalā*, *tattva* and *bhuvana*.
Śāradātilaka (Rāghavabhaṭṭa's comm. on it), V. 77.

Ādyā Śakti
Primeval energy conceived as a goddess.

Āgama
In Tantra, it generally stands for those works in which Pārvatī asks questions which are answered by Śiva.

Aghamarṣaṇa
Literally meaning the wiping off of the sin from the body. It is done by sprinkling water on different parts of the body.
Tantrasāra of Kṛṣṇānanda (on authority of *Mālinītantra*, p. 79).

Āghāta
Prāṇāyāma.

Aghora
(1) A form of Śiva, black and fierce, supposed to preside over the Southern region.
Prāṇatoṣiṇī, I. 9 (on authority of *Nirvāṇatantra*).
(2) Name of a Śaiva sect resorting to *Vāmācāra*.
Śaktisaṃgama, Tārā, 192-94.
(3) One of the two broad divisions of Tāntric *ācāras*, as distinct from *yoga*.

Āgneya-varṇa
Letters connected with the element of fire. These are from *Ya* to *Kṣa* in order.
Śāradātilaka (Rāghavabhaṭṭa's comm. on it), III. 1-3.

Ajapā
A form of effortless meditation. The sounds *haṃ* and *saḥ*, arising automatically due to inhalation and exhalation respectively, constitute this *mantra*. This automatic formation of the *haṃsa-mantra* takes place in *mūlādhāra*, *anāhata* and *ājñā cakras*. *Ajapā* is twofold, secret and open. The latter is subdivided into two categories, sound and sight.
Gheraṇḍa, V. 85.
Śāradātilaka, XIV. 91 (Rāghava's comm. on it).

Ājñā-cakra
The nerve-plexus between the eyebrows. Looking like a two-petalled white lotus, it is

symbolised by the letters *Ha* and *Kṣa*. *Ṣaṭcakranirūpaṇa*, XXXII.

Akṣamālā
A rosary of beads made of *Rudrākṣa*, crystals, etc.

Akula
Śiva aspect of Śakti.
Tantrāloka, III. 67.

Ali
Spirituous liquor used in Tāntric worship.

Ālīḍha
A posture in which the right leg is stretched forward and the left is slightly bent.

Āmnāya
Zone of Tāntric culture, five or six in number.
Kulārṇava, III. 7; *Śaktisaṃgama*, Sundarī, V. 182-87.

Anāhata
(1) A nerve-plexus (*Cakra*) in the region of the heart, supposed to look like a twelve-petalled red lotus.
(2) Name of a particular sound without anything being struck.

Anavasthollāsa
The last stage of spiritual progress, according to some Tāntric schools.
Paraśurāma-kalpasūtra, X. 68.

Āṇavī dīkṣā
A form of Tāntric initiation in which *mantra, arcanā, āsana, nyāsa, dhyāna* and various articles of worship are required. It is of various kinds, e.g., *Spārśī, Vācikī*, etc. *Śāradātilaka*, V. 127-40 (Rāghava's comm.), *Prāṇatoṣiṇī*, II. 4.

Aṅganyāsa
A method of feeling the limbs in a Tāntric rite. It is of five or six kinds. The centres are heart, head, protective symbol, eyes and intestine.
Nīlatantra, V. II.

Aṇimā
See *Siddhi*.

Antardaśāra
Internal body of mystic diagrams. Inner shade of the flames of *Cakras*, called *Bindu, Trikoṇa* and *Aṣṭakoṇa*. Manifest ray of the *Navatikoṇa* or *Navayonicakra* consisting of nine triangles.
Kāmakalāvilāsa, 30; *Nityāṣoḍaśīkārṇava*, VI. 15.

Antaryāga
Mental worship in which the *Pañcatattvas* are conceived as abstract and not tangible things.
Mahānirvāṇa, V. 143-49.
Gautamīya Tantra, IX.
Gāndharva Tantra, XII. 24-27.

Anukalpa
Substitute, e.g., coconut water for wine.

Āpyāyana
Processing of a *mantra*. Kṛṣṇānanda's *Tantrasāra*, p. 54.

Ārambha-ullāsa
First stage of spiritual attainment. *Paraśurāmakalpa*, X. 68.

Ardhaparyaṅka
A sitting posture in which both the legs are on the same pedestal, one knee being bent and the other raised.

Arka: *Jñāna-śakti*.

Asaṃprajñāta Samādhi
See *Samādhi*.

Āsana
Posture as an accessory of *yoga*.

Asmitā
See *Pañcakleśa*.

Aṣṭadala-padma
Eight-petalled lotus conceived as a symbol in the making of *Cakras* inside and outside human body as also in diagrams. The petals are stated to contain the letters *KA, CA, ṬA, TA, PA, YA, SA, LA*.

Aṣṭakoṇa-cakra
Octagonal diagram considered as representing both the gross and the subtle body of goddess. *Kāmakalā-vilāsa*, 29. *Cidvallī* on the same, 40 ff. The eight corners are supposed to be presided over by goddesses (Śakti), called Vaśinī, Kāmeśī, Modinī, Vimalā, Aruṇā, Jayinī, Sarveśī and Kaulinī. *Nityāṣoḍaśīkārṇava*, I. 191-92. The presiding deities are collectively called *Rahasya-yoginī*. Also see *Gandharva-tantra*, XVII. 74-76.

Aṣṭamātṛkā
Eight Mother-goddesses supposed to reside in the *Viṣṇurekhā* of *Bhūpura-yantra*, *Nityāṣoḍaśīkārṇava*, I. 169-71.

Aṣṭapāśa
Eight bonds of human existence, viz., *ghṛṇā* (hatred), *lajjā* (shame), *bhaya* (fear), *śaṅkā* (apprehension), *jugupsā* (aversion or reproach), *kula* (pedigree), *śīla* (conduct), *jāti* (birth or caste). *Paraśurāma-kalpasūtra*, X. 70. A list of 62 fetters is found in some Tantras. See *Saubhāgya-bhāskara* or *Lalitā-sahasra-nāma*, 129.

Aṣṭasiddhi
See *Siddhi*.

Astra: Same as *Astrabīja* (q.v.).

Astrabīja
Syllable *Phaṭ*. *Nīlatantra*, III. 8.

Aśvakrāntā (or, Gajakrāntā)

The vast tract of land extending from the Vindhyā hills to the great ocean. In the *Mahāsiddhasāratantra*, its western boundary is the river Karatoyā in Dinājpur district of West Bengal, and the eastern boundary is in Yavadvīpa or Java.

According to some authorities, it extends from above hill to the west, comprising Persia, Egypt and Rhodesia.

It is one of the three tracts into which India is divided in certain Tantras.

This region is said to have been so called as horse or elephant was the chief means of transport there.

Avadhūta

dvaita-jñāna-vihīno yaḥ
sarva-bhūta-hīte rataḥ/
tyakta-varṇāśramaḥ śāntaḥ
pāpa-leśa-parāṅmukhaḥ//
avalipto na kutrāpi
dhūtapāpaḥ sadaiva hi/
avadhūtaḥ sa vijñeyas-tatkṛte
cīna-sådhanam//

(1) A Tāntric devotee of a very high order.

An *Avadhūta* of the highest grade is called *Kulāvadhūta*.

Avadhūtas are divided into two classes: householders and recluses.

Kulārṇava, XVII.

Prāṇatoṣiṇī, VII. 4.

Mahānirvāṇa, VII. 271-83.

(2) Name of a nerve.

Avadhūtī

The central nerve, according to Buddhists, corresponding to *Suṣumnā* of Hindu Tantra.

Āvaraṇadevatā

Also called Yoginī, presiding over nine *Cakras* called *Prakaṭa*, *Gupta*, etc., which are different from the well-known *Ṣaṭcakras*.

Aityāṣoḍaśīkārṇava, I. 164-65 (*Setubandha* Comm.).

Avidyā

False knowledge, nescience. *Moha*.

Avira

Tāntric disciple belonging to the probationary stages of *ārambha*, *taruṇa*, *yauvana* and *prauḍha*.

Paraśurāma-kalpasūtra, X. 58 (Rāmeśvara's Comm.).

Āvṛti

Āvaraṇa. Veil of delusion.

Avyakta

Unmanifested. Denotes Prakṛti (q.v.).

Bahirdaśāra

External appearance of the mystic diagrams intended to represent five gross and five subtle elements. These elements are symbolised by ten letters beginning with *Ka*.

The ten triangles, representing the theme, are supposed to be presided over by ten goddesses, called Kulakaulayoginī.
Nityāṣoḍaśīkārṇava, I. 184-86, VI. 16.

Bahiryāga
External worship. Opposite to *Antaryāga* (q.v.).

Bāṇaliṅga
A form of Śiva-phallus, supposed to reside in the triangle of *Anāhata-cakra* (q.v.). So called as it is believed to be one of the 14 crores of *Śiva-liṅgas* established by demon Bāṇa at various places.
Ṣaṭ-cakra-nirūpaṇa, XXV.

Bhairava
(i) Paramaśiva, (ii) A human teacher who appears to have acquired perfect spiritual emancipation and become almost Śiva; their views are laid down in Tāntric *Yāmalas*.

Bhairavī
Female partner or Śakti of a Tāntric devotee.

Bhairavī Cakra
A ritual in which *Pañcatattvas* are used. In it, males and females participate and indulge in drinking and sexual intercourse.
Mahānirvāṇa, VIII. 54-206.
Kaulāvalī-nirṇaya, VII.
Kulārṇava, VIII.

Bhairavī Mudrā
It is that condition when everything is withdrawn into a person in the shape of his soul.

Bhāratī
Same as *Viśuddha* (q.v.).

Bhūmisparśa
A *mudrā* (q.v.) in which the palm of the right hand is turned inward, and the fingers outstretched with the tips of fingers touching the ground.

Bhūpura
A four-cornered figure with four doors and a triangle within.
Gandharva Tantra, V. 76.
Nityāṣoḍaśīkārṇava, I. 166 ff.

Bhūtāpsāraṇa
Warding off evil spirits and disturbances by means of *mantras*.
Śāradātilaka, IV. 10 (Rāghava's comm.).
Kṛṣṇānanda's *Tantrasāra*, p. 616.
Puraścaryārṇava, III. 154.

Bhūtaśuddhi
Part of a rite in which the five *bhūtas* or elements of the body are purified.
Nīlatantra, XVI. 56.

Bīja
(1) Mystic syllables like *Hrīṃ*, *Huṃ*, etc.
(2) Semen.
(3) Cidātman.

Bindu
(1) One dot represents undivided manifestation of Śiva.
(2) Double dot (*Visarga*) represents Śakti.
(3) According to Śaivas, an evolute of *Nāda*.
(4) In Kashmir Śaivism, one of the ten *Vidyā-tattvas*.
(5) *Prāṇa*. According to some, it has three forms, *Prakāśa* (static), *Vimarśa* (kinetic) and *Prakāśa-Vimarśa* (combination of both).
Śāradātilaka, I. 7 ff, II. 6, VII. 9.
Tantrāloka, I. 216.
Prapañcasāra, I. 41, III. 20-21.
Kāmakalāvilāsa, V-VII (*Cidvallī*).

Bodhicitta
Mind destined to attain enlightenment. It means the mind of the Buddha in his previous existences as Bodhisattva (q.v.).

Bodhisattva
A being destined to attain Buddhahood. Used to denote the various states of existence of Gautama or Siddhārtha prior to the attainment of Buddhahood.

Brahmadvāra
The passage through which *Kuṇḍalinī* (q.v.) moves.

Brahmagranthi
One of the three knots in the *Mūlādhāra-cakra*. *Nīlatantra*, XI. 22.

Brahmanāḍī
Same as *Suṣumnā* (q.v.).

Brahmapura: Human body.

Brahmarandhra
An aperture in the crown of the head, through which the soul or vital breath is supposed to escape on its leaving the body.

Brahmavartman
Same as *Suṣumnā* (q.v.).

Cakra
(a) The six mystical circles or nerve-plexuses, supposed to exist within the body from the lower extremity of the spinal cord up to the head. The circles in the ascending order are: *Mūlādhāra*, *Svādhiṣṭhāna*, *Maṇipura*, *Anāhata*, *Viśuddha*, *Ājñā*. The *Sahasrāra-padma* (1000-petalled lotus) is supposed to be located within the crown of the head.
(b) Designation of an assembly of Tāntric devotees for certain rites, e.g., *Bhairavī Cakra*.
(c) Endless rotation of Śakti.
(d) *Yantra* or mystic diagram, e.g., *Trikoṇacakra*, *Aṣṭakoṇacakra*.

See *Śaṭcakranirūpaṇa*.

Cakrapūjā
A Tāntric worship in the company of some Tāntric devotees under the leadership of the *Guru*.
Nīlatantra, IX. 3.

Cakrabheda
Literally, penetration of *Cakras*. Manifestation or activation which is necessary for keeping the body fit and for attainment of *Siddhis*. A Tāntric *Sādhanā*.

Cākṣuṣī dīkṣā
A form of initiation in which the *Guru* initiates his disciple by a mere glance.
Kulārṇava, XIV.
Śāradātilaka, V. 127-40 (Rāghava's comm.).

Cāndra
A Vāmācārī sect.
Śaktisaṃgama, Tārā, I. 92-94.

Candrakalā
Symbol of crescent moon supposed to exist on the crown of the goddess, from which nectar is believed to exude.
Mahānirvāṇa, XIII. 7.

Candranāḍī
Another name of *Iḍā* (q.v.), supposed to represent Śakti in the form of the moon.
Śaṭcakranirūpaṇa, I.

Caramālā
Rosary of *Rudrākṣa*, crystal, etc., for *Japa* or muttering the name of god.
Kṛṣṇānanda's *Tantrasāra*, p. 29.

Caturdaśāra
A diagram constituted by 14 triangles each of which is presided over by a goddess. Such goddesses are called Sampradāya-yoginīs. It is believed to lead to the acquisition of *Īśitva*, one of the *Siddhis* (q.v.).
Nityāṣoḍaśīkārṇava, IV. 149, VI. 17, XI. 179-83.
Gandharvatantra, V. 99, XVII. 49.

Caturviṃśatitattva
24 fundamental things also recognised in Tantra. These are five gross elements, five subtle elements, five sensory organs, five motor organs, mind, intellect, egotism, primordial substance (*prakṛti*).

Catuṣkūṭā
A particular arrangement of letters for use in the cult of Śrīvidyā.
Kṛṣṇānanda's *Tantrasāra*, p. 244.

Choṭikā
Syllable *Phaṭ*.

Cīnācāra
(Cīnakrama, Cīna-sādhana) Chinese ritual, chiefly relating to goddess Tārā, is the basis of Tāntric *Vāmācāra* (q.v.).

Tārātantra, p. 20 (of Kṛṣṇānanda); *Śaktisaṃgama*, Sundarī, I. 188 ff; *Puraścaryārṇava*, I. 20.

Citriṇī
: Name of a nerve, also called *Brahma-nāḍī*. Sometimes regarded as one of the three constituents of *Suṣumnā* (q.v.); often identified with *Suṣumnā*.
Prāṇatoṣiṇī, I. 4.

Cūḍācakra
: A kind of spiritual exercise for *Vīra* type of devotees. It involves *Laya-yoga* (q.v.).

Ḍākinī
: A class of minor deities, associated with Pārvatī, Chinnamastā, etc. Supposed to be the presiding deity of *Mūlādhāra*.
Prāṇatoṣiṇī, V. 6.
Kṛṣṇānanda's *Tantrasāra*, p. 338.
Ṣaṭcakranirūpaṇa, VIII.

Dakṣiṇācāra
: Orthodox way of spiritual attainment without *Pañcamakāra* in conformity with Veda, Smṛti and Purāṇa. *Vedācāra*, *Vaiṣṇavācāra* and *Śaivācāra* are included in it.

Dakṣiṇamārga
: Same as *Dakṣiṇācāra* (q.v.).

Dakṣiṇasrotatantra
: Tantras belonging to the southern current, viz., *Yoginījāla*, *Yoginīhṛdaya*, *Mantramālinī*, *Aghoreśī*, *Krīḍāghoreśvarī*, *Lākinīkalpa*, *Marīci*, *Mahāmarīci*.

Ḍāmara
: It denotes uproar, affray, riot, the bustle and confusion of festivity or strife. It stands for a class of Tantras, stated to have been narrated by Śiva.

Daśasaṃskāra
: See *Saṃskāra*.

Daśamahāvidyā
: Ten Tāntric goddesses: Kālī, Tārā, Ṣoḍaśī, Bhuvaneśvarī, Bhairavī, Chinnamastā, Dhūmāvatī, Vagalā, Mātaṅgī, Kamalā.
Prāṇatoṣiṇī, V. 6, p. 374.
The names differ in different Tantras.

Dehasādhana
: Same as *Kāyasādhana* (q.v.).

Devacakra
: A kind of *Cakra* ritual.

Devīcakra
: Same as *Cakra* (q.v.).

Devyastra
: The mystic syllables *Hrīṃ*, *Phaṭ*.
Nīlatantra, II. 7.

Dhāraṇayantra
: A diagram usually used as an amulet. It is drawn on a leaf, and dedicated to a deity.
Kṛṣṇānanda's *Tantrasāra*, p. 585.
Śaktīsaṃgama, Tārā, L. 1.2.

Dhāraṇī
Protective spell used by Tāntric Buddhists.

Dhātuśakti
Designation of Ḍākinī, Rākiṇī, etc., the presiding deities of *Cakras*.

Dhyāna
Meditation on a deity.
Basic element in Tāntric *Sādhana* and an accessory of *Yoga*.

Digambara
(1) A naked order of *Avadhūtas* (q.v.) having the quality of Śiva.
(2) A *Vāmācārī* sect.
Prāṇatoṣiṇī, VII. 7, p. 532.
Saundaryalaharī, 32 (*Lakṣmī* comm.).

Dīkṣā
Initiation. According to *Viśvasāra Tantra*, it is of four kinds, viz., *Kriyāvatī*, *Kalāvatī*, *Varṇamayī* and *Vedhamayī*.
Prāṇatoṣiṇī, II. 4.
According to *Kulārṇava* (XIV), it is sevenfold, viz., *Kriyā*, *Varṇa*, *Kalā*, *Sparśa*, *Vāk*, *Dṛk* and *Mānasa*. Each of these is subdivided.
According to *Rudrayāmala*, it is of three forms, viz., *Āṇavī*, *Śākti* and *Śāmbhavī*.
Prāṇatoṣiṇī, II. 4.
Other types are *Krama*, *Pañcāyatana* and *Ekamantra*, etc.

Dīpana
Processing of *mantra*.
Kṛṣṇānanda's *Tantrasāra*, p. 54.

Divya-bhāva
The highest spiritual attainment of a Tāntric devotee.

Divyacakra
Name of a *Cakra* ritual, in which the *Pañcatattvas* are used, meant for those who have made considerable spiritual progress.
Mahānirvāṇa, VIII. 204-19.

Divyamudrā
Same as *Khecarīmudrā* (q.v.).

Divya-pāna
One of the three modes of drinking of wine before the goddess, the other two being *Paśu* and *Vīra*.
Kulārṇava, VII; *Śaktisaṃgama*, Tārā, XXXIII. 6-8.

Divyatattva
A category of *Pañcatattva* (q.v.).

Divyaugha
A line of succession of Tāntric *gurus*.
Śyāmārahasya, III (quotation from *Bhāvacūḍāmaṇi*).

Dṛk-dīkṣā
Same as *Cākṣuṣī dīkṣā* (q.v.).

Dūtī
Same as *Latā* (q.v.).

Dūtīyāga
: Ritual union of a Tāntric devotee with his female partner. Her organ is fancied as sacrificial fire into which the semen of the male partner, conceived as clarified butter, is offered. *Paraśurāma-kalpasūtra*, X, 63.

Ekaliṅga
: A field or a place in which (up to five *krośas*) there is but one *Śivaliṅga*; designation of a *Śivaliṅga* at such a place.
Nīlatantra, III. 1.

Gajakrāntā
: Same as *Aśvakrāntā* (q.v.).

Gāṇapatyā-liṅga
: A class of Śiva-liṅgas, mentioned in the *Kāmikāgama*.

Gaudhāṣṭaka
: Eight fragrant substances taken together and used as substitute for wine of three kinds—*Śaktisambandhi*, *Śivasambandhi* and *Viṣṇusambandhi*.
Śāradātilaka, IV. 79-80.

Gauḍa Saṃpradāya
: A sect of Tāntric devotees belonging to eastern India and following *Vāmācāra*. It depends entirely on *Pañcatattva* (q.v.), and advocates the unity of *devatā*, *guru* and *mantra* as manifestations of the energy of the Great Goddess.
Puraścaryārṇava, IX, p. 866.
Śaktisaṃgama, Sundarī, III. 15-18.

Gaurīpaṭṭa
: Base upholding *Śivaliṅga*. Looking like the female organ, it is also called *yoni*.

Gāyatrī
: The basic *mantra* of an initiated *dvija*.
Ṛgveda, III. 62.10.

Gṛhāvadhūta
: An *Avadhūta* (q.v.) leading the life of a householder.
Prāṇatoṣiṇī, VII. 7, p. 532.

Guhyasādhana
: Performance of secret rituals by Tāntric devotees of the *Vīra* (q.v.) type. Those who are not initiated have no access to such a ritual.
Niruttara-tantra, X.

Guhya-samāja
: Secret assembly, in the Buddhist Saṃgha, of the members having faith in Tāntrism. They themselves wrote their scriptures. A Buddhist work bears this title.

Guṇaspanda
: Qualities of *Sattva*, etc.

Guptatarayoginī
: Designation of goddesses who are *Āvaraṇadevatās* (q.v.).
Gandharvatantra, V. 96.

Gupti

Keeping the *mantra* secret. Kṛṣṇānanda's *Tantrasāra*, p. 54.

Guru

(For female *Guru*, see *Stri-guru*)

A Tāntric preceptor. Qualifications of such a *guru*, female *guru*, characteristics of a hypocritical *guru* etc. have been dealt with in several Tāntric texts, e.g. *Kulārṇava*, XIII, XVI; *Rudrayāmala*, Uttara, II; *Prāṇatoṣiṇī*, II. 2, VI. 4; Kṛṣṇānanda's *Tantrasāra*, 2; *Tantrarāja*, I; *Śāradā-tilaka*, II, etc.

The *Gurutantra* deals exclusively with *Guru* — his glorification, propitiation, *Kulagurus* whose names end in Nātha etc.

The *Nirvāṇa-tantra* (III) mentions four kinds of *gurus*, viz. *Guru*, *Paramaguru*, *Parāparaguru* and *Parameṣṭhi-guru* (believed to be identical with Śiva).

Gurubīja

Letters H, S, Kh, M, L, V, R, Y, Ūm.

Hādividyā, Hādimata

Vidyā, denoting knowledge, *mantra* or deity, emanating from *Kāmarāja bīja*.

A school named after *Ha*, the symbol of Śiva, and influential in Kerala and Kashmir.

Śaktisaṃgama, Tārā, LVIII. 81.

Hākinī

Presiding deity of the *Ājñācakra* (q.v.), conceived as six-faced and white in complexion.

Ṣaṭcakranirūpaṇa.

Haṃsa

(1) Supreme Soul, Brahman.

(2) A symbolic *mantra* involving inhalation (*haṃ*) and exhalation (*sa*) of breath. Same as *Ajapā* (q.v.). Regarded as *Paramamantra*. It is of two kinds, *Vyakta* (manifest) and *Gupta* (hidden).

Haṃ is the symbol of *Bindu* (*Puruṣa*, Male Principle of Creation, and *Saḥ* of *Visarga* (*Prakṛti*, Female Principle).

Ṣaṭcakranirūpaṇa, XI. 111 (Observations of Kālīcaraṇa).

Haṃsa-mantra

Also called *Ajapā-mantra*. Name of the *mantra*, consisting of *haṃ* and *saḥ* symbolism, for the awakening of *Kuṇḍalinī* (q.v).

Haṃsapīṭha

Region of *Haṃsa*, supposed to exist within *Sahasrāra* (q.v.). Indicated by *A-KA-THA* triangle, and marked by letters *HA-LA-KṢA*. In it, the devotee should meditate on *guru* as identical with Śiva.

Pādukāpañcaka, I (Kālīcaraṇa's Comm.).

Hārdhakalā

(1) Sex-organ drawn on mystic diagrams. Also known as *Haṃsapāda* or *Yoni*. (2) Wave of bliss resulting from Śiva-Śakti union.

Hādi-mata (or -vidyā)

A Tāntric school which was very popular in Kerala and Kashmir. Those who belonged to this school claimed that their *vidyā* (knowledge, *mantra* and deity) was derived from a source known as *Kāmarāja-bīja*. *Ha* stands for Śiva; the school was named after *Ha*.

Cf. *Hakārāt Śiva-rūpatvaṃ tad-hādi-matamīritam/*

Śakti-saṃgama, Tārā, LVIII. 81.

Hākinī

The Presiding Deity (Śakti) of *Ājñā-cakra* (q.v.).

Haṃsa

See *Ajapā*.

Haṭhayoga

A kind of forced *yoga* or abstract meditation performed with great self-mortification, such as standing on one leg. In it, the mind is forced to withdraw from external objects.

In the *Yogaśīkhopaniṣad* (I.133), it is described as the unity of the sun (*Ha*) and the moon (*Ṭha*).

In the *Haṭhayoga-pradīpikā* (I. 10), it is regarded as the source of all kinds of *Yoga*.

Haviṣya

Food prepared with rice that has been dried in the sun. *Nīlatantra*, XI. 5.

Homa

A rite in which oblation is poured into fire. It is of various kinds, e.g., *Sthūla* (gross), *Sūkṣma* (subtle), *Parā* (transcendental), *Bāhya* (external), *Āntara* (internal), *Nigraha* (harmful act), *Saumya* (beneficial), etc.

Mātṛkābheda, XI. 8.

Tantrarāja, XXIX-XXXII.

Kṛṣṇānanda's *Tantrasāra*, IV.

Śāradātilaka, XVII-XVIII.

Tārābhakti-sudhārṇava, p. 247 ff.

Nīlatantra, XVI. 4.

Hotrī dīkṣā

A type of initiation in which the *guru* performs *homa* for purifying the six quarters. *Śāradātilaka*, V. 127-40.

Hsien (Chinese)

Immortality.

Hṛllekha

The *Bīja Hrīṃ*. *Nīlatantra*, V. 87.

Iḍā

One of the fourteen main nerves. Symbol of the moon, it is on the left of the spinal cord. Supposed to be of white colour. *Ṣaṭcakranirūpaṇa*, I.

Iddhi (from *Ṛddhi*)

Miraculous power stated in

Buddhist texts like the *Brahmajāla-sutta*, I. 26. *Cullavagga*, V. 8, etc.

Ilm (Arabic)
According to Sufis, knowledge gathered from experience.

Indrayoni
A nerve-plexus between *Viśuddha* and *Ājñā Cakras*.

Indu: *Kriyāśakti*.

Indubīja
Drāṃ.
Nīlatantra, V. 45.

Īśitva
A kind of *Siddhi* (q.v.).

Iṣṭamantra
The *mantra* taught by one's *guru*.

Itaraliṅga
A form of *Śiva-liṅga*.
Śāradātilaka, IV.

Japa
Muttering or repeating a *mantra*, or the name of a deity.
Kulārṇava, XVII.
Śaktisaṃgama, Tārā, XLVI. 2-3.
Gandharvatantra, XXIX. 9.
It is of three kinds, viz., *Vyakta* (expressed), *Avyakta* (unexpressed), *Sūkṣma* (subtle), also called, respectively, *Vācika*, *Upāṃśu* and *Mānasa*.

Jātakusuma
Menstrual blood of a woman.
Nīlatantra, XVII. 7.

Jātasūtaka
Newly born child. *Mantra* is conceived during initiation as a newly born child.
Śaktisaṃgama, Tārā, XLV. 7.

Jīvana
Processing a *mantra*.
Kṛṣṇānanda's *Tantrasāra*, p. 54.

Jīvanmukti
Liberation while alive.

Jīvaśakti
Name of *Cuṇḍālinī*, the vital energy within the body.
Tantrarāja Tantra, XXX. 34.

Jñānahoma
Homa performed in internal worship.
Prāṇatoṣiṇī, VII. 4, p. 535 (Quotation from *Nityātantra*).

Jyeṣṭhā
A destructive Śakti by which Śivahood of extremely enlightened persons is obstructed.

Jyotirdhyāna
Meditation on the Self, believed to reside in *Kuṇḍalinī* (q.v.) in the form of light. Also called *Tejodhyāna*.

Kādimata
A principal Tāntric school with *Ka* as its symbol. Texts in glorification of Mahātripurasundarī, especially those describing the mode of Her worship, etc., are known chiefly

under two divisions, one of which is *Madhumatīmata* or *Kādimata*. The *Tantrarāja*, *Mātṛkārṇava*, *Tripurārṇava* and *Yoginīhṛdaya* come under this class.
Śaktisaṃgama, Tārā, LVIII. 81-82.
Do, Kālī, V. 24-26.
For Tantras in this group see *Manoramā* comm. on *Kādimata-tantra*, I. 2 (ff), p. 2; *Tāntrik Texts*, VIII and Eng. Introduction, p. 2.

Kādividyā (Kādimata)
Knowledge deriving its name from the initial letter of *Vāgshava Bīja* (q.v.).
Śāradātilaka, I. 1 (comm.).

Kahādimata
One of the three main Tāntric doctrines.
Śaktisaṃgama, Tārā, LVIII. 81-82.

Kākinī
(1) Presiding deity of the *Anāhata Cakra* (q.v.), conceived as yellow and residing within a twelve-petalled red lotus.
Ṣaṭcakranirūpaṇa, XXIV.
(2) *Ka* is called *Kākinī Bīja*.

Kalā
(1) Aspect of the Great Mother Goddess, symbolically represented by *varṇa* or letter. 38 *Kalās* are supposed to have emanated from the three groups of letters, called *Saumya*, *Saura* and *Āgneya*.
Prapañcasāra, III. 11-12.
Śāradātilaka, I. III.
According to another tradition, 50 *Kalās* emanated from the five constituents of *Praṇava* (*Oṃkāra*), viz., *A*, *U*, *Ma*, *Bindu*, *Nāda*.
Śāradātilaka, II. 17.
(2) Prakṛti, Śakti, Māyā.
Śāradātilaka, I. 6.
Prapañcasāra, I. 26.
(3) Letters from *Ā* to *Kṣa*.
(4) *Nāda*.

Kālacakra
A minor nerve-cycle above *Viśuddha Cakra* (q.v.) but below the *Ājñācakra* (q.v.). Also known as *Lalanā-cakra*, it denotes the wheel of time and the chief deity of Tāntric Buddhists *Kālacakrayāna*.

Kalā(vatī) dīkṣā
A form of initiation in which the *guru* locates the five *Kalās*, called *Nivṛtti*, *Pratiṣṭhā*, *Vidyā*, *Śānti* and *Śāntyatīta* in different parts of the body of the disciple and anoints him.

Kālāmukha
A Vāmācārī Śaiva sect, much similar to Kāpālikas. They are known to have dwelt in South India.

Kalāmūrti
Fragmentary form of the figure of Śakti.

Śakti of any deity is divided into sixteen parts (*Kalā*). *Garland of Letters*, p. 194.

Kalānyāsa

Perception of the deity in different parts of the body of the female partner of the devotee. Kṛṣṇānanda's *Tantrasāra*, p. 128.

Kalā-tattva

The limited manifestation of Śiva in individuals. *Tantrāloka*, IX. 155.

Kālībīja

The syllable *Krīṃ*.

Kālīkula

A school of Tantra emphasising the importance of the cult of Kālī. The following are the scriptures of this school:

Jayadratha-yāmala, Kālajñāna, Kālottara, Mahākāla-saṃhitā, Śaktisaṃgama-tantra, Uttaratantra, Vyomakeśa-saṃhitā.

Kālīmata

Texts in glorification of Mahātripurasundarī, especially those describing the mode of her worship, etc., are known chiefly under two divisions, one of which is the *Kālīmata* or *Mālinīmata*.

Kāmabīja

The syllables *Klīṃ*, *Kroṃ*, etc.

Kāmakalā

(1) Sexual art.

(2) Imagined as Mahātripurasundarī, it is of the nature of *Cit* (consciousness), *Ānanda* (bliss), *Icchā* (will), *Jñāna* (knowledge) and *Kriyā* (action). It is supposed to be in a triangle within the *Candramaṇḍala* of the *Sahasrārapadma* (q.v.). It is regarded as a combination of the three *Bindus* of *Ravi*, *Agni* and *Soma*. In some Tantras, Kāma is the equilibrium of *Prakāśa* (static) and *Vimarśa* (dynamic) *Śakti* of Śiva. *Nityāṣoḍaśīkārṇava*, VI. 10.11 (*Setubandha* comm.). *Ṣaṭcakranirūpaṇa*, XL (Observations of Kālīcaraṇa). *Kāmakalāvilāsa*, VIII, *Cidvallī* (comm.).

Kāmamandira

House for union with *Śakti*. *Nīlatantra*, XX. 69.

Kāmarājabīja

Designation of letters *HA*, *SA*, *KA*, *HA*, *LA*, *HRĀÑ*, each symbolising an aspect of Śakti or Vidyā. *Śāradātilaka*, I.1 (comm.).

Kāmeśībīja or Kāmabīja

The syllable *Klīṃ* or *Klhrīṃ*.

Kāmika

Name of the seat for *Kāmya Japa* or the muttering of a

mantra or name of a deity for a special purpose. Made of the skin of deer, tiger or ram or of cane.
Puraścaryārṇava, VI, p. 420.

Kañcuka: *Pāśa*, evil, *Māyā*, etc. which are the causes of one's bondage.

Kāpālika
An extremist Śaiva resorting to the cult of Śakti, and drinking wine in human skulls.
Śaktisaṃgama, Kālī, VIII. 9-10.

Karamālā
The hand used as a rosary. Kṛṣṇānanda's *Tantrasāra*, pp. 27 ff.
Nīlatantra, XI. 29.

Karaṃkinī Mudrā
According to those, who have attained perfect knowledge, it is a mental state when the body of the five elements rests in the great firmament, and the world appears to be like a corpse and devoid of all actions.

Karaṇa
In astronomy it is the name given to half of a *tithi*.

Kāraṇa
Wine used in Tāntric rituals. The word means cause. Such wine is supposed to be the cause of knowledge of *dharma*, *artha*, *kāma* and *mokṣa*.
Prāṇatoṣiṇī, VII. 3, p. 510.

Karanyāsa
Part of a rite in which the hand is placed in a particular position. In it, the fingers and the reverse of the palm are used to invoke deities in the forms of letters.
Kṛṣṇānanda's
Tantrasāra, pp. 88 ff.
Nīlatantra, p. 11.

Kartari
A *mantra* of two letters.
Tantrarāja, XXXV. 28-29.

Kartrikā
A kind of *Astra* (q.v.) or weapon which is seen in the land of *Ādyā-Śakti*. *Nīlatantra*, IV. 17.

Kāśmīra Saṃpradāya
Tāntric devotees of Kashmir. Their doctrines and practices are set forth in the *Śaktisaṃgama*, Sundarī, III. 11 ff, and *Puraścaryārṇava*, IX, p. 866.
They follow also the texts of Kashmir Śaivism.

Kaula
One who performs Tāntric rites with five *Makāras*, i.e., follows *Kulācāra*.
Kaulas are divided into many sects, e.g., Kāpālika, Kṣapaṇaka, Digambara.
Nīlatantra, XVIII. 10.

Kaulamārga
A way of spiritual exercise (*ācāra*) confined within the

spiritual lineage of a particular group (*Kula*).
In it, the devotee worships with the *Pañcamakāras*.
It is of two kinds, wet and dry.
Kaulamārga-rahasya, p. 5.
Nirvāṇa-tantra, XI.
Kulārṇava, XVII.
Rudrayāmala, Uttara, XVII.
Kaulajñānanirṇaya, XIV, XVII, XXI.
Mahānirvāṇa, VII. 4.
Kaulāvalīnirṇaya, XXI, 189-190.
Prāṇatoṣiṇī, XIV.
Kṛṣṇānanda's *Tantrasāra*, p. 623.
Warning against abuse of *Kaulamārga*. *Paraśurāma-kalpasūtra*, III. 31 (comm.).
Mahānirvāṇa, I. 58-60.

Kaulika
Same as *Kaula* (q.v.).
One who follows the *Kula* or *Kaula* mode of *Sādhanā*. *Nirvāṇatantra*, XI; *Kulārṇava*, II, X, XI.
Nīlatantra, VI. 8.

Kaulika Śakti
Same as *Khecarī Śakti* (q.v.).

Kaulika Siddhi
Mokṣa according to *Kulamata* of Kashmir Śaivism.
Parātriṃśikā, p. 36.

Kaulinī
Same as *Kuṇḍalinī* (q.v.).

Kavaca
Prayer with certain mystic syllables supposed to protect the devotee as an armour protects the body. Protective spell.
Śyāmārahasya, IV.

Kerala Saṃpradāya
A Tāntric sect whose followers are spread over 19 countries from Āryāvarta to the sea.
Śaktisaṃgama, Kālī, IV. 3-1.
Siddhānta-saṃgraha.
Puraścaryārṇava, IX, p. 867.

Khapuṣpa
Menstrual blood.

Khecarī Mudrā
A Yogic posture which leads to spiritual attainment, and enables a person to overcome disease and death. By this *mudrā* movement on the outskirts of the sky of *Cit* becomes possible. *Gheraṇḍa*, III. 1-3.

Khecarī Śakti
Kha means Brahman.
The power, which moves as the kinetic energy of Brahman, is called *Khecarī*. Though one, it is manifested in various forms.
Parātriṃśikā, p. 30.

Kīlaka
Literally a small stick. It is a kind of *Nyāsa* (q.v.). *Nīlatantra*, VI. 2.
Kṛṣṇānanda's *Tantrasāra*, pp. 88 ff.

Kośa
Sheath. The human body is supposed to consist of the five sheaths as follows: *Annamaya*, *Prāṇamaya*, *Manomaya*, *Vijñānamaya*, *Ānandamaya*.

Kramadīkṣā
A type of initiation to the *mantras* of Kālī, Tārā and Tripurasundarī, meant for certain special kinds of devotees. *Prāṇatoṣiṇī*, II. 5.

Kramamata
A Tāntric system of Kashmir, dealt with in Abhinavagupta's *Kramakeli* and *Krama-stotra*. It is twofold according as it relates to Śaivism and Śāktism. *Tantrāloka*, IV. 157 ff.

Kriyāśakti
Three kinds of mystic power, viz., *Manojavitva* (having speed like mind), *Kāmarūpitva* (assuming forms at will), *Vikaraṇadharmitva* (infinite mental power to consume and transmit).

Kriyāvatī dīkṣā
A form of initiation in which many rituals are performed, and the *guru* sanctifies the disciple's body; inculcates his own consciousness into the disciple.
Prāṇatoṣiṇī, II.

Kriyāyoga
A kind of yogic exercise. *Śaktisaṃgama*, Sundarī, I. 197-200.

Krodhanī Mudrā
According to those, who have achieved success in *mantra*, it means that which is contained in the 24 *tattvas*.

Kṛtyā
An evil goddess supposed to cause harm.
Nīlatantra, V. 92.

Kula
(1) Family and the mode of worship handed down by the tradition of the family.
(2) Tāntric rite obtaining in a particular region with reference to a particular deity.
(3) The Śāstra which expounds the group of objects including the knower, the known and the knowledge or the worshipper and the object of worship.
(4) Body.
(5) *Ādhāracakra*. Constituents of the word are *Ku* (earth) and *līyate* (merges).
(6) Spiritual lineage from Paramaśiva to one's own *guru*. *Lalitāsahasranāma*, I (*Saubhāgyabhāskara* comm.).

Kulabhakta
One who is devoted to a *Kaulika Sādhaka*.
Nīlatantra, XI. 142.

Kulacakra
A kind of Tāntric rite in which several devotees assemble.
Nīlatantra, XIV. 13.

Kulācāra
Same as *Kaulamārga* (q.v.).
Nilātantra, XI. 128.

Kuladravya
Same as *Pañcatattva* (q.v.).
Kaulāvalīnirṇaya, VIII.
Nīlatantra, V. 7.

Kuladṛṣṭi
Sight of Kuladevī; *Kaulika's*. Sight of the desired deity..
Nīlatantra, XI. 100.

Kulajana
A devotee of the *Kaulika* class.
Nīlatantra, XI. 114.

Kulajña
One who knows *Kulācāra*.
Nīlatantra, XX. 56.

Kulajñāna
Knowledge of *Kulamārga*.
Paraśurāma-kalpasūtra, III. 31 (Rāmeśvara's comm.).

Kulakaulayoginī
Presiding goddesses of *Cakras* of the *Bahīr-dasāra* (q.v.) class.
Gandharvatantra, V. 102.

Kulakuṇḍalinī
Same as *Kuṇḍalinī* (q.v.).

Kulamārga
Same as *Kaulamārga* (q.v.).

Kulāmṛta
Nectar flowing down from the *Candramaṇḍala* within the head when *Kuṇḍalinī* (q.v.) penetrates the six *Cakras*.

Kulanāyaka
Best among the *Kaulika Sādhakas*. Here Śiva.
Nīlatantra, XVI. 11.

Kulapadma
Six-petalled lotus within *Sahasrāra* (q.v.).

Kulapatha
The passage through which *Kuṇḍalinī* (q.v.) ascends.
Saundaryalaharī, X.

Kulapūjana
Worship of the desired deity of a *Kaula* (q.v.).
Nīlatantra, XI. 77.

Kulapuṣpa
Flowers like *Rakta-javā* (red China rose); here it means the menstrual blood of a woman.
Nīlatantra, II. 3.

Kularasa
Svāyambhu-kusuma or menstrual blood of a woman.
Nīlatantra, IV. 2.

Kulasaṃketa
Technical mysteries of *Kaulamārga* (q.v.), e.g., *Kramasaṅketa*, *Pūjā-saṅketa*, *Mantrasaṅketa*, etc.
Niruttara, XII.
Kulārṇava, II.
Paraśurāma-kalpasūtra, VII. 1 (Rāmeśvara's comm.).

Kulaśāstra
Kulārṇava, Kaulāvalī-nirṇaya, etc.
Nīlatantra, XI. 128.

Kulasundara
Great *Kaulika* (q.v.).
Nīlatantra, XI. 90.

Kulasundarī
Feminine gender of *Kulasundara* (q.v.).

Kulatattva
Same as *Kuladravya.*

Kulāvadhūta
See *Avadhūta.*

Kulavidyā
The *mantra* used by a *Kaulika.*
Nīlatantra, XV. 13.

Kula-vṛkṣa
The following trees regarded as sacred by *Kaulas*:
Śleṣmātaka, Karañjaka, Nimba, Aśvattha, Kadamba, Plakṣa, Vaṭa, Udumbara, Ciñca.
Nīlatantra, XI. 116.

Kulayoṣit
Also called *Kaulinī,* it is the name of *Kuṇḍalinī* (q.v.).
Saundaryalaharī, VIII, XLI (Lakṣmīdhara's comm.).

Kullukā
Designation of a *mantra* recited before *japa* after the worship of *Mahāvidyā.*
Nīlatantra, V. 105.

Kulodaka
Semen.
Nīlatantra, II. 3.

Kumbhaka
A kind of *Prāṇāyāma* in which the breath is held up.
Nīlatantra, XVIII. 1.

Kuṇḍagolodbhava
'Menstrual blood, regarded as sacred for the Goddess. *Kuṇḍodbhava* is the blood of a married woman, and *Golodbhava* is of a widow.'
N.N. Bhattacharya, *Hist. of Tāntric Religion,* p. 443. The word *Kuṇḍa,* occurring in the *Manusmṛti,* iii. 156, 158, 178, and *Yājñavalkya-smṛti,* I. 10, 222, 224, has been interpreted as an illegitimate issue of a Brāhmin woman, whose husband is alive, by another Brāhmin male.
The word *Gola,* occuring in *Manusmṛti,* III. 156, 174 and *Yājñavalkya-smṛti,* I. 10, 222, has been taken to denote an offspring of the clandestine union of a Brāhmin widow and a Brāhmin male.

Kuṇḍalinī
The serpent, symbol of vital energy, supposed to coil around the *Mūlādhāra* (q.v.).
Tantrarājā, XXX. 65.
Gheraṇḍa, III. 44.
Ṣaṭcakranirūpaṇa, XI.
Śāradātilaka, XXV. 27.
Nīlatantra, IV. 9.
Prāṇatoṣiṇī, I.6.
Mātṛkābheda, XIV.

Rudrayāmala, Uttara, XXI.
Saundaryalaharī, X (Lakṣmīdhara).

Kūrcabīja
The mystic syllable *Huṃ*.

Kurukullā
Letters *A, E*.

Laghimā
See *Siddhi*.

Lākinī
Presiding deity of *Maṇipura Cakra* (q.v.).

Lakṣmī
Name of *bīja Śrīṃ*.
Nīlatantra, XV. 14.

Lalanācakra
See *Kālacakra, Lambikāgra*.

Lambikāgra
A nerve-circle located above the *Viśuddha* (q.v.) and below the *Ājñā* (q.v.). Also called *Lalanā* or *Kālacakra*.

Latā
Śakti or woman with whom one should associate or perform *Maithuna* as part of a Tāntric *Pūjā*.
Also called *Dūtī*.

Latāsādhana
Ritual involving.
Pañcamakāra.
Mahānirvāṇa, I. 52.

Layabhogāṅga-vidhāna
Process of separating *Malas* or *Pāśas* (q.v.) from the body. A part of *Smārtī dīkṣā* (q.v.).
Śāradātilaka, V. 127-40.
Puraścaryārṇava, V, p. 392.

Layasiddhiyoga-samādhi
State of perfect bliss. In it, the devotee acquires spiritual power, and enjoys the pleasure like sexual enjoyment leading to the realisation of identity with the Supreme Being.
Gheraṇḍa, VII. 12-13.

Layayoga
A form of *Haṭhayoga* which destroys all mundane desires, and leads to eternal bliss by bringing about the merger of one's mind in the Supreme Being.

Lelihāna Mudrā
According to Śāktas, that which licks everything again and again.

Liṅga
Male organ worshipped as Śiva-phallus.

Liṅgapuṣpa
The flower, called *Raktakaravī*, used as a substitute for sexual union.
Paraśurāma-kalpasūtra, X. 63 (Comm.).

Lopāmudrā
Mantras, relating to *Śrīvidyā*, consisting of 15 symbolic letters. Kṛṣṇānanda's *Tantrasāra*, pp. 242-43.

Madhyamā
A kind of sound midway between *Paśyantī* (q.v.) and *Vaikharī* (q.v.).

Connected with intellect. Represents equilibrium of *Parā* and *Paśyantī*. *Prapañcasāra*, II. 43 (Comm.). *Kāmakalāvilāsa*, XXVI (*Cidvallī*). *Lalitāsahasranāma*, 99 (*Saubhāgyabhāskara*).

Madhyamasrota Tantra
Tantras belonging to the middle current, viz., *Vijaya, Niḥśvāsa, Svāyambhuva, Vātūla, Vīrabhadra, Raurava, Makuta* and *Vīreśa*.

Madya
The first of the five *Makāras* in Tāntric *Pañca-makāra-sādhana*, wine. Of the various kinds of it, *Gauḍī* (prepared from molasses), *Paiṣṭī* (fermented from rice) and *Mādhvī* (prepared from the flowers of *Madhuka* plant — *Madhuka longifolia*) regarded as the best (*Kulārṇava*, V, *Mahānirvāṇa*, vi. 2-3). Thirteen kinds stated to have been used by the devotees from Gauḍa (*Śakti-saṃgama*, Kālī, IX. 46). Milk, honey and sugar-water recommended as substitutes of wine (*Mahānirvāṇa*, viii. 170-171). According to *Kulārṇava*, V, wine symbolises the flow of the essence of nectar from the union of Śiva-Śakti at the apex of the cerebrum.

Mahācakra
A *Cakra* ritual in which one's mother, sister, daughter, daughter-in-law and wife are to be worshipped as *Pañcaśakti*. *Niruttara*, X.

Mahācīnācāra, ahācīnakrama
Same as *Cīnācāra* (q.v.).

See *Nīlatantra*, Ch. xiii in Calcutta ed.

Mahāhrada
Pure *Cidātman*.

Mahāmāṃsa
Flesh of the following creatures, regarded as sacred for offering to the deity: man, cow, ram, horse, buffalo, boar, goat, deer. *Śyāmārahasya*, II. Kṛṣṇānanda's *Tantrasāra*, p. 630.

Mahāmudrā
(1) A form of posture. *Gheraṇḍa*, III. 1-3.
(2) Woman in general.
(3) Female organ.

Mahāpaśu
An uninitiated person. *Niruttara*, XII.

Mahāsāmrājya-dīkṣā
A form of initiation which is an essential prerequisite of *Kaula Sādhana*.

Mahāsetu
Designation of a *mantra* recited before *japa* after the worship of a *Mahāvidyā*.

Higher form of *Setu* (q.v.). *Nīlatantra*, V. 106.

Mahāsukha

According to Tāntric Buddhism, the *summum bonum* and the actual manifestation of *Bodhicitta* (q.v.). It can be brought about by the union of man and woman, the embodiments of *Upāya* and *Prajñā* respectively. In such a state, all mental action is suspended and the world is forgotten, and there is the most pleasant experience of non-duality.

Mahāvidyā

Ten Tāntric goddesses whose names vary in different texts. They are usually called *Kālī, Tārā, Ṣoḍaśī, Bhuvaneśvarī, Bhairavī, Chinnamastā, Dhūmāvatī, Vagalā, Mātaṅgī, Kamalā*. *Prāṇatoṣiṇī*, V. 6.

It is interesting to note that the term also denotes *Kevalānvayihetu*, i.e., a purely positive *probans* in logic or Nyāyaśāstra (vide *Mahāvidyā-viḍambana* of Vādīndra, ed. M.R. Telang, Baroda, 1920).

Mahāyoni

The sex organ of a woman; it is the assumed triangle of the *Sahasrāra-cakra* (q.v.). *Kaula-mārga-rahasya*, 256.

Mahimā

A kind of *siddhi* (q.v.).

Maithuna

Sexual intercourse, considered as one of the five *Makāras* in Tāntric rituals. *Mahānirvāṇa*, VI. 10 ff. *Prāṇatoṣiṇī*, VII. 4.

Makāra

See *Pañcamakāra*.

Mala

Fetters causing rebirth and suffering of worldly existence.

Threefold, viz., *Āṇava*, *Kārma* and *Māyīya*.

Mālinīmata

Same as *Kālīmata* (q.v.).

Mānasa dīkṣā

Same as *Manodīkṣā* (q.v.).

Mānavaugha

A line of succession of Tāntric *gurus*.

Maṇḍala

(1) A period of 49 days. *Nīlatantra*, XI. 64.

(2) A ritual *Cakra* in which the devotees, sitting with their female partners around the leader, indulge in the enjoyment of five *Makāras*. *Kaulāvalīnirṇaya*, VIII. *Mahānirvāṇa*, VIII. 154-156.

(3) Diagrams like *Sarvatobhadra*, used in Tāntric rituals.

Maṇipura

A *Cakra* near the navel region, also called *Nābhicakra*. Conceived as a 10-petalled lotus of blue

colour, each petal containing a letter. Within the lotus is conceived a triangle of the colour of the rising sun. The outer sides of the triangle are represented by three *svastika* symbols.
Ṣaṭcakra-nirūpaṇa, XIX, XXI.
Nīlatantra, V. 106.

Manodīkṣā
A form of initiation merely by the *guru's* thought and mental action.
Kulārṇava, XIV.

Manonmanī
Transcendental bliss coming out as a result of *bhaktiyoga-samādhi*.
Gheraṇḍa, VII. 14-15.

Mantra
Generally incantation relating to a deity.
The derivative meaning is *mananāt trāyate*, that which saves due to reflection. *Mantra* is equated by some with Brahman, the ultimate reality in the form of sound. It is believed to impart *Śakti* to a devotee who aspires after liberation.
Gandharva-tantra, XI.10, *Tantrarāja-tantra*, XXVI. 36-43 (Comm.), *Śāradātilaka*, I. 55; II. 57.

Mantra-adhva
Blood to be purified for *Sādhana*. *Adhva* denotes a constituent of the body which is of six kinds, viz., *Bhuvana* (cerebral organ), *Mantra* (blood and flesh), *Pada* and *Varṇa* (muscles and vein), *Dhātu* and *Reta* (bones and fluids). *Śāradātilaka*, V. 24-25 (Rāghavabhaṭṭa).

Mantracaitanya
Consciousness, inherent in *mantra*, to be roused by exertion.
Prāṇatoṣiṇī, IV. 1.
Gandharvatantra, XXIX. 24-25.

Mantrayāna
Name of Tāntric Buddhism.

Māntrī dīkṣā
A form of initiation in which the *guru* at first purifies himself and then consecrates his disciple.
Śāradātilaka, V. 127-40 (Rāghava).
Prāṇatoṣiṇī, II. 4.

Manu
Mantra.
Nīlatantra, XIV. 10.

Māraṇa
The rite for killing.

Marifat
According to Sufis, knowledge obtained through divine grace.

Mātṛ: Yoginī, Śakti Kalā.

Mātṛkā
(i) See *Aṣṭamātṛkā*.
(ii) Also the names of mystic letters.

Mātṛkānyāsa
Perception of *Mātṛkās* (q.v.) in the forms of letters in different parts of the body. Twofold — *Antarmātṛkā-nyāsa* and *Bahirmātṛkā-nyāsa*.
Kṛṣṇānanda's *Tantrasāra*, pp. 88 ff.

Mātṛkārṇa
Mātṛkāvarṇa; letter of the alphabet.
Nīlatantra, V. 114.

Mātṛkāvarṇa
See *Mātṛkārṇa*.

Matsya
Fish. One of the five *Makāras* (q.v.). Three kinds of fish are described as *Uttama*, *Madhyama* and *Adhama*.
Śyāmā-rahasya, III, *Mahānirvāṇa*, VI. 8.
Substitutes of fish are mentioned as a cake made of pulses and other substances.
Paraśurāma-kalpasūtra, X. 63 (commentary).

Māyā
Name of *Bīja Hrīṃ*.
Nīlatantra, XV. 14.

Māyābīja
Hrīṃ.
Nīlatantra, IV. 13.

Māyīya Mala: Such a feeling as 'I', 'Mine'.

Meru
The bead in a rosary, through which the ends of the thread pass before being tied in a knot.
Nīlatantra, XI. 22.

Mudrā
(i) Derived from root *Mud*, it literally means that which gives delight. Poses of hand or fingers used in worship, e.g., Matsya, Kūrma, Śaṃkha, etc.
The *Gheraṇḍa-saṃhitā* (III. 1-3) mentions 20 *Mudrās*.
(ii) Posture of the body at the time of *yoga*, e.g., *Aśviinī Mudrā*.
(iii) One of the five *Makāras* essential in Tāntric *Sādhana*. It means fried or parched cereals, e.g., *Yoginī-tantra*, ch. VI, or geometrical figures.
(iv) In Buddhist Tantra it denotes woman. The *Prajñopāya* and *Sekoddeśaṭīkā* (p. 56) take it to mean a woman with whom a Tāntric Yogin associates.

Mudrāvīrya
Condition of *Khecarī* (q.v.).

Mukta-triveṇī
Same as *Ājñā* (q.v.).

Mūla
(1) Also called *Mūlādhāra* (q.v.).
(2) *Mūlamantra* (q.v.).

Mūlacakra
Same as *Mūlādhāra* (q.v.).
Nīlatantra, V. 96.

Mūlādhāra
The lowest of the six *Cakras* (q.v.), supposed to be at the lowest extremity of the

spinal cord where *Kuṇḍalinī* (q.v.) is supposed to reside.
Ṣaṭcakranirūpaṇa, XIX.

Mūlamantra
The main or basic *mantra* imparted by one's spiritual preceptor at the time of initiation.

Mūlavidyā
Same as *Mūlamantra* (q.v.).
Nīlatantra, XI. 117.

Mursid
Guru or spiritual preceptor according to Sufis.

Nābhipadma
Same as *Maṇipura* (q.v.).
Ṣaṭcakranirūpaṇa, XIX.

Nāda
Sound. First vibration of Parā Śakti expressing itself in creation. Manifestation of the consciousness of the Supreme Being, revealed in sound.
Śāradātilaka, I. 6 ff.
Ṣaṭcakranirūpaṇa, XXXIX (Kālīcaraṇa)
Prapañcasāra, I. 41.

Nāda-brahman
Nāda (q.v.) imagined as Brahman in the form of primeval sound manifested in *Parā, Paśyantī, Madhyamā* and *Vaikharī*.
Kāmakalāvilāsa, IX (*Cidvallī*), *Saundarya-laharī*, XLI (comm. of Lakṣmīdhara).

Nāḍī
Artery or vein in the body. Supposed to be 72,000 in number. Of these, 72 are the major ones, of which again the three most important are *Iḍā, Pingalā*, and *Suṣumnā*.
Prāṇatoṣiṇī, I. 4.

Nakuli
Ha.

Nakulīśa
Ham.

Napuṃsaka mantra
A *mantra* which is neither male (i.e., meant for male deities) nor female (i.e., meant for female deities).
Śāradātilaka, II. 57-58.

Napuṃsaka Varṇa
Letters *R* and *L*.
Śāradātilaka, II. 5-7 (Rāghavabhaṭṭa).

Nārācamudrā
A hand-pose in which the tip of the right thumb is joined with the top mark of the right forefinger and then stretched out while other fingers are bent low.

Naṭī
Dancing woman, Goddess (Śakti) supposed to dance in delight at the performance of rituals in Her honour.
Niruttara, XV.

Navacakra
Nine *Cakras*, of which five belonging to Śakti and

pointing upward and four to Śiva pointing downward, constituting the *Śrīyantra* which is looked upon as the bodies of Śiva and Śakti, joined together.
Saundaryalaharī, IX (Lakṣmīdhara's comm.).
Nityāṣoḍaśīkārṇava, U, 47 (*Setubandha* comm.).

Navanāda
(1) Nine *Nādas* or special kinds of sound, supposed to reveal the nature of *Kuṇḍalinī*.
Kāmakalāvilāsa, XXVII (*Cidvallī*).
(2) Letter *A*, initial letter of each *Varga*, *Ya*, *Sa* and *Kṣa*.
Saundaryalaharī, XXXIV (Lakṣmīdhara).

Nigama
The class of Tantras in which Śiva asks questions, and Śakti answers them.

Nimeṣa Śakti
Will power, by which the concept of Sadāśiva is characterised in Kashmir Śaivism.
Īśvarapratyabhijñā, III. 1. 3.

Nirvikalpa Samādhi
Blissful state of mind in which the distinction of the knower, knowledge and object of knowledge is obliterated.

Nyāsa
(1) A part of Tāntric ritual, in which deities are placed (i.e., felt) on different limbs of the body.
There are various types of *Nyāsa*, e.g., *Mātṛkānyāsa* (feeling *Mātṛkās*), *Pīṭha-nyāsa* (feeling the holy resorts of Śakti), etc.
(2) Subtle identification with *Cakras*.
Kṛṣṇānanda's *Tantrasāra*, p. 339.
Nīlatantra, XI. 57.
Saubhāgya-bhāskara on *Lalitā-sahasra-nāma*, 2.4.
Gandharva-tantra, IX. 2.
Tārātantra, II. 3.
Śāradātilaka, VII.
Tārābhakti-sudhārṇava, V, p. 169.
See *Ṣoḍhānyāsa*.

Oḍra-puṣpa
Javā flower.
Also called *Japā*. China rose. Oḍra was the name of modern Orissa. Perhaps it was believed that this flower originally used to grow in Orissa.

Om
This syllable is regarded so sacred that a Vedic *mantra* is preceded and followed by it. The *Ṛgveda* commences with it — *Om agnimīḍe purohitam*, etc. It is constituted of the letters *A*, *U* and *M* symbolising the qualities of *Sattva*, *Rajas* and *Tamas* supposed to reside in Viṣṇu, Brahmā and Śiva respectively.

Also called *Praṇava*.
Even the Buddhists use *Om* in the beginning of their mystical formulae.
The *Bhagavadgītā* states (viii. 13) that this single syllable is Brahman.

Padmāsana
A sitting posture, in which the right foot is placed on the left thigh and vice versa.

Pañcabandhana
Five fetters as a result of *Avidyā* (false knowledge).

Pañcabhūta
Five gross elements, viz. Earth, Water, Fire, Wind and Ether.

Pañcagavya
Five products of the cow, viz. cowdung, cow's urine, milk, curd and ghee.
Nīlatantra, XVI, 47.

Pañcakalā
Five aspects of Śakti, viz. *Nivṛtti, Pratiṣṭhā, Vidyā, Śānti* and *Śāntyatīta*. *Śāradātilaka*, V. 79.

Pañcakañcuka
Five impure material elements, viz. *Kala, Niyati, Kala, Vidyā* and *Rāga*, which cause bondage of different kinds.

Pañcakleśa
Five fetters, viz. *Avidyā* (false knowledge), *Asmitā* (egotism), *Rāga* (attachment), *Dveṣa* (hatred), and *Abhiniveśa* (adherence).

Pañcakriyā or Pañcakṛtya
Five actions of Śakti, viz. *Sṛṣṭi* (Creation), *Sthiti* (Preservation), *Saṃhāra* (Destruction), *Tirodhāna* (Disappearance), *Anugraha* (Favour). *Tantrāloka*, I. 121.

Pañcamakāra
(also called Pañcatattva)
Five things, whose names begin with the letter *Ma*, necessary for Tāntric *Sādhana*. These are *Madya, Māṃsa, Matsya, Mudrā, Maithuna*.

Pañcāmnāya
Five *Āmnāyas* (zones) well-known for Tāntric culture.

Pañcamuṇḍī
An *āsana* (seat), for Tāntric *Sādhana*, made with the severed heads of two Caṇḍālas, one jackal, one monkey and one snake. According to *Yoginī-tantra* (chap. V), this *āsana* consists of the skulls of a jackal, a serpent, a dog, a bull and a man. As an alternative, five human skulls are prescribed.

Pañcāṅga-puraścaraṇa
Puraścaraṇa (q.v.) which consists in *japa, homa, tarpaṇa, abhiṣeka* and *viprabhojana*. The last one

means 'feeding Brāhmaṇas'. The other terms have been explained separately. Kṛṣṇānanda's *Tantrasāra*, 48.

Pañcāṅga-śuddhi

Fivefold purification, viz. *ātma-śuddhi, sthāna-śuddhi, deva-śuddhi, mantra-śuddhi, dravya-śuddhi. Kulārṇava*, VI.

Pañcarātra

Originally used, in *Śatapatha Brāhmaṇa*, as an adjective of *Puruṣamedha*, it later came to be used as an independent word meaning a sacrifice to be performed in five successive nights. The word has been interpreted in as many as eight different ways (vide K.D. Bharadvaja's paper 'Pañcarātra' in *Aruṇa Bhāratī*, A.N. Jani Fel. Vol., pp. 59 ff). The *Pañcarātra* deals with philosophy, meditation, temple architecture and iconography and some matters peculiar to the sect. Pāñcarātra is the name of a form of ritualistic Vaiṣṇavism.

Pañca Śakti

Mother, sister, daughter, daughter-in-law and preceptor's wife worshipped as five great Śaktis. *Niruttara*, X.

Pañca Preta

Brahmā, Viṣṇu, Rudra, Īśa, Sadāśiva, forming the seat of Goddess, together called *Pañca Preta*.

Pañcatanmātra

Five subtle elements, viz., *Śabda, Sparśa, Rūpa, Rasa, Gandha*, corresponding, respectively, to Sky or Ether, Wind, Fire, Water and Earth.

Pañcatattva

Same as *Pañcamakāra* (q.v.).

Pañcāyatanī dīkṣā

Initiation into the cults of Śiva, Śakti, Viṣṇu, Sūrya and Gaṇeśa. Kṛṣṇānanda's *Tantrasāra*, pp. 70-72.

Pañcopacāra

Five articles for worship, viz., *gandha* (sandal-paste and other fragrant substances), *puṣpa* (flower), *dhūpa* (incense), *dīpa* (lamp), *naivedya* (food offering). *Puraścaryārṇava*, III. 224.

Parā

A kind of sound. See *Śabda-brahman*. It is the initial stage of sound arising at *Mūlādhāra* (q.v.). Devoid of vibration, it is unmanifested but indestructible. *Cidvallī* on *Kāmakalā-vilāsa*, XX, XXIII.

Parakīyā

Wife of another person, sometimes taken by a devotee as his partner.

Paraliṅga

(1) Imaginary male organ in terms of which the *Bindu* or vacuum in the *Sahasrāra* triangle is conceived.

(2) A type of *Śivaliṅga*.

Paramahaṃsa
A devotee who has succeeded in *Haṃsa-mantra*.
There are two kinds of *Parama-haṃsa*, viz. (i) *Vidvat* — one who has realised Brahman; and (ii) *Vividiṣu* — one who is desirous of realisation.

Paramakula
Same as *Ājñā* (q.v.).

Parameṣṭhī Guru
The fourth spiritual ancestor of the *guru*.
Mahānirvāṇa, VI. 98.

Pāramitā
Perfection, transcendental virtue. Generally six or ten, viz., *Dama, Śīla, Kṣānti, Vīrya, Dhyāna, Prajñā*. To these are, sometimes, added *Satya, Adhiṣṭhāna, Maitra, Upekṣā*.

Paramudrā
Subtle form of *Mudrā*.
Tantrarāja, IV. 55.

Parāpara Guru
Third spiritual ancestor of the *guru*.
Mahānirvāṇa, VI. 98.

Parā Śakti
(1) Supreme Goddess. An aspect of Mother Goddess.
(2) Female partner of the Tāntric *Sādhaka*. *Śāradātilaka*, 1.7 (Comm.).
Nityāṣoḍaśīkārṇava, VI. 36. *Mahānirvāṇa*, V. 2. *Kulārṇava*, V. *Ṣaṭcakranirūpaṇa*, L (Kālīcaraṇa).

Pāśa
See *Aṣṭapāśa*.

Paśu
Anu. Jīva. That which is tied by pāśas or fetters.
A man in whom animal propensities are predominant.
Regarded as the weakest type of human beings.
A low class of Tāntric devotees. Twofold — *subhāva* (influenced by knowledge) and *vibhāva* (with a mark left by knowledge). A *paśu* may again be *dīkṣita* (initiated) or *adīkṣita* (uninitiated).
Pāśupatasūtra, I. 1, 7.
Kaulāvalīnirṇaya, XI, 187.
Nīlatantra, VIII. 18.

Paśubhāva
The attitude of a *Paśu* (q.v.).
Rudrayāmala, Uttara, VI. 50-51, XI. 28.

Paśucakra
A kind of *Cakra* ritual. *Niruttara*, X.

Paśu Śāstra
Tantras other than those belonging to the *Kaula* group.

Paśvācāra
General name of *Vedācāra, Vaiṣṇavācāra, Śaivācāra* and *Dakṣiṇācāra*.

Paśyantī
Belonging to the region of

the navel, it is the second stage of the development of sound within the body.
Prapañcasāra, II. 43 (comm.).

Pauṣṭika
A rite designed to cause prosperity.
Nīlatantra, XII. 26.

Piṇḍabrahmāṇḍa-mārga
Passage of the ascent of *Kuṇḍalinī* (q.v.).

Piṅgalā
One of the three principal arteries — rising from *Mūlādhāra* and reaching the right nostril. Possesses the characteristics of the Sun, it is also called *Sūryanāḍi*.
Śāradātilaka, XXV. 38 (Comm. of Rāghava).
Ṣaṭcakranirūpaṇa, I (*Sammohana Tantra*, quoted in Kālīcaraṇa's comm.).

Pīr (Persian)
Guru or spiritual preceptor, according to Sufis.

Pīṭha
A holy place in which a limb of the severed body of Satī (Śiva's consort) is supposed to have fallen.
Nīlatantra, III. 4.
Pīṭha means a place where a devotee of high order used to live or a seat on which such a devotee attained *Siddhi*. Generally 51 *Pīṭhas* are recognised. Of these, quite a few are in Bengal or in neighbouring areas.

Pīṭhanyāsa
See *Nyāsa*.

Pīṭhaśakti
Collective name of goddesses *Icchā*, *Jñāna*, etc., each representing an aspect of Śakti.
Śyāmārahasya, III.

Pradhāna-tattva
Equilibrium of the feeling of joy or sorrow.

Prajñā
The Female Principle in Tāntric Buddhism. *Hevajra-tantra*, X, *Prajñopāya*, 5, *Advaya-vajra-saṃgraha*, 2.26, 55, *Sādhanamālā*, 321, 329 ff, *Guhyasamāja*, 19, 158, *Śrīcakrasambhāra*, 28.

Prākāmya
A kind of *Siddhi* (q.v.).

Prakṛti
(1) Śakti, one's female partner in a Tāntric rite.
(2) Female Principle of creation.
(3) The Supreme Śakti according to Śāktas.
Nīlatantra, XXII. 18.

Praṇava
The Vedic syllable *Om* (q.v.).

Prāṇāyāma
Lit. the expansion of breath; a breathing exercise. It is of three kinds, viz. *Pūraka* (inhalation), *Kumbhaka* (holding the breath), *Recaka*

(exhalation). *Nīlatantra*, V. 9. *Prāṇatoṣiṇī*, VI. 1.

Pratyāhāra
Yogic process of withdrawing the senses from their contact with external objects.

Pratyālīḍha
A sitting posture in which the shooter has the left knee advanced and the right leg slightly bent and retracted. *Nīlatantra*, iv. 18.

Pṛthvībīja
The letter *La*.

Pūraka
A process of *prāṇāyāma* (q.v.).

Puraścaraṇa
A Tāntric rite designed to cause the potency of a *mantra*. It generally consists of ten parts, viz. *japa, homa, tarpaṇa, abhiṣeka, aghamarṣaṇa, sūryārghya, jalpana, praṇāma, pūjā, brāhmaṇabhojana*.
In it, the person concerned has to take *haviṣyānna* (q.v.) and *pañcagavya* (q.v.). *Kaulāvalīnirṇaya*, XV. *Nīlatantra*, X. 9.
It may consist of five parts also, viz. *Japa, Homa, Tarpaṇa, Abhiṣeka, Brāhmaṇabhojana*. Kṛṣṇānanda's *Tantrasāra*, p. 48.

Pūrṇābhiṣeka
Highest form of *Abhiṣeka* (q.v.).

Puruṣa-Prakṛti
Male and Female Principles of creation.

Pūrva-kaula
A sect of the *Kaulas* (q.v.).

Puryaṣṭaka
The eight gross and subtle elements constituting the body of the goddess, represented in *aṣṭakoṇa-cakra*. *Kāmakalā-vilāsa*, XI.

Puṣpa
Five kinds, viz.,
Para (flowers made of jewels, etc.),
Apara (made with cut pieces of variegated cloth),
Uttama (obtained from plants),
Madhyama (fruits),
Adhama (leaves, water).

Puṭita
A *mantra* in between two *Bījas*, one in the beginning, another at the end. *Nīlatantra*, V. 18.

Puṭīkṛta
Same as *puṭita* (q.v.).

Rahasya Yoginī
Eight presiding deities of the *Aṣṭakoṇa Cakra* (q.v.). *Gandharva*, XVII. 74.

Rājacakra
A form of *Cakra* worship.
In it, mother, sister, daughter, daughter-in-law and preceptor's wife are looked

upon as *Śaktis*.
Niruttara, X.

Rajanī
A special type of woman recommended for being worshipped in Tāntric rituals.
Niruttara-tantra, V. 3-4.

Rājayoga
A form of *yoga* in which the mind automatically merges in Brahman.
Prāṇatoṣiṇī, VI. 3.
Gheraṇḍa, VII. 16.

Rambhā
Designation of a woman of any of the four castes endowed with noble traits of character, eminently fit for Tāntric rites.
Niruttara-tantra, XI. 23-24.

Rathakrāntā
A vast stretch of land from the Vindhyas to Mahācīna including Nepal. China was called Mahācīna in the medieval period.
The region is said to have been renamed as *ratha* (chariot) was the means of transport there.

Recaka
A process of *prāṇāyāma* (q.v.).

Riktā
Name of a *tithi* of evil influence.
Nīlatantra, XII. 44.

Rudragranthi
A knot in the *Ājñā-cakra*, obstructing the ascent of *Kuṇḍalinī* (q.v.).
Lalitāsahasranāma, 89 (*Saubhāgyabhāskara* comm.).

Śabda-brahman
Eternal sound conceived as Brahman. It is fourfold, viz., *Parā*, *Paśyantī*, *Madhyamā* and *Vaikharī*. The terms have been explained separately.
It is the source of the letters of the alphabet, words and of other sounds through which thoughts are expressed. It is all-pervading.

Ṣaḍaṅga-nyāsa
Feeling the deity in six limbs, viz. heart, head, top of the head, protective amulet, eyes and intestines.

Sādhāraṇī
A public woman as the partner of a *Sādhaka*.

Sādi Vidyā
A branch of knowledge, so named after the initial letter of the *Śakti Bīja*.

Sahaja
(1) The easiest and most natural way of spiritual exercise.
(2) Ultimate reality according to the *Sahajiyās* or adherents of the *Sahaja* doctrine.

Sahasrāra
Thousand-petalled multicoloured lotus, supposed to exist in

Brahmarandhra (q.v.).
Ṣaṭcakranirūpaṇa, XLI-XLIII.
Nīlatantra, XVIII. 35.

Śaivācāra
A form of *Dakṣiṇācāra* emphasising the cult of Śiva-Śakti.
Vedic mode, eightfold Yogic practices and animal sacrifice; these are the characteristics of this *Ācāra*.
Prāṇatoṣiṇī, VII. 1.

Śākinī
Presiding Goddess of the *Viśuddha Cakra* (q.v.).
Ṣaṭcakranirūpaṇa, XXX (Kālīcaraṇa's comm.).

Śākteyī
A kind of *Dīkṣā* (q.v.).

Śakti
(1) The *Bīja Hrīṃ*.
(2) The female partner of a Tāntric *Sādhaka*.
Of three kinds, viz., *Svakīyā* (own wife), *Parakīyā* (another man's wife), *Sādhāraṇī* (prostitute).
(3) Female principle of creation.
(4) A limb of *Mantra*.
Kulārṇava, VII.
Niruttara, XIV.
Kṛṣṇānanda's *Tantrasāra*, p. 627.
Gandharva, XXIII. 19.
Prāṇatoṣiṇī, VII. 4.
Nīlatantra, II. 7.
Śrīvidyāratnasūtra, I (*Dīpikā* comm.).

Śaktibīja
Hrīṃ.

Śakticakra
Name of the five Śakti triangles in *Śrīyantra* (q.v.).
Saundaryalaharī (Lakṣmīdhara's comm. citing *Bhairavayāmala*).

Śakticālanī
A *mudrā* causing great success. By it the breath is held up by *Kumbhaka*. The wind so confined pushes *Kuṇḍalinī* upward.

Śaktidīkṣā
Initiation based on pure knowledge, in which there is no external rite. *Śāradātilaka*, IV. 1 (Rāghavabhaṭṭa).
Prāṇatoṣiṇī, II. 4.

Śakti-kāraṇavāda
The doctrine that Śakti is both the efficient and material cause of the universe.
Nityāṣoḍaśīkārṇava, IV. 5.
Śaktisaṃgama, Tārā, VIII. 28.
Saundaryalaharī, I.
Kaulamārgarahasya, p. 197.
Lalitāsahasranāma, 112 ff.

Śaktipāta
Touch of the lustre of Śiva, by which even a man of no strength can realise *Cit*. Also explained as the grace of Goddess with which a neophyte is favoured before initiation to Āgamānta Śaivism.

Śaktitrikoṇa
Śakti triangles conceived as existing in different parts of the body, the three lines of a triangle symbolising any set of three theories, and the angles supposed to be presided over by different goddesses.

Śaktivarṇa
Vowels.
Śāradātilaka, VI. 2 (comm.).

Śālagrāma
A special kind of stone, procured from rivers, especially the river Gaṇḍakī, and worshipped as a symbol of Nārāyaṇa.

Samādhi
An accessory of *Yoga*. State of intense concentration and bliss, in which the world of sense disappears. It is of two kinds, *Savikalpa* (q.v.) and *Nirvikalpa* (q.v.) which are also called *Saṃprajñāta* and *Asaṃprajñāta*, respectively.
Gheraṇḍa, VII. 1.
Gandharva, vi. 66 ff. *Kulārṇava*, 13-14.

Sāmarasya
Equilibrium of Śiva and Śakti (of *Upāya* and *Prajñā* in Buddhism), often conceived in sexual terms, the complete comprehension of which leads to the perception of non-duality.

Samaya (Pūjā)
Worship in and by the mind.

Samāyācāra
A mode of the *Śrīvidyā* cult.
Saundaryalaharī, vv. 31 ff (Lakṣmīdhara's comm.), (*Saubhāgyabhāskara* comm.).
Paraśurāma-kalpasūtra, vii. 1, X. 68, 80
(Rāmeśvara's comm.).

Śāmbhavī dīkṣā
A form of initiation of a superior level done by the mere touch, glance or will of the *guru*.
Related to the secret cult of *Kāmeśvarī*. *Nityotsava*, p. 9.

Saṃhāracakra
A part of *Navacakra* (q.v.).
Nityāṣoḍaśīkārṇava, I.

Śaṃkhinī
Name of a cerebral nerve.
Prāṇatoṣiṇī, I. 4, 33.

Saṃpradāyayoginī
See under *Caturdaśāra*.

Saṃprajñāta Samādhi
See *Samādhi*.

Sampuṭa
The desired *mantra*, recited before and after the name of the *Sādhya* (i.e., one against whom any of the six malevolent rites is performed).
Nīlatantra, XII. 25.

Saṃskāra
Sacrament, usually 10, prescribed for the three upper

classes of the Brāhmaṇical society.

Sandhyā (or, Saṃdhā)-bhāṣā (or, vacana)

Hevajra-tantra — chap. iii of the 2nd Kalpa of the Sanskrit text.
(1) Mystic language.
(2) Speech in which the intended meaning is hidden.
Saṃdhā seems to be the correct form.
For elaborate discussion, see V. Sastri in *IHQ*, 1928, pp. 287 ff and
P.C. Bagchi, *Studies in the Tantras*, pp. 27 ff.

Śāntā-Śakti

A form of *Śakti* containing will (*icchā*), knowledge (*jñāna*) and action (*kriyā*).

Śāntibīja

Svāhā.

Śastra

Syllable *Phaṭ*.

Ṣaṭcakrabheda

Same as *Cakrabheda* (q.v.).

Ṣaṭcakramārga

Same as *Piṇḍabrahmāṇḍa-mārga* (q.v.).

Ṣaṭ-kañcuka

Six causes of man's bondage, which are like veils over the Reality.

Ṣaṭkarma

Six acts calculated to do harm to an enemy:
Māraṇa (killing), *Stambhana* (causing paralysis), *Uccāṭana* (expulsion), *Vaśīkarana* (bringing others under control), *Vidveṣaṇa* (creating bad blood) and *Śānti* (pacification).
Nīlatantra, xii. 8;
Yoginī-tantra, IV;
Śāradātilaka, xxiii, 123 ff.

Śava-sādhana

Performance of a Tāntric rite with a corpse.
Kaulāvalī-nirṇaya, xiv; *Śyāmā-rahasya*, xiv; *Tārābhakti-sudhārṇava*, ix; *Puraścaryārṇava*, ix, *Nīlatantra*, xvi.

Savikalpa Samādhi

A state of perfect concentration and bliss in which a feeling of difference exists between the knower and the object of knowledge.

Sāvitrī

Mantra called *Gāyatrī* (q.v.).
Nīlatantra, II. 10.

Setu

(1) Designation of a *mantra* recited before *japa* after the worship of Mahāvidyā. So called as it is believed to be like a bridge for crossing the ocean of suffering. According to Kṛṣṇānanda's *Tantrasāra*, *Oṃkāra* precedes a *mantra*. According to *Prāṇatoṣiṇī*, *Praṇava* (*Oṃkāra*) is called *Setu* for Brāhmaṇas and Kṣatriyas. For Vaiśyas *Phaṭ* is *Setu*.

(2) Fourteen vowels followed by *anusvāra* and *nāda*. *Puraścaryārṇava*, VI, pp. 532-33. *Nīlatantra*, V. 105.

Siddha Vidyā

Same as *Mahāvidyā* (q.v.).

Siddha-mantra

The *mantra* which becomes effective instantaneously. If required, such a *mantra* can be adopted without regard to scriptural norms. *Rudrayāmala*, Uttara, III; Kṛṣṇānanda's *Tantrasāra*, IV.

Siddhāntācāra

A form of *Vāmācāra*, designed for devotees of the *Vīra* type. It lays greater stress on *antaryāga* than on external rites. Its adherents worship Viṣṇu by day while resorting to *pañcamakāra* at night. *Puraścaryārṇava*, I. 22; *Kaula-mārga-rahasya*, 10.

Siddhaugha

A line of succession of Tāntric *gurus*.

Siddhi

Mystical power. Supposed to be eight, viz. *Aṇimā* (assuming a very small form), *Laghimā* (making the body very light), *Prāpti* (power of obtaining anything), *Prākāmya* (irresistible will), *Mahimā* (increasing one's size at will), *Īśitva* (superiority, greatness), *Vaśitva* (bringing others under control), *Kāmāvasāyitā* (suppression of passion). Sometimes the number is given as ten, with the addition of *Bhuktisiddhi*, *Icchāsiddhi*. *Prapañcasāra*, XIX. 62-63.

Śiṣya

Disciple.
(i) Selection of *gurus* by — *Kulārṇava*, XI, XIV; *Rudrayāmala*, Uttara, II; *Prapancasāra*, XXXVI.
(ii) Test of, before initiation — Kṛṣṇānanda's *Tantrasāra*, 3; *Śāradātilaka*, II. 153.
(iii) Qualities of a good — *Śāradātilaka*, II. 145-50; *Tantrarāja*, I. 23, 24.
(iv) Characteristics of a bad disciple — *Rudrayāmala*, Uttara, II.
(v) Duties of — *Kulārṇava*, XII; *Kaulāvalī-nirṇaya*, X; *Paraśurāma-kalpasūtra*, X. 74.

Śivabīja

Name of mercury.

Śiva Cakra

The four Śiva triangles making the *Śrīyantra* (q.v.). *Viṣṇucakra*, *Aṣṭadala-padma*, *Bhūpura*, etc. are also called *Śivacakra*. *Saundaryalaharī*, IX (Lakṣmīdhara's comm.).

Smārtī dīkṣā

Initiation of the disciple in his absence. In it the

preceptor mentally renders the neophyte free from the threefold impurity of *āṇava*, *kārma* and *māyīya* types, and elevates his soul so as to enable it to be united with the Supreme Being.
Śāradātilaka, V. 127-40 (Rāghava's comm.).

Ṣoḍaśadala-padma
Sixteen-petalled lotus, each petal of which has a vowel representing a *Mātṛkā*.
Kāmakalā-vilāsa, XXXIII.

Ṣoḍaśopacāra
Sixteen articles for worship: *āsana, svāgata, pādya, arghya, ācamanīya, madhuparka, punarācamanīya, snānīya, vasana, bhūṣaṇa, gandha, puṣpa, dhūpa, dīpa, naivedya, vandanā.*
Mahānirvāṇa, XIII. 203-204.

Ṣoḍhānyāsa
A form of *Nyāsa* in which the deities are individually perceived in the body. It has six methods.
Tārābhakti-sudhārṇava, V, p. 163.
Śāradātilaka, VII.
Kṛṣṇānanda's *Tantrasāra*, pp. 272, 309 ff.
Puraścaryārṇava, XII. 1165.

Sparśa (Spārśanī) dīkṣā
Initiation of the disciple by the touch of the *guru*.
Kulārṇava, XIV.
Śāradātilaka, V. 127-40 (Rāghava's comm.).
Puraścaryārṇava, V. 391.

Śrīcakra
See *Śrīyantra*.

Śrīkula
A prominent Tāntric school to which texts like *Tripurārahasya*, *Prapañcasāra*, *Śāradātilaka*, etc., belong.

Śrīvidyā
(1) Mahāvidyā.
(2) A particular *mantra*.

Śrīyantra
The most important diagram relating to the cult of *Śrīvidyā*. Also called *Śrīcakra* and *Tripuracakra*.
It contains 9 triangles or *Yonis*, five connected with Śakti and four with Śiva, the former turned upward and the latter downward.
Nityāṣoḍaśīkārṇava, VI. 24.
Kāmakalāvilāsa, XXXVI.
Saundaryalaharī, IX (Lakṣmīdhara's comm.).

Srota
Branch (lit. current) of Tāntric tradition. Three currents are known, viz. *Dakṣiṇa* (right), *Vāma* (left) and *Madhyama* (middle). They are stated to represent the three *Śaktis* of Śiva.

Sṛṣṭicakra
One-third of *Śrīyantra*, representing the creative aspect of Śakti.
Setubandha comm. on *Nityāṣoḍaśīkārṇava*.

Stambhana
One of the six Tāntric rites, rendering the efforts of the enemy abortive or causing paralysis to his body.
Śāradātilaka, XXIII. 124.

Sthūladeha
Gross body.

Sthūla Dhyāna
Meditation based on an object like the image of the deity concerned.
Mahānirvāṇa, V. 139; *Śaktisaṃgama*, Sundarī, II. 126.

Strī-guru
Female preceptor.
(i) Characteristics of — *Rudrayāmala*, Uttara, II.
(ii) Benefit of initiation by — Kṛṣṇānanda's *Tantrasāra*, p. 3; *Śaktisaṃgama*, Tārā, LVIII. 7-8.
(iii) Verses for worship of — *Mātṛkābheda*, VII.
(iv) Mode of meditation on form of — *Prāṇatoṣiṇī*, III. 1, p. 155.

Strīvarṇa
Long vowels.
Śāradātilaka, II. 5-7 (comm.).

Śuddhatattva
Paramaśiva.

Śuddhavidyā
Knowledge of *Tattvas*.
That which imparts the knowledge of Śiva.

Śuddhi
Designation of meat, fish, *Mudrā*, fruits, roots, etc., offered while offering wine to the goddess.
Pañcamakāras (q.v.) are also called *Śuddhi*.

Sūkṣmadeha
Subtle body.

Śūlabīja
The mystic sound *Phaṭ*.

Śūnyatā
Void or vacuity conceived in terms of the Female Principle.

Sūrya Nāḍī
Another name of *Piṅgala* (q.v.).

Suṣumnā
A *Nāḍī* supposed to exist between *Iḍā* and *Piṅgalā*.
Also called *Brahmanāḍī* or *Brahmavartman*.
It extends from *Mūlādhāra* (q.v.) to *Brahmarandhra* (q.v.).
Through it *Kuṇḍalinī* ascends.

Svacchanda
Independent. Śiva.

Svādhiṣṭhāna
Name of a *Cakra* within the body, supposed to be located above *Mūlādhāra*. It looks like a six-petalled lotus.
Ṣaṭcakranirūpaṇa, XV-XVII (Lakṣmīdhara's comm.).
Nīlatantra, V. 96.
Ṣaṭcakranirūpaṇa, I.
Nīlatantra, XI. 28.

Svakīyā
Wife of the devotee as his partner in *Sādhana*.

Svapuṣpa

The first menstrual blood of a married woman, sacred to Goddess.

Svayaṃbhū Kusuma

Menstrual blood of a maiden.
Nīlatantra, XVIII. 7.

Tāḍana

Processing of a *mantra*. Each letter of it is recited 10 or 100 times.
Tāḍana is done also by writing the letters and sprinkling water of sandal wood over them.
Kṛṣṇānanda's *Tantrasāra*, p. 54.

Taijasa Varṇa

Āgneya Varṇa, i.e., *I, I, Ai, Kha, Cha, Ṭha, Tha, Pha, Ra, Kṣa;* stated to have originated from *tejas* (heat).

Tamas

Ātmābhimāna.

Tanmātra

Subtle elements, viz., *śabda, sparśa, rūpa, rasa, gandha.*

Taoism

A school of Chinese thought according to which Mother Goddess represents Yin, i.e., the Female Principle underlying creation.

Tārābīja

The mystic syllable *Kraṃ*.

Tārāṣodhā

A kind of *Nyāsa* used in the worship of Tārā.
Nīlatantra, V. 17.

Tāriṇimata

Same as *Kahādimata* (q.v.).

Tariqat

According to Sufis, the way of understanding the relation between God and the individual and with the material world.

Tarpaṇa

(1) Libation of water to deities, sages and forefathers.
Kṛṣṇānanda's *Tantrasāra*, pp. 81-82.
Mahānirvāṇa, V. 65.
(2) A method of processing *mantras*.
Tantrasāra, op. cit., p. 54.
Nīlatantra, VI. 5.

Tattvacakra

Same as *Divyacakra* (q.v.).

Tattvamudrā

The top of the ring-finger joined with the tip of the right thumb.
Nīlatantra, V. 56.

Tejodhyāna

Same as *Jyotirdhyāna* (q.v.).

Ṭha

An imitative sound, as if a metallic jar rolling down-steps.

Trailokyamohana-cakra

A form of *Śrīcakra* or *Śrīyantra* (q.v.).

Trikoṇa

(1) The mystic syllable *em*.
(2) Triangle, also called *yoni*,

necessary in Tāntric worship. *Parā Śakti* or *Vāk* is at the middle point. Three arms represent three forms of sound (*Paśyantī, Madhyamā, Vaikharī*), or, according to some Tantras, *Icchā* (desire), *Jñāna* (knowledge) and *Kriyā* (action). Three *Bījas*, three *Śaktis*, three goddesses, three *Pīṭhas*, and other concepts involving a triad. *Kuṇḍalinī* is called *Mahātrikoṇa*.
Kāmakalāvilāsa, XXII, XXIII.
Nityāṣoḍaśīkārṇava, VI. 36-40 (*Setubandha* comm.).
Paraśurāma-kalpasūtra, V. 1.
Gandharva-tantra, V. 112-13.
Tantrarāja-tantra, XXXV. 12-13.

Trilinga
Three phallus-symbols of Śiva, viz., *Bāṇa, Itara, Para*.
Kāmakalā-vilāsa, XIII, XIV.

Tripīṭha
Collective name of Kāmarūpa, Pūrṇagiri and Jālandhara Pīṭhas.
Kāmakalāvilāsa, XII, XIV.

Tripuracakra
Same as *Śrīcakra* or *Śrīyantra* (q.v.).

Tripurasundarīmata
Name of *Hādimata* (q.v.).
Śaktisaṃgama, Kālī, VI. 125.

Turīya
(1) Highest state.
(2) A very high state. A field of knowledge, which is also known as *turīya*, is supposed to be contained in the *Sahasrāra Cakra*.

Uccāṭana
One of the six malevolent rites, by which the expulsion or mental agitation of the enemy is ensured.
Śāradātilaka, XXIII. 125.

Unmanā, Unmanī
Sixth stage in spiritual exercise. The devotee, in this stage, experiences great joy in which his sense-organs stop functioning.

Upacāra
Articles for worship. These may range from five to sixty-four.
Śāradātilaka, IV. 92 (Rāghava's comm.).
Kṛṣṇānanda's *Tantrasāra*, pp. 551-52.
Mahānirvāṇa, VI. 78-79, XIII. 203 ff.

Upādānakāraṇa
Material cause.

Ullāsa
Stages of Tāntric *Sādhana*, viz., *Ārambha, Taruṇa, Yauvana, Prauḍha, Prauḍhānta, Unmana, Anavasthā*.
Paraśurāma-kalpasūtra, X. 68.

Unmanī (Unmanā)
The sixth stage of Tāntric *sādhana*. In this stage the devotee experiences great joy, and his sense organs apparently stop their function.

Kulārṇava, VIII; *Tārābhakti-sudhārṇava*, VI. 255.

Upacāra

Materials offered in worship. These may be five, seven, ten, twelve, sixteen, eighteen, thirty-six or sixty-four. *Puraścaraṇa*, III. 224-25; *Śāradā-tilaka*, IV. 92 (Rāghava's comm.), Kṛṣṇānanda's *Tantrasāra*, 551-52; *Mahānirvāṇa*, VI. 78-79, XIII. 203 ff.

Upāṃśu

Japa in a very low voice so that it cannot be heard.

Upāya

The Male Principle. The unity of *Upāya* with *Prajñā* (q.v.) was regarded as the ultimate reality in Tāntric Buddhism. In the *Guhyasamāja*, *Upāya* is called *vajrayoga* or means to the attainment of *bodhi* or enlightenment.

Uttarācāra

The way shown by Vedic injunction and the *Guru* who is *Jīvanmukta*.

Uttarakaula

A sect of *Kaula* worshippers.

Saundaryalaharī, XXIII, XXXIII (Lakṣmīdhara's comm.).

Uttarāmnāya

Northern zone of Tantra culture.

Vācikī (Vāk) dīkṣā

The form of initiation with *mantra*.

Śāradātilaka, V. 127-40 (Rāghava's comm.).

Vadhūbīja

Strīṃ.

Nīlatantra, V. 45.

Vāgbhava

It denotes *bījas*, and is also the name of a triangle.

Vahnijāyā

Svāhā.

Nīlatantra, XVII. 18.

Vaikharī

One of the four kinds of sounds. Carried by the wind inside the body, it is articulated in the throat as sentences.

Śāradātilaka, I.1 (Comm.).

Nityāṣoḍaśīkārṇava, VI. 10-11 (*Setubandha* comm.).

Vaiṣṇavācāra

A way of *Sādhana* to be followed by a Tāntric devotee. *Nīlatantra*, VIII. 19.

Vajra

(1) Thunderbolt, a weapon often found in the hands of the Tāntric Buddhist images. (2) Diamond.

In Tāntric Buddhism, it generally denotes *Śūnya* (Void) which, itself indestructible, is believed to destroy all evils. It also came to mean the real nature of things, and then the Supreme Being (Vajrasattva or Vajradhara). The idea led to the conception of the

Vajrakāya (q.v.) of the Buddha.
Advaya-vajra-saṃgraha, 24, 37.
Prajñopāya, III. 9, V. 45.
Vajra is also the name of a nerve within the *Suṣumnā* (q.v.).

Vajrapuṣpa
Diamond flower, valuable flower, the blossom of sesamum.
Nīlatantra, V. 25.

Vajrayāna
A form of Tāntric Buddhism.

Vāk-dīkṣā
See *Vācikī dīkṣā*.

Vāmācāra
A Tāntric way of *Sādhana*. Followers of it resort to *Pañcamakāra*.
Śaktisaṃgama, Tārā, I. 90 ff.
Śakti is worshipped as a personification of Śiva's wife. According to some, a rite in which a woman, who is placed on the left of the man, plays an important part, or is a crooked way practised secretly.
Vāma is of two kinds, *Madhyama* in which all the five *Makāras* are resorted to, and *Uttama* in which *Madya*, *Maithuna* and *Mudrā* are used.

Vāmamārga
Same as *Vāmācāra* (q.v.).

Varṇa(mayī) dīkṣā
The form of initiation in which the spirit of letters is infused into the different parts of the disciple's body.
Śāradātilaka, V. 116-21.

Vaśīkaraṇa
One of the six black rites by which a person is brought under control.
Śāradātilaka, XXIII. 123.

Vedācāra
A mode of *Sādhana*. In it the Vedic way is followed.
Prāṇatoṣiṇī, III. 1.

Vedha(mayī) dīkṣā
Same as *Manodīkṣā* (q.v.).

Veśyā
For technical meaning in Tantra, see our observations in connexion with the *Niruttara Tantra*.

Vibhāva
See under *Paśu*.

Vidveṣaṇa
A black rite by which animosity is created between persons.
Śāradātilaka, XXIII. 124.

Vidyā
(1) True knowledge.
(2) Female deity.
(3) *Mantra* relating to a female deity.
(4) Female partner of a Tāntric *Sādhaka*.
Nīlatantra, II. 2, XVIII. 34.

Vighnāpsāraṇa
Same as Bhūtāpsāraṇa (q.v.).

Vilāsa
A principal Tāntric school.

Vīra

A Tāntric *Sādhaka* of the second grade, who has advanced mental faculties, and follows *Vīrācāra* (q.v.).
Kulārṇava, XVII.
Rudrayāmala, Uttara, I. 136, LI. 20-21.
Paraśurāma-kalpasūtra, VI. 39 (comm.).
Nirvāṇatantra, XIV.
Kāmākhyātantra, IV.
Niruttara, XI.
Śaktisaṃgama, Sundarī, I. 197-200, Tārā, XL-III, 204.
Prāṇatoṣiṇī, VII. 1.

Vīrabhāva

A particular attitude of a Tāntric *Sādhaka*.

Vīracakra

A *Cakra* ritual in which five Śaktis, viz., mother (*Bhumīndra-kanyā*), daughter (*Rajakīsutā*), sister (*Śvapacī*), daughter-in-law (*Kapālī*) and wife (*Yoginī*) are worshipped.
Niruttara, X.

Vīrācāra

A way of *Sādhana* to be followed by a Tāntric devotee of the *Vīra* class (q.v.).

Vīrasādhana

Sādhana practised by a *Vīra* type of devotee.

Virāsana

Sitting posture in which one rests the body on the heels.

Visarga

It represents both *Parā* and *Aparā* aspects of Śakti.
Also called *Kaulika Śakti*, it is the Female Principle (*saḥ*) as complementary to the Male Principle (*haṃ*), *Bindu*.
Tantrā-loka, III. 120 ff, *Ṣaṭcakranirūpaṇa*, XL-III (Kālīcaraṇa's comm. quoting *Prapañcasāra*).

Viṣṇugranthi

A knot in the *Anāhata Cakra* (q.v.) which *Kuṇḍalinī* has to penetrate in its ascent.

Viṣṇukrāntā

The tract of land extending from the Vindhyas to Caṭṭala (Chittagong in Bangladesh) or, according to some, to Java in the Far East. Here, Viṣṇu means sea-going vessel, which is used in a journey to the Lord.

Viśuddha

One of the six *Cakras*, above the *Anāhata* (q.v.) in the region of the neck. Supposed to look like a sixteen-petalled lotus. Seat of Sarasvatī.
Ṣaṭcakranirūpaṇa, XXVIII, XXX.

Vitarka

Reflection like this—I am Śiva Himself.

Vyāpaka-nyāsa

See *Vyāpakatraya*.
Nīlatantra, V. 20.

Vyāpakatraya

A kind of *Nyāsa*. The three are:

1. Touching the head and foot with the hand.
2. From foot to head.
3. From head to foot.

Nīlatantra, V. 20.

Vyūha

According to the *Pāñcarātra Saṃhitās*, an emanative form of Vāsudeva in His act of creation. The principal forms were four, called Saṃkarṣaṇa etc. The total number of *Vyūhas* was twenty-four.

The *Ahirbudhnya Saṃhitā*, for instance, deals with the origin and development of the *Vyūhas*.

Yamala

Literally meaning 'pair', 'couple'.

Yang

The Male Principle in Chinese Philosophy.

Yantra

Diagram, geometrical figure, painted with various colours at the time of worship. The worshipper imagines that the deity, being worshipped for the time being, resides in the diagram. Diagrams differ according to the forms of the deities worshipped. Variously interpreted as instrument, the body and abode of a deity, amulet, mental faculty, pure consciousness, doctrinal niceties, microcosm of human body, etc.

Gandharva, V. 39-40.

Kulārṇava, VI, XVII.

Śaktisaṃgama, Tārā, XIII. 203, LL-2.

Kṛṣṇānanda's *Tantrasāra*, p. 312 ff.

Saundaryalaharī.

Nīlatantra, XVIII. 23.

Yantrapuṣpa

Flowers like *Javā*, *Aparājitā*, *Raktakaravīra*, etc.

Nīlatantra, XVIII. 23.

Yaugī dīkṣā

A form of initiation. In it, the *guru*, in a subtle form, enters the body of his disciple and identifies his personality with that of the disciple.

Śāradātilaka, V. 127-40 (Rāghava's comm.).

Yin

The Female Principle in Chinese philosophy.

Yoginī

(1) A class of goddesses, 64 in number, believed to be manifestations of the eight *Mātṛkās*.

(2) Female partner of the *Sādhaka*.

(3) Goddesses presiding over the *Cakras*.

(4) Name of a Tāntric school.

(5) A class of female ascetics spreading knowledge among the masses.

(6) Medicine woman.

(7) Woman possessed by the goddess.

Yoni

(1) Diagram resembling the female organ.
Nīlatantra, XII. 78.
(2) Fourfold Śakti, viz., *Ambā*, *Jyeṣṭhā*, *Raudrī*, *Vāmā*.
(3) Female organ. See *Gaurīpīṭha*.

Yonimudrā

(1) A finger-pose looking like the female organ.
(2) A posture of the body, in which the devotee fixes his anus on his left heel, tongue on the palate, and eyes on the tip of the nose. It is supposed to rouse *Kuṇḍalinī*.
Prāṇatoṣiṇī, I. 10.
Śāradātilaka, IX (Quotation from *Bhūtaśuddhi-tantra*).
Nīlatantra, VIII. 25.

Yonipuṣpa

Black *Aparājitā* flower symbolising sexual intercourse.
Paraśurāma-kalpasūtra, X. 63.

Yoniyugma

A triangle with its apex upward intersecting a triangle with its apex downward.
Nīlatantra, XIII. 79.

Yuganaddha

Male Principle united with Female Principle, a motif often represented in Tāntric Buddhist art.
The non-dual state of unity of *Śūnyatā* and *Karuṇā*.
Sādhanamālā, II, p. 505.

GLOSSARY OF SCIENTIFIC TERMS[1]

[Based mainly on the *Rasārṇava*. Occasionally consulted the *Yogataraṅgiṇī*, *Rasakāmadhenu*, *Rasasāra*, *Rasendracintāmaṇi*; *Paribhāṣā-pradīpa* and *Rasamārtaṇḍa* rarely adverted to.]

ADRIJA
Same as *Śilājatu* (q.v.).

ANDHAMŪṢĀ
A kind of closed crucible.

AMALA-MĀKṢIKA
Iron pyrites of silvery, radiated crystals.

AYASKĀNTA
Loadstone.

ĀRAṆĀLĀMLA
Sour gruel.

ĀROṬA
Well-purified, once killed mercury.

ĀSURĪ-LAVAṆA
Kālā nimak (lit. black salt).

ĀVĀPA
Throwing other things to the molten metals.

BADDHA
(Mercury) bound or fixed.

BĀLUKĀYANTRA
An apparatus.

BHASMAMŪṢĀ
A kind of crucible made of sesamum (2 parts) and brick-dust (1 part).

BHASMASŪTA
One of the seven stages of mercury.

BHĀNU
Copper.

BHĀVANĀ
Maceration of powders in fluids such as expressed juice of herbs, etc. The mixture is dried in the sun.

---

1. For the meaning of the terms, we have taken the Bibliotheca Indica ed. of *Rasārṇava* as our authority.

BHĀSKARA
Copper.

BHRAMARĀYANTRA or
BHRĀMARĪYANTRA
A kind of apparatus.

BHUJAGA
Lead.

BHŪCARA
Name of mercury properly calcined.

BHŪDHARA-YANTRA
An apparatus which is a crucible with mercury, placed in a pit, and is covered with *dīptopala* (gems?).

CAKRAYANTRA
An apparatus looking like a wheel.

CAṆAKĀNTAKA
Acid of *Cicer arictinum*, Linn.
Hindi *Canakloni*.
Bengali *Gāch-cholā*.

CAPALA
Mercury.

CĀRAṆA
A process of adding strength or efficacy to mercury, a part of *jāraṇa* (q.v.).

CUMBAKA
A sort of *Kāntapāṣāṇa* (q.v.).

CULIKĀLAVAṆA
A sort of salt, sometimes called *navasāra* (q.v.).

CHATRI
Disfigured mercury of the shape of an umbrella.

DARADA
Hiṅgula (q.v.). It is of three kinds, viz. *Carmāra*, *Śukatuṇḍaka* and *Haṃsapāda*. Each succeeding is of a better quality than the preceding one.

DALA
A preparation of several metals or minerals by purifying or refining them by other metals and minerals before they undergo the process of calcination.

DĪPAYANTRA
An apparatus, called Dīpikā, which occupies the place of *Tiryakpātana-yantra*.

DURMELI
Mercury not properly mixed.

DOLĀYANTRA
A suspension apparatus, vide P.C. Ray, *History of Hindu Chemistry*, I, p. 121.

DRĀVAṆA
Liquefaction, a way of refining mercury.

DVANDVANA
Compound of two metals or minerals.

DVANDVA-MELĀPANA (or, -MELĀPAKA)
An amalgam or compound of metals or minerals.

DHĀTU
Red ochre (*Giri-mṛttikā*, Bengali *Giri-māṭi*).

DHŪMĀVALOKIN
Mercury at a certain stage or at the best refined stage.

DHŪMOTTHA
Probably carbonate of potash.

DHŪLI
A stage of mercury.

GAGANADRUTI
Liquefaction of mica.

GAJAPUṬA
An apparatus for roasting metals or minerals in a pit in the ground.

GANDHAKA
Sulphur.

GANDHA-PĀṢĀṆA
Sulphur.

GARBHA-DRUTI
Liquefaction of metals or minerals within mercury.

GARBHA-YANTRA
An apparatus for calcination of paste.

GĀRA, GĀRĀ
Earth steeped in water.

GIRI
Bitumen.

GIRIJATU
Same as *Śilājatu* (q.v.).

GIRI-MASTAKA
(*Soraka*, according to *Rasakāmadhenu*. Nitre or Nitrate of potash. Bengali *sorā*).

GIRISĀMYA
Same as *Śilājatu* (q.v.).

GOROCANĀ
Concretions occasionally found in the gall-bladder of the ox or, according to some, in the brain of a cow.

GOSTANAMŪṢĀ
A crucible of the shape of the cow's udder.

HAṂSAPAKA
An apparatus for calcination of mercury.

HARAGAURĪ
Probably mercury and mica.

HARABĪJA
Mercury.

HARITĀLA
Orpiment.

HEMADALA
A preparation of gold with other minerals.

HEMABĪJA
A preparation of gold, purified by yellow and red dyeing plants or objects.

HIṄGU
Ferula asafoetida, Linn. Bengali *hiṅg*.

HIṄGULA
Cinnabar.

JATU
Same as *Śilājatu* (q.v.).

JANTUGHNA
Same as *Hiṅgu* (q.v.).

JALUKĀ (or, JALAUKĀ) BANDHA
One of the seven stages of mercury.

JĀRAṆA (or ṆĀ)
Calcination or oxydising metals or minerals.

KĀCA
Kind of salt, popularly called *Viṭ-lavaṇa*.

KACCHPA-YANTRA
Name of an apparatus.

KĀKAMĀCI
Solanum nigrum, Linn.

KALALA
Uterus, embryo.

KĀLIKĀ
An impurity of mercury or metals or minerals.

KALKA
Paste of vegetables ground and mixed with water.

KAÑCUKA
Impurity of mercury.

KĀÑJIKĀ
A sour gruel prepared from the acetous fermentation of pulverised paddy and other substances.

KĀṄKṢĪ
Same as *Saurāṣṭrī* (q.v.).

KAṄKUṢṬHA
One of the eight *Uparasas;* a coral-coloured medicinal earth.

KAṄKOLA
A fragrant spice, known as *Śītal cini*.

KANTALOHA
Cast iron.

KAPĀLĪ
One of the impurities of mercury.

KAPOTĀKHYA PUṬA
An apparatus (called Kapota) for roasting, digesting or sublimating metals, minerals or drugs.

KARĪṢĀGNI
Fire fuelled by dry cowdung.

KĀŚISA
Ferrous sulphate, sulphate of iron, two varieties, viz. *dhātukāśisa* (green vitriol) and *puṣpakāśisa* (yellow vitriol). Bengali *Hirākas*.

KAṬUTRAYA
Three spices taken together, viz., ginger, long pepper and black pepper.

KHAGA
Same as *Kaśisa* (q.v.).

KHECARA
Do.

KHECARATĀ
A certain state of mercury; the sky-going efficacy of mercury.

KHECARĪ
A mode of *jāraṇa* (q.v.).

KHOṬA
One of the seven stages of mercury. Bengali *jamak, phuṭ*.

KOṢṬHIKĀ
Koṣṭhī apparatus, vide P.C. Ray, *History of Hindu Chemistry*, I, p. 89. Bengali *Hāpar*.

KṢĀRATRAYA
Three kinds of alkali, viz. *sarjikṣāra* (natron), *yavakṣāra* (saltpetre) and *taṅkaṇakṣāra* (borax).

KṢĀRĀMLA
Alkali and acid.

KṢĀRĀṢṬAKA
Eight kinds of *Kṣāra* (alkali), viz. *Vajra* (alkali of Manasā or *Siju*), *Arka* (*Calatropis gigantea*), *Citraka* (*Plumbago zeylanica*), *Tumbi* (long gourd), *Arjuna* (*Terminalia arjuna*), *Sarja* (see above), *Yava* (see above), *Taṅkana* (see above).

KSETRAJA
A variety of gold.

KṢETRA-DOṢA
Impurity of mercury or other minerals obtained from the field or mine.

KVĀTHA
Decoction, generally prepared by boiling a certain quantity of vegetables in sixteen times of water till it is reduced to one-fourth.

LOHA
Any metal, especially iron.

LOHAKIṬṬA
Rust of iron or mandura.

LOHĀVARTA
A state of melted metals.

MANAḤŚILĀ
Realgar. Bengali *Manchāl*.

MAYŪRATUTTHA
Blue vitriol having the play of colours like the peacock's throat.

MAHĀRASA
Superior minerals, eight in number, viz., *mākṣika* (q.v.), *śilā* (rock), *capala* (probably some sulphurous minerals), *rasaka* (Calamine), *sasyaka* (q.v.), *darada* (q.v.), *sroto'ñjana* (q.v.) and *vimala* (q.v.).

MAHĀVIṢA
Virulent poison. Five kinds, viz. *saktuka* (Bengali *Chātāri viṣ*), *kālakūṭa* (Bengali *Kaṭhviṣ*), *sitamustā* (white guñjā or seed of *Abrus precatorius*, Linn.), *śṛṅgī* (Bengali *śṛṅgiviṣ*), *kṛṣṇaviṣ* (?).

MĀKṢIKA
Iron pyrites. See P.C. Ray, *History of Hindu Chemistry*, p. 138.

MEDINĪYANTRA
An apparatus, probably resembling *Pātāla yantra*.

MIŚRAKA
Mercury.

MṚTASŪTA
One of the seven stages of mercury.

MṚTASŪTAKA
Killed mercury.

MŪṢĀ
Crucible.

MŪṢĀYANTRA
Crucible apparatus.

NAVASĀRA
Nausadar, sal ammoniac.

NĀGA
Lead.

NIṢEKA
Dipping any hot metal into water.

NĪLAKĀCA
Black salt, popularly called *kāclavaṇ*.

PAÑCA-LAVAṆA
Five kinds of salt, viz. *Kāca, Saindhava, Sāmudra, Viḍa* and *Sauvarcala*.

PAÑCĀMLA
Aggregate of five acids, viz. *Kula, Dāḍimba, Tintiḍi, Cukaka* and *Amlavetasa*; or *Jambira, Nāraṅga, Amlavetasa, Tintiḍi, Bījapūraka*.

PAÑCĀVASTHĀ
Five stages of mercury, viz. *Dhūma, Ciṭiciṭi, Mandūka-pluti, Sakampa* and *Vikampa*.

PAṬU
Salt.

PAṬṬABANDHA
One of the seven stages of mercury; bound or fixed by a piece of cloth as it were.

PATAṄGĪ
A state of mercury.

PADMAYANTRA
An apparatus resembling a lotus.

PANNAGA
Lead.

PARIBĀLA
A kind of iron.

PĀTANĀYANTRA
An apparatus, called *Pātana*, vide P.C. Ray, *History of Hindu Chemistry*, I, p. 122.

PĀTĀLAYANTRA
An apparatus called *Pātāla*.

PĪTAVARGA
Aggregate of five yellow objects producing yellow dye.

PUṬAPĀKA
A particular method of preparing drugs, in which the various ingredients are wrapped up in leaves and, being covered with clay, are roasted in the fire.

PŪTIKA
Tin and lead, so called on account of their foetid odour.

PRAKĀŚAMŪṢĀ
A kind of open crucible as distinguished from *Andhamūṣā* (covered crucible).

PRATIVĀPA
The act of covering a melted metal.

RAVI
Copper.

RAVIJĪRṆA
(Mercury) Calcined with copper.

RAVINĀGA-KAPĀLĪ
A process of dyeing pure silver by the aid of copper

and lead, according to the practice of the Kāpālikas.

RASA
Mercury.

RASAJA
A variety of gold.

RASAKA
Calamine. Three kinds of it have been distinguished, viz., of the colour of earth, of the appearance of treacle, and of the colour of stone.

RASA-BHASMA-RASĀYANA
Medicinal effect of the calx of mercury.

RASAVĀDIN
Experts in chemistry or alchemy.

RASĀKṚṢṬI
A sort of preparation of mercury.

RĀJĀVARTA
One of the *Uparasas* (q.v.), a gem regarded as an inferior kind of diamond, *lapis lazuli*.

RĀMAṬHA
Same as *hiṅgu* (q.v.).

ŚILĀ
Same as *Manaḥśilā* (q.v.).

ŚILĀJATU
Bitumen of four kinds, viz. *Svarṇa, Raupya, Tāmra* and *Kṛṣṇāyas* (iron).

ŚUDDHĀBHRA-KAPĀLIN (or, ŚUBHRĀ)
A process of dyeing metals or minerals with the aid of white mica, according to the method of the *Kāpālikas*.

SARJA
Resinous exudation of *Śāl* tree (*Shorea robusta*, Gaertn.).

SASYAKA
Same as *Mayūra-tuttha* (q.v.).

SAINDHAVA
Rock-salt, originally obtained from the region called Sindhu.

SAURĀṢṬRĪ
A sweet-scented earth of Surat in Bombay Presidency.

SAUVARCALA
Sonchal or sochal, salt called *Kālānimak* (black salt) by the upcountry physicians.

SAUVĪRA
Galena or sulphide of lead, a sort of collyrium; its name is *Sauvīrāñjana*, being obtained from mountains of Sauvīra, a region along the Indus. This collyrium is popularly called *Kālā* (black) *Surmā*.

SROTOÑJANA
A kind of collyrium, produced in the bed of the Yamunā and other rivers. It is popularly called *Safed* (white) *Surmā*.

ŚULVA
Copper.

ŚULVAKAPĀLIKĀ
A process of dyeing metals or minerals with the aid of

copper, according to the method of the *Kāpālikas*.

SŪTA
Mercury.

SVEDANA
Application of heat to the skin or any substance for inducing perspiration.

TĀPYA
A sort of iron pyrite, sulphide of iron. So called as found in the bed of the river Tāpi or Tāpti.

TĀRA
Silver.

TĀRAJĪRṆA
Mercury calcined with silver.

TĀLA
Same as *Haritāla* (q.v.).

TĪKṢṆACŪRṆA
Iron-filings or iron-powder. Bengali *Lohacūrṇa*.

TĪKṢṆALOHA
Metal called *Tīkṣṇa* or iron, also called *Kānta* (or *Kānti* or *Kāñcī*) *loha*.

TĪKṢṆA ŚULVAKAPĀLIN
A process of dyeing metals or minerals with the aid of iron and copper, according to the method adopted by the Kāpālikas.

TUTTHA
Sulphate of copper. Bengali *tuñte.*

TUVARI
Alum-earth. Same as *Kāṅkṣī* (q.v.).

TRIKAṬU
Kaṭutraya (q.v.).

TRILOHA
Three metals taken together, viz. gold, silver, copper.

TRUṬI
Smallest weight and measure used by physicians.

UDGHĀṬA
A preparation of mercury devoid of all impurities.

UPARASA
Inferior or secondary minerals or metallic ores and earths (8 in number). These are *gandhaka* (sulphur), *tālaka* (orpiment), *śilā* or *manaḥśilā* (realgar), *saurāṣṭrī* (alum-earth), *khaga* (iron sulphate), *gairika* (red ochre), *rājāvarta* (lapis lazuli), *kaṅguṣṭha* (a medicinal earth).

UPAVIṢA
Minor or factitious poison. It is of different kinds, viz. *snuhi* (*Euphoria nerrifolia*, Linn.), *arka* (*Calatropis gigantea*), *unmattaka* (*Datura fastuosa* L.), *karavīra* (*Nerium indicum* Soland), *lāṅgali* (*Gloria superba*, Linn.).

ŪRDHVAPĀTANA
A kind of apparatus resembling *Pātana-yantra*, vide P.C. Ray, *History of Hindu Chemistry*.

VAṄGA
Tin.

VAIKRĀNTA-NĀGAKAPĀLĪ
A process of dyeing pure silver with the aid of *Vaikrānta* and *Nāga*, according to the practice of the *Kāpālikas*.

VAṄGA-TĪKṢṆA-KAPĀLĪ
A process of dyeing copper and silver with the aid of *Vaṅga* and *Tīkṣṇa*, according to the practice of the *Kāpālikas*.

VAṄGĀBHRAKA-KAPĀLĪ
A process of dyeing metals or minerals with the aid of tin and mica, according to the method of the *Kāpālikas*.

VIMALA
One of the eight *Mahārasas*. A variety of pyrites. May be white, yellow or red. Generally used to denote copper pyrites.

VAJRAMŪṢĀ
A hard crucible.

VARAMŪṢĀ
A kind of crucible.

VYOMAN
Mica.

YAVAKṢĀRA
Factitious carbonate of potash. See P.C. Ray, *History of Hindu Chemistry*, p. 45.

YAVĀGŪ
Gruel prepared by water (6 parts) and powdered rice (4 parts) boiled together. Used as *māṇḍa* (porridge), *peya* (drink) or *vilepī* (coating). Bengali *jāu*.

YOGAVĀHIN
A menstruum or medium of mixing metals or medicines.

SELECT BIBLIOGRAPHY

[In some secondary sources of our information, places of publication and/or dates have not been noted.]

It is divided into the following sections:

A. Texts, Lexicons and Translations
B. Books in Western Languages
C. Hindi Books
D. Bengali Books
E. Miscellaneous Books
F. Journals, Proceedings, Reports, Catalogues, etc.

As regards texts of Tantras, we have noted not only those mentioned in this work, but also other important titles known to have been published so that the reader may have an idea of the published materials.

A. TEXTS, LEXICONS AND TRANSLATIONS

Though it is a work on TANTRA, yet we have deemed it proper to include, in the Bibliography, some non-Tāntric works which deal with or are influenced by Tāntric matters.

Advaya-vajra-saṃgraha, GOS.

Ādyādi-mahālakṣmī-hṛdaya-stotra, in *Bṛhat-stotramuktāhāra*, pt. 2, *Bṛhat-stotraratnākara*, pt. 1.

Āgama-candrikā, ed. P. Sastri, Calcutta, 1985.

Agastya-saṃhitā, ed. R.N. Das, Lucknow, 1898; K.K. Smṛtitīrtha, Calcutta, 1910.

Ahīrbudhnya-saṃhitā, with Eng. trs. by Nityasvarūpānanda, Calcutta, 1964.

——, pub. from Adyar Library, Madras, 1966 (2nd ed.).

Ajitāgama, I, II, Pondicherry, 1963, 1967.

Ākāśabhairava-kalpa, N.C. Sharma.

Akulavīra-tantra, ed. P.C. Bagchi, Kaulajñāna-nirṇaya and some Minor Texts of the school of Matsyendranātha, Calcutta, 1934.

Ānanda-kāṇḍa, Tanjore Sarasvatī Mahal Series 15, 1952.

Ānandalaharī, ed. and trs. by A. Avalon, Madras, 1961 (5th ed.).

Aniruddha-saṃhitā, ed. A.S. Iyengar, Mysore, 1956.

Ārya-mañjuśrī-mūlakalpa, TSS, Trivandrum, 1920-25.

Aṣṭāvkra-saṃhitā, with Eng. trs., by Nityasvarūpānanda, Calcutta, 1964.

Aṣṭottara-śatopaniṣatsu Śākta Upaniṣad, Adyar, Madras, 1950.

Bhairava-Padmāvatī-kalpa, ed. K.V. Abhyankar, with comm. of Bandhusena in Jhavery, *Mantraśāstra*, pp. 1-74.

Bharadvāja-saṃhitā (Telugu), ed. P. Aiyyangar, Mysore.

——, from *Nārada-pañcarātra*, Veṅkaṭeśvara Press, Bombay, 1905.

Bhārgava Tantra, a Pañcarātra work, ed. R.P. Chowdhury.

Bhāskaravilāsa, Ptd. in NSP ed. of *Lalitā-sahasra-nāma*.

Bhāvopahāra, Cakrapāṇi, with *Vivaraṇa* by Ramyadeva, KSS, No. 14, 1918.

Bījanighaṇṭu, ed. A. Avalon, *Tāntrik Texts*, I.

Brahma-saṃhitā, Pub. in *Tāntrik Texts*, vol. XV.

Brahmasūtra with *Śaktibhāṣya*, see *Śaktibhāṣya*.

Bṛhadbrahma-saṃhitā (Devanāgarī), from *Nārada-pañcarātra*, ed. H.N. Apte, Ānandāśrama Series, No. 68 (Telugu), Tirupati, 1909.

Bṛhannīla-tantra, ed. M. Kaul, 1984.

Bṛhat-saṃhitā of Varāhamihira, with Bhaṭṭotpala's comm., ed. S. Dvivedi, Vizianagaram Sanskrit Series, 1985; Eng. trs. with notes, by M.R. Bhat, Delhi.

Bṛhat-tantrasāra of Kṛṣṇānanda, Calcutta, 1341 B.S., 10th ed.

Cakra-saṃbhāra-tantra, *Tāntrik Texts*, 7, Calcutta, 1919 (1st section); Tibetan Texts in *ibid.*, 11, Darjeeling, 1919.

Chinnamastā-tantra, Ptd. in *Śāktapramoda*, 1890, 1893.

Cidgagana-candrikā, with comm. of R. Misra, with *Divyacakorikā* comm., by K.A. Sastri, Letukura, East Godavari District, 1943, 2 pts.

Dakṣiṇāmūrti-saṃhitā, Varanasi, 1937 (Princess of Wales Sarasvatī Bhavana Texts, No. 61).

Dakṣiṇāmūrti-stotra, Śaṃkarācārya, with comm. of Svayaṃprakāśa and *Vārtika* of Sureśvarācārya, Bombay, 1902.

Dattātreya-tantra, with Hindi comm., Bombay, 1983.

Devī-bhāgavata, ed. (i) R. Pandeya, Varanasi, Saṃvat 1984; (ii) Veṅkaṭeśvara Press, with Nīlakaṇṭha's comm., *Tilaka*, Saṃvat 1984; (iii) Vaṅgavāsī, Calcutta, Śaka 1932 (=1910 A.D.), 2nd ed.

Devī-kālottarāgama, ed. with comm., by G. Kaviraj, in *Tantra-saṃgraha*, II, Varanasi, 1970, pp. 318-345.

Devī-purāṇa, ed. with Bengali trs. by P. Tarkaratna, Calcutta, 1334 B.S. (2nd ed.) with Hindi comm., Bombay, 1983.

Durgā-dakārādi-sahasra-nāma (from *Kulārṇava-tantra*), Ptd. Calcutta, 1921 (in a collection).

Durgā-saptaśatī, with seven Sanskrit commentaries, ed. K.K. Sharma, 1984.

Ekākṣarakośa (Puruṣottama), A. Avalon, *Tāntrik Texts*, I.

Gaṇapatitattva, Old Javanese Text, ed. with notes and Eng. trs. by S. Singhal, New Delhi, 1958.

Gandharvatantra, ed. Kak and Sastri, Srinagar, 1934.

Gandhottamā-nirṇaya (by son of Viśveśvara); ptd., Hardwar, 1900.

Gaurīkāñcalikā, Ptd., Calcutta, 1890, Bombay, 1907.

Gautamīya-tantra, ed. B. Jha, Varanasi, 1977.

Gāyatrī-kavaca, pub. Amritsar, 1902 (from *Vaśiṣṭha-saṃhitā* of Pañcarātra).

Gāyatrī-kavaca from *Rudrayāmala*, ptd. (i) *Bṛhat-stotra-muktāvalī*, Pt. 1, Stotra No. 245, 1st and 2nd ed., 1912, 1923; (ii) with *Surya-kavaca*, ptd. 29-31, 1918, in Telugu script.

Gāyatrī-rahasya, ed. B. Sarma Gaud.

Gāyatrī-tantra, ed. *Sulabha-tantra-prakāśa*, 1886. Also with Hindi comm., ed. M. Pal, Calcutta, Saṃvat 1948; with Hindi trs., Bombay, 1914.

Gopāla-mantra-kramadīpikā, Same as *Kramadīpikā* (q.v.).

Gorakṣa-siddhānta-saṃgraha, Sarasvatī Bhavana Texts, No. XVIII, Varanasi, 1925.

Guhyasamāja, GOS, LIII, 1931.

Guptasādhana-tantra, with Bengali trs., Calcutta, 1886; with Hindi comm., by B. Mishra, Bombay, 1922-23.

Gurutantra, ed. and trs. into Bengali by J. Tarkālaṃkāra, Calcutta, 1335 B.S.

Haṭhayoga-pradīpikā, Veṅkaṭeśvara Press, 1952.

Hayaśīrṣa-saṃhitā, Ādikāṇḍa, pub. by Varendra Research Society, Rajshahi, Bangladesh, in 2 vols., 1952, 1957.

Hevajra-tantra, ed. D.L. Snellgrove (with Eng. trs.), 2 vols., London, 1959.

Īśāna-śiva-gurudeva-paddhati, TSS, 69, 72, 77, 83.

Īśvara-pratyabhijñā-kārikā, Utpaladeva, with his own comm. up to 3.20, pub. with Siddhitrayī, KSS 34; ed. M.S. Kaul, 1921.

Īśvara-saṃhitā, Pub., Conjeevaram, 1923; Mysore, 1890 (Telugu script).

Jayadratha-yāmala, pub. in GOS, 54.

Jñānārṇava-tantra, ed. G.S. Gokhale, Poona, 1952.

Jñānasaṃkalinī (or, *-saṅkuli*)*-tantra*, with Beng. trs., in *Aruṇodaya*, Calcutta, 1891.

Jñānasiddhi, ptd. in GOS, XLIV, 1929.

Kākacaṇḍeśvarī-tantra, with Hindi trs., by V. Vaidyaraja, Etawah, 1930.

Kakṣapuṭa (or *-ṭi*), Pub. in *Aruṇodaya* (Part); pub. under the title *Siddha-nāgārjuna-kakṣapuṭa* in *Indrajālādisaṃgraha*, Vasumati, Calcutta (31 chs.), ptd. in Belgaum; with Telugu trs. by Venkatacalapati, Vijayawada, 1958; in 196 verses (perhaps only an extract). Extracts in P.C. Ray, *History of Hindu Chemistry*, II.

Kālacakra-tantra, ed., trs., J. Hopkins, London, 1985.

Kālacakra-tantrarāja, ed. B. Banerjee, Calcutta, 1985.

Kālikākalpa or *Kālīkalpa* in *Bṛhat-stotra-ratnākara*, I.

Kālikā-kula-sarvasva, in *Bṛhat-stotra-ratnākara*, II.

Kālikā-purāṇa, Venkatesvara Press, Bombay, Śaka 1829 (=1907 A.D.). Also ed. P. Tarkaratna, with Bengali trs., Calcutta, 1316 B.S.

Kālikārcā-mukura, by K. Nyāyaratna in *Ṣaṭ-cakranirūpaṇa*, p. 9, 1850.

Kālī-rahasya, with Hindi comm., ed. S. Mishra.

Kālī-tantra, with Skt. *Tippaṇī* and Beng. trs., Calcutta, 1922; in *Śāktapramoda*, Bombay. A different text of same title pub. by K.

Vidyaratna, Calcutta, 1892. A *Kālī-tantra*, with Hindi trs., Moradabad, 1902.

Kālī-vilāsa, London, 1917.

Kālī-vilāsa-tantra, *Tāntrik Texts*, VI, Calcutta, 1917.

Kalpa-cintāmaṇi of Dāmodara Bhaṭṭa, with Eng. trs., ed. N.N. Sharma, Delhi, 1979.

Kālyārcaṇa-candrikā of N. Lahidi, Murshidabad, 1877-79, in Bengali script.

Kāmadhenu-tantra in *Vividha-tantra-saṃgraha* and *Sulabha-mantra-prakāśa*, Calcutta, ed. R. Shukla.

Kāmakalā-vilāsa, Puṇyānandanātha, with comm. by Naṭanānanda-nātha; ed. with Eng. trs. and notes by A. Avalon, Madras, 1961.

Kāmākhyā-tantra, in *Tantrasāra*, 1877-84; Ptd. in *Sulabha-tantra-prakāśa*, 1886; *Vividha-tantra-saṃgraha*, Calcutta, 1877-81.

Kāmaratna-tantra of Nityanātha, Ptd. with Bengali trs., Calcutta, 1884; with Mārāṭhī trs., Calcutta, 1904; with Hindi trs., Lucknow, 1906; with Hindi commentary, Bombay, 1920; with Assamese trs., Shillong, 1928.

Kāmarūpa-tantra-mantra, with Beng. trs., Calcutta, 1912. Compiled by C. Vasak, with Beng. trs., Calcutta, 1929.

Kāmikāgama or *Kāmika Tantra*, (i) ptd. with Tāmil explanation in Grantha script, Kumbhakonam, 1916; (ii) in 2 vols. with Tāmil comm. and glossary, Madras, 1898-99; (iii) Pūrvabhāga, with Tāmil meaning and Uttarabhāga, Text only, by M. Alagappa Mudaliar, Madras, 1908; (iv) by K.S. Mudaliar.

Kapiñjala-saṃhitā, Cuddapet, 1896 (Telugu script).

Karaṅkiṇī-mahā-tantra, in ed. of *Rasaratnākara* (Rasangranthanmālā, Gondal, 1926), title *Kiṅkiṇī-merutantra*.

Karpūra-stava-rāja of Mahākāla, ed. S. Dikshit, Delhi.

Kāśyapa-jñānakāṇḍa, ed. R. Parthasarathi Bhattachar, Tirupati, 1948.

Kaula-jñāna-nirṇaya, ed. P.C. Bagchi, Calcutta, 1934.

Kaulamārga-rahasya, ed. S.C. Vidyābhūṣaṇa, Calcutta, Sāhitya Pariṣad Series, No. LXXVI.

Kaulāvalī-nirṇaya, *Tāntrik Texts*, XIV, Calcutta, 1928.

Kaulāvalītantra, ed. R.M. Chattopadhyay, Calcutta, 1283 B.S.

Kaulopaniṣad, with comm. in *Tāntrik Texts*, XI, London, 1922.

Kauśika-sūtra, ed. M. Bloomfield, New Haven, 1890. Important sections, referring to magic, trs. into German by W. Caland in *Altindisches Zauberritual*, Amsterdam, 1900.

Kauśikasūtra-dārilabhāṣya, ed. R.N. Dandekar, Poona, 1972.

Kramadīpikā, Chowkhamba Skt. Series, Varanasi, with comm., ed. D.P. Sukla, Varanasi, 1917.

Kramastotra, Abhinavagupta, published as Appendix C to *Abhinavagupta*, etc., by K.C. Pandey, 2nd ed., Varanasi, 1963.

Kriyoḍḍīśa-tantra, ed. L.M. Sarma, Bombay, V.S. 1981 (=A.D. 1924); 3rd rev. ed., by B.P. Misra, 1967.

Kubjikāmatatantra, J. Schoterman. Also pub. in Calcutta.

Kulacūḍāmaṇi-tantra, ed. *Tāntrik Texts*. IV, Calcutta, London, 1915; 2nd ed., Ganesh & Co., Madras, 1956.

Kulānanda-tantra, Ed. P.C. Bagchi, mentioned under *Akulavīra-tantra*.

Kulārṇava-tantra, *Tāntrik Texts*, V, London, 1917 ed., trs. T.K. Rai, Varanasi, 1983.

Kumāra-tantra, ed., trs. into French by J. Filliozat, Paris, 1937.

——, trs. by K.V. Zvelabil, *Adyar Library Bulletin*, 42, 1978.

Kumārī-tantra, in *Śāktapramoda*, compiled by Devānanda, 1980, ed. Krishnamacharya, with Hindi comm.; ed. A.K. Kalia.

Lakṣmī-tantra, with Hindi comm. of C.L. Gautam, Varanasi; Eng. trs. with notes, by S. Gupta, Leiden, 1972.

Lalitāsahasranāma, ed. V. Krishnamacharya, Adyar, 1959; with Bhāskararāya's comm. and Eng. trs. by R.A. Sastri, 3rd ed., Madras, 1951; with interpretive trs. from Kashmir Śākta viewpoint, by C.L. Raina, Delhi.

Luptāgama-saṃgraha, ed. G. Kaviraj, pt. I, Varanasi, Śaka 1892.

Mahābhāgavata-purāṇa, (i) Gujarati Ptg. Press, Bombay, 1913; (ii) ed. P. Tarkaratna, with Bengali trs., Calcutta, 1321 B.S.; (iii) cr. ed. with intro. and index by P. Kumar, Delhi, 1983.

Mahākāla-saṃhitā, pub. by G.N. Jha, Allahabad, 1971.

Mahānirvāṇa-tantra, ed. Ādi Brāhmasamāj, Calcutta, 1876. W. Alex, Delhi. Eng. trs. by Avalon, London, 1913. Prose Eng. trs. by M.N. Dutt, Calcutta, 1900.

Mahārthamañjarī, Maheśvarānanda, with *Parimala* comm., ed. Ganapati Sastri, TSS, No. 66, 1919.

Mahāvairocana-tantra, M.N. Dutta, A. Wayman.

Maheśvarīya-tantra, ed. L. Tikakar, with Hindi comm., Bombay, 1983; ed. R. Sharma (with Hindi comm.), Varanasi.

Mahimnaḥstotra of Puṣpadanta, with comm. of Madhusūdana Sarasvatī, Varanasi, 1964. Eng. trs. with comm. by A. Avalon, Madras, 1963.

Mālinī-vijayottara-tantra, ed. M.S. Kaul, Delhi, 1984.

Mālinī-vijayottara-vārtika, Abhinavagupta's comm. on *Mālinī-vijayottara-tantra*, ed. M.S. Kaul, 1911, KSS, No. XXXI.

Mantrābhidhāna (part of *Rudrayāmala*), ed. Avalon, *Tāntrik Texts*, I.

Mantramahārṇava, with Hindi trs. by R.K. Rai, Devīkhaṇḍa, Miśrakhaṇḍa (shortly).

Mantra-mahā-vijñāna, pts. 1-4.

Mantramahodadhi of Mahīdhara, with Skt. comm., Bombay, 1983; with *Naukāṭīkā* and Eng. Intro., ed. J.W. Dejong, Canberra (3 vols., in one). Eng. trs. by T.V.P. Iyer, ed. with *Naukā* comm., Hindi trs. and Hindi comm. by S. Chaturvedi, Varanasi, 1981, text and comm. with Eng. trs. by a Board of Scholars, 1988.

Mantrayogasaṃhitā, text and Eng. trs. by R.K. Rai.

Mātaṅgaparameśvarāgama, I, Vidyāpāda, with comm. of Rāmakaṇṭha, ed. N.R. Bhatta, Pondicherry, 1977.

Śivasūtravārtika, comm. by Bhāskara, ed. J.C. Chatterji, 1916.

Śivasūtra-vārtika, comm. by Varadarāja, ed. M.S. Kaul, KSS, No. XLIII, 1925.

Śivasūtra-vimarśinī, Kṣemarāja, ed. J.C. Chatterji, KSS, I.

——, Eng. trs. by P.T.S. Iyengar, 1911, Allahabad, 1912.

Spanda-kārikā, with Kallaṭa's *Vṛtti* and *Śiva-sūtra-vārtika* of Bhāskara, ed. J.C. Chatterji, 1916.

Spanda-kārikā-vivṛti, Rāmakaṇṭha, ed. J.C. Chatterji, KSS, VII, 1913.

Spanda-nirṇaya, comm. of Kṣemarāja on *Spanda-kārikā*, ed. with Eng. trs. by M.S. Kaul, KSS, No. XLII, 1925.

Spanda-pradīpikā, comm. of Bhaṭṭa Utpala or Utpala Vaiṣṇava, ed. V. Islampurkar, 1898.

Spanda-sandoha, Kṣemarāja's comm. on the first verse of *Spanda-kārikā*, ed. M.R. Shastri, KSS, XVI, 1917.

Śrīdevī-rahasya, ed. R.C. Kak (with *Jvālāmukha-sahasranāmādi-bṛhat-pariśiṣṭa*).

Śrīgurutantra, with Hindi trs., Hardwar, 1967.

Śrīpraśna-saṃhitā (Kumbhakonam, 1904) (Grantha script), ed. J.R. Bhattacharya, with Hindi trs., Hardwar, 1967.

Mātṛkābheda-tantra, ed. C. Bhattacharya, Calcutta, 1933. Ed. R.K. Rai, Varanasi, 1983. Eng. trs. by M. Magee.

Mātṛkācakra-viveka of Svatantrānandanātha, Pub. in *Sarasvatī Bhavana Series*, Benares, 1934.

Mātṛkānighaṇṭu, ed. Avalon, *Tāntrik Texts*, I.

Māyātantra, Calcutta.

Meghamālā, ed. R.V. Sarma, Bombay, 1911, also ptd. in Varanasi, 1878.

Merutantra, Veṅkaṭeśvara Press, Bombay, 1908. Rep. 1940.

Mṛgendrāgama (Kriyāpāda and Caryāpāda), with comm. of Bhaṭṭa Nārāyaṇa Kaṇṭha, ed. N.R. Bhatt, Pondicherry, 1962.

——, Section on Yoga, with comm. of Bhaṭṭa Nārāyaṇakaṇṭha and *Dīpikā* of Aghora Śivācārya, ed. with translation and notes by H. Hutin, Pondicherry, 1980.

Mṛgendra-tantra (Vidyāpāda-yogapāda), with comm. of Bhaṭṭa Nārāyaṇakaṇṭha, ed. M.S. Kaul, 1930.

Mudrānighaṇṭu (from *Vāmakeśvara Tantra*), ed. Avalon, *Tāntrik Texts*, I.

Mudrāprakāśa, ptd. Varanasi, V.S. 1941 = A.D. 1884-85.

Muṇḍamālā Tantra, Calcutta, 1387 B.S. Also ed. R.M. Chattopadhyay.

Nārada-pañcarātra, ed. K.M. Banerji, Calcutta, 1963. Trs. into Eng. in *SBH*, 23, 1921. Also ed., with Hindi comm., by R.K. Rai.

Nāradīya Saṃhitā, ed. R.P. Choudhari.

Netratantra, ed. V. Dvivedi, with comm. of Kṣemarājācārya, Delhi, 1985; ed. J. Das, with Bengali trs., Calcutta, 1388 B.S.; ed. M.S. Kaul, Bombay, I, 1926; II, 1939.

Nīlatantra, ed. (in Bengali script) with Bengali trs., by J.L. Das, Calcutta, 1388 B.S.

Niruttaratantra, *Bṛhannīlatantra*, ptd. Srinagar, 1938, ed. D. Tripathi, with Bengali trs., Calcutta, 1385 B.S. B. Sarma, Prayag, V.S. 2017 = A.D. 1960-61.

Nirvāṇatantra, ed. N. Smṛtitīrtha, with Bengali trs., Calcutta, 1385 B.S.

——, G. Kaviraj (*Tantra-saṃgraha*, II) in 15 chaps. B. Sarma, Prayag, V.S. 2021 = A.D. 1964-65, 14 chaps.

Niṣpannayogāvalī, ed. B. Bhattacharya, Baroda, 1949.

Nityāṣoḍaśīkārṇava, ed. with *Setubandha* comm. of Bhāskararāya and Vidyānanda, ed. V.V. Dvivedi, included in *Yoga-tantra-saṃgraha*, Varanasi, 1968.

Nityotsava of Umānanda (*Paraśurāma-kalpasūtra*, II), GOS, XXIII, 1923, 3rd ed., 1948.

Padmatantra, Bangalore, 1927 (2 vols.), Telugu script; Mysore, 1891 (Telugu script).

Pādukāpañcaka, *Tāntrik Texts*, II, 1913.

Pañcarātrāgama, I, II.

Paramānanda-tantra, with comm. of Maheśvarānandanātha, ed. R. Mishra.

Parama-puruṣa-saṃhitā, ed. P. Sitaramacarya, Bhadrachalam.

Paramārtha-sāra, Abhinavagupta, with comm. of Yogarāja; ed. J.C. Chatterji, KSS, VII, 1916; with Eng. trs. and notes by L.D. Barnett, London, 1910.

Parameśvara-saṃhitā, Srirangam, 1953.

Pārānanda-sūtra, pub. in GOS, 56, 1931.

Parāparaveśikā of Kṣemarāja, with notes by M.R. Sastri, 1918.

Parāśara-saṃhitā (Telugu), ed. Raghavacharya, I, Bangalore, 1898.

Paraśurāmakalpasūtra, ed. with Rāmeśvara's comm., GOS, 22, 1923; 2nd rev. and enlarged ed. by S.Y. Dave, 1950.

Parātantra, ed. (9 chaps. containing 526 verses), by D.S. Jang Bahadur Rana, Prayag (Allahabad), 2016 V.S. = 1959-60 A.D.

Parātriṃśikā, Kashmir Series, No. 18, 1918.

Parātriṃśikā-vivaraṇa, Abhinavagupta, ed. with notes, by M.R. Shastri, KSS, No. XVIII, 1918.

Pauṣkara-saṃhitā, A.S. Iyengar and M.C. Thirumalachariar.

Pheṭkāriṇī-tantra, ptd. in *Vividha-tantra-saṃgraha*, Calcutta, 1877-84; *Sulabha-tantra-prakāśa*, Calcutta, 1886; ed. G.N. Kaviraj in *Tantra-saṃgraha*, Varanasi, Śaka 1892 = A.D. 1970. Vol. II, pp. 161-306.

Pracaṇḍacandrikā, Same as *Chinnamastā*.

Parātriṃśikā-laghuvṛtti of Abhinavagupta, ed. J.D. Jadoo, 1947.

Prajñopāya-viniścaya-siddhi, ptd. in *GOS*, XL, IV, 1929.

Prāṇatoṣiṇī, ed. J. Vidyasagara, Calcutta, 1989; with Hindi trs. by R.D. Shukla, Pub. by Navabharata Publishers, Calcutta, 1991 (in Bengali script).

Prapañcasāra, ed. with *Vivaraṇa* comm. of Padmapāda, *Prayogakrama-dīpikā* comm. on *Vivaraṇa*, Intro. by Avalon, by A. Sarasvati, Delhi, 1981.

Pratyabhijñā-hṛdaya of Kṣemarāja, with Eng. trs. and notes, by Thakur J. Singh, Delhi, 1963. With Eng. trs. and comm. (under title *The Secret of Self-realisation*): I.K. Taimni, Adyar, Madras, 1974.

Puraścaraṇa-dīpikā of Kāśīnātha or Śivānandanātha, Varanasi, 1973.

Puraścaryārṇava, ed. P. Varma, 3 Pts., Calcutta, 1901, 1902, 1904; by Pratap Sinha; ed. M. Jha.

Puruṣottama-saṃhitā, ed. P. Sitaramacharya, Bhadrachalam, 1932 (Telugu script).

Rādhātantra, ed. K. Mukhopadhyay, Calcutta, 1383 B.S.; Puri Das, Calcutta, 1954; K.P. Vidyaratna, Calcutta, 1313 B.S. = 1906 A.D.

Rasārṇava-tantra, ed. P.C. Ray and H.C. Kaviratna, Calcutta, 1910 (Bib. Ind.); ed. I, Patna, Varanasi, 1939. Reptd., I, 1985.

Rasārṇavaṃ nāma Rasa-tantram, with gloss, called Bhagīratha and Hindi exposition, called *Rasacandrikā* by I. Tripathi.

Rasārṇavakalpa, Eng. trs. by M. Ray; B.B. Subbarayappa.

Rauravajāmala, I, II, Pondicherry, 1961, 1972, ed. N.R. Bhatt.

Ṛgvidhāna, ed. R. Meyer, Berolini, 1878.

Rudrayāmala-tantra, with Hindi comm., Bombay, 1983; *Uttaratantra*, ed. J. Vidyasagara, Calcutta, 1937; *Uttaratantra*, ed. R.K. Rai, Varanasi, 1986.

Sādhanamālā, ed. B. Bhattacharya, 2 vols., *GOS*, Baroda, 1925-28.

Sādhanarahasya, I, compiled by A. Kavibhusana, Śaka 1852 (1930 A.D.).

Sādhanarahasya-pariśiṣṭa, compiled by A. Kavibhusana.

Śāktānanda-taraṅgiṇī, ed. P. Sastri (with Beng. trs.), Calcutta, 1349 B.S., ed. R. Chattopadhyay. *Vividhatantra-saṃgraha*, Calcutta, 1881-86; R.N. Tripathi, Varanasi, Append. (*Yogatantra Granthamālā*, Vol. II).

Śāktapramoda, ed. by R. Singh, 1951.

Śākta Upaniṣads, ed. A.G.K. Warri, Adyar, Madras.

Śāktavijñāna of Somānandanātha, ed. J.D. Jadoo, 1947.

Śaktibhāṣya (on *Brahmasūtra*) by P. Tarkaratna, Chap. I, Śaka 1859; Chap. II, 1861.

Śakti-mīmāṃsā, ptd., Sarasvatī Bhavana Texts, No. 11, Benares, 1924.

Śaktisaṃgama-tantra, ed. B. Bhattacharya, Kālīkhaṇḍa, *GOS*, 61, 1932; Tārākhaṇḍa, *GOS*, 91, 1941; Sundarakhaṇḍa, *GOS*, 104, 1947; Chinnamastā-khaṇḍa, *GOS*, 166, 1979.

Sāmrājya-lakṣmī-pīṭhikā, Ptd. in Tanjore Sarasvatī Mahal Ser. 58.

Samūrtārcanādhikaraṇa, ed. P. Raghunatha Cakravarti Bhattacharya; M.R. Kavi, Tirupati.

Sanatkumāra-saṃhitā, ed. B. Krishnamacharya.

Sannyāsatantra, Swami S. Saraswati.

Śāradātilaka of Lakṣmaṇa Deśika, ed. A. Avalon, Delhi, 1982 (with comm. of Rāghava Bhaṭṭa); ed. with Hindi exposition, C. Gautam; Eng. trs. by a Board of Scholars, 1988.

Sarasvatītantra, Calcutta.

Sarva-durgati-pariśodhana-tantra, Skt., Tibetan text romanised with Eng. trs., intro., notes, ed. T. Skorupski, Delhi, 1983.

Sarvānanda-taraṅgiṇī, ed. A.B. Tarkatīrtha, with Beng. trs., Calcutta, 1932.

Sarvollāsa, ed. R.M. Chakravarti, and D.C. Bhattacharya, Comilla (now in Bangladesh), 1941. Also ed. by G. Kaviraj.

Śata-ratna-saṃgraha, Ed. A. Avalon, *Tāntrik Texts*, XXII, Calcutta, 1944.

Ṣaṭcakranirūpaṇa, *Ṣaṭcakravivṛti* (Part of *Śrītattvacintāmaṇi* of Pūrṇānanda), ed. T.N. Vidyāratna, Calcutta/London, 1913. Eng. trs. by Avalon in *The Serpent Power*, Madras, 1972.

Ṣaṭcakravivṛti, ed. T.N. Vidyāratna, *Tāntrik Texts*, II, Calcutta, 1913.

Ṣaṭ-karma-dīpikā, ptd. with Bengali trs., along with *Dattātreya-tantra*, Calcutta, 1885; ed. J. Vidyāsāgara's sons in *Indrajāla-vidyā-saṃgraha*, Calcutta, 1915.

Sāttvata-saṃhitā, ed., with Skt. comm., by Trivedi, Varanasi; ed. P.B. Anathachariar, Conjeevaram, 1902.

Sāttvata-tantra, ed. A.S. Phadke, Varanasi, 1934.

Saubhāgyalakṣmī-tantra, Calcutta.

Saubhāgya-subhagodaya (or- *sudhodaya*), ed. V.V. Dvivedi, in his ed. of *Nityāṣoḍaśīkārṇava*, pp. 306-321.

Saundaryalaharī of Śaṃkarācārya, ed., with comm. and Eng. trs., by Woodroffe, Adyar, 1937; ed. N. Brown, with Eng. trs., Cambridge Mass., 1958; ed., with nine expositions, Eng. trs., notes, Hindi trs. etc., by Kuppusvami, Delhi, 1976; ed., with three comms., Eng. trs. and notes, by R.A. Sastri and R.K. Guru, Madras, 1957.

Siddhalaharītantra, Same as *Kālīvilāsa* (q.v.).

Siddha-nāgārjuna-kakṣapuṭa, See *Kakṣapuṭa*.

Siddhasiddhānta-saṃgraha, G.N. Kaviraj.

Siddha-siddhānta-paddhati and other works of Nātha Cult, by Mullick, Poona, 1954.

Siddhāntasāra, Collected by B.L. Sarkar, Pub. by S.L. Sarkar, Calcutta.

Śiva-dṛṣṭi, Somānanda, with Utpaladeva's comm., ed. M.S. Kaul, KSS, LIV, 1934, Chap. I, trs. and comm. by R. Gnoli, pub. in *East and West*, New Series, VIII, 1957.

Śivasūtra, Vasugupta, with five commentaries, ed. K. Sagar with Kṣemarāja's comm. and Eng. trs., 1384 B.S.; ed. P. Sastri, Calcutta, 1313 B.S.; with Hindi trs. by H. Shankar, S. Sankar, 1926.

Śrītantranidhi, Śaktinidhi, with Eng. trs. by B.R. Srivastava.

Śrītattva-cintāmaṇi, Calcutta Skt. Series, No. 19; with comm. by Bhuvana on chs. I-XVIII and by Cintāmaṇi on chs. XIX-XXVI, Delhi, 1994.

Śrīvidyāratnasūtra, Varanasi, 1924.

Sulabha-tantraprakāśa, Calcutta, 1887.

Svacchanda-tantra, ed., with Kṣemarāja's comm., by V.V. Dvivedi, Pts. I, II.

Śyāmārahasya, with Bengali trs., ed. S. Tirthanatha, Calcutta, 1389 B.S.

Tantra of Svayambhu Vidyāpāda, with comm. of Sadyojyoti, Delhi.

Tantrābhidhāna, with Eng. trs. by R.K. Rai.

Tantrakaumudī of Devanātha, ed. R. Jha, Darbhanga, 1969.

Tantrāloka of Abhinavagupta, ed., with Jayaratha's *Viveka* comm., by K. Sagar; ed. with Skt. comm., Eng. Intro. and indices, by R.C. Dwivedi and N. Rastogi in 8 vols., Delhi.

Āhnika IV, with *Viveka* comm. of Jayaratha, ed. M.S. Kaul, KSS, No. XXX, 1921.
It is learnt that the *Tantrāloka* has been translated into Italian by R. Gnoli. Ed. L. Shastri, Intro. by Avalon, Delhi, 1981 (with comm.).

Tantra-saṃgraha of Nīlakaṇṭha Somayājī, with *Yuktidīpikā*, and *Laghuvivṛti* of Śaṃkara, cr. ed. K.V. Sarma, Part I, Hoshiarpur, Punjab, 1977.
Ed. R.P. Tripathi, Pt. III, Varanasi, 1979; V.V. Dvivedi, Pt. IV.

Tantrasāra-saṃgraha of Nārāyaṇa, Madras, 1950.

Tantrasamuccaya (Nārāyaṇa) with comms. of Śaṃkara and *Vivaraṇa*, TSS, Nos. 67, 71, 151, 169.
Partial text in N.V. Mallya's *Studies in Sanskrit Texts on Temple Architecture, with special reference to Tantrasamuccaya*, Chidambaram, Annamalai University, 1949.

Tantrasāra of Kṛṣṇānanda, Same as *Bṛhat-tantrasāra* (q.v.), ed. P.K. Sastri, 3rd ed., R.M. Chatterji, Calcutta, 1929.

Tantrasāra of Abhinavagupta, ed. with notes, M.R. Sastri, 1918, under the title 'Essenza dei Tantra'.

Tantrasāra of Abhinavagupta, trs. into Italian by P. Boringhieri, with exhaustive introduction by R. Gnoli, Torino, 1960.

Tantra-śuddha-prakaraṇa, ed. T. Ganapati Sastri, Trivandrum, 1915.

Tantra-vaṭa-dhānikā, Abhinavagupta, ed. M.R. Sastri, KSS, XXIV, 1918.

Tāntrika Abhidhāna, Svami, S.N., Calcutta, 1910 B.S.

Tārābhaktisudhārṇava, *Tāntrik Texts*, Vol. XXI, Calcutta, 1940.
Ed. P. Bhattacharya, Delhi, 1983 (Reprint).

Tārārahasya of Brahmānanda, ed. P.C. Pal and others, Calcutta, 1948 V.S.; ed. J. Vidyasagara, Calcutta, 1896; ed. T. Giritirtha, with Bengali trs., Calcutta, 1384 B.S.; ed. P. Sastri, Calcutta, 1313 B.S.; with Hindi trs. by H. Shankar, S. Sankar, 1926.

Tārārahasya-vṛttikā, Varendra Research Society, Rajshahi (Bangladesh), 1961.

Tārātantra, ed. A.K. Maitra, Delhi, 1983. Pub. by Varendra Res. Soc., Rajshahi (Bangladesh); ed. with Hindi Notes.

Toḍala-tantra, ed. B. Sarma, Prayag (Allahabad), V.S. 2018=A.D. 1961/62; G. Kaviraj in *Tantra-saṃgraha*, II, pp. 63-94.

Tripurā-rahasya, ed. G. Kaviraj (Jñānakhaṇḍa), with *Tātparyadīpikā* comm. of Śrīnivāsa, Varanasi, 1965.

—— (Jñānakhaṇḍa), with Hindi comm., by S.D. Maharaj.

——, Eng. trs. and comparative study of the process of individuation by A.U. Vasavada, Varanasi, 1965.

—— (Māhātmya Khaṇḍa), Varanasi, 1932.

Tripurasundarī-daśaka, ptd. in *Stotrārṇava*, p. 654, Madras.

Tripurāsāra-samuccaya of Nāgabhaṭṭa, with Skt. commentary of Govindācārya, Varanasi, 2nd ed., Calcutta, 1897.

Tripuropaniṣad, with comm. of Bhāskarācārya, Varanasi.

Ucchiṣṭa-gaṇeśa-sahasra-nāma-stava, Ed. V. Raghavan, Madras, 1959. Ptd. in a collection of *Ucchiṣṭa-Gaṇapati* Texts, Veṅkaṭeśvara Press, Bombay, 1931.

Uḍḍāmara-tantra, Varanasi, 1897.

Uddhārakośa (A dictionary of the Secret Code of Tāntric Syllabic Code), Raghuvir and Shodo Taki, 1978.

Uḍḍīśa Tantra, In 20 chaps. ptd. in *Indrajālādi-saṃgraha*, Cal., 1879. *Sulabha-tantra-prakāśa*, Calcutta, 1887, Lucknow 1822, with Hindi trs., Moradabad, 1898; with Hindi comm. of S. Mishra, Varanasi.

Ugratārā-sahasra-nāma, Pub. by Varendra Res. Society, Rajshahi, Bangladesh.

Ūrdhvāmnāya-saṃhitā, ed. A.C. Tarkanidhi, Calcutta, 1285 B.S.=1878 A.D.

Vāmakeśvara-tantra, Ed. (1) K.S. Agase, Poona, 1908, with Bhāskara's comm., rev. ed., 1970; (2) V.V. Dvivedi, with a learned intro. and comms. of Śivānanda and Vidyānanda, Varanasi, 1968; (3) M.K. Sastri, Srinagar (under the title *Vāmakeśvara-mata*) with Jayaratha's comm.

Vāmakeśvarī-mata, with *Vivaraṇa* by Jayaratha; ed. M.K. Sastri, 1945.

Varivasyā-rahasya of B. Makhin, ed. S.C. Sastri, with author's own comm., Eng. trs. and notes, Adyar, Madras, 1948.

Vāsanā-tattva-bodhikā, Same as *Tārā-rahasya-vṛttikā* (q.v.).

Vātulanātha-sūtra, with comm. by Ananta Śaktipāda, ed. and trs. into French by L. Silburn, Paris, 1959.

Vidyākalpasūtra, Same as *Paraśurāma-kalpasūtra* (q.v.).

(*Śrī*) *Vidyārṇava-Tantra*, ed. B. Sarma, Prayag (Allahabad), V.S. 2023=1966/67 A.D., in 2 pts.

Vijñānabhairava, with Beng. trs. and exposition, by R.C. Adhikari, Burdwan, West Bengal, 1980; with Eng. trs. by J. Singh; with comm. by Kṣemarāja upto verse 23 and by Śivopādhyāya onwards, ed. with notes, by M.R. Shastri, 1918; with comm. of Ānanda Bhaṭṭa, ed. with notes, by M.R. Shastri, KSS, No. IX, 1918; text and comm., trs. with notes into French by L. Silburn, Paris, 1961, with subtitle *Samagra Bhāratīya Yogaśāstra* and with Skt. and Hindi comm., ed. V.V. Dvivedi, Delhi, 1978.

Vīṇāśikha-tantra (Śaiva Tantra of left current), ed. T. Goudriaan, Delhi, 1988, with Intro., Romanised text, Eng. trs., notes, index of half-Ślokas (odd *pādas*) and index of Sanskrit words.

Viṣṇusaṃhitā, Trivandrum Sanskrit Series, 1925.

Viṣṇutilaka (Telugu), Bangalore, 1896.

Yantra-cintāmaṇi, with Hindi comm., Varanasi.

Yogaratnamālā of Nāgārjuna, P. Kumar.

Yogatantra-granthamālā, ed. Shukla, Varanasi, 1970.

Yoginī-hṛdaya (being chaps. VI-VIII of *Nityāṣoḍaśīkārṇava*), with *Dīpikā* of Amṛtānanda and *Setubandha* of Bhāskara Rāya, ed. G. Kaviraj, Varanasi (1963); ed. K. Chattopadhyay, 2nd ed., Varanasi, 1963.

Yoginī-tantra, ed., with Hindi trs., K. Misra, Bombay, 1983; B.N. Sastri, 1982; ed. B. Sastri (with intro. in Eng.), ed. R.M. Chatterji.

Yonitantra, ed. J. A. Schoterman, New Delhi, 1980.

B. BOOKS IN WESTERN LANGUAGES

Aiyer, K.N.: *Thirty-two Vidyās*.

Allen, M.R.: *The Cult of Kumārī*.

Alpar, H.R.: *Understanding Mantras*, Delhi.

Anand, M.R.: *Kamakala*, New York, 1958; *Tantric Magic* (with A. Mookherjee), New Delhi, 1977.

Angiras, R.S.: *Trilogy of Tantra*, Haryana, 1989.

Arguelles & Arguelles: *Maṇḍala*, etc.

Arundale, G.S.: *Kuṇḍalinī*.

Avalon, A. (John Woodroffe) ed. *Tāntrik Texts Series*: *Principles of Tantra*, Madras, 1960 (2 vols.); (Eng. trs. of *Tantra-tattva* of Śiva Candra

Vidyārṇava); *Intro. to Kaulajñānanirṇaya*, Calcutta, 1934; *Shakti and Shākta*, Madras; *The Great Liberation*, Madras, 1956; *Mahāmāyā*; *Intro. to Tantraśāstra*, *The World as Power*, Madras, 1957; *Serpent Power*, Madras, 1957; *Wave of Bliss* (Eng. trs. of *Ānandalaharī*, and comm.), Madras, 1957; *Chakras*.

Ayyar, C.V.H.: *Origin and Early History of Śaivism in South India*, Madras, 1974.

Bagchi, P.C.: *Studies in the Tantras*, Pt. I, Calcutta, 1939, Rep. 1975.

Bagchi, S.: *Eminent Indian Śākta Pīṭhas*, etc., in the background of the *Pīṭhas* of Kālīghāṭ, Vakreśwar and Kāmākhyā, Calcutta, 1980.

Bajpai, Ira: *The Philosophy of Tantrāloka* (Āhnikas 1-3 with Eng. trs.), Ph.D. thesis, 1971, Lucknow University.

Bandyopadhyay, P.: *The Goddess of Tantra*, 2nd ed.

Banerji, J.N.: *Purāṇic and Tāntric Religion, Early Phase*, Calcutta.

——: *Development of Hindu Iconography*, Calcutta, 1956.

Banerji, S.C.: *Tantra in Bengal*, Calcutta, 1978.

——: *Fundamentals of Ancient Indian Music and Dance*, Ahmedabad, 1976.

——: *A Brief History of Tantra Literature*, Calcutta.

——: *Kālidāsa Apocrypha*, Varanasi.

——: *Cultural Heritage of Kashmir*, Calcutta.

Barnard, T.: *Haṭhayoga*, London, 1950.

Barth, A.: *The Religions of India*, London, 1989.

Basu, M.: *Tantras, A General Study*, Calcutta, 1976.

——: *Fundamentals of the Philosophy of Tantra*, Calcutta, 1986.

Beane, W.C.: *Cult and Symbols in Śākta Hinduism, A Study of the Indian Mother Goddess*, Leiden, 1977.

Bedekar, V.M.: See Hinze.

Benard, E.A.: *Chinnamastā*, the Awful Buddhist and Hindu Tāntric Goddess, 1994.

Beyer, G.: *The Cult of Tārā*, London, 1973 (Magic and Ritual in Tibet).

Bhandarkar, R.G.: *Vaiṣṇavism, Śaivism and Minor Religious Systems*, Strasbürg, 1913, Varanasi, 1965.

Bharah, A.: *The Tāntric Tradition*, London, 1965.

——: *The Ochre Robe*, London, 1961.

Bhat, M.S.: *Vedic Tāntrism, A Study of Ṛgvidhāna of Śaunaka* (with text, trs.), Delhi.

Bhattacharya, B.: *Indian Buddhist Iconography, Mainly Based on Sadhanamala and Cognate Tantric Texts of Rituals*, 2nd ed., Calcutta, 1958.

——: *Introduction to Buddhist Esoterism.*

——: *World of Tantra.*

Bhattacharya, D.: *Mythological and Ritual Symbolism* — a study with reference to the Vedic and Tantric Agni.

Bhattacharya, D.C.: *Tantric Buddhist Iconographic Sources* — A Study with reference to the Vedic and Tantric Agni, New Delhi, 1974.

Bhattacharya, N.N.: *History of Sakta Religion*, New Delhi, 1974.

——: *Tantric Buddhism* (Centennial Tributes to Benoytosh Bhattacharya), ed. in collaboration with A. Ghosh.

——: *The Indian Mother Goddess*, 2nd ed., New Delhi, 1977.

——: *History of Tāntric Religion*, New Delhi, 1982.

——: *History of Indian Cosmogonical Ideas*, New Delhi, 1971.

——: *History of Indian Erotic Literature*, New Delhi, 1973.

——: *Rituals and their Social Contents*, New Delhi, 1975.

——: *A Glossary of Indian Religious Terms and Concepts*, New Delhi, 1990.

Bhattasali, N.K.: *Iconography of Buddhist and Brahmanical Sculptures in Dacca Museum*, 1972.

Bloomfield, J.: *Mantras* (Sacred Words of Power).

——: *The Way of Power — A Practical Guide to Tantric Mysticism of Tibet*, London, 1970.

Bose, N.K.: *Canons of Orissan Architecture*, pp. 92, 154.

Bose, M.M.: *Caitanya Sahajiya Cults of Bengal*, Calcutta, 1930.

Bose, P.: *Indian Teachers of Buddhist Universities*, Adyar, 1923.

Bose and Halder: *Tantras — Their Philosophy and Occult Secrets*, Calcutta, 1956.

Brahma, N.K.: *Philosophy of Hindu Sadhana*, Calcutta, 1932.

Breaux, C.: *Journey into Consciousness, the Chakras, Tantra and Jungian Psychology.*

Briggs, G.W.: *Gorakhnath and the Kanphata Yogis*, Calcutta, 1938.

Brooks, D.R.: *Auspicious Wisdom: The Texts and Traditions of Srividya.*

——: *Sakta Tantrism in South India.*

——: *The Secret of the Three Cities — an intro. to Hindu Sakta Tantrism.*

Brunner, H.: Importance de la litterateur agamique pour l'etude des religious vivantes de l'Inde, in *Indologica Taurinensia*, III-IV, Torino, 1977, pp. 107-124.

Capra, F.: *The Tao of Physics*, 1979.

Carlstedt, G.: *Studies in Kularnava-tantra*, Upsala, 1974.

Chakrabarti, C.: *The Tantras, Studies on their Religion and Literature*, Calcutta, 1963.

Chakrabarti, P.C.: *Doctrine of Sakti in Indian Literatures*, Calcutta, 1940.

Chakravarti, C.: *Tantras*, etc., Calcutta, 1963.

Chakraborti, H. (ed.): *Pāśupata-sūtra*, Calcutta, 1970.

——: *Śākta Tāntrik Cult in India.*

Chandra, L.: *Maṇḍalas of the Tantrasamuccaya.*

Chatterji, J.C.: *Kashmir Śaivism*, KSS, II, 1944, Delhi, 1959.

Chattopadhyay, A.: *Atīśa and Tibet*, Calcutta, 1967.

Chattopadhyay, S.: *Reflections on the Tantras.*

Chaudhuri, L.R.: *Practicals of Mantras and Tantras.*

Chen, C.M.: *Discrimination between Buddhist and Hindu Tantras.*

Coburn, T.B.: *Devī-māhātmya, Crystallisation of the Goddess Tradition*, 1984.

Dasgupta, S.N.: *A History of Indian Philosophy*, Vol. III.

Dasgupta, S.B.: *Introduction to Tāntric Buddhism*, Calcutta, 1958.

——: *Aspects of Indian Religious Thoughts*, Calcutta, 1957.

——: *Obscure Religious Cults as Background of Bengali Literature*, Calcutta, 1962.

De, S.K.: *Early History of Vaiṣṇava Faith and Movement in Bengal*, Calcutta, 1969.

Desai, D.: *Erotic Sculptures of India*, New Delhi, 1975.

Desika, N.R.: *Śrīvidyā-Upāsanā* (Lalitā-sahasra-nāma Stotra), Bangalore, 1992.

Devasenapati, V.A.: *Śaiva Siddhānta*, Madras, 1958.

Diksitar, V.R.R.: *The Lalitā Cult*, Madras, 1942.

Dimock, E.C.: *The Place of the Hidden Moon: Erotic Mysticism in the Vaiṣṇava Sahajiyā Cult of Bengal*, Chicago and London, 1966.

Douglas, N.: *Tantrayoga*, New Delhi, 1971.

Dutt, S.: *Buddhist Monks and Monasteries of India*, London, 1962.

Dutta, M.N. (Trs.): *Mahānirvāṇa Tantra*.

Dvivedi, V.V.: *Tantra-yātrī* (Essays on Tantra), Varanasi, 1982.

Dvivedi and Shahni: *Bauddha Tantrakośa*, Pt. I, Varanasi, 1990.

Dyczkowski, M.S.G.: *The Doctrine of Vibration*, State University of New York Press.

——: *The Canon of Śaivāgama and the Kubjikā Tantras of the Western Kaula Tradition*.

Ehrenfels, O.R.: *Mother-right in India*, Hyderabad, 1941.

Eliade, M.: *Yoga — Immortality and Freedom*, 2nd ed., New York, 1958.

Eliot: *Hinduism and Buddhism*.

Encyclopaedia Britannica, Vols. dealing with Tantra and its different aspects.

Evanscoentz, W.Y.: *Tibetan Yoga and Secret Doctrines*.

Farquhar, J.N.: *An Outline of the Religious Literature of India*, London, 1920.

Farrow and Menon: *The Concealed Essence of the Hevajratantra*, Delhi.

Foucher, A.: *Etude sur l'Iconographic Boudhique de l'Inde*, 2 pts.

Frawley, D.: *Tāntric Visions of the Divine Feminine*, Delhi.

Freud, S.: *Kuṇḍalinī energie*, etc.

Garrison, O.V.: *Tantra, the Yoga of Sex*.

Gavin and Frost: *Tāntric Yoga*, the royal path to raising Kuṇḍalinī Power, Delhi, 1994.

Geden, A.S.: *Tantras* (Entry in *Ency. of Rel. and Ethics*, T. Hastings, Vol. XII, 1951).

Getty, A.: *Gods of Northern Buddhism*, New York, 1964.

Gode, P.K.: *Studies in Indian Literary History*, 3 vols., Bombay, 1953-56.

Goel, B.S.: *Third Eye and Kuṇḍalinī*, Kuruksetra, 1985.

Gonda, J. (ed.): *A History of Indian Literature*, Vol. I, Fasc. 1, Wiesbaden, 1977, Vol. II, Fasc. 2, Wiesbaden, 1981.

——: *Die Religionen Indiens*, 2 vols., Stuttgart, 1960-63.

Gopi Krishna: *Kuṇḍalinī*.

Goudriaan, T. and Gupta, S.: *Hindu Tāntric and Śākta Literature*, Pub. in the Series *History of Indian Literature*, Vol. II, Fasc. 2, Wiesbaden, 1981.

Guenther, H.V. and C. Trungpa: *Dawn of Tantra*, ed. M. Kohn, 1975; *Yuganaddha, the Tāntric View of Life*, Benares, 1964; *The Tāntric View of Life*, Berkeley and London, 1972.

Gupta, Goudriaan and Moens: *Hindu Tāntrism*, Leiden, 1979.

Hartmann, C.G.: *Aspects de la deesse Kālī dans son culte, et dans la litterature indienne*, Helsinki, 1969.

Hazra, R.C.: *Studies in the Upapurāṇas*, 2 vols., Calcutta, 1958-63.

Hinze, O.M.: *Tantra-vidyā* (Trs. V.M. Bedekar).

Hopkins, J.: *The Tāntric Destination*, an intro. to Tibetan Buddhism, ed. A.C. Klain, London, 1984.

James, E.O.: *The Cult of the Mother Goddess*, London, 1959 (pp. 99-124 deal with India).

Jash, P.: *History of Śaivism*, Calcutta, 1974; *Pratyabhijñā system* — its religious and philosophic background, 1960; Some controversial viewpoints, 1959, 1960.

Jha, S.K.: *A Critical and Comparative Study of Pratyabhijñā Philosophy* (Ph.D. Thesis, 1972, Darbhanga).

Jhavery, M.B.: *Comparative and Critical Study of Mantrashāstra* (with special treatment of Jain *Mantra-vāda*), Ahmedabad, 1944.

Jung, C.G.: Maṇḍala Symbolism in Śrī Bhairava-Padmāvatī-kalpa. Trs. R.F.C. Hull, Princeton, 1972.

Kakati, B.K.: *The Mother Goddess Kāmākhyā*, Gauhati, 1961.

Kandoi, B.R. (ed.): *A Peep into Tantras*, Sashidhar Sarma Fel. Ser., Pt. 9, Chandigarh.

Kane, P.V.: *History of Dharmaśāstra*, 5 vols., Poona, 1930-62.

Kapur, T.B.: *Dhyānamaṇḍala*.

Kaviraj, G.N.: *Śākta Philosophy*; *History of Philosophy, Eastern and Western*, ed. Radhakrishnan, London, 1952-53; *Philosophy of Tripura-tantra*, Varanasi, 1931; *Some Aspects of the Philosophy of Śākta Tantra*, Varanasi, 1967.

Kavory, M.B.: *Comparative and Critical Study of Mantra-śāstra*, 1944.

Kaw, R.K.: *The Doctrine of Recognition*, Hoshiarpur, 1967.

Khanna, M.: *Yantra*, London, 1979.

Kinsley, D.: *Tantric Vision of the Divine Feminine — the Ten Mahāvidyās*.

Kramrisch, S.: *Unknown in India; Ritual Art in Tribe and Village*, Philadelphia, 1968.

Krishna, G.: *Kuṇḍalinī, in Time and Space*, New Delhi; *Secrets of Kuṇḍalinī in Pāncastavī; Kuṇḍalinī: the Biological Basis of Religion and Genus*.

Kumar, P.: *Tāntric Goddess Tārā; Shakti Cult in Ancient India; Śāktism — A Study; Śakti and Her Episodes*, 1981.

Kundu, N.L.: *Non-dualism in Śaiva and Śākta Philosophy*, Calcutta.

Lal, K.: *The Cult of Desire*, Delhi, 1966 (2nd ed.).

Lal, P.: *Hindu Religion and Iconology*.

Lansdowne, Z.F.: *The Chakras and Esoteric Healing*, Delhi, 1993.

La Vallee Poussin: *Bouddhisme Etudes et Materiaun*, Mem. Ac. Belgique, 1897.

Leedbeater, C.W.: *Cakras*, Adyar, 1927.

Lele, W.K.: *Doctrine of the Tantryukti*.

Lennoy, R.: *The Eye of Love*, London, 1977.

Lessing and Wayman: *Introduction to Buddhist Tāntric Systems*, Delhi, 1983.

Lorenzen, D.N.: *The Kāpālikas and Kālāmukhas*, New Delhi, 1972.

Mahadevan, T.M.P.: *Kashmir Śaivism*, 1952; *Gauḍapāda*, Madras, 1952.

Mahajan, S.N.: *The Science of Yoga and Consciousness*.

Majithia, S.S.: *The Great Yogic Sermon*, 1969.

Majumdar, R.C. (ed.): *History of Bengal*, I, Dacca, 1943.

Malik, A.D.: *Kuṇḍalinī and Meditation*, Delhi, 1991.

Marr, G.S.: *Sex in Religion*, London, 1936.

Matsubara, M.: Pañcarātra-saṃhitā and Early Vaīṣṇava Theology, with trs. and critical notes from chapters on theology in Ahirbudhnya saṃhitā.

Matsunaga, Y.: *The Guhyasamāja Tantra*.

Mehta, R.J.: *Konark Sun-Temple of Love*, Bombay, 1969.

Mehta, Rohit: *The Secret of Self-transformation: A Synthesis of Tantra and Yoga*.

Menon, C.A.: *Kālī-worship in Kerala*, Madras, 1959.

Mishra, K.: *Significance of Tāntric Tradition*, Varanasi, 1981.

Mishra, R.: *Advaya-siddhi—the Tāntrik view of Lakṣmīṅkarā*, Delhi, 1995.

Mishra, T.N.: *Impact of Tantra on Religion and Art*.

Mitra, R.: *The Sanskrit Buddhist Literature of Nepal*, Calcutta, 1971.

Mookherjee, A.: *Tantra Art*, Delhi, 1966; *Tantra Āsana*, Basel, New York, 1971; *The Tāntric Way* (with M. Khamara); *Kuṇḍalinī*, Delhi, 1982; *Kālī, the Feminine Force*, London, 1988.

Mookherji, Khanna: *Tāntric Way — Art, Science, Ritual*, London, 1989.

Mukherji, S.C.: *A Study of Vaiṣṇavism*.

Muller, Ortega P.E.: *The Triardic Heart of Śiva*, Kaula Tāntricism of Abhinavagupta in the non-dual Śaivism of Kashmir, Albany, 1989.

Mullin, G.H. and Richards, M. (ed.): *Meditations on Lower Tantras*, Dharamsala, 1983.

Mullin, G.H. (Comp. and trs.): *Bridging the Sūtras and Tantras*, a collection of Ten Minor Works by the First Dalai Lama (1319-1474), Dharamsala, 1981.

Muses, C.A.: *Esoteric Teachings of the Tibetan Tantra*, trs. C.C. Chi, York Beach, 1982.

Nagaswamy, R.: *Tāntric Cult of South India*, Delhi, 1980.

Nandimath, S.C.: *Hand-Book of Vīra Śaivism*, Dharwar, 1942.

Nawels, S.M.: *Jaina Paintings*, Vol. 1, Ahmedabad, 1980.

Needham, J.: *Science and Civilisation in China*, 2 vols., Cambridge, 1954-56.

Neuman, E.: *The Great Mother*, New York, 1961.

Nihom, M.: *Studies in Indian and Indonesian Tāntrism* (The Kunjarakarma-dharma-katha in the Yoga Tantra).

Osho: *Tantra, the Supreme Understanding*.

Padoux, A.: *Vāc, the concept of the word in selected Hindu Tantras* (Trs. from French original by J. Gontier), Albany.

——: *Recherches sur la symbolique et l'energie de la parole dans certaines textestantriques*, Paris, 1975.

Pandey, K.C.: *An Outline of History of Śaiva Philosophy*.

——: *Abhinavagupta*, Varanasi, 1963.

Pandit, M.P.: *More on Tantras*, New Delhi, 1985; *Gems from the Tantra*, Pts. I, II; *Thoughts of a Shākta; Lights on the Tantra; Tāntric Sādhana*, 1964; *Studies in the Tantras and the Veda*, Madras, 1964.

Pandit, B.N.: *Aspects of Kashmir Śaivism*, Srinagar, Kashmir, 1947; *Comparative Study of Kashmir Śaivism* (Thesis for Ph.D. 1964, Punjab University).

Paranjoti, V.: *Śaiva Siddhānta*, London, 1954.

Pathak, V.S.: *Śaiva Cult in Northern India*, Varanasi, 1960.

Pott, P.H.: *Yoga and Yantra, their interrelation and their significance for Indian Archaeology*, The Hague, 1966.

Prabhavananda, Swami: *The Spiritual Heritage of India*, London, 1962.

Prajnananda, Swami: *Historical Study of Indian Music*, Calcutta, 1975.

Prem Saran: *Tantra, Hedonism in Indian Culture*, New Delhi, 1998 (2nd ed.).

Radhaswami, S.: *Kuṇḍalinī-yoga*, Delhi; *Mantras, Words of Power*, Delhi.

Rajneesh: *The Book of Secret Discourses on Vishana Bhairava-Tantra*, 5 vols., Poona, 1974, ed. A. Prem, A. Teerth.

Rao, S.K.R.: *Tantra, Mantra, Yantra; Tāntric Tradition; Elements of Hindu Iconography*, Madras, 1916; *Yantras, Text and Plates*, 1988; *Śrī Chakras, Text and Plates*, 1989; *Meditation on Lalitā-sahasra-nāma*, Bangalore, 1990.

Rao, T.A.G.: *Elements of Hindu Iconography*, 2 vols., New Delhi, 1968.

Rastogi, N.: *Tantric Thought of Kashmir, A Framework of the Monistic Culture; Krama Tantricism of Kashmir*, Vol. I, Delhi, 1979, Vol. II, shortly; *Introduction to the Tantrāloka; Kālī as a Metaphysical Concept in the Krama System of Kashmir*, 1965, 1966.

Rawlinson, R.: *Tantra*, London, 1973; *Erotic Art of the East*, New York, 1968.

Ray, N.R.: *Sanskrit Buddhism in Burma*.

Ray, P.: *History of Chemistry in Ancient and Medieval India*, Calcutta, 1956 (ed. P.C. Ray's work of the same title).

Regmi, D.R.: *Medieval Nepal*, 3 vols., Calcutta, 1965-66.

Rele, V.G.: *Mysterious Kuṇḍalinī*, Bombay, 1927.

Rend, C.I.P.: *Introduction to the Cakras*, 1974.

Rendel, P.: *Introduction to the Cakras*, Northamptonshire, 1974.

Rudrappa, J.C.: *Kashmir Śaivism*, Bangalore.

Samuel, G. etc.: *Tantra and Popular Religion in Tibet*, New Delhi, 1994.

Sankaranarayanan, S.: *Śrīckara*, 1970; *Glory of the Divine Mother*, Delhi.

Santideva, S.: *Encyclopaedia of Tantra*, 3 vols.

Saran, P.: *Tantra, Hedonism in Indian Culture*, New Delhi, 1994.

Sarasvati, Swami S.: *Meditation from the Tantras; Kuṇḍalinī Tantra*, Munger (Bihar), 1984; *Light on Guru-Disciple Relationship*, 1984; *Āsana, Prāṇāyāma, Mudrā Bandha*, Monghyr (Bihar), 1983.

Sarasvati, Swami Shankaradevananda: *Yogic Management of Asthma and Diabetes*, Munger (Bihar), 1984.

Sarasvati, P. and Woodroffe: *Sādhana for Self-realisation* (*Mantras, Yantras* and *Tantras*), Madras, 1963.

Saraswati, S.K.: *Tantrayāna Art Album*, Calcutta, 1979.

Saraswati, B. (ed.): *Prakṛti*, vol. iii (The Āgamic Tradition and the Arts), New Delhi, 1995.

Sastri, H.: *Origin and Cult of Tārā*, Calcutta, 1925.

Sastri, H.C.: *Tantra Darshan*.

Sastri, K.T.V.: *Further Lights: The Veda and the Tantra*, 1951.

Sastri, M.R.: *Tantrasāra of Abhinavagupta*, Bombay, 1918.

Sastry, K.: *The Veda and the Tantra*, Madras, 1951.

Sastry, T.V.K.: *Sidelights on the Tantra*, Pondicherry, 1971; *The Tāntric Practices in Śrīvidyā*, etc., Bangalore, 1990.

Satpathy, S.: *Daśamahāvidyā and Tantraśāstra*.

Saunders, E.D.: *Mudrā*, London, 1966.

Scharpes, E.: *Tāntrik Doctrine of Immaculate Conception*, 1933.

Schrader, F.O.: *Introduction to the Pāncarātra and the Ahirbudhnya-saṃhitā*, Madas, 1916.

Schultz, F.A.: Die philosophischtheologischen Lehren des Pāśupata-systems nach dem Pañcarātra-bhāṣya un der Ratnaṭīkā, Walldrof, 1958.

Sen Sharma, D.B.: *Studies in Tantrayoga*, 1985.

Shah, P.R.: *Tantra: Its Therapeutic Aspect*, Calcutta, 1987.

Shastri, V.D.: *Mālinīvijayottara-tantra* — source-book, etc. (Ph.D. Thesis, 1956, Punjab University).

Sharma, L.N.: *Kashmir Śaivism*, Varanasi, 1972.

Sharma, P.K.: *Śakti and Her Episodes*, etc., Delhi, 1981; *Śakti Cult in Ancient India*, Varanasi, 1974.

Sharma, S.R.: *Tāntric Mahāvijñāna*, Bareilly, 1970.

Shaw, M.: *Passionate Enlightenment, Women in Tāntric Buddhism*, Princeton, 1994.

Shende, J.N.: *Religion and Philosophy of the Atharvaveda*, Poona, 1952.

Shivananda: *Tantra-yoga, Nāda-yoga and Scientific Basis*.

Shubhakaran, K.T.: *Mystical Formulae*, Pt. II, *Yantras*, New Delhi, 1992.

Siddhantasastri, R.K.: *Śaivism Through the Ages*, Delhi, 1975.

Silburn, L.: *Kuṇḍalinī, the power of depths*.

Singh, L.P.: *Tantra: Its Mystic and Scientific Basis*, Delhi, 1976.

Sinha, A.K.: *Science and Tantrayoga*, Kuruksetra, 1981.

Sinha, J.: *Śākta Monism; Cult of Shakti; Schools of Śaivism*, Calcutta, 1970.

Sircar, D.C.: *The Shākta Pīṭhas*, Delhi, 1973; *Shakti Cult and Tārā*, Calcutta, 1960.

Sivapriyananda, Svami: *Secret Power of Tāntric Breathing*, 1983.

Smith, H.D.: *Descriptive Bibliography of the Printed Texts of the Pañcarātrāgama*, Vol. I, Baroda, 1975, GOS, Vol. 158.

Snellgrove, D.L.: *The Hevajra Tantra, a critical study*, 2 vols., 1980 — Vol. I: Bibliography, Diagrams, Glossary, Index (Intro. and Eng. trs.); Vol. II: Romanised text.

Srinivasan, M.S.: *The Yogic Vision of Tantra*.

Srivastava, B.: *Iconography of Sakti; Tantra, the Supreme Understanding* (Discourses of Tilopa's Song of Mahāmudrā); *Tāntric Mysticism of Tibet*, New York, 1974; *Tāntricism, its Secret Principles and Practices*, Northamptonshire, 1982.

Taimini, T.K.: Śiva-sūtra with Eng. trs. and comm. (Ultimate Reality and Realisation).

Tāranātha: *History of Buddhism in India*, trs. into German by A. Schiefner, St. Petersburg.

Tattvananda (Swami): *The Vaiṣṇava Sects*, 1989; *The Śaiva Sects, Mother-worship*; *The Tantra Vision* (Discourse on the Royal Song of Suraha).

Thomas, P.: *Kāmakalpa*, 1963; *Kāmakalpa*, Bombay, 1960; *Incredible India*, Bombay, 1966.

Thomas, E.J.: *History of Buddhist Thought*, Reprint, 1953.

Trungpa, C.; *Journey without Goal, Tāntric Wisdom of the Buddha*, Boston, 1985.

Tsong Ka-pa: *Tantra in Tibet — The Great Exposition of Secret Mantra*, trs. into Eng. under the title *Tantra in Tibet*, by J. Hopkins, London, 1977.

Tsuda (ed.): *The Saṃvarodaya-tantra*, Tokyo, 1974.

Tucci, G.: *Theory and Practice of Maṇḍala*, London, 1961; *Ratilīlā*, an interpretation of the Tāntric images of the temples of Nepal, Geneva, 1969.

Tulkes, D. and Mullin, G.H.: *Atīśa and Buddhism in Tibet*.

Türstig, Hans-Georg: *Yantracintāmaṇi* of Dāmodara (on magic related to Tāntrism), Stuttgart, 1988.

Upadhyay, R.K.: *Concept of God in the Śaiva Tantra*.

Vajapeya, K.: *Science of Mantras*.

Vasavada, A.U.: *Tripurā-rahasya* (Jñānakhaṇḍa — Eng. trs. and a comparative study of the process of individuation).

Vasu, S.C.: *Gheraṇḍa-saṃhitā* (trs.), 1979.

Vira, R.V. and Taki, S.: *A Dictionary of Secret Tāntric Syllabic Code*, Lahore, 1938.

Viṣṇutīrtha, Swami: *Devātmā Śakti*, 1949.

Waddel, L.A.: *Lamaism*, London, 1985.

Walker, B.: *Tāntricism, its Secret Principles and Practices*.

Wall, O.A.: *Sex and Sex-worship*, London, 1919.

Warder, A.K.: *Indian Buddhism*.

Warrier, A.G.K. (trs.): *Śākta Upaniṣads*, Adyar, 1967.

Wayman, A.: *Yoga of Guhyasamāja-tantra*, ed. K.V. Sarma, Hoshiarpur, 1979; Text in Roman script with Eng. trs.: Buddhist Tantras (Light on Indo-Tibetan Esotericism, New York, 1973).

——: *Foundation of the Buddhist Tantras*, Delhi, 1990.

——: *The Buddhist Tantras.*

White, J. (ed.): *Kuṇḍalinī, Evolution and Enlightenment*, New York, 1979.

Winternitz: *History of Indian Literature*, Vol. I, Delhi, 1990 (Rep. of ed. of 1981); Vol. II, Delhi (Rep. of rev. ed. of 1983).

Woodroffe, J.: See Avalon.

——: *Śakti and Shākta* — essays and addresses on the Shākta Tantraśāstra, Madras and London, 1927.

——: *Tantrarāja-tantra and Kāmakalāvilāsa*, Madras, 1971.

Woodroffe and Mukhopadhyay: *Mahāmāyā*, Madras, 1954.

Yeshe, Lama T.: *Introduction to Tantra.*

Zannas, E. and Auboyer, J.: *Khajuraho*, The Hague, 1960.

Zimmer, H.: *Myths and Symbols in Indian Art and Civilisation*, ed. J. Campbell; *Kunstform und yoga im indischen Kultbild*, Berlin.

C. HINDI BOOKS

Avasthi, S.S.: *Mantra aur Mātṛkāon kā Rahasya.*

Kaviraj, G.N.: *Tāntrik Vaṅmay men Śākta-dṛṣṭi*, Patna, 1963; *Tantra aur Āgam Śāstron kā Digdarśan*, Trs. by H.K. Tiwari, Varanasi; *Tāntrik Sādhana aur Siddhānta*, Trs. by H.K. Tiwari, Varanasi; *Tāntrik Sāhitya*, Varanasi; *Bhāratīya Saṃskṛti aur Sādhanā*, Varanasi.

Kamalesh, S.: *Śaktibhāṣya kā Adhyayan.*

Sastri, G.: *Tantradarśan.*

Sastri, D.: *Tantrasiddhānta aur Sādhanā.*

Vasavada, A. (Hindi rendering by B.S. Upadhyay): *Tripurārahasya kā Tantra-viśleṣaṇa*, Varanasi.

D. BENGALI BOOKS

Bandyopadhyay, S.C.: *Śaktiraṅga Vaṅgabhūmi*, Calcutta, 1398 B.S.

Bandyopadhyay, J.N.: *Pañcopāsanā*, Calcutta, 1960.

Basu, Manoranjan: *Rāmakṛṣṇa-Sādhana-Parikramā*, Calcutta, 1978.

Bhattacharya, Mahendranath: *Bhāratīya Dharmer Itihās*, Calcutta, 1977.

Bhattacharya, S.: *Tantra Paricaya*, Santiniketan, 1359 B.S.

Brahmachari, T.P.: *Tāntrik Sādhanā O Tantrakāhinī*, Calcutta.

Chakravorty, C.: *Tantrakathā*, Calcutta, 1362 B.S.

Chakraborty, J.K.: *Śākta Padāvalī O Śakti-sādhanā*, Calcutta, 1382 B.S. (5th ed.); *Prācīn Bhāratīya Sāhitya O Vāṅgālīr Uttarādhikār*, 1382 B.S. (2nd ed.).

Chakravorty, S.: *Mehārer Sarvānanda*, Calcutta.

Chatterjee, R.M.: *Vividha-Tantra-Saṃgraha*, Calcutta, 1981-86.

Das, U.K.: *Śāstramūlak Bhāratīya Śakti-sādhanā*, 2 vols., Birbhum, 1373 B.S.

Das Gupta, Nalini: *Vāṅgalāy Bauddha-Dharma*.

Das Gupta, S.B.: *Bhārater Śakti-sādhanā O Śākta Sāhitya*, Calcutta, 1367 B.S.

Datta, Mahendra (Śrīma): *Śrīśrī Rāmakṛṣṇa Kathāmṛta*.

Ghosh, N.: *Dasa Mahāvidyā*, Calcutta.

Kaviraj, G.N.: *Tāntrik Sādhanā O Siddhānta*, I, 2nd ed., Burdwan, 1983, II, 2nd ed.; *Tantra O Āgama-Śāstrer Digdarśan*, Vol. I, Calcutta, 1963.

Majumdar, R.C.: *Vāṃlādeśer Itihās*, Vols. I, II, Calcutta, 1377 B.S. Portions dealing with Tantra.

Mitra, S.: *Aviśvāsya Satya*, Calcutta; *Daśamātṛkā*, Calcutta.

Nandi, Sunil: *Kālī-rahasya*, Calcutta.

Nigudhananda: *Khunje Phiri Kuṇḍalinī*, Calcutta; *Mahātīrtha Ekānna Pīṭher Sandhāne*, Calcutta; *Ekānna Pīṭher Sādhak*, Calcutta; *Śaktikṣetra Cavviś Upapīṭher Sandhāne*, Calcutta.

Raghuvir and Shodotaki: *Uddhārakośa of Dakṣiṇāmūrti*, 1978.

Ray, A.: *Śāktapadāvalī*, Calcutta.

Ray, Diptimay: *Paścim Vaṅger Kālī O Kālīkṣetra*, Calcutta.

Sanyal, N.: *Bhāratīya Bhāskarye Mithun*, Calcutta.

(Svami) Saradananda: *Gītātattva O Bhārate Śaktipūjā*, Calcutta, 1983.

Sarasvati, Padmanath: *Prabandhāṣṭaka*.

Sarkar, M.: *Tantrer Ālo*, Calcutta, 1354 B.S.

Sastri, H.P.: *Bauddha Gān O Dohā*, Calcutta, 1916.

Sastri, S.: *Tantraparicay*, Calcutta, 1359 B.S.

Sen, K.M.: *Vāṃlār Sādhanā*, Calcutta, 1352 B.S.

Siddhantabhusana, S.C.: *Kaula-mārga-rahasya*, Calcutta, 1335 B.S.

Svami, S.N.: *Tāntrik Abhidhāna*, Calcutta, 1910.

Vidyabhusan, A.C.: *Sarasvatī*, I, 1340 B.S.

Vidyarnava, S.C.: *Tantratattva*, I, 1317 B.S.

E. MISCELLANEOUS BOOKS

A Cat. of Skt. MSS in Private Libraries of North Western Provinces, Pt. I, Benares, 1874.

C.K. Raja Pres. Vol., pp. 271-284.

Jha Commemoration Vol. (articles by C. Chakravarti).

K.B. Pathak Comm. Vol. (articles by C. Chakravarti).

Volume of Studies Presented to F. Thomas (articles by B. Bhattacharya).

V. Bhattacharya's *Āchārya Ray Commemoration Vol.* (article captioned Sanskrit Treatises on Alchemy as translated into Tibetan; K.C. Viraraghava's article entitled The Study of Alchemy).

Memoirs of Archaeological Survey of India, No. 66 Encyclopaedia of Indo-Aryan Research, Vol. III, 6 (R.G. Bhandarkar's article on The Pañcarātra or Bhāgavata System), 1913.

Aruṇa Bhāratī — A.N. Jani Fel. Vol.:
- (i) Paper on Pañcarātra by K.D. Bharadwaj
- (ii) Dhal's paper — Virajākṣetra — a Śākta Pīṭha
- (iii) Joshi's paper — Śākta Tāntrism in Gupta Age
- (iv) Desai's paper — Mother Goddess and Her Partner.

Cultural Heritage of India, R.K. Mission Institute of Culture, Calcutta, 4 vols., Calcutta, 1953-62.
Evolution of Tantras — P.C. Bagchi, vol. iv.
The Spirit and Culture of the Tantras, A.B. Ghosh, vol. iv.
Śakti Cult in South India — K.R. Venkataraman, vol. iv.

History and Culture of the Indian People, Bombay.
Tāntrik Religion in vol. iv (in *The Age of Imperial Kanauj*).

Essays in Classical and Modern Hindu Law, II, Leiden, 1977.

A Juridical Fabrication of Early British India: *The Mahānirvāṇa Tantra* — J.D.M. Derrett.

Studies in honour of A. Padover, Albany, New York (G. Bühnemann — On *Puraścaraṇa*, *Kulārṇava Tantra*, ch. 15, in Goudriaan's ed.).

Tantra and Taoist Studies in honour of R. Stein, Vol. I, ed. M. Strickmann, 1981 (A. Padoux — Un Japa tantrique; Yoginīhṛdaya 3.172-190).

F. JOURNALS, PROCEEDINGS, REPORTS, CATALOGUES, ETC.

English

A journal, entitled *Ancient Tantra*, dealing exclusively with Tāntric matters, is published from Ancient Tantra, 130 Adarsh Nagar, Jalandhar-144 008.

The magazine, entitled *Kuṇḍalinī*, on Tantra-yoga, is published by Kuṇḍalinī Research and Publication Trust, New Delhi.

ABORI, IX, XV, XVI (articles by R.C. Hazra).

ABORI, X, 1930 (article by B. Bhattacharya). Also see XIII, pp. 208-11.

ABORI Diamond Jubilee Vol. 1978 (article by S.A. Dange).

ABORI, XIX, 1938 (A.K. Coomaraswamy, The Tāntric Doctrine).

Adyar Library Bulletin, I, 3, pp. 92-95; XX (article by C. Chakravorty); XXVII, pp. 1-17.

Annual Reports of Faculty of Arts and Letters, Tohuk University, 1958 (H. Hadamo, Human existence in Tāntric Buddhism).

Archaeological Survey of India Report, IX (Temple of 64 Yoginīs in Bheraghat).

Bhāratakaumudī, II, Allahabad, 1947 (U.P. Shah, A Peep into the Early History of Tantra in Jaina Literature).

Catalogue of India Office Printed Books.

Cunningham, *Archaeological Survey Report*, IX.

Bulletin of R.K. Mission Institute of Culture, Calcutta, D. Sen's paper on Advaitism in Tantra.

Bulletin of School of Oriental and African Studies, London, LIV, pt. 2, 1991 (G. Bühnemann, Selecting and Perfecting *Mantras* in Hindu Tāntrism).

Bulletin de l'Ecole Francaise d'Extreme-Orient, Paris, 65, 1978, pp. 65-85 [A. Padoux — Contribution a l'etude du Mantrasastra, I: La selection des mantra (mantroddhara)].

Bulletin of R.V. Res. Inst., X, ii, p. 80, Trichur.

Eranos Jahrbuch, I, Zurich, 1933 (H. Zimmer, Zue Bedentong des Indischen Tantra Yoga).

Glory of India (Pub. by Motilal Banarasidass, Delhi), Vol. VI, 1-4 (Article — Lakṣeśvara Rath, a lesser known Tāntric by P. Mishra).

Harvard Journal of Asiatic Studies, VII, 1945 (Chou-yi liang, Tāntrism in China).

IHQ, V, p. 390, VI (P.C. Bagchi, On some Tāntric texts studied in Ancient Kambuja); VII, 1931 (D.R. Sastri, The Lokāyatas and Kāpālikas); IX, 1933 (R.C. Hazra, Influence of Tantra on *Tattvas* of Raghunandana); pp. 1-10 (H. Winternitz, Notes on the Guhyasamaja-Tantra and the Age of Tantras); XII, 1936 (S. Levi, On a Tāntric fragment from Kucha); VI, X, XXVII (articles by C. Chakraborty); Sept. 1951 (Śākta festivals of Bengal); XXXI, 1935 (Matsyendranātha and his Yoginī Cult by Karambelkar); XXXII, 1956 (article by B. Bhattacharya).

Indian Antiquary, IV, 101 ff (Eng. trs. of portions of Tāranātha's *History of Buddhism*).

Indian Culture, II, 1934 (Przylusky, J. Mudra).

Indologica Taurinensia, I, Torino, 1973, pp. 61-69.

JA, 1935, CCXXVI, pp. 1-66.

JAOS, VI, 23, 1902 (A.H. Ewing, The Śāradā-Tilaka Tantra).

JASB, Letters, XVII (article by B. Banerji).

JASB, New Series, XXVI, p. 130; XXIX (article by C. Chakravarti).

JASB, New Series, XVIII-IX.

JBORS, XXI, i, xxiii (pp. 40-44).

JOR, Madras, XIX, Pt. 4, 1950 (Tāntric Cult in Epigraphs by B.P. Desai).

JRAS, 1894 (L.A. Waddell, The Indian Buddhist Cult of Avalokita and His Consort Tārā).

JRAS, 1910 (On Tantras in Malabar).

JRAS, 1911 (A.G. Svamin's paper — The Pañcarātras or Bhāgavat-Śāstra).

JRASB, XIV, p. 74 ff.

Journal of Assam Res. Soc., III, IV, p. 121.

Journal of Music Academy, Madras, XI, 1-4, 1940.

Journal of Ganganath Jha Res. Inst., I, p. 177 ff.

Journal of Indian Society of Oriental Art, Calcutta, IX (pp. 151-93), X (pp. 210-52).

Journal of Indian and Buddhist Studies, II, pp. 512-13.

Journal of Oriental Institute, Baroda, XIII.1, Appendix; XVI.

Lalitakalā, 1-2, 1955 (P. Chandra, The Kaula-Kapotika Cult at Khajuraho).

Marg, Bombay, March, 1965 (Plastic Situation by M. Anand; Sculptures of Nāgārjuna-Konda, A. Roy).

Marg, June, 1963 (The Lesser Vehicle, etc., by M. Anand).

MASI, No. 20 (H. Sastri, Origin and Cult of Tārā).

Melanges Chinois et Bouddhiques, III, Brussels, 1934-35 (Tucci, G., Some Glosses upon the *Guhyasamāja*).

Mitteilungen des Instituts fur Orient forschunger, I, 1953, pp. 424-73.

Nepal Catalogue of MSS I.

New Indian Antiquary, I, 1938 (S.K. De, The Buddhist Tāntric Sanskrit Literature of Bengal).

New Catalogus Catalogorum, Madras.

Notices of Skt. MSS, 2nd Series, by H.P. Shastri.

Notices of Skt. MSS, by R.H. Mitra.

Ostasiatesche Zeolgchrift, XII, N.S. Berlin, 1936 (H.V. Glasenapp, Tantrismus and Śaktismus).

Oxf., II.

Poona Orientalist, XXI, pp. 47-49 on Śaktisaṃgama-Tantra.

Proc. of Indian Hist. Cong., VIII (Panigrahi, K.C., Obscene Sculptures of Orissan Temples).

Proc. of All India Oriental Conference, XX, vol. ii; vol. vi.

Proc. of All India Oriental Conference — Summaries, XI, pp. 111-112.

Quest, XXV, 1962 (A. Bharati, Metaphysics of Tāntrism).

RASB Des. Cat. of Skt. MSS in Royal Asiatic Soc. of Bengal.

Rupam, 1920 (*Mithuna in Indian Art* by O.C. Gangoli), Summaries of Papers, 5th World Skt. Con., 1981 (Tāntrism, Śakti Cult, Śākambhari, Classification of Śaiva Tantras).

Skt. Sāhitya Pariṣat Patrikā, Calcutta, XIV, pp. 269-274.

Studies in honour of A. Padover, Albany, New York (G. Bühnemann — On *Puraścaraṇa*, *Kulārṇava Tantra*, chap. 15 in Goudriaan's ed.).

Tāntric and Taoist Studies in honour of R. Stein, Vol. I, ed. M. Strickmann, 1981 (A. Padoux — Un Tapa tantrique: Yoginīhṛdaya, 3.172-190).

ZDMG, Supplement, III, 2 (1977), paper by J.A. Schoterman — Some Remarks on *Kubjikā-mata-tantra*.

Bengali

Bābā Tāraknāth (Monthly journal published from Tārakeśvar Math, Hughly, West Bengal), V. II, 1392 B.S.; K.K. Sen Gupta's paper on Śaktivād O Durgāpūjā.

Desh, Calcutta Weekly, dated 17-10-87, p. 15; B.N. Mukherji's paper on Kālīdevīr Mūrti-tattva.

Vaṅgīya Sāhitya Pariṣat Patrikā, Calcutta, 58, iii-iv; 59, pp. 68-72.

INDEX

Abhayākaragupta 89
Abhinavagupta 89–90
Ādikarma-pradīpa 233
Advaya-siddhi 233
Advayavajra 90–91
Āgamacandrikā 117
Āgama-tattva-vilāsa 117
Agastya 91
Agastya-saṃhitā 117–118
Ahirbudhnya-saṃhitā 118–120
Ākāśa-bhairava-kalpa 120–121
Akulavīra-tantra 121
Amara Maitra 91–92
Amara-saṃgraha 121
Āmarī-saṃhitā 121
Amṛtānandanātha 92
Anaṅgavajra 92
Annadā-kalpa-tantra 121–122
Anupamavajra 92
Ārya-mañjuśrī-mūlakalpa 233–234
Aṣṭamī-vrata-vidhāna 234
Atīśa 92–93

Bhairavānanda 93
Bhairava-padmāvatī-kalpa 122
Bhairava Tripāṭhin 93
Bhāskararāya 93-94
Bhāskara-vilāsa 122
Bhāsurānanda-Nātha 94
Bhūta-ḍāmara-tantra 122–123
Bodhibhadra 94
Brahmānanda Giri 95
Brahma-saṃhitā 123
Brahma-yāmala 123

Cakra-saṃvāra-tantra 234–235
Chinnamastā-tantra 123
Cidgagana-candrikā 123–124

Dakṣiṇāmūrti-saṃhitā 124
Devānanda Siṃha 95
Devanātha Ṭhakkura Tarkapañcānana 95
Devīkālottarāgama 124
Divākaracandra 95
Durgārāma 95

Ekallavīra-caṇḍa-mahāroṣaṇa-tantra 235

Gaṇapati-tattva 125
Gandharva-tantra 125
Gauḍapāda 95–96
Gauḍapāda-sūtra 125
Gaurī-kāñcalikā 125–126
Gautama-tantra 126
Gāyatrī-tantra 126–127
Gīrvāṇendra Sarasvatī II 96
Gorakṣanātha 96

Gorakṣa-siddhānta-saṃgraha 127
Govinda Śarman 96
Govinda Vidyāvinoda 96
Guhya-samāja 235–237
Guhyasiddhi 237
Gupta-sādhana tantra 127–129
Guru-tantra 129

Halāyudha 96–97
Haṃ sa Miṭhu 97
Haragovinda Rāya 97
Hari 97
Hariharānandanātha Tīrthasvāmin 97
Hārītāyana 97
Hevajra-tantra 237–238

Indrabhūti 98
Īśāna-Śiva-Gurudeva-Miśra 98
Īśānaśiva-gurudeva-paddhati 130

Jālandharapāda 98–99
Jayaratha 98
Jayadratha-yāmala 130
Jayākhya-saṃhitā 130–131
Jayasaṃhitā 131
Jetāri 99
Jīva Gosvāmin 99
Jñāna-dīpikā 131
Jñānalakṣmī 131
Jñānānanda Paramahaṃsa 99
Jñānārṇava-tantra 131
Jñānasaṃkalinī-tantra 132
Jñānasiddhi 238–239
Jñānendranātha 99

Kākacaṇḍī-tantra 132–133
Kālacakra-tantra 239–241
Kālidāsa 99–100
Kālī-tantra 133
Kālī-tattva 134
Kālīvilāsa-tantra 134–135
Kālottara-tantra 135–136
Kālyarcana-candrikā 136
Kāmadhenu-tantra 136
Kāmakalā-vilāsa 136–138
Kāmākhya-tantra 138
Kāmaratna 139
Kāmikāgama-tantra 139–140
Kāmya-yantroddhāra 140
Kaṅkālamālinī-tantra 140
Karapātrisvāmin 100
Kāśinātha Bhaṭṭa Bhaḍa 100
Kaula-gaja-mardana 141
Kaula-jñāna-nirṇaya 141
Kaulāvalī-nirṇaya 141–143
Kaulopaniṣad 143–144
Keśava 100–101
Keśava Bhaṭṭa Gosvāmin 101
Kramadīpikā 144
Kriyoḍḍīśa-tantra 144
Kṛṣṇamohana 101
Kṛṣṇānanda Āgama 101
Kṛṣṇapāda 101–102
Kṛṣṇa Vidyāvāgīśa Bhaṭṭācārya 102
Kṣemarāja 102
Kubjikā-mata-tantra 144–146
Kubjikā-tantra 146–147
Kukkuripāda 102
Kulacūḍāmaṇi 147–148
Kula-mūlāvatāra 148–149
Kulānanda-tantra 149
Kulārṇava-tantra 149–152
Kumāracandra 102
Kumāra-tantra 152
Kumārī-tantra 153–154

Lakṣmaṇadeśika 103
Lakṣmaṇa Rāṇāḍe 103

Lakṣmīdhara 103
Lakṣmīṃkarā 103
Lakṣmī-tantra 154–155

Mādhavācārya 103
Mādhavānandanātha 104
Mahā-cīnā-cāra-tantra 155–156
Mahākāla-tantra 241
Mahānirvāṇa-tantra 156–157
Mahīdhara 104
Mālinīvijayottara-tantra 157–159
Mallasena 104
Mañjuśrī-mūlakalpa 241–242
Mantramahodadhi 159
Mātaṅga-Pārameśvarāgama 159–161
Mātṛkābheda-tantra 161–162
Mātṛkā-cakra-viveka 162
Matsya-sūkta 162
Matsyendranātha 104
Meghamālā 162
Merutantra 163
Mīnanātha 104
Mṛgendra-tantra 163–164
Mudrā-prakāśa 164
Murāri 104

Naḍapāda 105
Nāgabhaṭṭa 105
Nāgabodhi 105
Nāgārjuna 105
Narasiṃha Ṭhakkura 105
Nārāyaṇa 105
Nārāyaṇa Kaṇṭha 105
Naṭanānanda Nātha 106
Netratantra 166–167
Niḥśvāsa-tattva-saṃhitā 164–66
Nīlakamala Lāhiḍī 106
Nīlakaṇṭha Caturdhara 106
Nīlatantra 167–169
Nirañjana Siddha 106
Niruttara-tantra 170–175
Nirvāṇa-tantra 175–176
Niṣpanna-yogāvalī-nāma 242
Nityānandanātha 107
Nityanātha Siddha 107
Nityaprajña 107
Nityāṣoḍaśīkārṇava-tantra 176
Nityotsava-tantra 176

Padmapādācārya 107
Padmavajra 107
Pañcakrama 242
Pañcama-veda-sāra-nirṇaya 176
Paṇḍita Kāṇha 107
Paramānanda-tantra 177
Pārānanda 107
Pārānanda-sūtra 178–179
Paraśurāma-kalpasūtra 179–182
Parātantra 178
Parivrājakācārya 108
Pārvatīputra 108
Pheṭkāriṇī-tantra 182
Piṅgalāmata 182–183
Pīṭha-nirṇaya 183
Pīṭha-sthānas 247
Prajñāvarman 108
Prajñopāya-viniścaya-siddhi 242–243
Prakāśānanda Deśika 108
Prāṇamañjarī 108
Prāṇatoṣiṇī 183–186
Prapañca-sāra-tantra 187–189
Premanidhi Pantha 108
Puṇyānandanātha 109
Pūrṇānanda 109–110
Putali 110

Rādhā-tantra 189
Rāghavabhaṭṭa 110

Raghunātha Tarkavāgīśa
  Bhaṭṭācārya 110
Rahasya-pūjā-paddhati 189
Rāmakiśora 110
Rāmakṛṣṇa Tarkālaṃkāra 111
Rāmānanda 111
Rāmatoṣaṇa Vidyālaṃkāra 111
Rāmeśvara 111
Rasārṇava 190
Ratnākaraśānti 112
Rāvaṇa 112
Rudrayāmala 190

Sadāśiva Śukla 112
Sādhana-mālā 243–244
Śaiva-kalpadruma 191
Śāktakrama 191
Śāktānanda-taraṅgiṇī 191–192
Śākta-pramoda 192
Śakti-mīmāṃsā 192
Śakti-saṃgama-tantra 192–195
Śaktisūtra 195
Śaṃkara 112
Śaṃkarācārya 112–113
Śaṃkarānandanātha 113
Sammoha tantra 195
Sāmrājya-lakṣmī-pīṭhikā 195
Saṃvarodaya-tantra 244
Śāntarakṣita 113
Sarasvatī-Tīrtha 113
Sarvānanda 113–114
Sarvānanda-taraṅgiṇī 196
Sarvollāsa 196
Śata-ratna-saṃgraha 196–197
Ṣaṭ-karma-dīpikā 197
Ṣaṭkarmollāsa 197
Sātvata-tantra 197–199
Saubhāgya-kalpadruma 200
Saubhāgya-subhagodaya 200
Sekoddeśaṭīkā 244
Siddhanātha 114
Śīlabhadra 114
Śivānanda 114
Śrīcakra-saṃbhāra-tantra 244
Śrīkaṇṭha 114
Śrīnaḍapāda 114
Śrīnātha 114
Śrīnivāsa 114
Śrīrāja Devānanda Siṃha 115
Śrī-tattva-cintāmaṇi 200–201
Śrīvidyā-ratna-sūtra 202
Subhagānandanātha 115
Subhagodaya 202
Sudhā-vidyotinī 202
Śukla Mathurānātha 115
Svacchanda-tantra 203
Svatantrānandanātha 115
Śyāmā-rahasya 203–204

Tailikapāda 115
Tantra(s)
  and Vedic literature 31–32
  antiquity of 13–14
  authors of 89–116
  Buddhist 233–245
  classification of 18–19
  contents of 19–30
  Hindu 117–231
  in foreign countries 85–87
  meaning of 11
  miscellaneous tāntric works
    and commentaries 248–249
  number of 17
  place of origin of 14–17
  rationale behind composition of 11–13
  society reflected in 81–84
Tantra, science in
  art and architecture 70–77
  music and dance 68–69

rise of Sahajiyā cult 77
Śabda and Dhvani 77
Sufism 78–79
Tantra and Āyurveda 66–67
tāntric therapeutics 67–68
Tantra-cūḍāmaṇi 204
Tantrāloka 204
Tantra-paddhati 205
Tantrarāja-tantra 205–208
Tantrasāra 208–209
Tantrasāra-saṃgraha 209–210
Tāntric elements in post-Vedic Sanskrit literature
the Great Epics 33
miscellaneous works 33–37
Tāntric lexicons 61–63
Tāntric Śaivism of Kashmir
Krama tāntricism 49–55
philosophy of 55–59
Śaiva works 39–43
Śiva-sūtras 43–46
Spanda-kārikā 46–49
Tārā-bhakti-sudhārṇava 210
Tārārahasya 210–211
Tārā-rahasya-vṛtti 211
Tārātantra 211–212, 245
Tattvānanda-taraṅgiṇī 212
Toḍala-tantra 212
Tripurā-rahasya 212–214
Tripurāsāra-samuccaya 214

Uḍḍīśa-tantra 214–215
Umānandanātha 115–116
Umāpati Śivācārya 116
Ūrdhvāmnāya 215

Vāmācāra-mata-khaṇḍana 216
Vāmakeśvara-tantra 216
Varivasyā-rahasya 217
Vidyānandanātha 116
Vidyāraṇya 116
Vidyārṇava-tantra 217–219
Vijñānabhairava-tantra 219–222
Vīṇāśikha-tantra 222–223
Viṣṇu-saṃhitā 223
Vyāsa 116

Yadunātha 116
Yoginī-hṛdaya-dīpikā 223
Yoginī-tantra 224–228
Yoni-tantra 229–231